EX LIBRIS
Lynne Rudder Baker
Philosopher
1944 - 2017

The future of folk psychology

The essays in this volume are concerned with our everyday and developed scientific systems of explanation of human behavior in terms of beliefs, attitudes, memories, and the like. The volume provides an introduction to the lively contemporary debate about the status and theoretical viability of such forms of "folk-psychological" explanation, in the light of recent developments in neurobiology and cognitive science. It can be used as a textbook for advanced courses in the philosophy of mind, psychology, and cognitive science.

The future of folk psychology
Intentionality and cognitive science

Edited by

John D. Greenwood
City College and Graduate School, CUNY

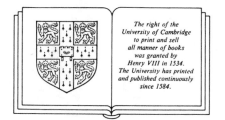

The right of the
University of Cambridge
to print and sell
all manner of books
was granted by
Henry VIII in 1534.
The University has printed
and published continuously
since 1584.

Cambridge University Press
Cambridge
New York   Port Chester   Melbourne   Sydney

Published by the Press Syndicate of the University of Cambridge
The Pitt Building, Trumpington Street, Cambridge CB2 1RP
40 West 20th Street, New York, NY 10011, USA
10 Stamford Road, Oakleigh, Melbourne 3166, Australia

First published 1991

Printed in Canada

Library of Congress Cataloging-in-Publication Data
The future of folk psychology: intentionality and cognitive science /
edited by John D. Greenwood.
   p. cm.
Includes index.
ISBN 0-521-40335-9. – ISBN 0-521-40898-9 (pbk.)
1. Psychology – Philosophy. 2. Ethnopsychology. 3. Cognitive
science. 4. Intentionality (Philosophy) I. Greenwood, John D.
BF38.F88 1991
150 – dc20   90-27907
                                                                    CIP

British Library Cataloguing in Publication Data
The future of folk psychology: intentionality and cognitive science.
1. Cognitive psychology.
I. Greenwood, John D.
153

ISBN 0-521-40335-9 hardback
ISBN 0-521-40898-9 paperback

Contents

Contributors

Jonathan Bennett
Department of Philosophy
Syracuse University

Simon Blackburn
Department of Philosophy
University of North Carolina
  at Chapel Hill

Paul M. Churchland
Department of Philosophy
University of California, San
  Diego

Daniel C. Dennett
Center for Cognitive Studies
Tufts University

Jerry A. Fodor
Department of Philosophy
Graduate School, City University
  of New York

Joseph Garon
Department of Philosophy
University of California, San
  Diego

John D. Greenwood
Department of Philosophy
City College and Graduate School,
  City University of New York

John Heil
Department of Philosophy
Davidson College

Terence Horgan
Department of Philosophy
Memphis State University

Richard McDonough
Department of Philosophy
National University of Singapore

Joseph Margolis
Department of Philosophy
Temple University

William Ramsey
Department of Philosophy
University of Notre Dame

Jay Rosenberg
Department of Philosophy
University of North Carolina
  at Chapel Hill

Stephen Stich
Department of Philosophy
Rutgers University, New Brunswick

James Woodward
Department of Humanities and
  Social Sciences
California Institute of Technology

Preface

This book is based on the principal contributions to a conference on the future of folk psychology sponsored by the Department of Philosophy of the University of North Carolina at Greensboro, April 15–17, 1988. The essays by Paul Churchland, by William Ramsey, Stephen Stich, and Joseph Garon, by Daniel Dennett, by Jonathan Bennett, and by Simon Blackburn are based on the principal papers of the conference. The essays by John Greenwood, by John Heil, and by Jay Rosenberg are based on commentaries delivered at the conference. The other commentators at the conference were Jeff Coulter and Sydney Shoemaker.

The essays by Jerry Fodor and by Terence Horgan and James Woodward were published previously: Fodor's originally appeared in *Mind* in 1985; Horgan and Woodward's originally appeared in *The Philosophical Review* in 1985. The essays by Joseph Margolis and by Richard McDonough were written specially for this volume.

I am grateful to all the speakers, commentators, and moderators who participated in the Greensboro symposium. I also thank Jarrett Leplin for providing me with the opportunity to convene the symposium during my sojourn at the University of North Carolina at Greensboro, and the University of North Carolina at Greensboro for its financial support of the Annual Symposium in Philosophy.

Introduction: Folk psychology and scientific psychology

John D. Greenwood

This volume is about the future of folk psychology. It concerns the likely intellectual fate of our everyday conceptual scheme for accounting for our own and others' actions in terms of beliefs, desires, emotions, and motives, and developed scientific psychological forms of explanation that employ analogous references to contentful and causally efficacious psychological states.

I

Despite the impression created by many recent critics of folk psychology, its serious treatment as a form of causal explanatory theory by philosophers and psychologists is a relatively new phenomenon. For many years, philosophy of mind had little to say about intentional psychological states such as beliefs, desires, emotions, and motives. Through the 1950s and 1960s, the central debate concerned the mind–brain identity theory, but only rarely did the discussion focus on intentional psychological states. Most philosophers were almost exclusively concerned with the question of whether the qualitative aspects of sensations such as pain or sense impressions could be reduced to brain states (Smart 1959). Although the neo-Wittgensteinians generated famous debates about our knowledge of other minds and the possibility of a logically private language, and developed detailed conceptual analyses of psychological concepts such as emotion (Kenny 1963) and motivation (Peters 1958), these did little to further our understanding of the causal-explanatory role of references to intentional psychological phenomena. Indeed, a central thesis of many neo-Wittgensteinian accounts was that folk-psychological references to intentional psychological states are not causal explanatory (Peters 1958; Louch 1966). According to such accounts, a folk-psychological explanation is a logically distinct kind of explanation, one that explicates the social meaning of human actions or renders them "intelligible" in the light of rules and reasons.

Philosophy of mind, as such, had little to say that would have interested the practicing psychologist. In any case, the practicing psychologist would not have been much interested, because for an equally long period psychologists themselves were not particularly concerned with intentional psychological states. For many years psychologists were committed to some form of behaviorism, either rejecting references to psychological states outright as "explanatory fictions" (Skinner 1953), or insisting on their strict operational definition in terms of observable environmental stimuli and behavioral responses (Kendler 1952). The logical consequence was the methodological exclusion of substantive cognitive theories referencing contentful and causally efficacious psychological states. The only philosophical analyses held to be relevant to scientific psychology were apparent philosophical justifications of some form of logical behaviorism (Ryle 1949), or philosophical critiques of the principles of behavioral conditioning theory (Taylor 1964). During this period there was little philosophical analysis that could be properly described as philosophy of psychology, insofar as such a discipline is regularly held to be centrally concerned with the theoretical psychological states postulated by psychologists. The reason is that during this period there was scarcely any first-order theoretical domain that could become the object of philosophical analysis.

Now there is such a domain, and with a vengeance. The reason is the 'cognitive revolution' in psychology, which began in the 1950s and has continued to grow at an exponential pace into the multidisciplined enterprise that is contemporary 'cognitive science'. On the metatheoretical level, many researchers became dissatisfied with the sterile and restrictive conception of theoretical psychological descriptions avowed by traditional empiricist and behaviorist accounts. Thus in a classic paper in the *Psychological Review*, MacCorquodale and Meehl (1948) distinguished between "intervening variables" that are wholly definable in terms of observable stimulus–response sequences and that serve a merely logically integrative function, and "hypothetical constructs" that are not wholly definable in terms of such sequences, and whose "surplus meaning" can be developed to generate novel empirical predictions (cf. Hempel 1985).

The fertility of such "open" theoretical constructs was demonstrated by the success of substantive theories of cognition based upon an "information-processing" perspective (Miller 1956; Broadbent 1958). A powerful impetus for this development was the parallel development of the study of 'artificial intelligence' in computers, providing psychologists with a theoretical model of human cognition in terms of internally processed 'programs' (Newell, Shaw, & Simon 1958). The success of cognitive theories based upon a general information-processing approach, and the ability to simulate many cognitive achievements in computers, convinced many practitioners of both the utility of psychological theoretical constructs and the reality of the structures and processes putatively described by them: "The basic reason for studying the cognitive processes has become as clear as the reason for studying anything else: because they are there" (Neisser 1967, p. 12).

Of course, many psychologists remained hypercautious, given their traditional antipathy toward cognitive theories. Thus for example, Lachman, Lachman, and Butterfield, in their oft-cited introductory text in cognitive psychology, *Cognitive Psychology and Information Processing* (1979), spend about 500 pages describing in great detail the experimental evidence favoring specific theories of cognitive processing, and then rather lamely conclude that it is too early to tell whether such processes really exist. This hypercaution had much to do with traditional associations of cognitive theory and discredited forms of 'introspective psychology'. Many felt that cognitive psychology was bound to be unscientific because it must depend upon the introspection of psychological states and processes by experimental subjects. The substantial theoretical achievements of cognitive psychology, however, demonstrated that the link between cognitive theory and introspection was one of association only and not of methodological entailment, for the theoretical successes of cognitive psychology were achieved largely without reference to the accounts of introspecting subjects.[1]

Indeed it is arguably one of the theoretical achievements of cognitive psychology that it has demonstrated that experimental and lay subjects have rather poor introspective access to cognitive processes. Thus, for example, theorists such as Evans and Wason (1976) have developed theoretical models of logical reasoning that successfully predict normal errors as well as achievements, strongly suggesting that heterogeneous subject explanations are rationalizations of their errors rather than descriptions of the cognitive processes that generated them. Analogously, theorists such as Nisbett and Wilson (1977) and Nisbett and Ross (1980) have documented a whole range of experimental studies in cognitive and social psychology that strongly suggest that subjects have very poor introspective access to the distal stimuli and cognitive processes that influence their choices, and produce largely erroneous explanations of their behavior that are based not on introspection of cognitive processes but on socially learned "a priori causal theories."

Contemporary philosophy of mind has moved in a similar direction, and in the process has very largely developed into philosophy of psychology. Philosophical interest has shifted from sensational phenomena such as pain and sense-data to intentional psychological phenomena such as beliefs and desires etc. Davidson's (1963, 1967) seminal papers on the explanation of human action have led to a new consensus that folk-psychological explanations referencing 'propositional attitudes'[2] are a species of causal explanations that may play an entirely legitimate role in a scientific psychology (whatever Davidson's reservations about its prospects). Nowadays most philosophers treat intentional psychological phenomena as theoretical entities and endorse a realist (as opposed to an 'instrumentalist' or 'fictionalist') account of their descriptions, debating the acceptability of alternative 'functionalist' accounts of their metaphysics and semantics in terms of their causal role.

These psychological and philosophical developments came together in Jerry Fodor's *The Language of Thought* (1975). In this work, Fodor articulated what he claimed are the ontological commitments of contemporary theories of cognitive science. According to Fodor, cognitive science largely is and ought to be committed to *intentional realism:* the doctrine that propositional attitudes are contentful ("semantically evaluable") and causally efficacious (functional) states instantiated in neural systems (and perhaps other forms of physical systems, such as computers). Fodor also articulated what he held to be the basic form of many cognitive theories in psychology: that information processing essentially involves rule-governed computations performed upon mental representations. Although Fodor's own detailed account of cognition has always been a subject of controversy, his general perspective did integrate a number of central assumptions shared by very many philosophers and cognitive scientists.

II

These developments went on swimmingly for a short while. But only for a short while, for there was a price to pay for granting intentional psychological descriptions a causal-explanatory theoretical status. It was the price paid by any genuine explanatory theory: the risk of falsification. It could no longer be maintained – as it was maintained by the neo-

Wittgensteinians – that references to propositional attitudes have a privileged conceptual position with respect to the explanation of human action. Indeed it could no longer be presumed that propositional attitudes have *any* explanatory role to play in developed psychological science. The behaviorists may have been wrong to reject explanatory references to contentful psychological states on dubious epistemological and semantic grounds. Modern cognitive science may, however, be correct to reject such references on sound empirical grounds, because of their inaccuracy or inadequacy as causal explanations. Or at least so argue the contemporary critics of folk psychology, such as Paul and Patricia Churchland (P. M. Churchland 1979, 1981, 1984; P. S. Churchland 1986) and Steven Stich (1983).

The future of folk psychology, conceived as a body of causal-explanatory theoretical references to contentful psychological states employed by layfolk and scientific psychologists, is threatened by a number of related arguments. It is argued that our folk-psychological explanations are, or are likely to turn out to be, generally inaccurate or inferior to alternative theoretical explanations of human behavior in terms of neurophysiological processes. If this proves to be the case, it is argued that we ought to abandon our cherished forms of folk-psychological explanation and the ontology of contentful psychological states they presuppose. It is also argued that it is, or is likely to be, the case that the posits of our best theories in cognitive science will not be identifiable with the posits of folk-psychological explanations. Thus we are, or are likely to be, forced to conclude that there are no entities that have the essential properties traditionally attributed to folk-psychological phenomena.

Paul and Patricia Churchland have tended to emphasize the first form of argument; Stephen Stich, the second. There is a third and more general form of argument common to both and most other critics of folk psychology (cf. Rosenberg 1981). It is claimed that folk-psychological phenomena do not form 'natural kinds' that support universal causal laws that could in principle be reduced to neurophysiological laws. This is often expressed via the claim that everyday or scientific folk-psychological references to intentional psychological phenomena do not reduce "smoothly" to neurophysiological explanatory kinds, or that such phenomena are not identifiable with the "naturally isolable" mechanisms described by neurophysiological theories. The "intentional categories" of folk psychology "stand magnificently alone, without any visible prospect of reduction" (Churchland 1981, p. 75). Folk-psychological phenomena thus appear to be ontologically discontinuous with the rest of physical nature. This creates an intolerable situation for the hard-nosed cognitivist scientist, one that critics of folk psychology argue can be resolved only by the abandonment of folk psychology and the ontology of contentful psychological states. Together these arguments are employed to support the position known as 'eliminative materialism'. (For early approximations and statements see Sellars 1956; Feyerabend 1963; and Rorty 1965.)

The first two forms of argument are based upon conditional premises, the truth of which is generally accepted by most contributors to the debate. Thus most parties agree that if folk psychology is a body of inaccurate or stagnant causal-explanatory theory, then it – and the ontology it postulates – ought to be abandoned. Critics of folk psychology affirm the antecedent of this conditional and derive the consequent. Defenders of folk psychology deny the antecedent, either by denying the claim that folk psychology is a body of theory or by denying that it is a body of inaccurate or stagnant theory. Most parties also agree that if folk psychology postulates psychological states that are contentful and causally efficacious, and if cognitive science suggests that there are not or are unlikely to be any psychological states with these properties, then we are obliged to abandon the ontology posited by folk-psychological explanations. Again critics of folk psychology affirm the antecedents and derive the consequent. Defenders of folk psychology deny the antecedents, either by denying that folk-psychological phenomena are individuated by such properties, or by affirming that there are psychological states with such properties.

Most critics and defenders of folk psychology endorse the materialist assumption that intentional psychological phenomena – if they exist at all – are incarnated in the human brain. Most critics and defenders of folk psychology also assume that folk-psychological explanations will not "smoothly" reduce to neurophysiological explanations. Critics of folk psychology see this "failure" as a reason for rejecting the postulated ontology of folk psychology, whereas defenders of folk psychology see it as a reason for maintaining the autonomy of folk-psychological explanation. Those who endorse eliminative materialism tend to have a negative view of the empirical adequacy and fertility of autonomous folk-psychological explanation. Those who reject eliminative materialism naturally tend to take a much more optimistic view.

Recent developments in cognitive science have added some spice to these arguments, by providing a live theoretical alternative to traditional computational theories of cognition. 'Connectionist' or 'parallel distributed processing' (PDP) theories of cognitive functions (Rumelhart & McClelland 1986) advance accounts of how neural networks represent reality that do not involve the neural system's performing computations on mental representations; that is, they do not involve the system's performing operations on stored symbols in the fashion of modern digital computers. According to these accounts, representations of real-⌐ ity are neurally constructed and developed via patterns of excitatory and inhibitory stimuli and the strength of their connections. Critics of folk⌐ psychology such as Churchland and Stich have been quick to exploit this development, suggesting that connectionist theory is inconsistent with folk psychology. Defenders of folk psychology doubt this, suggesting that connectionist theories are best conceived as accounts of the neural implementation of systems that perform computations over representations (Fodor & Pylyshyn 1988).

III

All these forms of argument are discussed in some shape or form by the various contributors to this volume. In the first chapter, "Fodor's Guide to Mental Representation: The Intelligent Auntie's Vade-Mecum," Jerry Fodor provides a conceptual map of the basic philosophical positions adopted in the present debate, as well as a fairly succinct statement of his own distinctive position. What unites most of the defenders of folk psychology is a commitment to realism with respect to propositional attitudes: They hold that there are contentful psychological states that play a causal role in the generation of human behavior. What unites most of the critics of folk psychology is their commitment to antirealism with respect to propositional attitudes: They deny that there are any psychological states that have the semantic and causal properties conventionally attributed to them. Of course, there are important differences between proponents of these basic positions, as Fodor notes, and indeed the details of his own position are not shared by many contemporary realists. There are also those, such as Dan Dennett (1979, 1987), who attempt to steer a middle course by denying the literal reality of contentful psychological states such as beliefs and desires while maintaining their instrumental utility as predictively powerful theoretical constructs.

Paul M. Churchland's essay, "Folk Psychology and the Explanation of Human Behavior" (Chapter 2), provides an economical statement of what has come to be known as the "theoretical view" of folk psychology. According to Churchland, folk psychology is a "framework of concepts, roughly adequate to the demands of everyday life, with which the humble adept comprehends, explains, predicts, and manipulates a certain domain of phenomena." As such, it ought to be rejected "in its entirety" if it can be demonstrated to be generally inaccurate or inferior to alternative neurophysiological theories of human behavior.

Churchland defends this view against a variety of familiar alternative analyses of folk-psychological discourse that treat such accounts as serving a normative or social-performative function, or as nonempirical or noncausal explanations based on conceptual connections between folk-psychological explanantia and explananda. Churchland deals in a little more detail with one objection which he claims has more bite, and which has motivated him to modify his own position. To account for the fact that few ordinary folk can articulate the body of universally quantified laws relating folk-psychological states and behaviors that are said to constitute the body of folk-psychological knowledge, Churchland argues that our theoretical knowledge is not so "linguistic as we have chronically assumed," and suggests an alternative connectionist account in terms of subsumption under a "prototype."

In "Two Contrasts: Folk Craft Versus Folk Science, and Belief Versus Opinion" (Chapter 6), Daniel C. Dennett remarks that if the principles of explanation and prediction employed by layfolk are not linguistically articulated as a body of propositions, then "that's a pretty good reason for not calling it a theory." In my own contribution to this volume, entitled "Reasons to Believe" (Chapter 3), I focus on some problems generated by Churchland's rather liberal and sometimes ambiguous employment of the term 'theoretical'. Although Churchland is correct to insist against normative and performative theorists that folk-psychological discourse is theoretical in the sense that it is descriptive, he requires a much stronger and very specific philosophical interpretation of the term 'theoretical' to sustain the eliminativist argument. We are obliged to abandon the ontology of folk psychology in the face of explanatory failure, only if, as Churchland claims, the semantics and truth conditions of folk-psychological descriptions are determined by the causal-explanatory propositions in which they regularly figure, that is, given this familiar account of theoretical meaning. I argue that this is not the case with respect to our theoretical descriptions of contentful psychological states, nor is it the case with respect to the theoretical descriptions of natural science. Consequently, even if most or all of our folk-psychological explanations turned out to be inaccurate or inadequate, this would not oblige us to abandon the ontology of folk-psychological states. We could, rather, conclude that such 'hypothetical' or 'postulated' theoretical states exist (to employ two other familiar senses of the term 'theoretical') but do not have the causal properties we formerly attributed to them.

Of course, Churchland would be correct to insist that in order to maintain our commitment to the ontology of folk psychology rationally in such circumstances, we ought to have independent grounds for postulating such contentful states. I suggest that we do in fact have adequate independent grounds. I also note that Churchland makes a rather poor case for the empirical inadequacy of folk psychology and I suggest that the primary threat to folk psychology is not empirical but conceptual: It derives precisely from the restrictive methodological principles that underpin the doctrine of eliminative materialism.

In "Connectionism, Eliminativism, and the Future of Folk Psychology" (Chapter 4), Ramsey, Stich, and Garon distinguish between *ontologically conservative* and *ontologically radical* theory changes. In the case of ontologically conservative theoretical changes, we come to recognize that particular theoretical entities (e.g., planets) do not have some of the properties we formerly attributed to them (e.g., circular motions in Ptolemaic theory), but we continue to maintain our commitment to the existence of such entities. In ontologically radical theoretical changes, we come to recognize that nothing has the properties we formerly attributed to postulated theoretical entities (e.g., the elasticity of caloric), and consequently abandon our commitment to the existence of such entities. They suggest that acceptance of a certain class of connectionist theories of memory would constitute an ontologically radical theory change with respect to the propositional attitudes posited by layfolk and traditional cognitive scientists.

According to Ramsey, Stich, and Garon, folk psychology is committed to *propositional modularity:* the view that propositional attitudes "are *functionally discrete, semantically interpretable* states that play a *causal role* in the production of other propositional attitudes, and ultimately in the production of behavior." Although these criteria seem to be satisfied by many of the theoretical posits of contemporary cognitive theories, such as semantic network theories of memory (Collins & Quillian 1972), they do not appear to be satisfied by the theoretical posits of at least a certain subclass of connectionist theories. If a certain subclass of connectionist theories of memory are correct, they argue, then we ought to eliminate theoretical references to propositional attitudes from this explanatory domain, for the mechanisms postulated by such theories are distributed and subsymbolic; that is, they do not have the essential properties of propositional attitudes.

In "Being Indiscrete" (Chapter 5), John Heil doubts that connectionist theories are in fact seriously at odds with traditional cognitive theories referencing propositional attitudes. Although the modes of representation described by connectionist theories may be "widely distributed," such states may still be taken to have the restricted causal roles traditionally attributed to propositional attitudes. Heil also casts doubt on the claim that folk psychologists are committed to any strong "discreteness" requirement. Although this characterization is perhaps true of some particular theorists, most notably Fodor, it does not seem to be true of many others. He notes that according to Davidson, for example, folk-psychological description and explanation are necessarily holistic. These considerations lead Heil to conclude that "connectionist models of cognition seem most naturally interpretable as hypotheses about the underlying dynamics of beliefs, desires, and other propositional attitudes."

Daniel Dennett, in "Two Contrasts: Folk Craft Versus Folk Science, and Belief Versus Opinion" (Chapter 6), also notes that connectionist theories are inconsistent only with particular species of folk-psychological explanation, not with folk-psychological explanation per se: "It is really rather curious to say, 'I'm going to show you that folk psychology is false by showing you that Jerry Fodor is mistaken.' " Dennett distinguishes between folk-psychological explanation as craft, which he is at pains to stress is an "extraordinarily powerful source of prediction," and particular theories or ideologies that account for the success of the craft of folk-psychological explanation. He doubts that developments in cognitive science would ever oblige us to abandon the craft of folk-psychological explanation, given its "prodigious" predictive power. He agrees with Ramsey, Stich, and Garon that developments in neuroscience or connectionist theory may turn out to be inconsistent with particular ideologies that explain the general success of the craft of folk psychology, such as Fodor's computational account in terms of discrete, semantically interpretable, and causally efficacious states.

Dennett claims that the success of folk psychology as an explanatory craft is perhaps best explained by treating beliefs and desires *instrumentally*, as "*abstracta* – more like centers of gravity than individualizable concrete states of a mechanism." Dennett also gives some reasons for questioning the current enthusiasm for connectionist theories of cognition, and makes a critical distinction between 'beliefs' that may be (instrumentally) attributable to all "intentional systems" (animal, vegetable, mechanical, or human) and linguistically infected states or 'opinions' that are attributable only to language users, and he suggests that the causal architecture required for the "psychology of opinions" is likely to be rather different from the causal architecture sufficient for the "psychology of beliefs."

In "Folk Psychology Is Here to Stay" (Chapter 7), Terence Horgan and James Woodward claim that it is in fact doubtful that folk psychology exhibits "explanatory failures on an epic scale" (Churchland 1981, p. 76), or that it is a "stagnant or degenerating research program" (p. 75). Many theories of contemporary cognitive and social psychology that employ references to contentful psychological states represent substantive achievements recognized by the relevant 'scientific communities'.

Horgan and Woodward also go to the heart of the matter: the ancient metaphysical issue of the relation between the psychological and the physical, and the age-old inclination of materialists to deny the ontological and explanatory autonomy of the psychological. They claim that both Churchland and Stich place quite unjustified and excessively restrictive conditions on theoretical psychological explanation. Churchland claims that folk psychology is probably false and the entities it postulates nonexistent if it does not reduce "smoothly" to neurophysiology via bridge statements linking psychological and neurophysiological types. Horgan and Woodward claim that this argument is simply fallacious, representing nothing more than a dogma of eliminative materialism. They also argue that Stich's (1983) "modularity requirement" – that psychological states must be identifiable with naturally isolable neurophysiological states if they are to be accorded ontological status – is too stringent. All that is required of legitimate theoretical posits such as contentful psychological states is that they be identifiable with neurophysiological states whose *components* are naturally isolable. They assert that this is the only reasonable reductive constraint that can be imposed on any form of scientific theory.

Horgan and Woodward argue that if folk-psychological explanations are false, it is because the particular "causal architectures" postulated by folk-psychological explanations do not exist. Such claims can be independently tested at the psychological level without any reference to the prospects of neurophysiological reduction. If this is so, then an empirically successful folk psychology need not be concerned about the possible reductive failures stressed by the Churchlands and Stich.

Such philosophical presuppositions about reductive constraints on psychological theory mark the great divide between eliminative and noneliminative materialists, whatever their opinion of the actual explanatory achievements of folk psychology. Eliminativists seem unable or unwilling to countenance an autonomous and empirically successful level of folk-psychological explanation. Noneliminative materialists appear to take this achievement for granted and espouse its independent virtues. Thus the chapters by Jonathan Bennett and by Simon Blackburn stress the virtues of explanations that cross-cut ontologies of physical composition.

In "Folk-Psychological Explanations" (Chapter 8), Jonathan Bennett characterizes folk-psychological explanations as explanations that bring "conceptual unity" to a set of facts about a system that are not unifiable under a single mechanistic or physical account. According to Bennett, "a system x's intentionality is genuine only if some class of x's inputs/outputs falls under a single intentional account . . . and does not fall under any one mechanistic generalization." Bennett's analysis appears diametrically opposed to those of Churchland and of Stich, both of whom treat the failure to fall under one physicalist or mechanistic account as a mark of the inadequacy of any form of explanation. Indeed, one may wonder if Bennett has not made too strong a claim in the opposite direction, by denying genuine intentionality to systems whose intentional description coincides with a single mechanistic account. But Bennett notes that the issue is not simply about single versus multiple mechanistic accounts. (Since multiple mechanisms may be accidentally related under an intentional description, they are insufficient for genuine intentionality.) He stresses the role played by evolutionary origin and educability – two grounds for the explanatory employment of intentional descriptions – in determining genuine intentionality.

In "Losing Your Mind: Physics, Identity, and Folk Burglar Prevention" (Chapter 9), Simon Blackburn also stresses the unifying role played by folk-psychological explanations. He claims that eliminativist strategies are based on what he calls the "Tractarian error": the notion that the identity of physical and psychological states consists in the spatial configuration of particles. In contrast, Blackburn claims that "physical thinking is essentially a question of finding one state that covers many realizations." Physics itself deals rarely with compositional kinds but more often with relational, dispositional, and functional kinds whose predicates unify by classifying across differences in physical composition. He also stresses that such unifying concepts play a central role in physics, providing scope for theories of conservation over changes of phase from solid to liquid or gas. (Compare the concepts of energy and entropy.)

Accordingly, for Blackburn, the multiple realizability of contentful psychological states poses no threat at all to their ontological status. If causal explanatory descriptions of beliefs and desires unify neurophysiological compositional differences, they are merely doing the same job as explanatory concepts in physics such as temperature and energy. To recognize that "thinking of Vienna" may be neurophysiologically realized in one way in one person and in another way in another person no more impugns the "empirical integrity" of such folk-psychological concepts than the fact that "acceleration" is realized in one material form in a stone and in another material form in a feather impugns the "empirical integrity" of the concept of "acceleration."

In " 'Tractarian States' and Folk-Psychological Explanation" (Chapter 10), Jay Rosenberg wonders if the error Blackburn cites is truly Tractarian and suggests that there is nothing in Wittgenstein's *Tractatus* (1917) to warrant identifying its "configuration of objects" with spatial arrays. He also suggests that what he redescribes as the "structuralist intuition" is not so obviously an error after all: that ultimately the "intelligibility of *how* a physical system does whatever it (functionally) does depends on the in-principle availability of an account of *what* that system (compositionally) *is*." He says that what is wrong with the eliminativist position is not the notion that temperature or psychological states are in some sense identical with their physical or neurophysiological realizations, but a particular essentialist conception of these theoretical identifications. Whether or not this is true, Rosenberg is surely correct to follow Blackburn in suggesting that the issue of eliminativism hangs largely on unresolved philosophy-of-science issues about theoretical reduction and the proper analysis of theoretical identifications.

It is not clear that Blackburn would deny Rosenberg's claim. He might accept the necessity of some compositional account without abandoning his central claim that the explanatory power of many explanations in physics and folk psychology is not parasitic upon the detailing of the multiple forms of physical realization of the relational or functional kinds of things referenced by such explanations. In "The Autonomy of Folk Psychology" (Chapter 11), Joseph Margolis also insists that the explanatory power of folk psychology is independent of specific neurophysiological accounts of the physical realization of psychological states, since according to Margolis there is little prospect of this form of reductive compositional analysis.

Margolis does not deny materialism. He assumes that intentional psychological states are physically incarnated and multiply realized. Nevertheless, he insists that the cultural domain of folk-psychological explanation cannot be reduced to the purely physiological or biological order or, for that matter, to the informational regularities postulated by computational theories. He holds that "human intelligence is a complex, relatively stable, developmentally open-ended, verbally realized, not systematically closed organization that exhibits *culturally formed aptitudes.*" In contrast, the reductive stratagems of computational cognitive science and neurophysiology are "contextless, ahistorical, completely extensional": They simply cannot accommodate psychological phenomena located in the social space of a historically functioning culture.

Margolis clearly holds that the irreducibility of folk-psychological explanations does not impugn their explanatory integrity. What he essentially denies is the equation of ontological and explanatory continuity made by Churchland and Stich, who appear to treat explanatory continuity as a condition of ontological continuity. Once we reject this notion, Margolis suggests, most of our problems disappear: We can recognize that folk-psychological accounts – which may be autonomously successful – are explanatorily discontinuous with neurophysiological accounts, while granting that our human psychology is materially continuous with our neurobiology and the rest of physical nature.

In "A Culturalist Account of Folk Psychology," the final chapter in this volume, Richard McDonough takes the defense of folk psychology to its extreme: the suggested elimination of neurophysiological explanations from the domain of intelligent human behavior. McDonough launches a major attack on contemporary philosophical conceptions of folk-psychological explanations. He argues that most such conceptions presuppose a mechanistic metaphysics of "internalism" that is simply not a feature of everyday folk-psychological explanations. Everyday explanations of human actions do not presuppose that agents have *in* them (in any sense) beliefs and desires that cause their actions.

Adopting a Wittgensteinian perspective on what he calls "personalist psychology," McDonough argues that if psychological contents are modeled on linguistic usage, and if linguistic usage is embedded in, and individuated with respect to, human culture (social institutions, practices, etc.), then psychological states cannot be inner entities that can be individuated independently of their cultural context. According to McDonough, the relational or "holistic" nature of psychological phenomena renders folk-psychological explanations irreducible to neurophysiological explanations, indeed to *any* form of mechanistic explanation in terms of internal states.

For McDonough, the ascription of a contentful psychological state to an agent is a description of a form of cultural embeddedness. He does not deny that such ascriptions are causal explanatory, since they can be successfully employed in the prediction of intelligent human behavior. What he denies is that intelligent human behavior can be explained by reference to causally potent internal states.

Both Margolis and McDonough recognize the context dependence of folk-psychological descriptions. This marks another major difference between the critics and some of the defenders of folk psychology. Stich (1983), for example, treats the context relativity of folk-psychological explanations as a demonstration of their inadequacy as theoretical posits. Margolis and McDonough treat it as a reflection of an ontological fact about human psychology that derives from its social embeddedness in a historically evolving culture.

IV

Many more issues are addressed and arguments advanced in all of these essays, whose contents I have only briefly characterized. Moreover, my characterizations have not been designed to be comprehensive or even synoptic. I have, rather, tried to provide the reader with a conceptual guide to their relations by stressing common or divergent themes, leaving the authors to speak for themselves in articulating their own distinctive positions and arguments.

Nor have I attempted any adjudication of the debate. I do, however, want to close this introduction by highlighting a number of points that seem to emerge from this cursory survey of the variety of positions advocated by the contributors to this volume.

Despite the eliminativist rhetoric, most of the current debate about the future of folk psychology is not really directed toward an assessment of the empirical adequacy of our everyday or developed scientific psychological explanations of human actions in terms of beliefs, desires, emotions, and motives. Neither the Churchlands nor Stich attempts to document in detail the supposedly de facto inaccuracies of everyday folk-psychological explanations, nor do they, for example, engage in an extended methodological critique of the evidential basis of generally accepted theories in cognitive, social, and clinical psychology that make essential reference to intentional psychological states. They tend to rest content with dismissive references to the "stagnancy" of folk psychology that only already committed eliminativists find convincing.

Most of the current debate concerns two issues. The first is theoretical and empirical, concerning what is or is likely to be our best current or future theory of cognitive processing. It concerns the question of whether our best theories of cognitive abilities do or are likely to postulate the symbolic states of computational theories, or the subsymbolic states of connectionist theories, or some combination or variant. This issue cannot of course be resolved by philosophical argument, although philosophers acquainted with the explanatory domain and available evidence can (and frequently do) engage in critical assessments of the comparative adequacy of competing theories. Since no consensus appears to be emerging among researchers, this issue is likely to remain a live theoretical controversy for the foreseeable future.

The second issue is a philosophical or metaphysical question about the ontological status of the psychological in relation to the physical. Ultimately, it is a philosophy of science issue concerning whether there are reductive constraints on theory selection at the psychological level: whether we ought to restrict our ontological commitments to include only those theoretical posits that reduce "smoothly" to neurophysiology or "naturally isolable" kinds. It has been noted that most of the critics of folk psychology suppose that there are such constraints, and most of the defenders of folk psychology deny it. Since there does not appear to be any sign of emerging consensus among philosophers of science or mind, this is also likely to remain a live issue for the foreseeable future (and, no doubt, beyond).

But what is the poor folk psychologist to do in the meantime? Surely, it is business as usual for ordinary folk and most scientific psychologists, who cannot wait upon the distant pronouncements of cognitive science or philosophy of science. Eliminativists tend to be dismissive of the 'isolationalism' of lay and scientific practitioners of folk psychology. Yet their relative neglect of both these issues may be largely justified.

It seems pretty clear, for example, that our everyday explanations of human actions in terms of beliefs, desires, and the like do not, for example, involve any ontological commitments to "propositional modularity" with respect to psychological states. At best we employ a very rudimentary theory of information processing that is little more than a gross philosophical gloss on folk-psychological explanation. Since lay folk psychological explanations of human action simply do not presuppose any specific theoretical claims about cognitive processing, the explanatory adequacy of such accounts cannot be assessed by reference to the debate about the posits of cognitive science.

Much the same is true of scientifically developed folk-psychological explanations of human actions. The closest scientific analogue of folk-psychological explanation is in fact not cognitive psychology but social psychology. The routine concern of cognitive psychology is the explanation of cognitive processing. The routine concern of social psychology is the explanation of human actions such as aggression, dishonesty, conformity, and cooperation. Since such explanations do not involve specific ontological commitments to either computational or connectionist accounts of cognitive processing, the empirical adequacy of such explanations likewise cannot be decided by reference to the outcome of debates about the posits of cognitive science.

Folk psychologists may therefore legitimately ignore as irrelevant some of the complaints of eliminativist critics. Churchland, for example, claims that folk psychology exhibits "explanatory failures on an epic scale" because, inter alia, it cannot explain "the common ability to catch an outfield fly ball on the run . . . the internal construction of a 3-D visual image . . . the rich variety of perceptual illusions" (1981, p. 73). As Horgan and Woodward note in Chapter 7, cognitive psychology does not do a bad job of explaining these phenomena by reference to contentful psychological states. It is, however, quite inappropriate to consider the failure to explain such phenomena as demonstrative of the inadequacy of everyday folk psychology or social psychology, which just isn't in the business of explaining such phenomena. This would be comparable to considering that the (miserable) failure of neurophysiology to explain "bystander apathy" (Latané & Darley 1970) or "impression management" (Goffman 1959) is indicative of the inadequacy of neurophysiological theory.

The eliminativist might object that since the contentful psychological states postulated by social psychology must be identified with the contentful states postulated by computational cognitive science and cognitive psychology, their ultimate legitimacy rests on the outcome of the cognitive debate. Yet it is far from obvious that we should suppose this unless we are already committed to the eliminativist principle about reductive constraints. Undoubtedly, information-bearing states are ontologically grounded in our neurophysiology, and undoubtedly, our achievement motives are ontologically grounded in these information-bearing states (and ultimately in our neurophysiology). We are, however, obliged to accept their reduction to each other only if we already accept the eliminativist restraints on theoretical selection at the psychological level or (as these remarks suggest) levels.

Practitioners of any science perhaps ought to be aware of any philosophical and a priori legislation about such reductive constraints on adequate explanations. If any theory is spectacularly successful by ordinary empirical standards (successful prediction and fertility), then that surely is and will always remain the best reason for embracing its ontology, even if it does not reduce to whatever categories are held to be ontologically fundamental at that moment in historical time.

If we reject such reductive constraints, then the following possibility for the future of folk psychology suggests itself: It may turn out that our best theoretical explanations of cognitive processing do not require us to postulate contentful psychological states (at least in the form of mental representations that are computationally processed). It may also turn out that our best explanations of human actions do. Or it may turn out that some of our cognitive achievements are best explained in terms of subsymbolic connectionist systems, whereas others are best explained in terms of computations over internal representations (cf. Bechtel 1988), and that some human actions are best explained in terms of contentful opinions and motives, whereas others are best explained in terms of operant conditioning, physiological reactions, and biologically inherited behavioral propensities.

I suspect that if we keep an open mind, something very much like this will turn out to be the case: "Everyone has won, so all must have prizes." I also doubt whether any philosophical intuition that precludes it ought to be trusted. Yet at this point I no doubt betray my own prejudices and predilections – a prudent point at which to close.

In any case, the hour is premature for any philosophical or theoretical synthesis. The present volume is, rather, intended as an entry into an ongoing debate. I hope the quality of the arguments advanced in the following pages convinces the reader of the greatest virtue of the contemporary debate about the future of folk psychology: It has forced philosophers and psychologists to articulate and develop in much fuller detail the ontological and metaphysical commitments of their explanatory references to contentful psychological states such as beliefs, desires, emotions, and motives. In consequence, it is now not only true that philosophy of psychology has an object. It also has its own increasingly rich content.

Notes

1. This is not to deny the utility of using subject 'protocols' (Ericsson & Simon 1984) to suggest theories of cognitive processing, or the legitimacy of employing them as evidential grounds (in at least some cases) for preferring one cognitive theory over its rivals.
2. 'Propositional attitude' is the conventional term employed by philosophers to reference contentful psychological states such as beliefs, desires, and hopes. I follow the conventional usage throughout this introduction. The reader should, however, be cautioned that this characterization does imply a particular theoretical position, by presupposing that the contentful psychological states of folk psychology involve an attitude to the content of a proposition. Although this analysis works well for most beliefs, it doubtfully generalizes to other contentful psychological states, such as emotions and motives. Love and the motive of revenge appear to be contentful psychological states that essentially involve attitudes toward other people rather than toward propositions.

   This no doubt explains one peculiarity of the debate about the future of folk psychology: the fact that emotions and motives are rarely referenced as illustrative examples, despite their central role in folk-psychological explanation. This is itself perhaps best explained by the almost exclusive focus on cognitive psychology in current debates (beliefs conceived as propositional attitudes can be readily incorporated into computational theories of cognition), despite the fact that social psychology perhaps represents the closest scientific analogue of everyday folk-psychological explanation. Cf. Section IV of this introduction.

References

Bechtel, W. (1988). "Connectionism and Rules and Representation Systems: Are They Compatible?" *Philosophical Psychology*, 1:5–16.
Broadbent, D. E. (1958). *Perception and Communication*. Oxford: Pergamon Press.
Churchland, P. M. (1979). *Scientific Realism and the Plasticity of Mind*. Cambridge: Cambridge University Press.
Churchland, P. M. (1981). "Eliminative Materialism and Propositional Attitudes." *Journal of Philosophy*, 78:67–90.
Churchland, P. M. (1984). *Matter and Consciousness*. Cambridge, Mass.: MIT Press.
Churchland, P. S. (1986). *Neurophilosophy: Towards a Unified Science of the Mind–Brain*. Cambridge, Mass.: MIT Press.
Davidson, D. (1963). "Actions, Reasons and Causes." *Journal of Philosophy*, 60:685–700.
Davidson, D. (1967). "Causal Relations." *Journal of Philosophy*, 64:691–703.
Dennett, D. C. (1978). *Brainstorms*. Cambridge, Mass.: MIT Press.
Dennett, D. C. (1987). *The Intentional Stance*. Cambridge, Mass.: MIT Press.
Ericsson, K. A., & Simon, H. A. (1984). *Protocol Analysis*. Cambridge, Mass.: MIT Press.

Evans, J. St. B. T., & Wason, P. C. 1976). "Rationalization in a Reasoning Task." *British Journal of Psychology*, 67:479–486.

Feyerabend, P. K. (1963). "Materialism and the Mind–Body Problem." *Review of Metaphysics*, 17:49–67.

Fodor, J. A. (1975). *The Language of Thought*. Cambridge, Mass.: Harvard University Press.

Fodor, J. A., & Pylyshyn, Z. W. (1988). "Connectionism and Cognitive Architecture: A Critical Analysis." *Cognition*, 28:3–71.

Goffman, E. (1959). *The Presentation of Self in Everyday Life*. New York: Doubleday.

Hempel, C. G. (1958). "The Theoretician's Dilemma: A Study in the Logic of Theory Construction." In H. Feigl, M. Scriven, & G. Maxwell, eds., *Minnesota Studies in the Philosophy of Science*, Vol. 2. Minneapolis: University of Minnesota Press.

Kendler, H. H. (1952). " 'What Is Learned?': A Theoretical Blind Alley." *American Psychologist*, 59:269–277.

Kenny, A. (1963). *Action, Emotion, and Will*. London: Routledge & Kegan Paul.

Lachman, R., Lachman, J., & Butterfield, E. (1979). *Cognitive Psychology and Information Processing*. Hillsdale, NJ: Erlbaum.

Latané, B., & Darley, J. M. (1970). *The Unresponsive Bystander: Why Doesn't He Help?* New York: Appleton-Century-Crofts.

Louch, A. (1966). *Explanation and Human Action*. Oxford: Basil Blackwell.

MacCorquodale, K., & Meehl, P. E. (1948). "On a Distinction Between Hypothetical Constructs and Intervening Variables." *Psychological Review*, 55:95–107.

Miller, G. A. (1956). "The Magical Number Seven, Plus or Minus Two: Some Limits on Our Capacity for Processing Information." *Psychological Review*, 63:81–97.

Neisser, U. (1967). *Cognitive Psychology*. New York: Appleton-Century-Crofts.

Newell, A., Shaw, J. C., & Simon, H. A. (1958). "Elements of a Theory of Problem Solving." *Psychological Review*, 65:151–166.

Nisbett, R. E., & Ross, L. (1980). *Human Inference: Strategies and Shortcomings of Social Judgement*. Englewood Cliffs, N.J.: Prentice Hall.

Nisbett, R. E., & Wilson, D. D. (1977). "Telling More Than We Can Know: Verbal Reports on Mental Processes." *Psychological Review*, 84:231–259.

Peters, R. S. (1958). *The Concept of Motivation*. London: Routledge & Kegan Paul.

Rorty, R. (1965). "Mind–Body Identity, Privacy, and Categories." *Review of Metaphysics*, 19:24–54.

Rosenberg, A. (1981). *Sociobiology and the Preemption of Social Science*. Baltimore: Johns Hopkins University Press.

Rumelhart, D. E., & McClelland, J. L. (1986). *Explorations in the Microstructure of Cognition*, Vol. 1: *Foundations*. Cambridge, Mass.: MIT Press.

Ryle, G. (1949). *The Concept of Mind*. London: Hutchinson.

Sellers, W. (1956). "Empiricism and the Philosophy of Mind." In H. Feigl & M. Scriven, eds., *Minnesota Studies in the Philosophy of Science*, Vol. 1. Minneapolis: University of Minnesota Press.

Skinner, B. F. (1953). *Science and Human Behavior*. New York: Macmillan.

Smart, J. J. C. (1959). "Sensations and Brain Processes." *Philosophical Review*, 68: 141–156.

Stich, S. P. (1983). *From Folk Psychology to Cognitive Science: The Case Against Belief*. Cambridge, Mass.: MIT Press.

Taylor, C. (1964). *The Explanation of Behaviour*. London: Routledge & Kegan Paul.

Wittgenstein, L. (1917). *Tractatus-Logico-Philosophicus*, trans. D. F. Pears and B. F. McGuinness. London: Routledge & Kegan Paul.

1 Fodor's guide to mental representation: the intelligent auntie's vade-mecum

Jerry A. Fodor

It rained for weeks and we were all *so* tired of ontology, but there didn't seem to be much else to do. Some of the children started to sulk and pull the cat's tail. It was going to be an *awful* afternoon until Uncle Wilifred thought of Mental Representations (which was a game that we hadn't played for *years*) and everybody got *very* excited and we jumped up and down and waved our hands and all talked at once and had a perfectly *lovely* romp. But Auntie said that she couldn't stand the noise and there would be tears before bedtime if we didn't please calm down.

Auntie rather disapproves of what is going on in the Playroom, and you can't entirely blame her. Ten or fifteen years of philosophical discussion of mental representation has produced a considerable appearance of disorder. Every conceivable position seems to have been occupied, along with some whose conceivability it is permissible to doubt. And every view that anyone has mooted someone else has undertaken to refute. This does *not* strike Auntie as constructive play. She sighs for the days when well-brought-up philosophers of mind kept themselves occupied for hours on end analysing their behavioural dispositions.

But the chaotic appearances are actually misleading. A rather surprising amount of agreement has emerged, if not about who's winning, at least about how the game has to be played. In fact, everybody involved concurs, pretty much, on what the options are. They differ in their hunches about which of the options it would be profitable to exercise. The resulting noise is of these intuitions clashing. In this paper, I want to make as much of the consensus as I can explicit; both by way of reassuring Auntie and in order to provide new participants with a quick guide to the game: Who's where and how did they get there? Since it's very nearly true that you can locate all the players by their answers to

This essay was originally published in *Mind* in 1985, as the first in a series of "State of the Art" articles. It is reprinted by permission of the publisher and the author.

quite a small number of diagnostic questions, I shall organize the discussion along those lines. What follows is a short projective test of the sort that self-absorbed persons use to reveal their hitherto unrecognized proclivities. I hope for a great success in California.

First question: How do you feel about propositional attitudes?

The contemporary discussion about mental representation is intimately and intricately involved with the question of Realism about propositional attitudes. Since a goal of this essay is to locate the issues about mental representation with respect to other questions in the philosophy of mind, we commence by setting out this relation in several of its aspects.

The natural home of the propositional attitudes is in 'common-sense' (or 'belief/desire') psychological explanation. If you ask the Man on the Clapham Omnibus what precisely he is doing there, he will tell you a story along the following lines: 'I wanted to get home (to work/to Auntie's) and I have reason to believe that there – or somewhere near it – is where this omnibus is going.' It is, in short, untendentious that people regularly account for their voluntary behaviour by citing beliefs and desires that they entertain; and that, if their behaviour is challenged, they regularly defend it by maintaining the rationality of the beliefs ('Because it *says* it's going to Clapham') and the probity of the desires ('Because it's *nice* visiting Auntie'). That, however, is probably as far as the Clapham Omnibus will take us. What comes next is a philosophical gloss – and, eventually, a philosophical theory.

First philosophical gloss

When the ordinary chap says that he's doing what he is because he has the beliefs and desires that he does, it is reasonable to read the 'because' as a *causal* 'because' – whatever, exactly, a causal 'because' may be. At a minimum, common sense seems to require belief/desire explanations to support counterfactuals in ways that are familiar in causal explanation at large: if, for example, it is true that Psmith did A because he believed B and desired C, then it must be that Psmith would *not* have done A if either he had not believed B or he had not desired C. (*Ceteris paribus*, it goes without saying.) Common sense also probably takes it that if Psmith did A because he believed B and desired C, then – *ceteris paribus* again – believing B and desiring C is causally sufficient for doing A. (However, common sense does get confused about this since – though believing B and desiring C was what caused Psmith to do A – still it is common sense that Psmith could have believed B and desired C and *not* done A had he so decided. It is a question of some interest whether common sense can have it both ways.) Anyhow, to a first approximation the common-sense view is that there is mental causation, and that mental causes are subsumed by counterfactual-supporting generalizations of which the practical syllogism is perhaps the paradigm.

Closely connected is the following: Everyman's view seems to be that propositional attitudes cause (not only behaviour but also) other propositional attitudes. Thoughts cause desires (so that thinking about visiting Auntie makes one want to) and – perhaps a little more tendentiously – the other way around as well (so that the wish is often father to the thought, according to the common-sense view of mental genealogy). In the paradigm mental process – viz. thinking – thoughts give rise to one another and eventuate in the fixation of beliefs. That is what Sherlock Holmes was supposed to be so good at.

Second philosophical gloss

Common sense has it that beliefs and desires are semantically evaluable; that they have *satisfaction-conditions*. Roughly, the satisfaction-condition for a belief is the state of affairs in virtue of which that belief is true or false and the satisfaction-condition for a desire is the state of affairs in virtue of which that desire is fulfilled or frustrated. Thus, *that it continues to rain* makes true the belief that it is raining and frustrates the desire that the rain should stop. This could stand a lot more sharpening, but it will do for the purposes at hand.

It will have occurred to the reader that there are other ways of glossing common-sense belief/desire psychology. And that, even if this way of glossing it is right, common-sense belief/desire psychology may be in need of emendation. Or cancellation. Quite so, but my purpose isn't to defend or criticize; I just want to establish a point of reference. I propose to say that someone is a *Realist* about propositional attitudes iff (a) he holds that there are mental states whose occurrences and interactions cause behaviour and do so, moreover, in ways that respect (at least to an approximation) the generalizations of common-sense belief/desire psychology; and (b) he holds that these same causally efficacious mental states are also semantically evaluable.

So much for common-sense psychological explanation. The connection with our topic is this: the full-blown Representational Theory of

Mind (hereinafter RTM, about which a great deal presently) purports to explain how there *could be* states that have the semantical and causal properties that propositional attitudes are commonsensically supposed to have. In effect, RTM proposes an account of what the propositional attitudes *are*. So, the further you are from Realism about propositional attitudes, the dimmer the view of RTM that you are likely to take.

Quite a lot of the philosophical discussion that's relevant to RTM, therefore, concerns the status and prospects of common-sense intentional psychology. More, perhaps, than is generally realized. For example, we'll see presently that some of the philosophical worries about RTM derive from scepticism about the semantical properties of mental representations. Putnam, in particular, has been explicit in questioning whether coherent sense could be made of such properties. (See Putnam, MH; Putnam, CPIT.) I have my doubts about the seriousness of these worries (see Fodor, BD); but the present point is that they are, in any event, misdirected as arguments against RTM. If there is something wrong with meaning, what that shows is something *very* radical, viz. that there is something wrong with propositional attitudes (a moral, by the way, that Quine, Davidson, and Stich, among others, have drawn explicitly). That, and *not* RTM, is surely the ground on which this action should be fought.

If, in short, you think that common sense is just plain *wrong* about the aetiology of behaviour – i.e. that there is *nothing* that has the causal and semantic properties that common sense attributes to the attitudes – then the questions that RTM purports to answer don't so much as arise for you. You won't care much what the attitudes are if you take the view that there aren't any. Many philosophers do take this view and are thus united in their indifference to RTM. Among these Anti-Realists there are, however, interesting differences in motivation and tone of voice. Here, then, are some ways of not being a Realist about beliefs and desires.

First Anti-Realist option

You could take an *instrumentalist* view of intentional explanation. You could hold that though there are, *strictly speaking*, no such things as beliefs and desires, still talking as though there were some often leads to confirmed behavioural predictions. Everyman is therefore licensed to talk that way – to adopt, as one says, the intentional stance – so long as he doesn't take the ontological commitments of belief/desire psychology literally. (Navigators talk geocentric astronomy for convenience, and nobody holds it against them; it gets them where they want to go.) The great virtue of instrumentalism – here as elsewhere – is that you get all the goodness and suffer none of the pain: you get to use propositional-attitude psychology to make behavioural predictions; you get to 'accept' all the intentional explanations that it is convenient to accept; but you don't have to answer hard questions about what the attitudes *are*.

There is, however, a standard objection to instrumentalism (again, here as elsewhere): it's hard to explain why belief/desire psychology works so well if belief/desire psychology is, as a matter of fact, not true. I propose to steer clear, throughout this essay, of general issues in the philosophy of science; in particular of issues about the status of scientific theories at large. But – as Putnam, Boyd and others have emphasized – there is surely a presumptive inference from the predictive successes of a theory to its truth; still more so when (unlike geocentric astronomy) it is the *only* predictively successful theory in the field. It's not, to put it mildly, obvious why this presumption shouldn't militate in favour of a Realist – as against an instrumentalist – construal of belief/desire explanations.

The most extensively worked out version of instrumentalism about the attitudes in the recent literature is surely owing to D. C. Dennett. (See the papers in Dennett, B; especially the essay 'Intentional Systems'.) Dennett confronts the 'if it isn't true, why does it work?' problem (in Dennett, TB), but I find his position obscure. Here's how I *think* it goes: (a) belief/desire explanations rest on very comprehensive rationality assumptions; it's only fully rational systems that such explanations could be literally true of. These rationality assumptions are, however, generally contrary to fact; *that's* why intentional explanations can't be better than instrumental. On the other hand, (b) intentional explanations *work* because we apply them only to evolutionarily successful (or other 'designed') systems; and if the behaviour of a system didn't at least *approximate* rationality it wouldn't *be* evolutionarily successful; what it would be is extinct.

There is a lot about this that's problematic. To begin with, it's unclear whether there really is a rationality assumption implicit in intentional explanation and whether, if there is, the rationality assumption that's required is so strong as to be certainly false. Dennett says in 'Intentional Systems' (Dennett, IS) that unless we assume rationality we get no behavioural predictions out of belief/desire psychology since without rationality any behaviour is compatible with any beliefs and desires.

Clearly, however, you don't need to assume *much* rationality if all you want is *some* predictivity; perhaps you don't need to assume more rationality than organisms actually have.

Perhaps, in short, the rationality that Dennett says that natural selection guarantees is enough to support *literal* (not just instrumental) intentional ascription. At a minimum, there seems to be a clash between Dennett's principles (a) and (b) since if it *follows from* evolutionary theory that successful organisms are pretty rational, then it's hard to see how attributions of rationality to successful organisms can be construed purely instrumentally (as merely a 'stance' that we adopt towards systems whose behaviour we seek to predict).

Finally, if you admit that it's a matter of fact that some agents are rational to some degree, then you have to face the hard question of how they *can* be. After all, not *everything* that's 'designed' is rational even to a degree. Bricks aren't for example; they have the wrong kind of structure. The question what sort of structure is required for rationality does, therefore, rather suggest itself and it's very unclear that that question can be answered without talking about structures of beliefs and desires; intentional psychology is the only candidate we have so far for a theory of how rationality is achieved. This suggests – what I think is true but won't argue for here – that the rational systems are a species of the intentional ones rather than the other way around. If that is so, then it is misguided to appeal to rationality in the analysis of intentionality since, in the order of explanation, the latter is the more fundamental notion. What with one thing and another, it does seem possible to doubt that a coherent instrumentalism about the attitudes is going to be forthcoming.

Second Anti-Realist option

You could take the view that belief/desire psychology is just plain false and skip the instrumentalist trimmings. On this way of telling the Anti-Realist story, belief/desire psychology is in competition with alternative accounts of the aetiology of behaviour and should be judged in the same way that the alternatives are; by its predictive successes, by the plausibility of its ontological commitments, and by its coherence with the rest of the scientific enterprise. No doubt the predictive successes of belief/desire explanations are pretty impressive – especially when they are allowed to make free use of *ceteris paribus* clauses. But when judged by the second and third criteria, common-sense psychology proves to be

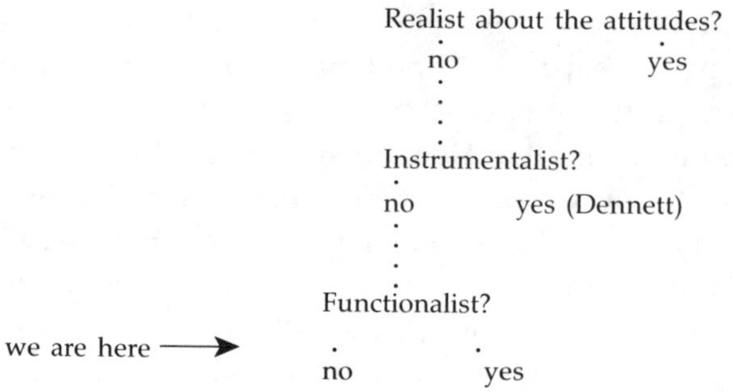

Realist about the attitudes?
no   yes

Instrumentalist?
no   yes (Dennett)

Functionalist?

we are here ⟶
no   yes

Figure 1.

a *bad* theory; 'stagnant science' is the preferred epithet (see Churchland, EMPA; Stich, FFPTCS). What we ought therefore to do is get rid of it and find something better.

There is, however, some disagreement as to what something better would be like. What matters here is how you feel about Functionalism. So let's have that be our next diagnostic question.

(Is everybody still with us? In case you're not, see the decision tree in Figure 1 for the discussion so far. Auntie's motto: a place for every person; every person in his place.)

Second question: How do you feel about Functionalism?

(This is a twice told tale, so I'll be quick. For a longer review, see Fodor, MBP; Fodor, SSA.)

It looked, in the early 1960s, as though anybody who wanted psychology to be compatible with a physicalistic ontology had a choice between some or other kind of *behaviourism* and some or other kind of *property-identity theory*. For a variety of reasons, neither of these options seemed very satisfactory (in fact, they still don't) so a small tempest brewed in the philosophical teapot.

What came of it was a new account of the type/token relation for psychological states: psychological-state tokens were to be assigned to psychological-state types *solely* by reference to their causal relations to proximal stimuli ('inputs'), to proximal responses ('outputs'), and to one another. The advertising claimed two notable virtues for this theory:

first, it was *compatible* with physicalism in that it permitted tokenings of psychological states to be identical to tokenings of physical states (and thus to enjoy whatever causal properties physical states are supposed to have). Secondly, it permitted tokens of one and the same psychological-state type to differ arbitrarily in their physical kind. This comforted the emerging intuition that the natural domain for psychological theory might be physically heterogeneous, including a motley of people, animals, Martians (always, in the philosophical literature, assumed to be silicon-based) and computing machines.

Functionalism, so construed, was greeted with audible joy by the new breed of 'Cognitive Scientists' and has clearly become the received ontological doctrine in that discipline. For, if Functionalism is true, then there is plausibly a *level of explanation* between common-sense belief/ desire psychology, on the one hand, and neurological (circuit-theoretic; generally 'hard-science') explanation on the other. Cognitive Scientists could plausibly formulate their enterprise as the construction of theories pitched at that level. Moreover, it was possible to tell a reasonable and aesthetically gratifying story about the relations *between* the levels: common-sense belief/desire explanations *reduce to* explanations articulated in terms of functional states (at least the true ones do) because, according to Functionalism, beliefs and desires *are* functional states. And, for each (true) psychological explanation, there will be a corresponding story, to be told in hard-science terms, about how the functional states that it postulates are 'realized' in the system under study. Many different hard-science stories may correspond to one and the same functional explanation since, as we saw, the criteria for the tokening of functional states abstract from the physical character of the tokens. (The most careful and convincing Functionalist manifestos I know are Block, WIF; and Cummins, NPE; q.v.)

Enthusiasm for Functionalism was (is) not, however, universal. For example, viewed from a neuroscientist's perspective (or from the perspective of a hard-line 'type-physicalist') Functionalism may appear to be merely a rationale for making do with bad psychology. A picture many neuroscientists have is that, if there really are beliefs and desires (or memories, or percepts, or mental images or whatever else the psychologist may have in his grab bag), it ought to be possible to 'find' them in the brain; where what *that* requires is that two tokens of the same *psychological* kind (today's desire to visit Auntie, say, and yesterday's) should correspond to two tokens of the same *neurological* kind (today's firing of neuron #535, say, and yesterday's). Patently, Functionalism relaxes that requirement; relaxes it, indeed, to the point of invisibility. Functionalism just *is* the doctrine that the psychologist's theoretical taxonomy doesn't need to look 'natural' from the point of view of any lower-level science. This seems to some neuroscientists, and to some of their philosopher friends, like letting psychologists get away with murder. (See, for example, Churchland, EMPA, which argues that Functionalism could have 'saved' alchemy if only the alchemists had been devious enough to devise it.) There is, for once, something tangible at issue here: who has the right theoretical vocabulary for explaining behaviour determines who should get the grants.

So much for Functionalism except to add that one can, of course, combine *accepting* the Functionalist ontology with *rejecting* the reduction of belief/desire explanations to functional ones (for example, because you think that, though *some* Functionalist psychological explanations are true, no common-sense belief/desire psychological explanations are). Bearing this proviso in mind, we can put some more people in their places: if you are Anti-Realist (and anti-instrumentalist) about belief/desire psychology, *and* you think there is no Functional level of explanation, then probably you think that behavioural science is (or, anyhow, ought to be) neuroscience.[1] (*A fortiori*, you will be no partisan of RTM, which is, of course, way over on the other side of the decision tree.) The Churchlands are the paradigm inhabitants of this niche. On the other hand, if you combine eliminativist sentiments about propositional attitudes with enthusiasm for the functional individuation of mental states, then you anticipate the eventual *replacement* of common-sense belief/desire explanations by theories couched in the vocabulary of a Functionalist psychology; replacement rather than *reduction*. You are thus led to write books with such titles as *From Folk Psychology to Cognitive Science* and are almost certainly identical to Steven Stich.

One more word about Anti-Realism. It may strike you as odd that, whereas instrumentalists hold that belief/desire psychology works so well that we can't do anything without it, eliminativists hold that it works so badly ('stagnant science' and all that) that we can't do anything *with* it. Why, you may ask, don't these Anti-Realists get their acts together?

This is not, however, a real paradox. Instrumentalists can agree with eliminativists that *for the purposes of scientific/serious explanation* the attitudes have to be dispensed with. And eliminativists can agree with instrumentalists that for *practical* purposes, the attitudes do seem quite indispensable. In fact – and here's the point I want to stress just now –

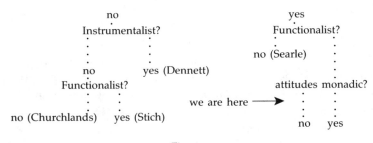

Figure 2.

what largely motivates Anti-Realism is something deeper than the empirical speculation that belief/desire explanations won't pan out as science; it's the sense that there is something intrinsically wrong with the intentional. This is so important that I propose to leave it to the very end.

Now for the other side of the decision tree. (Presently we'll get to RTM.)

If you are a Realist about propositional attitudes then, of course, you think that there are beliefs and desires. Now, on this side of the tree too you get to decide whether to be a Functionalist or not. If you are not, then you are probably John Searle, and you drop off the edge of this paper. My own view is that RTM, construed as a species of Functionalist psychology, offers the best Realist account of the attitudes that is currently available; but this view is – to put it mildly – not universally shared. There are philosophers (many of whom like Searle, Dreyfus, and Haugeland are more or less heavily invested in Phenomenology) who are hyper-Realist about the attitudes but deeply unenthusiastic about both Functionalism and RTM. It is not unusual for such theorists to hold (a) that there *is* no currently available, satisfactory answer to the question 'how could there be things that satisfy the constraints that common sense places upon the attitudes?'; and (b) that finding an answer to this question is, in any event, not the philosopher's job. (Maybe it is the psychologist's job, or the neuroscientist's. See Dreyfus, WCCD; Haugeland, NPC; Searle, MBP.)

For how the decision tree looks now, see Figure 2.

If you think that there are beliefs and desires, and you think that they are functional states, then you get to answer the following diagnostic question:

Third question: Are propositional attitudes monadic functional states?

This may strike you as a *silly* question. For, you may say, since propositional attitudes are by definition relations to propositions, it follows that propositional attitudes are by definition not monadic. A propositional attitude is, to a first approximation, a *pair* of a proposition and a set of intentional systems, viz. the set of intentional systems which bear that attitude to that proposition.

That would seem to be reasonable enough. But the current ('Naturalistic') consensus is that if you've gone this far you will have to go further. Something has to be said about the place of the semantic and the intentional in the natural order; it won't do to have unexplicated 'relations to propositions' at the foundations of the philosophy of mind.

Just *why* it won't do – precisely what physicalist or Naturalist scruples it would outrage – is, to be sure, not very clear. Presumably the issue isn't Nominalism, for why raise that issue *here;* if physicists have numbers to play with, why shouldn't psychologists have propositions? And it can't be worries about individuation since distinguishing propositions is surely no harder than distinguishing propositional attitudes and, for better or worse, we're committed to the latter on this side of the decision tree. A more plausible scruple – one I am inclined to take seriously – objects to unreduced *epistemic* relations like *grasping* propositions. One really doesn't want psychology to presuppose any of *those;* first because epistemic relations are pre-eminently what psychology is supposed to *explain,* and second for fear of 'ontological danglers'. It's not that there aren't propositions, and it's not that there aren't graspings of them; it's rather that graspings of propositions aren't plausible candidates for ultimate stuff. If they're real, they must be really something else.

Anyhow, one might as well sing the songs one knows. There *is* a reductive story to tell about *what it is* for an attitude to have a proposition as its object. So, metaphysical issues to one side, why not tell it?

The story goes as follows. Propositional attitudes are monadic, functional states of organisms. Functional states, you will recall, are type-individuated by reference to their (actual and potential) causal relations; you know everything that is essential about a functional state when you know which causal generalizations subsume it. Since, in the psychological case, the generalizations that count for type individuation are the ones that relate mental states to one another, a census of mental states would imply a network of causal interrelations. To specify such a network would be to constrain the nomologically possible mental histories of an organism; the network for a given organism would exhibit the possible patterns of interaction among its mental states (insofar, at least, as such patterns of interaction are relevant to the type individuation of the states). Of necessity, the actual mental life of the organism would appear as a path through this network.

Given the Functionalist assurance of individuation by causal role, we can assume that each mental state can be identified with a node in such a network: for each mental state there is a corresponding causal role and for each causal role there is a corresponding node. (To put the same point slightly differently, each mental state can be associated with a formula (e.g. a Ramsey sentence; see Block, op. cit.) which uniquely determines its location in the network by specifying its potentialities for causal interaction with each of the other mental states). Notice, however, that while this gives a Functionalist sense to the individuation of propositional attitudes, it does not, in and of itself, say what it is for a propositional attitude to have the propositional content that it has. The present proposal is to remedy this defect by reducing the notion of propositional content to the notion of causal role.

So far, we have a network of mental states defined by their causal interrelations. But notice that there is also a network generated by the *inferential relations that hold among propositions;* and it is plausible that its inferential relations are among the properties that each proposition has essentially. Thus, it is presumably a non-contingent property of the proposition that Auntie is shorter than Uncle Wilifred that it entails the proposition that Uncle Wilifred is taller than Auntie. And it is surely a non-contingent property of the proposition that P & Q that it entails the proposition that P and the proposition that Q. It may also be that there are evidential relations that are, in the relevant sense, non-contingent; for example, it may be constitutive of the proposition that many of the G's are F that it is, *ceteris paribus,* evidence for the proposition that all of the G's are F. If it be so, then so be it.

The basic idea is that, given the two networks – the causal and the inferential – we can establish partial isomorphisms between them. Under such an isomorphism, *the causal role of a propositional attitude mirrors the semantic role of the proposition that is its object.* So, for example, there is the proposition that John left and Mary wept; and it is partially constitutive of this proposition that it has the following 'semantic' relations: it entails the proposition that John left; it entails the proposition that Mary wept; it is entailed by the pair of propositions {John left, Mary wept}; it entails the proposition that somebody did something; it entails the proposition that John did something; it entails the proposition that either it's raining or John left and Mary wept . . . and so forth. Likewise there are, among the potential episodes in an organism's mental life, states which we may wish to construe as: (S^1) having the belief that John left and Mary wept; (S^2) having the belief that John left; (S^3) having the belief that Mary wept; (S^4) having the belief that somebody did something; (S^5) having the belief that either it's raining or John left and Mary wept . . . and so forth. The crucial point is that it constrains the assignment of propositional contents to these mental states that the latter exhibit an appropriate pattern of causal relations. In particular, it must be true (if only under idealization) that being in S^1 tends to cause the organism to be in S^2 and S^3, that being in S^1 tends to cause the organism to be in S^4, that being (simultaneously) in states (S^2, S^3) tends – very strongly, one supposes – to cause the organism to be in state S^1, that being in state S^1 tends to cause the organism to be in state S^5 (as does being in state S^6, viz. the state of believing that it's raining). And so forth.

In short, we can make non-arbitrary assignments of propositions as the objects of propositional attitudes because there is this isomorphism between the network generated by the semantic relations among propositions and the network generated by the causal relations among mental states. The assignment is non-arbitrary precisely in that it is constrained to preserve the isomorphism. And because the isomorphism is perfectly objective (which is not, however, to say that it is perfectly unique; see below), knowing what proposition gets assigned to a mental state – what the object of an attitude is – is knowing something useful. For, within the limits of the operative idealization, *you can deduce the causal consequences of being in a mental state from the semantic relations of its propositional object.* To know that John thinks that Mary wept is to know that it's highly probable that he thinks that somebody wept. To know that Sam thinks that it's raining and that Sam thinks that if it's raining it is well to carry an umbrella is to be far along the way to predicting a piece of Sam's behaviour.

It may be, according to the present story, that preserving isomorphism between the causal and the semantic networks is *all* that there is to the assignment of contents to mental states; that nothing constrains the attribution of propositional objects to propositional attitudes *except* the requirement that isomorphism be preserved. But one need not hold that that is so. On the contrary, many – perhaps most – philosophers who like the isomorphism story are attracted by so-called 'two-factor' theories, according to which what determines the semantics of an attitude is not just its functional role but also its causal connections to objects 'in the world'. (This is, notice, still a species of Functionalism since it's still causal role alone that counts for the type individuation of mental states; but two-factor theories acknowledge as semantically relevant 'external' causal relations, relations between, for example, states of the organism and *distal* stimuli. It is these mind-to-world causal relations that are supposed to determine the denotational semantics of an attitude: what it's about and what its truth-conditions are.) There are serious issues in this area, but for our purposes – we are, after all, just sightseeing – we can group the two factor theorists with the pure functional role-semanticists.

The story I've just told you is, I think, the standard current construal of Realism about propositional attitudes.[2] I propose, therefore, to call it 'Standard Realism' ('SR' for convenience). As must be apparent, SR is a compound of two doctrines: a claim about the 'internal' structure of attitudes (viz. that they are *monadic* functional states) and a claim about the source of their semantical properties (viz. that some or all of such properties arise from isomorphisms between the causal role of mental states and the implicational structure of propositions). Now, though they are usually held together, it seems clear that these claims are orthogonal. One could opt for monadic mental states without functional-role semantics; or one could opt for functional-role semantics together with some non-monadic account of the polyadicity of the attitudes. My own view is that SR should be rejected wholesale: that it is wrong about both the structure *and* the semantics of the attitudes. But – such is the confusion and perversity of my colleagues – this view is widely thought to be eccentric. The standard Realistic alternative to Standard Realism holds that SR is right about functional semantics but wrong about monadicity. I propose to divide these issues: monadicity first, semantics at the end.

If, in the present intellectual atmosphere, you are Realist and Functionalist about the attitudes, but you don't think that the attitudes are *monadic* functional states, then probably you think that to have a belief or a desire – or whatever – is to be related in a certain way to a Mental Representation. According to the canonical formulation of this view: for any organism O and for any proposition P, there is a relation R and a mental representation MP such that: MP means that (expresses the proposition that) P; and O believes that P iff O bears R to MP. (And similarly, R desires that P iff O bears some *different* relation, R', to MP. And so forth. For elaboration, see Fodor, PA; Fodor, LOT; Field, MR.)

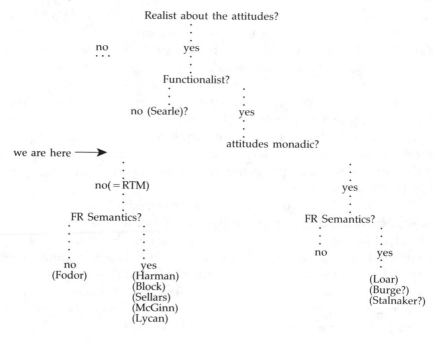

Figure 3.

This is, of course, the doctrine I've been calling full-blown RTM. So we come, at last, to the bottom of the decision tree. (See Figure 3.)

As compared with SR, RTM assumes the heavier burden of ontological commitment. It quantifies not just over such mental states as believing that P and desiring that Q, but also over mental representations; symbols in a 'Language of Thought'. The burden of proof is thus on RTM. (Auntie holds that it doesn't matter who has the burden of proof because the choice between SR and RTM isn't a *philosophical* issue. But I don't know how she tells. Or why she cares.) There are two sorts of considerations which, in my view, argue persuasively for RTM. I think they are the implicit sources of the Cognitive Science Community's commitment to the mental representation construct.

First argument for RTM: productivity and constituency

The collection of states of mind is productive: for example, the thoughts that one actually entertains in the course of a mental life comprise a relatively unsystematic subset drawn from a vastly larger variety of thoughts that one could have entertained had an occasion for them arisen. For example, it has probably never occurred to you before that no grass grows on kangaroos. But, once your attention is drawn to the point, it's an idea that you are quite capable of entertaining, one which, in fact, you are probably inclined to endorse. A theory of the attitudes ought to account for this productivity; it ought to make clear what it is about beliefs and desires in virtue of which they constitute open-ended families.

Notice that Naturalism precludes saying 'there are arbitrarily many propositional attitudes because there are infinitely many propositions' and leaving it at that. The problem about productivity is that there are arbitrarily many propositional attitudes that one can *have*. Since relations between organisms and propositions aren't to be taken as primitive, one is going to have to say what it is about organic states like believing and desiring that allows them to be (roughly) as differentiated as the propositions are. If, for example, you think that attitudes are mapped to propositions in virtue of their causal roles (see above), then you have to say what it is about the attitudes that accounts for the productivity *of the set of causal roles*.

A natural suggestion is that the productivity of thoughts is like the productivity of natural languages, i.e. that there are indefinitely many thoughts to entertain for much the same reason that there are indefinitely many sentences to utter. Fine, but how do natural languages manage to be productive? Here the outlines of an answer are familiar. To a first approximation, each sentence can be identified with a certain sequence of sub-sentential constituents. Different sentences correspond to different ways of arranging these sub-sentential constituents; new sentences correspond to new ways of arranging them. And the meaning of a sentence – the proposition it expresses – is determined, in a regular way, by its constituent structure.

The constituents of sentences are, say, words and phrases. What are the constituents of propositional attitudes? A natural answer would be: other propositional attitudes. Since, for example, you can't believe that P and Q without believing that P and believing that Q, we could take the former state to be a complex of which the latter are the relatively (or perhaps absolutely) simple parts. But a moment's consideration makes it clear that this won't work with any generality: believing that P or Q doesn't require either believing that P or believing that Q, and neither does believing that if P then Q. It looks as though we want propositional attitudes to be built out of *something;* but not out of other propositional attitudes.

There's an interesting analogy to the case of speech-acts (one of many such; see Vendler, RC). There are indefinitely many distinct assertions (i.e. there are indefinitely many propositions that one can assert); and though you can't assert that P and Q without asserting that P and asserting that Q, the disjunctive assertion, P or Q, does not imply the assertion of either of the disjuncts, and the hypothetical assertion, if P then Q, does not imply the assertion of its antecedent or its consequent. So how do you work the constituency relation for *assertions?*

Answer: you take advantage of the fact that making an assertion involves using symbols (typically it involves *uttering* symbols); the constituency relation is defined for the symbols that assertions are made by using. So, in particular, the standard (English-language) vehicle for making the assertion that either John left or Mary wept is the form of words 'either John left or Mary wept'; and, notice, this complex linguistic expression *is*, literally, a construct out of the simpler linguistic expressions 'John left' and 'Mary wept'. You can assert that P or Q without asserting that P or asserting that Q, but you can't utter the form of words 'P or Q' without uttering the form of words 'P' and the form of words 'Q'.

The moral for treatments of the attitudes would seem to be straightforward: solve the *productivity* problem for the attitudes by appealing to constituency. Solve the *constituency* problem for the attitudes in the same way that you solve it for speech-acts: tokening an attitude involves tokening a symbol, just as tokening an assertion does. What kind of symbol do you have to token to token an attitude? A mental representation, of course. Hence RTM. (Auntie says that it is crude and preposterous and *unbiological* to suppose that people have sentences in their heads. Auntie always talks like that when she hasn't got any arguments.)

Second argument for RTM: mental processes

It is possible to doubt whether, as functional-role theories of meaning would have it, the propositional contents of mental states are reducible to, or determined by, or epiphenomena of, their causal roles. But what *can't* be doubted is this: the causal roles of mental states typically closely parallel the implicational structures of their propositional objects; and the predictive successes of propositional-attitude psychology routinely exploit the symmetries thus engendered. If we know that Psmith believes that P $\rightarrow$ Q and we know that he believes that P, then we generally expect him to infer that Q and to act according to his inference. Why do we expect this? Well, because we believe the business about

Psmith to be an instance of a true and counterfactual-supporting generalization according to which believing P and believing P → Q is causally sufficient for inferring Q, *ceteris paribus*. But then: *what is it about the mechanisms of thinking in virtue of which such generalizations hold?* What, in particular, could believing and inferring be, such that thinking the premisses of a valid inference leads, so often and so reliably, to thinking its conclusion?

It was a scandal of mid-century Anglo-American philosophy of mind that though it worried a lot about the nature of mental states (like the attitudes) it quite generally didn't worry much about the nature of mental *processes* (like thinking). This isn't, in retrospect, very surprising given the behaviourism that was widely prevalent. Mental processes are causal sequences of mental states; if you're eliminativist about the attitudes you're hardly likely to be Realist about their causal consequences. In particular, you're hardly likely to be Realist about their *causal interactions*. It now seems clear enough, however, that our theory of the structure of the attitudes *must* accommodate a theory of thinking; and that it is a pre-eminent constraint on the latter that it provide a mechanism for symmetry between the inferential roles of thoughts and their causal roles.

This isn't, by any means, all that easy for a theory of thinking to do. Notice, for example, that the philosophy of mind assumed in traditional British Empiricism was Realist about the attitudes and accepted a form of RTM. (Very roughly, the attitudes were construed as relations to mental images, the latter being endowed with semantic properties in virtue of what they resembled and with causal properties in virtue of their associations. Mental states were productive because complex images can be constructed out of simple ones.) But precisely because the mechanisms of mental causation were assumed to be associationistic (and the conditions for association to involve pre-eminently spatiotemporal propinquity), the Empiricists had no good way of connecting the *contents* of a thought with the effects of entertaining it. They therefore never got close to a plausible theory of thinking, and neither did the associationistic psychology which followed in their footsteps.

What associationism missed – to put it more exactly – was the similarity between trains of thoughts and *arguments*. Here, for an example, is Sherlock Holmes doing his thing at the end of 'The Speckled Band':

. . . I instantly reconsidered my position when . . . it became clear to me that whatever danger threatened an occupant of the room could not come either from the window or the door. My attention was speedily drawn, as I have already remarked to you, to this ventilator, and to the bell-rope which hung down to the bed. The discovery that this was a dummy, and that the bed was clamped to the floor, instantly gave rise to the suspicion that the rope was there as a bridge for something passing through the hole, and coming to the bed. The idea of a snake instantly occurred to me, and when I coupled it with my knowledge that the Doctor was furnished with a supply of the creatures from India I felt that I was probably on the right track . . .

The passage purports to be a bit of reconstructive psychology, a capsule history of the sequence of mental episodes which brought Holmes first to suspect, then to believe, that the Doctor did it with his pet snake. Now, back when Auntie was a girl and reasons weren't allowed to be causes, philosophers were unable to believe that such an aetiology could be literally true. I assume, however, that liberation has set in by now; we have no philosophically impressive reason to doubt that Holmes's train of thoughts went pretty much the way that he says it did.

What is therefore interesting, for our purposes, is that Holmes's story isn't *just* reconstructive psychology. It does a double duty since it also serves to assemble *premisses* for a plausible inference to the *conclusion* that the doctor did it with the snake. ('A snake could have crawled through the ventilator and slithered down the bell-rope'; 'the Doctor was known to keep a supply of snakes in his snuff box', and so forth.) Because this train of thoughts is tantamount to an argument, Holmes expects Watson to be *convinced* by the considerations which, when they occurred to him, caused Holmes's own conviction. (Compare the sort of mental history that goes 'Well, I went to bed and slept on it, and when I woke up in the morning I found that the problem had solved itself'. Or the sort that goes: 'Bell-ropes always make me think of snakes, and snakes make me think of snake oil, and snake oil makes me think of doctors; so when I saw the bell-rope it popped into my head that the Doctor and a snake might have done it between them'. That's mental causation perhaps; but it's not *thinking*.)

What connects the causal-history aspect of Holmes's story with its plausible-inference aspect is precisely the parallelism between trains of thought and arguments: the thoughts that effect the fixation of the belief that P provide, often enough, good *grounds* for believing that P. (As Holmes puts it in another story, 'one true inference invariably suggests others'.) Were this not the case – were there not this general harmony between the semantical and the causal properties of thoughts – there wouldn't, after all, be much profit in thinking.

What you want to make thinking worth the while is that trains of thoughts should be generated by mechanisms that are generally truth-preserving (so that 'a true inference (generally) suggests other inferences *that are also true*'). Argument is generally truth-preserving; that, surely, is the teleological basis of the similarity between trains of thoughts and arguments. The associationists noticed hardly any of this; and even if they had noticed it, they wouldn't have known what to do with it. In this respect, Conan Doyle was a far deeper psychologist – far closer to what is essential about the mental life – than, say James Joyce (or William James, for that matter).

When, therefore, Rationalist critics (including, notably, Kant) pointed out that thought – like argument – involves judging and inferring, the cat was out of the bag. Associationism was the best available form of Realism about the attitudes, and associationism failed to produce a credible mechanism for thinking. Which is to say that it failed to produce a credible theory of the attitudes. No wonder everybody gave up and turned into a behaviourist.

Cognitive Science is the art of getting the cat back in. The trick is to abandon associationism and combine RTM with the 'computer metaphor'. In this respect I think there really has been something like an intellectual breakthrough. Technical details to one side, this is – in my view – the *only* respect in which contemporary Cognitive Science represents a major advance over the versions of RTM that were its eighteenth- and nineteenth-century predecessors.

Computers show us how to connect semantical with causal properties *for symbols*. So, if the tokening of an attitude involves the tokening of a symbol, then we can get some leverage on connecting semantical with causal properties *for thoughts*. Here, in roughest outline, is how the story is supposed to go.

You connect the causal properties of a symbol with its semantic properties via its syntax. The syntax of a symbol is one of its second-order physical properties. To a first approximation, we can think of its syntactic structure as an abstract feature of its (geometric or acoustic) *shape*. Because, to all intents and purposes, syntax reduces to shape, and because the shape of a symbol is a potential determinant of its causal role, it is fairly easy to see how there could be environments in which the causal role of a symbol correlates with its syntax. It's easy, that is to say, to imagine symbol tokens interacting causally *in virtue of* their syntactic structures. The syntax of a symbol might determine the causes and effects of its tokenings in much the way that the geometry of a key determines which locks it will open.

But, now, we know from formal logic that certain of the semantic relations among symbols can be – as it were – 'mimicked' by their syntactic relations; that, when seen from a very great distance, is what proof-theory is about. So, within certain famous limits, the semantic relation that holds between two symbols when the proposition expressed by the one is implied by the proposition expressed by the other can be mimicked by syntactic relations in virtue of which one of the symbols is derivable from the other. We can therefore build machines which have, again within famous limits, the following property: the operations of such a machine consist entirely of transformations of symbols; in the course of performing these operations, the machine is sensitive solely to syntactic properties of the symbols; and the operations that the machine performs on the symbols are entirely confined to alterations of their shapes. Yet the machine is so devised that it will transform one symbol into another if and only if the symbols so transformed stand in certain *semantic* relations; e.g. the relation that the premisses bear to the conclusion in a valid argument. Such machines – computers, of course – just *are* environments in which the causal role of a symbol token is made to parallel the inferential role of the proposition that it expresses.[3]

I expect it's clear how this is all supposed to provide an argument for quantifying over mental representations. Computers are a solution to the problem of mediating between the causal properties of symbols and their semantic properties. So *if* the mind is a sort of computer, we begin to see how you can have a theory of mental processes that succeeds where associationism (to say nothing of behaviourism) abjectly failed; a theory which explains how there could regularly be non-arbitrary content relations among causally related thoughts.

But, patently, there are going to have to be mental representations if the proposal is going to work. In computer design, causal role is brought into phase with content by exploiting parallelisms between the syntax of a symbol and its semantics. But that idea won't do the theory of *mind* any good unless there are *mental* symbols; mental particulars possessed of semantic *and syntactic* properties. There must be mental symbols because, in a nutshell, only symbols have syntax, and our best available theory of mental processes – indeed, the *only* available theory of mental processes that isn't *known* to be false – needs the picture of the mind as a syntax-driven machine.[4]

A brief addendum before we end this section: the question of the extent to which RTM must be committed to the 'explicitness' of mental representation is one that keeps getting raised in the philosophical literature (and elsewhere; see Dennett, CCC; Stabler, HAGR). The issue becomes clear if we consider real computers as deployed in Artificial Intelligence research. So, to borrow an example of Dennett's, there are chess machines which play as though they 'believe' that it's a good idea to get one's Queen out early. But there needn't be – in fact, there probably wouldn't be – anywhere in the system of heuristics which constitutes the program of such a machine a symbol that *means* '(try and) get your Queen out early'; rather the machine's obedience to that rule of play is, as it were, an epiphenomenon of its following many *other* rules, much more detailed, whose joint effect is that, *ceteris paribus*, the Queen gets out as soon as it can. The moral is supposed to be that though the contents of *some* of the attitudes it would be natural to attribute to the machine *may* be explicitly represented, none of them *have* to be, *even assuming the sort of story about how computational processes work that is supposed to motivate RTM*. So, then, what exactly *is* RTM minimally committed to by way of explicit mental representation?

The answer should be clear in light of the previous discussion. According to RTM, mental processes are transformations of mental representations. The rules which determine the course of such transformations may, but needn't, be themselves explicitly represented. But the mental contents (the 'thoughts', as it were) that get transformed *must be* explicitly represented or the theory is simply false. To put it another way: if the occurrence of a thought is an episode in a mental process, then RTM is committed to the explicit representation of the content of the thought. Or, to put it still a third way – the way they like to put it in AI – according to RTM, programs may be explicitly represented and data structures have to be.

For the sake of a simple example, let's pretend that associationism is true; we imagine that there is a principle of Association by Proximity in virtue of which thoughts of salt get associated with thoughts of pepper. The point is that even on the assumption that it subsumes mental processes, the rule 'associate by proximity' need not itself be explicitly represented; association by proximity may emerge from dynamical properties of ideas (as in Hume) or from dynamical properties of neural stuff (as in contemporary connectionism). But what *must* be explicit is the Ideas – of pepper and salt, as it might be – that get associated. For, according to the theory, mental processes are actually *causal sequences of tokenings of such Ideas;* so, no Ideas, no mental processes.

Similarly, *mutatis mutandis*, for the chess case. The rule 'get it out early' may be emergent out of its own implementation; out of lower-level heuristics, that is, any one of which may or may not itself be explicitly represented. But the representation of the board – of actual or possible states of play – over which such heuristics are defined *must* be explicit or the representational theory of chess playing is simply false. The theory says that a train of chess thoughts is a causal sequence of tokenings of chess representations. If, therefore, there are trains of chess thoughts but no tokenings of chess representations, it *follows* that something is not well with the theory.

So much, then, for RTM and the polyadicity of the attitudes. What about their semanticity? We proceed to our final diagnostic question:

Fourth question: How do you feel about truth-conditions?

I remarked above that the two characteristic tenets of SR – that the attitudes are monadic and that the semanticity of the attitudes arises from isomorphisms between the causal network of mental states and the inferential network of propositions – are mutually independent. Similarly for RTM; it's not mandatory, but you are at liberty to combine RTM with functional-role ('FR') semantics if you choose. Thus, you could perfectly well say: 'Believing, desiring, and so forth are relations between intentional systems and mental representations that get tokened (in their heads, as it might be). Tokening a mental representation has causal consequences. The totality of such consequences implies a network of causal interrelations among the attitudes . . .' and so on to a functional-role semantics. In any event, it's important to see that RTM needs *some* semantic story to tell if, as we have supposed, RTM is going to be Realist about the attitudes and the attitudes have their propositional objects essentially.

Which semantic story to tell is, in my view, going to be *the* issue in mental representation theory for the foreseeable future. The questions here are so difficult, and the answers so contentious, that they really fall outside the scope of this paper; I had advertised a tour of an intellectual landscape about whose topography there exists some working consensus. Still, I want to say a little about the semantic issues by way of closing. They are the piece of Cognitive Science where philosophers feel most at home; and they're where the 'philosophy of psychology' (a discipline over which Auntie is disinclined to quantify) joins the philosophy of language (which, I notice, Auntie allows me to spell without quotes).

There are a number of reasons for doubting that a functional-role semantic theory of the sort that SR proposes is tenable. This fact is currently causing something of a crisis among people who would like to be Realists about the attitudes.

In the first place – almost, by now, too obvious to mention – functional-role theories make it seem that empirical constraints must underdetermine the semantics of the attitudes. What I've got in mind here isn't the collection of worries that cluster around the 'indeterminacy of translation' thesis; if that sort of indeterminacy is to be taken seriously at all – which I doubt – then it is equally a problem for *every* Realist semantics. There are, however, certain sources of underdetermination that appear to be built into functional-role semantics as such; considerations which suggest either that there is no unique best mapping of the causal roles of mental states on to the inferential network of propositions or that, even if there is, such a mapping would nevertheless underdetermine assignments of contents to the attitudes. I'll mention two such considerations, but no doubt there are others; things are always worse than one supposes.

Idealization

The pattern of causal dispositions actually accruing to a given mental state must surely diverge very greatly from the pattern of inferences characteristic of its propositional object. We don't, for example, believe all the consequences of our beliefs; not just because we haven't got time to, and not just because everybody is at least a little irrational, but also because we surely have some false beliefs about what the consequences of our beliefs are. This amounts to saying that some substantial idealization is required if we're to get from the causal dispositions that mental states actually exhibit to the sort of causal network that we would like to have: a causal network whose structure is closely isomorphic to the inferential network of propositions. And now the problem is to provide a non-circular justification – one which does not itself appeal to semantical or intentional considerations – for preferring *that* idealization to an infinity or so of others that ingenuity might devise. (It won't do, of course, to say that we prefer that idealization because it's the one which allows mental states to be assigned the intuitively plausible propositional objects; for the present question is precisely whether anything besides prejudice underwrites our common-sense psychological intuitions.) Probably the idealization problem arises, in some form or other, for any account of the attitudes which proposes to reduce their semantic properties to their causal ones. That, alas, is no reason to assume that the problem can be solved.

Equivalence

Functionalism guarantees that mental states are individuated by their causal roles; hence by their position in the putative causal network. But *nothing* guarantees that *propositions* are individuated by their *inferential* roles. Prima facie, it surely seems that they are not since equivalent propositions are *ipso facto* identical in their inferential liaisons. Are we therefore to say that equivalent propositions are identical? Not, at least, for the psychologist's purposes since attitudes whose propositional objects are equivalent may nevertheless differ in their causal roles. We need to distinguish, as it might be, the belief that P from the belief that P & (Q v – Q), hence we need to distinguish the *proposition* that P from the proposition that P & (Q v – Q). But surely what distinguishes these propositions is not their inferential roles, assuming that the inferential role of a proposition is something like the set of propositions it cntails and is entailed by. It seems to follow that propositions are not individuated by their position in the inferential network, hence that assignments of propositional objects to mental states, if constrained only to preserve isomorphism between the networks, *ipso facto* underdetermine the contents of such states. There are, perhaps, ways out of such equivalence problems; 'situation semantics' (see Barwise, SA) has recently been advertising some. But all the ways out that I've heard of violate the assumptions of FR semantics; specifically, they don't identify propositions with nodes in a network of inferential roles.

In the second place, FR semantics isn't, after all, much of a panacea for Naturalistic scruples. Thought it has a Naturalistic story to tell about how mental states might be paired with their propositional objects, the semantic properties of the propositions themselves are assumed, not explained. It is, for example, an intrinsic property of the proposition that Psmith is seated that it is true or false in virtue of Psmith's posture. FR semantics simply takes this sort of fact for granted. From the Naturalist's point of view, therefore, it merely displaces the main worry from 'What's the connection between an attitude and its propositional object?' to 'What's the connection between the propositional object of an attitude and whatever state of affairs it is that makes that proposition true or false?' Or, to put much the same point slightly differently, FR semantics has a lot to say about the mind-to-proposition problem but nothing at all to say about the mind-to-world problem. In effect FR semantics is content to hold that the attitudes inherit their satisfaction-conditions from their propositional objects and that propositions have *their* satisfaction-conditions *by stipulation*.

And, in the third place, to embrace FR semantics is to raise a variety of (approximately Quinean) issues about the individuation of the attitudes; and these, as Putnam and Stich have recently emphasized, when once conjured up are not easily put down. The argument goes like this: according to FR semantic theories, each attitude has its propositional object in virtue of its position in the causal network: 'different objects iff different loci' holds to a first approximation. Since a propositional attitude has its propositional object essentially, this makes an attitude's identity depend on the identity of its causal role. The problem is, however, that we have no criteria for the individuation of causal roles.

The usual sceptical tactic of this point is to introduce some or other form of slippery-slope argument to show – or at least to suggest – that there *couldn't be* a criterion for the individuation of causal roles that is other than arbitrary. Stich, for example, has the case of an increasingly senile woman who eventually is able to remember about President McKinley only that he was assassinated. Given that she has no *other* beliefs about McKinley – given, let's suppose, that the *only* causal consequence of her believing that McKinley was assassinated is to prompt her to produce and assent to occasional utterances of 'McKinley was assassinated' and immediate logical consequences thereof – is it clear that she in fact has *any* beliefs about McKinley at all? But if she *doesn't* have, *when, precisely, did she cease to do so?* How much causal role does the belief that McKinley was assassinated have to have to be the belief that McKinley was assassinated? And what reason is there to suppose that this question has an answer? (See Stich, FFPTCS and also Putnam, CPIT.) Auntie considers slippery-slope arguments to be in dubious taste and there is much to be said for her view. Still, it looks as though FR semantics has brought us to the edge of a morass and I, for one, am not an enthusiast for wading in it.

Well then, to summarize: the syntactic theory of mental operations promises a reductive account of the *intelligence* of thought. We can now imagine – though, to be sure, only dimly and in a glass darkly – a psychology which exhibits quite complex cognitive processes as being constructed from elementary manipulations of symbols. This is what RTM, together with the computer metaphor, has brought us; and it is, in my view, no small matter. But a theory of the *intelligence* of thought does not, in and of itself, constitute a theory of thought's *intentionality*. (Compare such early papers as Dennett, IS, where these issues are more or less comprehensively run together, with such second thoughts as Fodor, SSA and Cummins, NPE where they more or less aren't.) If RTM is true, the problem of the intentionality of the mental is largely – perhaps exhaustively – the problem of the semanticity of mental representations. But of the semanticity of mental representations we have, as things now stand, no adequate account.

Here ends the tour. Beyond this point there be monsters. It may be that what one descries, just there on the furthest horizon, is a glimpse of a causal/teleological theory of meaning (Stampe TCTLR; Dretske, KFI; Fodor, SWS; Fodor, P); and it may be that the development of such a theory would provide a way out of the current mess. At best, however, it's a long way off. I mention it only to encourage such of the passengers as may be feeling queasy.

('Are you finished playing now?'
'Yes, Auntie.'
'Well, don't forget to put the toys away.'
'No, Auntie.')

Notes

1. Unless you are an eliminativist behaviourist (say Watson) which puts you, for present purposes, beyond the pale.
   While we're at it: it rather messes up my nice taxonomy that there are philosophers who accept a Functionalist view of psychological explanation, and are Realist about belief/desire psychology, but who reject the reduction of the latter to the former. In particular, they do not accept the identification of any of the entities that Functionalist psychologists posit with the propositional attitudes that common sense holds dear. (A version of this view says that functional states 'realize' propositional attitudes in much the way that the physical states are supposed to realize functional ones. See, for example Matthews, TR.)
2. This account of the attitudes seems to be in the air these days; and, as with most doctrines that are in the air, it's a little hard to be sure exactly who holds it. Far the most detailed version is in Loar, MM; thought I have seen variants in unpublished papers by Tyler Burge, Robert Stalnaker, and Hartry Field.
3. Since the methods of a computational psychology tend to be those of proof theory, its limitations tend to be those of formalization. Patently, this raises the well-known issues about completeness; less obviously it connects the Cognitive Science enterprise with the Positivist programme for the formaliza-

tion of inductive (and, generally, non-demonstrative) styles of argument. (On the second point, see Glymour, AE.)

4. It is possible to combine enthusiasm for a syntactic account of mental processes with any degree of agnosticism about the attitudes – or, for that matter, about semantic evaluability itself. To claim that the mind is a 'syntax-driven machine' is precisely to hold that the theory of mental processes can be set out in its entirety without reference to any of the semantic properties of mental states (see Fodor, MS), hence without assuming that mental states *have* any semantic properties. Steven Stich is famous for having espoused this option (Stich, FFPTCS). My way of laying out the field has put the big divide between Realism about the attitudes and its denial. This seems to me justifiable, but admittedly it underestimates the substantial affinities between Stich and the RTM crowd. Stich's account of what a good science of behaviour would look like is far closer to RTM than it is to, for example, the eliminative materialism of the Churchlands.

References

Barwise, SA: Barwise, J. and Perry, J., *Situations and Attitudes*. MIT Press (1983).

Block, WIF: Block, N., 'What is Functionalism?' in Block, N. (ed.), *Readings in Philosophy of Psychology*, Vol. 1. Harvard University Press (1980).

Churchland, EMPA: Churchland, P., 'Eliminative Materialism and Propositional Attitudes', *Journal of Philosophy*, 78 (1981), 2.

Cummins, NPE: Cummins, R., *The Nature of Psychological Explanation*. MIT Press (1983).

Dennett, B: Dennett, D., *Brainstorms*. Bradford Books (1978).

Dennett, CCC: Dennett, D., 'A Cure for the Common Code?', in *Brainstorms*. Bradford Books (1978).

Dennett, IS: Dennett, D., 'Intentional Systems', in *Brainstorms*. Bradford Books (1978).

Dennett, TB: Dennett, D., 'True Believers: The Intentional Strategy and Why It Works', in *Scientific Explanation, Papers Based on Herbert Spencer Lectures Given in the University of Oxford*. Clarendon Press (1981).

Dretske, KFI: Dretske, F., *Knowledge and the Flow of Information*. MIT Press (1981).

Dreyfus, WCCD: Dreyfus, H., *What Computers Can't Do*. Harper & Row (1979).

Field, MR: Field, H., 'Mental Representation', *Erkenntnis*, 13 (1978), 9–61; also in Block, N. (ed.), *Readings in Philosophy of Psychology*, Vol. 2. Harvard University Press (1980).

Fodor, BD: Fodor, J., 'Banish DisContent'. Unpublished.

Fodor, LOT: Fodor, J., *The Language of Thought*. Thomas Y. Crowell Co., Inc. (1975) and Harvard University Press, paperback (1979).

Fodor, MBP: Fodor, J., 'The Mind–Body Problem', *Scientific American*, 244 (1981), 515–31.

Fodor, MS: Fodor, J., 'Methodological Solipsism', *The Behavioral and Brain Sciences* 3 (1980). Reprinted in Fodor, J., *Representations*. Harvester (1981).

Fodor, P: Fodor, J., 'Psychosemantics, Or Where Do Truth Conditions Come From?' Unpublished.

Fodor, PA: Fodor, J., 'Propositional Attitudes', *The Monist*, 61 (1978). Reprinted in Fodor, J., *Representations*. Harvester (1981).

Fodor, SSA: Fodor, J., 'Something on the State of the Art'. Unpublished.

Fodor, SWS: Fodor, J., 'Semantics, Wisconsin Style', *Synthese*, 59 (1991), 231–50.

Glymour, AE: Glymour, C., 'Android Epistemology'. Unpublished.

Haugeland, NPC: Haugeland, J., 'The Nature and Plausibility of Cognitivism', *The Behavioural and Brain Sciences*, 2 (1981), 215–60.

Loar, MM: Loar, B., *Mind and Meaning*. Cambridge University Press (1981).

Matthews, TR: Matthews, R., 'Troubles with Representationalism', forthcoming in *Social Research*.

Putnam, CPIT: Putnam, H., 'Computational Psychology and Interpretation Theory,' in *Philosophical Papers, Vol. III: Realism and Reason*. Cambridge University Press (1983).

Putnam, MH: Putnam, H., 'Meaning Holism', mimeograph, Harvard University.

Searle, MBP: Searle, J., 'Minds, Brains and Programs', *The Behavioral and Brain Sciences*, 3 (1980), 417–24.

Stabler, HAGR: Stabler, E., 'How are Grammars Represented?' *The Behavioral and Brain Sciences* 6 (1983), 391–402.

Stampe, TCTLR: Stampe, D., 'Towards a Causal Theory of Linguistic Representation', *Midwest Studies in Philosophy*, II (1977), 42–63.

Stich, FFPTCS: Stich, S., *From Folk Psychology to Cognitive Science*. MIT Press (1983).

Vendler, RC: Vendler, Z., *Res Cogitans*. Cornell University Press (1972).

2 Folk psychology and the explanation of human behavior

Paul M. Churchland

Folk psychology, insist some, is just like folk mechanics, folk thermo-dynamics, folk meteorology, folk chemistry, and folk biology. It is a framework of concepts, roughly adequate to the demands of everyday life, with which the humble adept comprehends, explains, predicts, and manipulates a certain domain of phenomena. It is, in short, a folk *theory*. As with any theory, it may be evaluated for its virtues or vices in all of the dimensions listed. And as with any theory, it may be rejected in its entirety if it fails the measure of such evaluation. Call this the "theoretical view" of our self understanding.

Folk psychology, insist others, is radically unlike the examples cited. It does not consist of laws. It does not support causal explanations. It does not evolve over time. Its central purpose is normative rather than descriptive. And thus, it is not the sort of framework that might be shown to be radically defective by sheerly empirical findings. Its assimilation to theories is just a mistake. It has nothing to fear, therefore, from advances in cognitive theory or the neurosciences. Call this the "antitheoretical view" of our self-understanding.

Somebody here is deeply mistaken. The first burden of this essay is to argue that it is the antitheoretical view that harbors most, though not all, of those mistakes. In the thirty years since the theoretical view was introduced (see especially Sellars 1956; Feyerabend 1963; Rorty 1965; P. M. Churchland 1970, 1979, 1981) a variety of objections have been leveled against it. The more interesting of those will be addressed shortly. My current view is that these objections motivate no changes whatever in the theoretical view.

The second and more important burden of this essay, however, is to

An abridged version of this essay first appeared in *Proceedings of the Aristotelian Society*, supplementary vol. 62 (1988). Section 3 is a short commentary on Daniel C. Dennett's *Intentional Stance*. It first appeared in *Behavioral and Brain Sciences* 11 (1989), no. 3, under the title, "On the Ontological Status of Intentional States: Nailing Folk Psychology to Its Perch."

outline and repair a serious failing in the traditional expressions of the theoretical view, my own expressions included. The failing, as I see it, lies in representing one's commonsense understanding of human nature as consisting of *an internally stored set of general sentences*, and in representing one's predictive and explanatory activities as being a matter of *deductive inference* from those sentences plus occasional premises about the case at hand.

This certainly sounds like a major concession to the antitheoretical view, but in fact it is not. For what motivates this reappraisal of the character of our self-understanding is the gathering conviction that little or *none* of human understanding consists of stored sentences, not even the prototypically *scientific* understanding embodied in a practicing physicist, chemist, or astronomer. The familiar conception of knowledge as a set of propositional attitudes is itself a central aspect of the framework of folk psychology, according to the reappraisal at hand, and it is an aspect that needs badly to be replaced. Our self-understanding, I continue to maintain, is no different in character from our understanding of any other empirical domain. It is speculative, systematic, corrigible, and in principle replaceable. It is just not so specifically *linguistic* as we have chronically assumed.

The speculative and replaceable character of folk psychology is now somewhat easier to defend than it was in the sixties and seventies, because recent advances in connectionist artificial intelligence (AI) and computational neuroscience have provided us with a fertile new framework with which to understand the perception, cognition, and behavior of intelligent creatures. Whether it will eventually prove adequate to the task of replacing folk psychology remains to be seen, but the mere possibility of systematic alternative conceptions of cognitive activity and intelligent behavior should no longer be a matter of dispute. Alternatives are already in the making. Later in the paper I shall outline the main features of this novel framework and explore its significance for the issues here at stake. For now, let me acquiesce in the folk-psychological conception of knowledge as a system of beliefs or similar propositional attitudes, and try to meet the objections to the theoretical view already outstanding.

1. Objections to the theoretical view

As illustrated in my 1970, 1979, and 1984 publications, a thorough perusal of the explanatory factors that typically appear in our commonsense explanations of our internal states and our overt behavior sustains the quick "reconstruction" of a large number of universally quantified conditional statements, conditions with the conjunction of the relevant explanatory factors as the antecedent and the relevant explanandum as the consequent. It is these universal statements that are supposed to constitute the "laws" of folk psychology.

A perennial objection is that these generalizations do not have the character of genuine causal/explanatory laws; rather, they have some other, less empirical status (e.g., that of normative principles or rules of language or analytic truths). Without confronting each of the many alternatives in turn, I think we can make serious difficulties for any objection of this sort.

Note first that the concepts of folk psychology divide into two broad classes. On the one hand, there are those fully intentional concepts expressing the various propositional attitudes, such as belief and desire. And on the other hand, there are those nonintentional or quasi-intentional concepts expressing all of the other mental states, such as grief, fear, pain, hunger, and the full range of emotions and bodily sensations. Where states of the latter kind are concerned, I think it is hardly a matter for dispute that the common homilies in which they figure are causal/explanatory laws. Consider the following.

- A person who suffers severe bodily damage will feel pain.
- A person who suffers a sudden sharp pain will wince.
- A person denied food for any length will feel hunger.
- A hungry person's mouth will water at the smell of food.
- A person who feels overall warmth will tend to relax.
- A person who tastes a lemon will have a puckering sensation.
- A person who is angry will tend to be impatient.

Clearly these humble generalizations, and thousands more like them, are causal/explanatory in character. They will and regularly do support simple explanations, sustain subjunctive and counterfactual conditionals, and underwrite predictions in the standard fashion. Moreover, concepts of this simple sort carry perhaps the major part of the folk-psychological burden. The comparatively complex explanations involving the propositional attitudes are of central importance, but they are surrounded by a quotidian whirl of simple explanations like these, all quite evidently of a causal/explanatory cast.

It won't do, then, to insist that the generalizations of folk psychology are on the whole nonempirical or noncausal in character. The bulk of them, and I mean thousands upon thousands of them, are transparently causal or nomological. The best one can hope to argue is that there is a central core of folk-psychological concepts whose explanatory role is somehow *discontinuous* with that of their fellows. The propositional attitudes, especially belief and desire, are the perennial candidates for such a nonempirical role, for explanations in their terms typically display the explanandum event as "rational." What shall we say of explanations in terms of beliefs and desires?

We should tell essentially the same causal/explanatory story, and for the following reason. Whatever else humans do with the concepts for the propositional attitudes, they do use them successfully to predict the future behavior of others. This means that, on the basis of presumed information about the current cognitive states of the relevant individuals, one can nonaccidentally predict at least some of their future behavior some of the time. But any principle that allows us to do this – that is, to predict one empirical state or event on the basis of another, logically distinct, empirical state or event – *has* to be empirical in character. And I assume it is clear that the event of my ducking my head is logically distinct both from the event of my perceiving an incoming snowball, and from the states of my desiring to avoid a collision and my belief that ducking is the best way to achieve this.

Indeed, one can do more than merely predict: one can control and manipulate the behavior of others by controlling the information available to them. Here one is bringing about certain behaviors by steering the cognitive states of the subject, by relating opportunities, dangers, or obligations relevant to that subject. How this is possible without an understanding of the objective empirical regularities that connect the internal states and the overt behaviors of normal people is something that the antitheoretical position needs to explain.

The confused temptation to find something special about the case of intentional action derives primarily from the fact that the central element in a full-blooded action explanation is a configuration of propositional attitudes in the light of which the explanandum behavior can be seen as sensible or rational, at least from the agent's narrow point of view. In this rational-in-the-light-of-relation we seem to have some sort of supercausal *logical* relation between the explanans and the explanandum, which is an invitation to see a distinct and novel type of explanation at work.

Yet while the premise is true – there is indeed a logical relation between the explanandum and certain elements in the explanans – the conclusion does not begin to follow. Students of the subject are still regularly misled on this point, for they fail to appreciate that a circumstance of this general sort is *typical* of theoretical explanations. Far from being a sign of the nonempirical and hence nontheoretical character of the generalizations and explanations at issue, it is one of the surest signs available that we are here dealing with a high-grade theoretical framework. Let me explain.

The electric current *I* in a wire or any conductor is causally determined by two factors: it tends to increase with the electromotive force or voltage *V* that moves the electrons down the wire, and it tends to be reduced according to the resistance *R* the wire offers against their motion. Briefly, $I = V/R$. Less cryptically and more revealingly,

> *(x)(V)(R)[(x is subject to a voltage of (V)) & (x offers a resistance of (R))*
> $\supset$ *(∃I) ((x has a current value of (I)) & (I = V/R))]*

The first point to notice here is that the crucial predicates – *has a resistance of (R), is subject to a voltage of (V),* and *has a current of (I)* – are what might be called "numerical attitudes": they are predicate-forming functors that take singular terms for numbers in the variable position. A complete predicate is formed only when a specific numeral appears in the relevant position. The second point to notice is that this electrodynamical law exploits a relation holding on the domain of numbers in order to express an important empirical regularity. The current *I* is the *quotient* of the voltage *V* and the resistance *R*, whose values will be cited in explanation of the current. And the third point to notice is that this law and the explanations it sustains are typical of laws and explanations throughout science. Most of our scientific predicates express numerical attitudes of the sort displayed, and most of our laws exploit and display relations that hold primarily on the abstract domain of numbers. Nor are they limited to numbers. Other laws exploit the abstract relations holding on the abstract domain of vectors, or on the domain of sets, or groups, or matrices. But none of this means they are nonempirical, or noncausal, or nonnomic.

Action explanations, and intentional explanations in general, follow the same pattern. The only difference is that here the domain of abstract objects being exploited is the domain of propositions, and the relations displayed are logical relations. And like the numerical and vectorial attitudes typical of theories, the expressions for the propositional attitudes are predicate-forming functors. *Believes that P*, for example, forms a complete predicate only when a specific sentence appears in the variable position *P*. The principles that comprehend these predicates have the same abstract and highly sophisticated structure displayed by our most typical theories. They just exploit the relations holding on a different domain of abstract objects in order to express the important empirical regularities comprehending the states and activities of cognitive creatures. That makes folk psychology a very interesting theory, perhaps, but it is hardly a sign of its being *nontheoretical*. Quite the reverse is true. (This matter is discussed at greater length in Churchland 1979, section 14, and 1981, pp. 82–84.)

In sum, the simpler parts of folk psychology are transparently causal or nomic in character, and the more complex parts have the same sophisticated logical structure typical of our most powerful theories.

But we are not yet done with objections. A recurrent complaint is that in many cases the reconstructed conditionals that purport to be sample "laws" of folk psychology are either strictly speaking false, or they border on the trivial by reason of being qualified by various *ceteris paribus* clauses. A first reply is to point out that my position does not claim that the laws of folk psychology are either true or complete. I agree that they are a motley lot. My hope is to see them replaced entirely, and their ontology of states with them. But this reply is not wholly responsive, for the point of the objection is that it is implausible to claim the status of an entrenched theoretical framework for a bunch of "laws" that are as vague, as loose, and as festooned with *ceteris paribus* clauses as are the examples typically given.

I will make no attempt here to defend the ultimate integrity of the laws of folk psychology, for I have little confidence in them myself. But this is not what is required to meet the objection. What needs pointing out is that the "laws" of folk theories are *in general* sloppy, vague, and festooned with qualifications and *ceteris paribus* clauses. What the objectors need to do, in order to remove the relevant system of generalizations from the class of empirical theories, is to show that folk psychology is significantly *worse* in all of these respects than are the principles of folk mechanics, or folk thermodynamics, or folk biology, and so forth. In this they are sure to be disappointed, for these other folk theories are even worse than folk psychology (see McKloskey 1983). In all, folk psychology may be a fairly ramshackle theory, but a theory it remains. Nor is it a point against this that folk psychology has changed little or none since ancient times. The same is true of other theories near and dear to us. The folk physics of the twentieth century, I regret to say, is essentially the same as the folk physics of the ancient Greeks (McKloskey 1983). Our conceptual inertia on such matters may be enormous, but a theory remains a theory, however many centuries it may possess us.

A quite different objection directs our attention to the great many things beyond explanation and prediction for which we use the vocabulary and concepts of folk psychology. Their primary function, runs the objection, is not the function served by explanatory theories, but rather the myriad social functions that constitute human culture and commerce. We use the resources of folk psychology to promise, to entreat, to congratulate, to tease, to joke, to intimate, to threaten, and so on. (See Wilkes 1981, 1984.)

The list of functions is clearly both long and genuine. But most of these functions surely come under the heading of control or manipulation, which is just as typical and central a function of theories as is either explanation or prediction, but which is not mentioned in the list of theoretical functions supplied by the objectors. Though the image may be popular, the idle musings of an impotent stargazer provide a poor example of what theories are and what theories do. More typically, theories are the conceptual vehicles with which we literally come to grips with the world. The fact that folk psychology serves a wealth of practical purposes is no evidence of its being nontheoretical. Quite the reverse.

Manipulation aside, we should not underestimate the importance for social commerce of the explanations and predictions that folk psychology makes possible. If one cannot predict or anticipate the behavior of one's fellows at all, then one can engage in no useful commerce with them whatever. And finding the right explanations for their past behavior is often the key to finding the appropriate premises from which to anticipate their future behavior. The objection's attempt to paint the functions of folk psychology in an exclusively nontheoretical light is simply a distortion born of tunnel vision.

In any case, it is irrelevant. For there is no inconsistency in saying that a theoretical framework should also serve a great many nontheoretical purposes. To use an example I have used before (1986), the theory of *witches, demonic possession, exorcism,* and *trial by ordeal,* was also used for a variety of social purposes beyond strict explanation and prediction. For example, its vocabulary was used to warn, to censure, to abjure, to accuse, to badger, to sentence, and so forth. But none of this meant that demons and witches were anything other than theoretical entities, and none of this saved the ontology of demon theory from elimination when its empirical failings became acute and different conceptions of human pathology arose to replace it. Beliefs, desires, and the rest of the folk-psychological ontology all are in the same position. Their integrity, to the extent that they have any, derives from the explanatory, predictive, and manipulative prowess they display.

It is on the topic of explanation and prediction that a further objection finds fault with the theoretical view. Precisely what, begins the objection, is the observable behavior that the ontology of folk psychology is postulated to explain? Is it bodily behavior as *kinematically* described? In some cases, perhaps, but not in general, certainly, because many quite different kinematical sequences could count as the same intentional action, and it is generally the *action* that is properly the object of folk-psychological explanations of behavior. In general, the descriptions of human behavior that figure in folk-psychological explanations and pre-dictions are descriptions that *already* imply perception, intelligence, and personhood on the part of the agent. Thus, it must be wrong to see the relation between one's psychological states and one's behavior on the model of theoretical states postulated to explain the behavior of some conceptually independent domain of phenomena (Haldane 1988).

The premise of this objection is fairly clearly true: a large class of behavior descriptions are not conceptually independent of the concepts of folk psychology. But this affords no grounds for denying theoretical status to the ontology of folk psychology. The assumption that it does reflects a naive view of the relation between theories and the domains they explain and predict. The naive assumption is that the concepts used to describe the domain to be explained must always be concep-tually independent of the theory used to explain the phenomena within that domain. That assumption is known to be false, and we need look no farther than the special theory of relativity (STR) for a living counterex-ample.

The introduction of STR brought with it a systematic reconfiguration of all of the basic observational concepts of mechanics: spatial length, temporal duration, velocity, mass, momentum, etc. These are all one-place predicates within classical mechanics, but they are all replaced by two-place predicates with STR. Each ostensible "property" has turned out to be a *relation*, and each has a definite value only relative to a chosen reference frame. If STR is true, and since the early years of this century it has seemed to be, then one cannot legitimately describe the observation-al facts of mechanics save in terms that are drawn from STR itself.

Modern chemistry provides a second example. It is a rare chemist who does not use the taxonomy of the periodic table and the combinatorial lexicon of chemical compounds to describe both the observable facts and their theoretical underpinnings alike. For starters, one can just smell hydrogen sulphide, taste sodium chloride, feel any base, and identify copper, aluminum, iron, and gold by sight.

These cases are not unusual. Our theoretical convictions typically reshape the way we describe the facts to be explained. Sometimes it happens immediately, as with STR, but more often it happens after long familiarity with the successful theory, as is evidenced by the idioms casually employed in any working laboratory. The premise of the objection is true. But it is no point at all against the theoretical view. Given the great age of folk psychology, such conceptual invasion of the explanandum domain is only to be expected.

A different critique of the theoretical view proposes an alternative account of our understanding of human behavior. According to this view, one's capacity for anticipating and understanding the behavior of others resides not in a system of nomically embedded concepts, but rather in the fact that one is a normal person oneself, and can draw on one's own reactions, to real or to imagined circumstances, in order to gain insight into the internal states and the overt behavior of others. The key idea is that of empathy. One uses oneself as a simulation (usually imagined) of the situation of another and then extrapolates the results of that simulation to the person in question (see Gordon 1986; Goldman 1989).

My first response to this line is simply to agree that an enormous amount of one's appreciation of the internal states and overt behavior of other humans derives from one's ability to examine and to extrapolate from the facts of one's own case. All of this is quite consistent with the theoretical view, and there is no reason that one should attempt to deny it. One learns from every example of humanity one encounters, and one encounters oneself on a systematic basis. What we must resist is the suggestion that extrapolating from the particulars of one's own case is the fundamental ground of one's understanding of others, a ground that renders possession of a nomic framework unnecessary. Problems for this stronger position begin to appear immediately.

For one thing, if *all* of one's understanding of others is closed under extrapolation from one's own case, then the modest contents of one's own case must form an absolute limit on what one can expect or explain in the inner life and external behavior of others. But in fact we are not so limited. People who are congenitally deaf or blind know quite well that normal people have perceptual capacities beyond what they themselves possess, and they know in some detail what those capacities entail in the way of knowledge and behavior. People who have never felt profound grief, say, or love, or rejection, can nonetheless provide appropriate predictions and explanations of the behavior of people so afflicted. And so on. In general, one's immediately available understanding of human psychology and behavior goes substantially beyond what one has experienced in one's own case, either in real life or in pointed simulations. First-person experience or simulation is plainly not *necessary* for understanding the behavior of others.

Nor is it *sufficient*. The problem is that simulations, even if they motivate predictions about others, do not by themselves provide any explanatory understanding of the behavior of others. To see this, consider the following analogy. Suppose I were to possess a marvellous miniature of the physical universe, a miniature I could manipulate in order to simulate real situations and thus predict and retrodict the behavior of the real universe. Even if my miniature unfailingly provided accurate simulations of the outcomes of real physical processes, I would still be no further ahead on the business of *explaining* the behavior of the real world. In fact, I would then have two universes, both in need of explanation.

The lesson is the same for first-person and third-person situations. A simulation itself, even a successful one, provides no explanation. What explanatory understanding requires is an appreciation of the *general patterns* that comprehend the individual events in both cases. And that brings us back to the idea of a moderately general *theory*.

We should have come to that idea directly, since the empathetic account of our understanding of others depends crucially on one's having an initial understanding of oneself. To extrapolate one's own cognitive, affective, and behavioral intricacies to others requires that one be able to conceptualize and spontaneously to recognize those intricacies in oneself. But one's ability to do this is left an unaddressed mystery by the empathetic account. Self-understanding is not seen as a problem; it is other-understanding that is held up as the problem.

But the former is no less problematic than the latter. If one is to be able to apprehend even the *first-person* intricacies at issue, then one must possess a conceptual framework that draws all of the necessary distinctions, a framework that organizes the relevant categories into the appropriate structure, a framework whose taxonomy reflects at least the more obvious of the rough nomic regularities holding across its elements, even in the first-person case. Such a framework is already a theory.

The fact is, the categories into which any important domain gets divided by a learning creature emerge jointly with an appreciation of the rough nomic regularities that connect them. A nascent taxonomy that supports the expression of no useful regularities is a taxonomy that is soon replaced by a more insightful one. The divination of useful regularities is the single most dominant force shaping the taxonomies developed by any learning creature in any domain. And it is an essential force, even in perceptual domains, since our observational taxonomies are always radically underdetermined by our untrained perceptual mechanisms. To suppose that one's conception of one's *own* mental life is innocent of a network of systematic expectations is just naive. But such a network is already a theory, even before one addresses the issue of others.

This is the cash value, I think, of P. F. Strawson's insightful claim, now thirty years old, that to be in a position to pose any question about other minds, and to be in a position to try to construct arguments from analogy with one's own case, is already to possess at least the rudiments of what is sought after, namely, a general conception of mental phenomena, of their general connections with each other and with behavior (Strawson 1959). What Strawson missed was the further insight that such a framework is nothing other than an empirical theory, one justified not by the quasi-logical character of its principles, as he attempted unsuccessfully to show, but by its impersonal success in explaining and predicting human behavior at large. There is no special justification story to be told here. Folk psychology is justified by what standardly justifies *any* conceptual framework: namely, its explanatory, predictive, and manipulative success.

This concludes my survey of the outstanding objections to the theoretical view outlined in the opening paragraph of the present chapter. But in defending this view there is a major difference between my strategy in earlier writings and my strategy here. In my 1970 paper, for example, the question was framed as follows: "Are action explanations *deductive-nomological* explanations?" I would now prefer to frame the question thus: "Are action explanations of the same general type as the explanations typically found in the sciences?" I continue to think that the answer to this second question is pretty clearly yes. My reasons are given above. But I am no longer confident that the deductive-nomological (D-N) model itself is an adequate account of explanation in the sciences or anywhere else.

The difficulties with the D-N model are detailed elsewhere in the literature, so I shall not pause to summarize them here. My diagnosis of its failings, however, locates the basic problem in its attempt to represent knowledge and understanding by sets of sentences or propositional attitudes. In this, the framers of the D-N model were resting on the basic assumptions of folk psychology. Let me close this paper by briefly exploring how we might conceive of knowledge, and of explanatory understanding, in a systematically different way. This is an important undertaking relative to the concerns of this chapter, for there is an objection to the theoretical view, as traditionally expressed, that seems to me to have some real bite. It is as follows.

If one's capacity for understanding and predicting the behavior of others derives from one's internal storage of thousands of laws or nomic generalizations, how is it that one is so poor at enunciating the laws on which one's explanatory and predictive prowess depends? It seems to take a trained philosopher to reconstruct them! How is it that children are so skilled at understanding and anticipating the behavior of humans in advance of ever acquiring the complex linguistic skills necessary to express those laws? How is it that social hunters such as wolves and lions can comprehend and anticipate each other's behavior in great detail when they presumably store no internal sentences at all?

We must resist the temptation to see in these questions a renewed motivation for counting folk psychology as special, for the very same problems arise with respect to any other folk theory you might care to mention: folk physics, folk biology, whatever. It even arises for theories in the highly developed sciences, since, as Kuhn has pointed out, very little of a scientist's understanding of a theory consists in his ability to state a list of laws. It consists, rather, in the ability to apply the conceptual resources of the theory to new cases, and thus to anticipate and perhaps manipulate the behavior of the relevant empirical domain. This means that our problem here concerns the character of knowledge and understanding in general. Let us finally address that problem.

2. An alternative form of knowledge representation

One alternative to the notion of a universal generalization about F is the notion of a *prototype* of F, a central or typical example of F which all other examples of F resemble, more or less closely, in certain relevant aspects. Prototypes have certain obvious advantages over universal generalizations. Just as a picture can be worth a thousand words, so a single complex prototype can embody the same breadth of information concerning the organization of co-occurrent features that would be contained in a long list of complex generalizations. Furthermore, prototypes allow us a welcome degree of looseness that is precluded by the strict logic of a universal quantifier: not *all* Fs need be Gs, but the standard or normal ones are, and the nonstandard ones must be related by a relevant similarity relation to those that properly are G. Various theorists have independently found motive to introduce such a notion in a number of cognitive fields: they have been called 'paradigms' and 'exemplars' in the philosophy of science (Kuhn 1962), 'stereotypes' in semantics (Putnam 1970, 1975), 'frames' (Minsky 1981) and 'scripts' (Schank 1977) in AI research, and finally 'prototypes' in psychology (Rosch 1981) and linguistics (Lakoff 1987).

Their advantages aside, prototypes also have certain familiar problems. The first problem is how to determine just what clutch of elements or properties should constitute a given prototype, and the second problem is how to determine the metric of similarity along which closeness to the central prototype is to be measured. Though they pose a problem for notions at all levels, these problems are especially keen in the case of the so-called "basic" or "simple" properties, because common sense is there unable even to articulate any deeper constituting elements (for example, what elements "make up" a purple color, a sour taste, a floral smell, or the phoneme /ā/?). A final problem concerning prototypes is a familiar one: how might prototypes be effectively represented in a real cognitive creature?

This last question brings me to a possible answer, and to a path that leads to further answers. The relevant research concerns the operations of artificial neural networks, networks that mimic some of the more obvious organizational features of the brain. It concerns how they learn to recognize certain types of complex stimuli, and how they represent what they have learned. Upon repeated presentation of various real examples of the several features to be learned (*F*, *G*, *H*, etc.), and under the steady pressure of a learning algorithm that makes small adjustments in the network's synaptic connections, the network slowly but spontaneously generates a set of internal representations, one for each of the several features it is required to recognize. Collectively, those representations take the form of a set or system of similarity spaces, and the central point or volume of such a space constitutes the network's representation of a *prototypical F, G,* or *H.* After learning is completed, the system responds to any *F*-like stimulus with an internal pattern of neuronal activity that is *close to* the prototypical pattern in the relevant similarity space.

The network consists of an initial "sensory" layer of neurons, which is massively connected to a second layer of neurons. The sizes or "weights" of the many connections determine how the neurons at the second layer collectively respond to activity across the input layer. The neurons at the second layer are connected in turn to a third layer (and perhaps a fourth layer, etc., but I shall limit the discussion here to three-layer networks). During learning, what the system is searching for is a configuration of weights that will turn the neurons at the second layer into a set of *complex feature detectors.* We then want the neurons at the third or "output" layer to respond in turn to the second layer, given any *F*-like stimuli at the input layer, with a characteristic pattern of activity. All of this is achieved by presenting the network with diverse examples of *F*s, and slowly adjusting its connection weights in the light of its initially chaotic responses.

Such networks can indeed learn to recognize a wide variety of surprisingly subtle features: phonemes from voiced speech, the shapes of objects from grey-scale photos, the correct pronunciation of printed English text, the presence of metallic mines from sonar returns, and grammatical categories in novel sentences. Given a successfully trained network, if we examine the behavior of the neurons at the second or intermediate layer during the process of recognition, we discover that each neuron has come to represent, by its level of activity, some distinct aspect or dimension of the input stimulus. Taken together, their joint activity constitutes a multidimensional analysis of the stimuli at the input layer. The trained network has succeeded in finding a set of dimensions, an *abstract space,* such that all more-or-less typical Fs produce a characteristic profile of neuronal activity across those particular dimensions, while deviant or degraded Fs produce profiles that are variously *close* to that central prototype. The job of the third and final layer is then the relatively simple one of distinguishing that profile-region from other regions in the larger space of possible activation patterns. In this way, artificial neural networks generate and exploit prototypes. It is now more than a suggestion that real neural networks do the same thing. (For a summary of these results and how they bear on the question of theoretical knowledge, see Churchland 1989a. For a parade case of successful learning, see Rosenberg and Sejnowski 1987. For the *locus classicus* concerning the general technique, see Rumelhart et al. 1986.)

Notice that this picture contains answers to all three of the problems about prototypes noted earlier. What dimensions go into a prototype of F? Those that allow the system to respond to diverse examples of F in a distinctive and uniform way, a way that reduces the error messages from the learning algorithm to a minimum. How is similarity to a prototype measured? By geometrical proximity in the relevant parameter space. How are prototypes represented in real cognitive creatures? By canonical activity patterns across an appropriate population of neurons.

Note also that the objective features recognized by the network can also have a temporal component: a network can just as well be trained to recognize typical *sequences* and *processes* as to recognize atemporal patterns. Which brings me to my final suggestion. A normal human's understanding of the springs of human action may reside not in a set of stored generalizations about the hidden elements of mind and how they conspire to produce behavior, but rather in one or more prototypes of the deliberative or purposeful process. To understand or explain someone's behavior may be less a matter of deduction from implicit laws, and more a matter of recognitional subsumption of the case at issue under a relevant prototype. (For a more detailed treatment of this view of explanation, the *prototype activation model*, see Churchland 1989b.)

Such prototypes are no doubt at least modestly complex, and presumably they depict typical configurations of desires, beliefs, preferences, and so forth, roughly the same configurations that I have earlier attempted to express in the form of universally quantified sentences. Beyond this, I am able to say little about them, at least on this occasion. But I hope I have succeeded in making intelligible to you a novel approach to the problem of explanatory understanding in humans. This is an approach that is grounded at last in what we know about the brain. And it is an approach that ascribes to us neither reams of universally quantified premises, nor deductive activity on a heroic scale. Explanatory understanding turns out to be not quite what we thought it was, because cognition in general gets characterized in a new way. And yet explanatory understanding remains the same *sort* of process in the case of human behavior as in the case of natural phenomena generally. And the question of the *adequacy* of our commonsense understanding remains as live as ever.

3. Addendum: Commentary on Dennett

I focus here on one of the relatively few issues that still divide Dennett and me: the ontological status of intentional states. We both accept the premise that neuroscience is unlikely to find "sentences in the head," or anything else that answers to the structure of individual beliefs and desires. On the strength of this shared assumption, I am willing to infer that folk psychology is false, and that its ontology is chimerical. Beliefs and desires are of a piece with phlogiston, caloric, and the alchemical essences. We therefore need an entirely new kinematics and dynamics with which to comprehend human cognitive activity, one drawn, perhaps, from computational neuroscience and connectionist AI. Folk psychology could then be put aside in favor of this descriptively more accurate and explanatorily more powerful portrayal of the reality within. Certainly, it will be put aside in the lab and in the clinic, and eventually, perhaps, in the marketplace as well.

But Dennett declines to draw this eliminativist conclusion, despite his firm acceptance of the premise cited, and despite his willingness to contemplate unorthodox forms of cognitive theory. He prefers to claim a special status for the various intentional states, a status that will permit us to be "realists" about beliefs and desires despite their projected absence from our strict scientific ontology.

This impulse in Dennett continues to strike me as arbitrary protectionism, as ill-motivated special pleading on behalf of the old and familiar. His initial rationale for exempting folk psychology from the usual scientific standards involved assigning it a purely instrumental status, but this swiftly brought him all kinds of grief, as he himself explains (1987, pp. 71–72). Instrumentalism is first and foremost an *anti*realist position, hardly a welcome port given Dennett's aims, a fact Dennett now appreciates in more detail. Accordingly, his current rationale draws a much more narrowly focused analogy between intentional states and geometrical *abstracta* such as the centers of gravity, axes of rotation, equators, etc., that are postulated to such good effect in mechanics. As Dennett sees it, these latter are not real in the same sense that *concreta* like bricks and trees are real (you can't trip over them, for example), but they can reasonably be said to be real even so. Intentional states are real in the same sense, claims Dennett.

The reality of equators, centers, and rotational axes I am happy to grant. They are all places or loci of some sort that are decisively specifiable by reference to the shape or behavior of the relevant concrete object. But the alleged similarity of these items to beliefs, desires, and other intentional states escapes me entirely. In what respects are they similar, and why should they be grouped together in advance of the issue here at stake? That is, in advance of any hopes of finding an exculpatory status for intentional states?

Dennett is quick to point out that folk psychology has some nontrivial predictive power, especially in its central domain of normal human behavior, despite the lack of any neural *concreta* answering to the propositional attitudes. He emphasizes, quite correctly, that it is an objective fact about humans that a significant amount of their behavior is accurately predictable in intentional terms.

But I think he overvalues this fact wildly. We must not forget that all sorts of false theories, with wholly chimerical ontologies, can boast very impressive predictive power in various proprietary domains. But this buys their ontology no special status. It is an objective fact that much of the behavior of metals and ores is predictable in terms of the alchemical essences, that most of the behavior of the visible heavens is predictable in terms of nested crystal spheres, that much of the behavior of moving bodies is predictable in terms of impetus, and so forth. And yet there are no alchemical essences, nor any crystal spheres, nor any impetus. We could, of course, set about insisting that these three "things" are real and genuine after all, though mere *abstracta* to be sure. But none of us is tempted to salvage *their* reality by such a tortured and transparent ploy. Why should we be tempted in the case of the propositional attitudes?

This disagreement between us on the status of folk psychology dates from several letters now a full decade old. However, one point on which we then agreed was that neither of us could clearly imagine a systematic alternative to folk psychology. At the time I ascribed this inability to the natural poverty of our imaginations. Dennett was inclined to suspect a deeper reason. But since then the materials available to imagination have improved dramatically. The microstructure of the brain and the recent successes of connectionist AI both suggest that our principal form of representation is the high-dimensional activation vector, and that our principal form of computation is the vector-to-vector transformation, effected by a matrix of differently weighted synapses. In place of propositional attitudes and logical inferences from one to another, therefore, we can conceive of persons as the seat of vectorial attitudes and various nonlinear transformations from one vector to another. We can already see how such a vectorial system can do many of the things that humans and other animals do swiftly and easily, such as recognize faces and other highly complex stimuli, or control a complex body with both relevance and grace. The possibility of a real alternative now seems beyond dispute: we are already building it.

What remains an issue is how our familiar folk psychology will fare in light of what the new conception will reveal. Retention through reduction remains a real possibility, though the character of the theoretical developments just cited make this seem increasingly unlikely. If we rule out reduction, then elimination emerges as the only coherent alternative, Dennett's resistance notwithstanding.

In the end, Dennett's steadfast insistence that folk psychology is not just another false theory, but rather an "abstract stance" of some kind, one with striking predictive powers, reminds me of the shopkeeper in the Monty Python sketch about the distraught customer trying to return a recently purchased but very dead parrot. Python fans will remember the shopkeeper's deliciously shifty-eyed insistence. "Naw, naw, it's not *dead!* It's just *resting!* It's just *pining* for the fiords! . . . Lovely *plumage,* the Norwegian Blue."

References

Churchland, P. M. (1970). "The Logical Character of Action Explanations." *Philosophical Review,* 79 (2):214–236.

Churchland, P. M. (1979). *Scientific Realism and the Plasticity of Mind.* Cambridge: Cambridge University Press.

Churchland, P. M. (1981). "Eliminative Materialism and the Propositional Attitudes." *Journal of Philosophy,* 78 (2):67–90.

68   *Paul M. Churchland*

Churchland, P. M. (1984). *Matter and Consciousness*. Cambridge, Mass.: MIT Press.

Churchland, P. M. (1986). "On the Continuity of Science and Philosophy." *Mind and Language*, 1 (1):5–14.

Churchland, P. M. (1989a). "On the Nature of Theories: A Neurocomputational Perspective." In W. Savage, ed., *Scientific Theories: Minnesota Studies in the Philosophy of Science*, Vol. 14. Minneapolis: University of Minnesota Press.

Churchland, P. M. (1989b). "On the Nature of Explanation: A PDP Approach." In *A Neurocomputational Perspective: The Nature of Mind and the Structure of Science*. Cambridge, Mass., The MIT Press.

Dennett, D. (1987). *The Intentional Stance*. Cambridge, Mass.: MIT Press.

Feyerabend, P. K. (1963). "Materialism and the Mind–Body Problem." *Review of Metaphysics*, 17:49–66.

Goldman, A. (1989). "Interpretation Psychologized." *Mind and Language*, 4:161–185.

Gordon, R. (1986). "Folk Psychology as Simulation." *Mind and Language* 1 (2): 158–171.

Haldane, J. (1988). "Understanding Folk." *Proceedings of the Aristotelian Society* [Suppl.], 62:222–246.

Kuhn, T. S. (1962). *The Structure of Scientific Revolutions*. Chicago: University of Chicago Press.

Lakoff, G. (1987). *Women, Fire and Dangerous Things*. Chicago: University of Chicago Press.

McKloskey, M. (1983). "Intuitive Physics." *Scientific American*, 248 (4):122–130.

Minsky, M. (1981). "A Framework for Representing Knowledge." In J. Haugeland, ed., *Mind Design*. Cambridge, Mass.: MIT Press.

Putnam, H. (1970). "Is Semantics Possible?" In H. Kiefer & M. Munitz, eds., *Languages, Belief, and Metaphysics* (Albany: State University of New York Press). Reprinted in H. Putnam, *Mind, Language and Reality*. Cambridge: Cambridge University Press.

Putnam, H. (1975). "The Meaning of 'Meaning.'" In K. Gunderson, ed., *Language, Mind and Knowledge: Minnesota Studies in the Philosophy of Science*, Vol. 7. Reprinted in H. Putnam, *Mind, Language and Reality*. Cambridge: Cambridge University Press.

Rorty, R. (1965). "Mind–Body Identity, Privacy, and Categories." *Review of Metaphysics*, 19:24–54.

Rosch, E. (1981). "Prototype Classification and Logical Classification: The Two Systems." In E. Scholnick, ed., *New Trends in Cognitive Representation: Challenges to Piaget's Theory*. Hillsdale, NJ: Lawrence Erlbaum.

Rosenberg, C. R., & Sejnowski, T. J. (1987). "Parallel Networks That Learn To Pronounce English Text." *Complex Systems*, 1:145–168.

Rumelhart, D. E., Hinton, G. E., & Williams, R. J. (1986). "Learning Internal Representations by Error Propagation." In D. E. Rumelhart & J. L. McClelland, eds., *Parallel Distributed Processing: Explorations in the Microstructure of Cognition*. Cambridge, Mass.: MIT Press, 1986.

Schank, R., & Abelson, R. (1977). *Scripts, Plans, Goals, and Understanding*. New York: John Wiley.

Sellars, W. (1956). "Empiricism and the Philosophy of Mind." In H. Feigl & M. Scriven, eds., *Minnesota Studies in the Philosophy of Science*, Vol. 1. Minneapolis: University of Minnesota Press. Reprinted in W. Sellars, *Science, Perception and Reality*. London: Routledge & Kegan Paul, 1963.

Strawson, P. F. (1959). *Individuals*. London: Methuen.

Wilkes, K. (1981). "Functionalism, Psychology, and the Philosophy of Mind." *Philosophical Topics*, 12 (1):147–167.

Wilkes, K. (1984). "Pragmatics in Science and Theory in Common Sense." *Inquiry*, 27 (4):339–361.

3 Reasons to believe

John D. Greenwood

The thesis that the language of folk psychology is *theoretical* is central to Paul Churchland's (1979, 1981) statement of the doctrine of eliminative materialism. Churchland claims that since the explanations advanced by folk psychology are – or are likely to prove – generally inaccurate or inadequate, the entities postulated by folk-psychological explanations of behavior – beliefs, desires, motives, and other contentful psychological states – ought to be eliminated from mature science, in favor of the neurophysiological entities postulated by superior neurophysiological theories.

There are those who would dispute this thesis. I do not. I take it for granted that the language of folk psychology is theoretical, at least in a number of everyday senses of the term 'theoretical'. In this chapter, I argue that the possible explanatory failure of folk psychology would not oblige us – and ought not to incline us – to reject the ontology of contentful psychological states postulated by folk psychology.

I do this via a consideration of two natural objections to Churchland's conclusion that we ought to abandon the ontology of intentional psychological phenomena in the manner that we came to abandon the ontological items postulated by Ptolemeic theory, caloric theory, phlogiston theory, and so forth. The first of these objections is to the effect that since our classificatory descriptions of human action employ the resources of folk psychology, we cannot abandon folk psychology without abandoning the attempt to explain human action. The second objection is to the effect that it is absurd to suggest that we abandon the ontology of folk psychology, since we all know very well at least our own beliefs, wishes, motives, and so forth, and express them even in denials of the ontology of folk psychology. Churchland treats these objections as mere products of "conceptual inertia" or as philosophically naive attempts to deny the theoretical nature of folk psychology. In the next three sections of this chapter, I suggest that these objections have considerably more substance than Churchland gives them credit for. In

Section IV, I briefly consider Churchland's claim (Chapter 2, this volume) that our theoretical knowledge is "not so specifically *linguistic* as we have chronically assumed." In the final section, I suggest that the primary threat to folk psychology is not empirical but conceptual: It derives precisely from the common commitment to the principles that underpin the doctrine of eliminative materialism.

I

The first objection may be stated in the following fashion: Many practicing psychologists (despite their frequent rhetorical avowals to the contrary) are not particularly concerned with the explanation of human behaviors or physical movements per se. They are instead concerned to provide empirically supported explanations of socially meaningful human actions such as aggression, dishonesty, helping, child abuse, and suicide. They are concerned with the explanation of those behaviors that are constituted as human actions by their intentional direction and social location (Greenwood 1990a). Thus, for example, diverse behaviors such as raising an arm, moving a switch on a shock generator, and tampering with a colleague's brake cable are all constituted as *aggressive actions* by being represented by the agent as directed toward the injury of another. Diverse behaviors such as keeping the wrong change, shoplifting, and intentionally neglecting to remind our moving-out-of-state neighbors that we still have the garden tools we borrowed from them are all constituted as *dishonest actions* by being represented by the agent as involving the removal or receipt of goods that rightly belong to another. The explanatory domain of much psychological science is defined and constituted according to the representational dimensions documented by folk-psychological classificatory descriptions. To abandon the ontology of folk psychology would be to abandon the very *subject matter* of much psychological science.

Paul Churchland has a ready answer to this objection. However, he misses the point of it. He sees it as yet another attempt to argue that folk psychology is nontheoretical, and an attempt that is based upon a naive and outdated conception of theory that postulates a sharp distinction between the theoretical and the observational. He argues that such classificatory descriptions, like other classificatory descriptions in science, are 'theory-informed' (Hanson 1958; Kuhn 1970). Since they are informed by what he considers to be an inadequate theory – namely folk psychology – they ought to be abandoned along with the theory.

But although it is true that we frequently do *redefine* the explanatory domain of many sciences in terms of our best theoretical explanations, it is simply not true that our original classifications of explanatory domains presuppose theoretical explanations of them. This is not regularly the case in natural science, and it is just as well, for otherwise we could not have competing theoretical explanations of the same diseases and depressions, the recognized properties of a vacuum, or agreed deviations in the orbit of Mercury, etc.

This is not to deny that our classificatory descriptions of explanatory domains are theory-informed. Of course they are. Thus, for example, competing theories of 'evolution' in terms of punctuated equilibrium versus continuity presuppose a particular theoretical characterization of 'evolution'. What should be noted, however, is that both competing theories presuppose the same theoretical characterization of 'evolution' (in terms of adaptive changes, etc.), and that neither explanatory theory is presupposed by it. Moreover, although the critical observations that frequently enable scientists to adjudicate between competing explanatory theories are frequently theoretically informed, they are rarely informed by competing explanatory theories. Thus the telescopic observations of the stellar parallax that enabled scientists to adjudicate between geocentric and heliocentric theories were informed by the theory of the telescope, but did not presuppose the accuracy of either the geocentric or heliocentric theory. The X-ray diffraction discriminations of the structure of DNA that supported the Watson–Crick theory of the structure of DNA over its rivals were informed by the theory of X-ray diffraction but did not presuppose the accuracy of the Watson–Crick theory or any of its rivals. The first feature accounts for the fact that explanatory theories can be competing. The second feature accounts for the fact that the observational evaluation of explanatory theories can be objective (Greenwood 1990b).

Churchland in fact confounds two distinct senses of the term 'theoretical'. We must be careful to distinguish between the use of the term 'theoretical' to characterize any description of postulated properties or relations (see, e.g., Churchland 1984, p. 80), and the use of the term 'theoretical' to characterize descriptions of postulated *causal-explanatory* dimensions with respect to a particular domain (see, e.g., Churchland 1984, p. 56).

Now it is doubtless true that in the former sense of 'theoretical', all our classificatory descriptions of human action are theory-informed. This seems a minimal condition of their having semantic contents and truth values. Certainly it would be a self-defeating exercise to try to defend the ontology of folk psychology by denying this. This is why Churchland has such an easy time dealing with most of the antitheoretical objections. However, it is just not true that most classificatory descriptions presuppose theoretical causal explanations of the phenomena clas-sified, and it is certainly not the case with respect to our folk-psychological classificatory descriptions of human action.

Our classifications of certain actions as instances of aggression, dis-honesty, and so forth do not presuppose any theoretical explanation of such actions. The classification of an action as an instance of aggression or dishonesty does not presuppose any of a possible variety of compet-ing causal explanations of aggression or dishonesty. There is, for exam-ple, no inconsistency in supposing that some instances of aggression are best explained in terms of motives of revenge, that other instances are best explained in terms of exposure to "violent stimuli" (Berkowitz & LePage 1967), and that others still are best explained in terms of excita-tions of the lateral hypothalamus, because the correct description of an action as an instance of aggression does not presuppose any of these competing causal explanations of aggression.

This is not of course to deny that such classificatory descriptions are theoretical: To characterize an action as aggressive is to attribute to it an intentional direction. It is to deny that such theoretical descriptions are causal explanatory: To characterize an action as aggressive does not furnish or presuppose any causal explanation of aggressive actions. Philosophers have been correct to identify intentionality as a constitu-tive feature of human action (Goldman 1970; McGinn 1979) but have been quite wrong to suppose that the intentional nature of human ac-tion can be explicated in terms of causal-explanatory reasons for ac-tion.

It might be objected that the constitutive intentional states referenced by folk-psychological classifications of actions may also be interpreted as referencing causal-explanatory states – states that are causally necessary or sufficient conditions for actions such as aggression and dishonesty. Even if this were the case, it should be noted that such classifications would still not presuppose any of a possible variety of competing causal explanations of actions so constituted. Even if we classified aggressive actions as actions that are caused by "intentions to harm another," it would still remain an open question whether such actions are them-selves caused by motives of revenge, violent stimuli, or excitations of the lateral hypothalamus.

Moreover, it is not the case. Aggressive actions are constituted as aggressive actions not by antecedent intentions to harm another but, rather, by contemporaneous representations of behavior as directed toward the injury of another. If an agent does not represent his or her behavior as directed to the injury of another, that behavior does not constitute an aggressive action, whatever the prior intention. This is perhaps easier to see in the case of dishonest actions. An action is dishonest if it involves the removal, receipt, or retention of goods represented as rightly belonging to another. My action of retaining a video recorder incorrectly mailed to me is dishonest if I represent the video recorder as rightly belonging to another. But my retention of the video recorder becomes dishonest the moment I recognize that it rightfully belongs to another while continuing to retain it. I do not need to have had a prior intention to retain it, or a prior recognition that it rightfully belongs to another.

This is not to deny that references to constitutive intentional states *may* function as adequate causal explanations of actions. Perhaps the best explanation of some, many, or all instances of aggression is in terms of the agent's aim to harm another. Some persons may be aggressive for no other reason or cause: They may be aggressive for its own sake, as it were. Analogously the best explanation of some, many, or all instances of 'helping', defined in terms of behaviors aimed to relieve the distress of another, may be in terms of the agent's aim to relieve the distress of another simpliciter. Some persons may help others for no other reason or cause. The latter forms of action are likely rarer than we would like to imagine: Many, no doubt, have additional (or ulterior) motives. The former forms of action are hopefully as rare as we would like to imagine. However, the adequacy of these particular causal explanations of acts of aggression and helping is an empirical question. Their empirical adequacy is not vouchsafed by the classification of human actions as instances of aggression and helping.

To claim that our theoretical classificatory descriptions of human action are not causal explanatory is not to deny that they are subject to empirical evaluation. If it had turned out that there was no empirical evidence for the intentional direction of human actions, then no doubt we ought to have abandoned our folk-psychological classifications of actions and replaced them with purely physical forms of behavioral description. Yet, there is plenty of evidence for the intentional direction of human action. The contents of the constitutive representations of behavior that are referenced by action descriptions are revealed daily in our everyday discourse about the likely consequences of behaviors. Agents articulate their knowledge of the likely harmful effects of certain behaviors, honestly avow that they are aiming to harm another, and engage in behaviors likely to cause harm to another. We have a wealth of evidence to support the claim that agents regularly act intentionally, that they direct their behaviors to the goals they avow.

Since our classificatory descriptions of human actions do presuppose an ontology of contentful psychological states but do not presuppose the adequacy of any causal explanations of human actions in terms of contentful psychological states, the demonstrated inaccuracy or inadequacy of our folk-psychological explanations of human actions (e.g., in terms of motives of revenge or other motives postulated by social or clinical psychology, etc.) would not oblige us to abandon our classificatory descriptions of human actions or the ontology of contentful psychological states presupposed by them. Nor would it incline us to do so, since we have empirical grounds for maintaining our classificatory descriptions and the ontology of contentful psychological states presupposed by them that are independent of the empirical adequacy of folk-psychological explanations of human actions.

II

I think the argument of Section I is sufficient to resist Churchland's eliminativist conclusion, but I also want to make a stronger claim: Even if all our folk-psychological explanations of human actions turned out to be inaccurate or inadequate, we would not be obliged – nor should we be inclined – to reject the particular contentful psychological states postulated by such *explanations*.

Consider the competing explanations of aggressive actions noted earlier, in terms of motives of revenge, violent stimuli, and excitations of the lateral hypothalamus. Let us suppose, for the sake of argument, that aggressive actions are in fact never caused by motives of revenge, defined as representations of actions as restitutions for some prior injury or offense. Would this explanatory failure oblige us to accept that there are no such things as motives of revenge, or even incline us toward this? Not a bit. There is no contradiction or absurdity in supposing that motives of revenge are rarely effective, or indeed never effective. The point is perhaps clearer to grasp if we consider the other competing theoretical explanations of aggression. Even if our experimental evidence suggested that aggressive actions are never caused by the presence of violent stimuli, defined as stimuli that are symbolic of violence (e.g., guns and pictures of boxers), this would not oblige or incline us to deny that there are such things as violent stimuli. Analogously, if we discovered that excitations of the lateral hypothalamus are not responsible for any instances of aggression, this fact would not oblige or incline us to deny that there are excitations of the lateral hypothalamus.

The reason is that phenomena such as motives of revenge, violent stimuli, and excitations of the lateral hypothalamus are individuated *independently* of their postulated causal-explanatory dimensions with respect to human aggression. Consequently, we are not obliged to deny their existence if we determine that they do not have the causal-explanatory dimensions we formerly attributed to them.

Churchland's eliminativist argument presupposes that the semantics and truth conditions of theoretical descriptions are fixed by reference to the causal-explanatory propositions in which they figure. This is why he holds that we are obliged to reject the entities postulated by such descriptions when the causal-explanatory propositions in which they figure turn out to be false. This is a very specific and contentious account of theoretical meaning, albeit one much favored by traditional empiricists and neo-empiricists. Churchland calls himself a realist, but he adopts a modified Quinean account of the semantics of theoretical descriptions. According to this account, the meaning of theoretical descriptions in any science is determined by the "network" of causal-explanatory "laws/principles/generalizations in which they figure" (Churchland 1984, p. 56).

This is a very doubtful account of theoretical meaning. The semantics of a great many theoretical descriptions in science is determined by the theoretical model employed (Harré 1970; Hesse 1976). These descriptions ascribe to postulated entities some of the properties of already familiar phenomena, and exploit the semantics of our familiar descriptions of them. These descriptions of properties and relations are meaningful independently of the causal-explanatory purposes they are eventually employed to serve.

Thus Bohr's theory of the atom, for example, involves the descriptive claim that elements are composed of atoms that have some of the properties of planetary systems (on a much smaller scale): They are composed of discontinuous particles with a nucleus (of protons and neutrons) that maintains other particles (electrons) in orbit via attractive forces. The meaning and truth conditions of these claims are quite independent of the meaning and truth conditions of the empirical laws governing the spectral emissions of hydrogen and helium that theoretical references to the structure of the atom were originally employed to explain. Bohr's theoretical descriptions of the atom are true if and only if there are atoms and they have the compositional properties and relations ascribed to them by these descriptions.

This account of theoretical meaning explains how many persons can understand the ontological claims of Bohr's theory (they can understand, via the theoretical model, what it claimed and what must be the case for these claims to be true) without having any inkling of the spectral emission laws it was introduced to explain. Analogously, many people understand the ontological claims of Freud's theory (about un-conscious psychological states) but have little knowledge of the empiri-cal phenomena (conversion hysterias, etc.) the theory was introduced to explain. It also explains how we can come to recognize empirically that certain phenomena do not have the causal-explanatory dimensions we ascribe to them: "Marsh vapors" exist but do not cause malaria or other tropical fevers. It also explains our recognition of a whole range of theoretical entities for which we have no presently adequate knowledge of their causal dimensions: We recognize the existence of Golgi bodies and myelin sheaths, although we presently do not have much under-standing of their biological and neurophysiological function. Ironically, the most obvious examples come from biology and neurophysiology, where we recognize many structures and processes whose causal or functional role we are trying desperately hard to understand. When we abandon tentative hypotheses about the causal-explanatory role of such phenomena, we never for a moment consider their ontological elimina-tion, as we are supposed to do in the case of folk psychology. This is just as well for biology. One of the earliest documented forms of folk psy-chology is biological in nature. According to the folk psychology of Plato's *Timeus,* our emotional life is to be explained in terms of the swelling of the heart, and the function of the liver is to reflect the contents of our thoughts. This has long been demonstrated to be false, yet few have rushed to conclude that there are no such things as hearts or livers.

It is equally wrong to suppose that the semantics of our folk-psychological theoretical descriptions is fixed by reference to the causal-explanatory propositions in which they regularly figure. The properties referenced by our folk-psychological descriptions are modeled upon some of the properties of linguistic propositions – specifically, their sense and reference. In ascribing beliefs and motives to self and others, we ascribe (intensional) contents directed upon (intentional) objects in the natural and social psychological world. Thus, in attributing to myself the belief that the Empire State Building is the tallest building in the world, I mean that I represent the Empire State Building (intentional object) *as* the tallest building in the world (intensional content). In attributing shame to another, I mean that that person represents some action of his or hers (intentional object) *as* personally humiliating and degrading (intensional content). Such attributions are true if and only if agents represent particular aspects of reality in the particular ways attributed to them, *irrespective of the adequacy of causal explanations referenc-ing such psychological states.*

Since the semantics and truth conditions of theoretical descriptions in natural and psychological science are logically independent of the semantics and truth conditions of the causal-explanatory propositions in which such descriptions may figure, we are not obligated to reject the ontological claims of a theory when we recognize the inaccuracy or inadequacy of its causal-explanatory claims. In the case of folk psychology, we would not be obliged to reject the ontological claims of folk psychology if we came to recognize the inaccuracy or inadequacy of many (or all) of our folk-psychological explanations. We could consistently maintain our powerful intuition that there are such things as contentful beliefs, emotions, and motives, even though we may think it possible or likely that our current (lay or scientific) causal-explanatory references to these phenomena will turn out to be inaccurate or inadequate.

To say this is merely to stress the semantic independence of theoretical descriptions in natural and psychological science from the causal-explanatory propositions in which they regularly figure. Theoretical descriptions that are employed to furnish explanations must of course be testable if they are to be of any scientific value: They must license empirical predictions. I do not deny this testability requirement. But this reasonable requirement does not itself require that such predictions be derivable from theoretical descriptions alone – a condition that in fact is rarely (if ever) satisfied. The descriptions of the spectral line emissions of hydrogen and helium are not derivable from the theoretical descriptions of Bohr's theory alone: A good many additional causal posits and auxiliary hypotheses are required. The same is true with respect to theoretical descriptions of intentional psychological states. Indeed, in this case it is perhaps even more obvious, since cross-cultural psychologists appear to be able to reidentify emotions such as shame and anger in different cultures (Triandis 1980), although the actions generated by agents who are ashamed or angry may differ quite dramatically because of differences in local rules governing appropriate responses and 'display rules' governing expression (Harris 1989). Actions based upon emotions simply cannot be predicted from the theoretical description of an emotion alone.

I do not, however, mean to suggest that the ontological commitments of folk psychology can be preserved by an appeal to the so-called *Quine–Duhem* thesis. According to at least some statements of this thesis, it is always possible to retain theoretical explanations that are faced with failed predictions by modifying or replacing auxiliary hypotheses employed in the derivation of such predictions. I have argued elsewhere (Greenwood 1990b) that the Quine–Duhem thesis does not offer an epistemologically viable strategy for preserving theoretical *explanations* in the face of apparent falsifications. Moreover, I would agree with Churchland that when the avowed accuracy or adequacy of theoretical explanations is our only evidential grounds for commitment to the ontology presupposed by them, then we ought to abandon our commitment to this ontology if we come to recognize the general inaccuracy or inadequacy of such explanations.

What I would deny is that the avowed explanatory success of folk psychology is our only evidential grounds for accepting the ontology of intentional psychological states posited by folk-psychological descriptions. Consider the favorite examples of rejected theoretical posits referenced by critics of folk psychology: the posits of phlogiston theory, caloric theory, and the theory of witches. A common feature of all these theories is that their proposed explanatory success with respect to particular domains was the sole evidential grounds for accepting the ontologies posited by these theories. Thus it was rational to abandon these ontologies along with the discredited explanations avowed by such theories.

This is patently not the case, however, with respect to the objects of a great many of our theoretical descriptions. Often these phenomena can be perceptually discriminated more or less directly or via sense-extending instruments: The causal or functional role of such entities then becomes a matter of empirical investigation. This is the case with respect to many of the examples previously cited: marsh vapors, Golgi bodies, violent stimuli, and so forth. It also seems fairly obviously not true of our theoretical descriptions of psychological states. Even if we recognized that all our folk-psychological explanations of human action are inaccurate, we would still have good reason to maintain the existence of intentional psychological states. One reason is self-knowledge of such states, which I consider in the next section. The second reason is that persons can articulate and communicate their psychological states.

Now one might be inclined to reject the evidence of agent accounts as itself based on a presumption about the adequacy of folk-psychological explanations. Yet this inclination ought to be resisted. Our discrimination of contentful psychological states via agent accounts, like our discrimination of Golgi bodies via microscopic staining, is of course 'theory-informed'. But neither form of theory-informed discrimination presupposes the adequacy of causal explanations referencing psychological states or Golgi bodies: This feature explains why it is possible to entertain alternative and competing theories of their causal or functional role.

If it is insisted that our discriminations of contentful psychological states via agent accounts still presuppose the accuracy of one particular form of folk-psychological explanation that causally relates contentful psychological states and agent accounts, then it may be replied that this particular folk-psychological explanation has far greater epistemic warrant than our everyday folk-psychological explanations of human actions such as aggression and dishonesty. There is not a shred of psychological or neurophysiological evidence to undermine it.

Moreover, it ought to be stressed that what is at issue is the existence of contentful psychological states, not the accuracy of particular explanations of particular agent-accounts by reference to them. Our legitimate treatment of agent accounts of their beliefs and motives as evidence for contentful psychological states does not require that we suppose that such accounts are always or even regularly accurate: It does not require that folk-psychological explanatory generalizations relating particular psychological states and particular agent accounts are themselves accurate. Even if such accounts are regularly biased, distorted, or self-deceiving, we may reasonably treat such accounts as good evidence for the existence of contentful psychological states simpliciter, perhaps remaining more cautious in treating particular accounts as good evidence for the existence of particular states. That is, it is not a necessary condition for treating human talk as evidence of the existence of contentful psychological states that we have any theory of the undoubtedly complex etiology of the causal production of talk. It is surely sufficient that we are in causal contact with the talk of others in a language that we comprehend.

If this is so, then we could meaningfully ascribe folk-psychological states to ourselves and others and have evidence for their existence, even if we had no theory of their causal relation to discourse or action, or if our folksy theories turned out to be generally inadequate or inaccurate. Churchland's account of the semantics of theoretical psychological descriptions rules this out as a conceptual possibility, by tying the semantics of such descriptions to their causal-explanatory employment. According to Churchland, we grasp the semantics of folk-psychological descriptions by learning their causal-explanatory employment "at our mother's knee."

This does not, in fact, appear to be the case. Developmental psychologists have demonstrated that children can employ folk-psychological discourse from about age two or three. By that time, most children have an extensive psychological vocabulary (words like "want," "need," "hope," "believe," "suppose," "think," etc., see Olson & Astington 1986), and can employ this vocabulary to attribute contentful psychological states to themselves and others. However, it is not until about age four that children develop mastery of the causal-explanatory employment of intentional psychological descriptions. As Leslie (1988, pp. 37–38) notes:

Very young children can take a causal view of the world. As far as the behaviour of people is concerned, they include as possible causes of behaviour only concrete objects and events. Independently of this causal view, these children can also formulate representations of mental states.

About four years of age, these two independent capacities are brought together; children enlarge their notion of "possible causes of behaviour" to include mental states. From this point, mental states can be treated as both *causes* of behaviour and *effects* of perceptual exposure to a situation.[1]

If this is so, then very young children can ascribe psychological states to self and others and have evidence for them (via talk) without having any grasp of causal-explanatory theory. And if this is so, it is surely possible for adults and psychological scientists to ascribe psychological states to self and others meaningfully and to have evidence for them (via talk), even if their causal-explanatory theories of discourse and action turn out to be inaccurate or inadequate.

III

The preceding discussion leads us to consideration of the second objection to eliminativism. It may be argued that we would not be obliged to abandon the ontology of folk psychology even if our folk-psychological explanations turned out to be generally inaccurate or inadequate, since we have independent grounds for maintaining the existence of folk-psychological phenomena, in the form of self-knowledge of beliefs, emotions, and so forth.

Now Churchland (1979, 1984) has a ready answer to this objection. He claims that it simply begs the question and is based upon a naive view about the directness of perception, including any form of "internal perception" or introspection. Churchland argues that all forms of perception are 'theory-informed'. Accordingly, self-knowledge – "the perception of our internal states" – is also theory-informed. Unfortunately, it is informed by a bad theory – folk psychology – and would be greatly advanced if it came to be informed by a superior theory, namely neurophysiology.

Churchland does not deny that there is something to be internally perceived in the case of self-knowledge. Indeed, it is central to his argument that there is, for he wants to treat self-knowledge of psychological states as analogous to the theory-informed perceptions of medieval astronomers. In the latter case, there was *something* to see, but the Ptolemaic theoretical interpretation of it was wrong. In the former case, there is something that is perceived ("cortical states"), but our folk-psychological theoretical interpretation of it is wrong (Churchland 1986, p. 219). Consequently, Churchland argues that our self-knowledge would be much improved if it were informed by superior neurophysiological theory. Just as we can be taught to observe the heavens in ways informed by Copernican rather than Ptolemaic theory, we can be taught to observe our internal states in ways informed by neurophysiological theory.

In this case, however, it appears to be Churchland who is begging the question. In the first place, if the arguments of the preceding section are sound, the possible theory informity of self-knowledge would not constitute any grounds for doubting its accuracy. Even if self-knowledge of intentional psychological states is informed by theoretical conceptions of such states, the accuracy of self-knowledge is not impugned by the possible inaccuracy or inadequacy of folk-psychological explanations, if the accuracy of such theories is logically independent of their causal-explanatory employment. Recall that young children do appear to be able to provide accounts of their beliefs and fears before they can master the causal-explanatory theories that reference them.

In the second place, Churchland's argument is based on the doubtful assumption that self-knowledge of intentional psychological states is analogous to self-knowledge of sensations such as pain, that it involves a form of perception of 'internal states' informed by theoretical conceptions of them. Thus Churchland (1984, p. 73) argues that self-knowledge (or "self-perception") improves with practice and the increasing sophistication of our theoretical classifications:

Accordingly, the self-awareness of a young child, though real, will be much narrower or coarser than that of a sensitive adult. What is simply a dislike for someone, for a child, may divide into a mixture of jealousy, fear, and moral disapproval of someone, in the case of an honest and self-perceptive adult.

Yet self-knowledge of intentional psychological states cannot be so readily assimilated to self-knowledge of internal states such as pain. The reason young children do not have self-knowledge of jealousy, fear, and moral disapproval is not due to their introspective inexperience or the poverty of their theoretical conceptions of internal states. Rather, young children are simply not jealous, do not have adult fears, and do not express moral disapproval. In order to have self-knowledge of these states, they must first learn to be jealous, have adult fears, and express moral disapproval. In order to do this, they do not have to learn to represent their internal states in any fashion. Rather they have to learn how to represent *social reality* in the conventional ways that are constitutive of these sentiments in any form of human life.

Consider self-knowledge of shame, for example. This is not a matter of the practiced discrimination of internal states informed by theories about them. Shame, unlike sensations such as pains or itches, does not occur and recur independently of representation. Rather, we have to learn to be ashamed: We have to learn to treat certain actions (or failures to act) as personally degrading and humiliating. When young children have learned to be ashamed, they know their shame when they can articulate this form of representation of social reality. Moreover, this is all they need to know in order to know their shame: They do not need to know that it is conventionally classified as "shame" in their form of social life.

That is, it is not a necessary condition of self-knowledge of shame that agents employ any form of theoretical conception of their shame, far less any causal-explanatory theory referencing their shame. Children can know their shame before they learn that it is descriptively classified as "shame." Many agents in primitive societies seem to have self-knowledge of their rich psychological lives, but largely eschew discourse about psychological states (Hallpike 1979; Levy 1984).

Contra Churchland, theories about internal states do not appear to be an integral feature of self-knowledge. The reason is that self-knowledge of shame and other intentional psychological states does not appear to involve any form of perception of internal states. In order to know my shame, I need to know how I represent *external reality* (my actions or failure to act). I do not need to know how I represent any internal states.

This point may be illustrated in the following indirect fashion. Let us suppose, for the sake of argument, that we can discriminate internal states by some form of perception informed by neurophysiological theory. What would this tell us in the case of shame, for example, or our belief that the value of the dollar will fall? Our perceptual judgments based upon such hypothetical internal discriminations would be articulations of the intentional direction and intensional content of our neurophysiological theories about our internal states. However, what we need to know is the intentional direction and the intensional content of our *shame* and *belief*. We need to know how we represent our actions and what we think will happen to the dollar. We need to know how we represent the properties of phenomena *external* to us. We do not need to know the properties, or how we represent the properties, of any *internal* phenomena. That is, such hypothetical internal perception would be necessarily focused in the wrong direction (Greenwood 1990c; 1991a).

Moreover, in order to have knowledge of such hypothetical internal states, in the form of articulable and communicable knowledge, it must be the case that the agent is able to articulate the intentional direction and intensional content of his or her perceptual *beliefs*. However, this is to presuppose precisely the ability – and folk-psychological ontology – that such an account is designed to deny. (Alternatively, it presupposes an infinite regress of internal perceptions of internal perceptions in order to determine the contents and objects of theories informing our perceptions.)

One way of expressing this point is as follows: Self-knowledge of intentional psychological phenomena is not analogous to forms of perception informed by theory but is formally identical to our knowledge of the contents and objects of the theories that frequently do inform our perceptions. It is nothing more or less than the ability to articulate the contents and objects of our beliefs, emotions, and so forth. To say this is not, of course, to advocate or endorse any account of the causal grounding of this ability; it is to note the incoherence of supposing that it is causally grounded upon theoretically informed perceptions of internal states.

To say this is not to affirm the infallibility of self-knowledge; no doubt we err often enough in articulating the contents of our psychological states. Yet it is difficult to suppose that we regularly err or that we might universally err. If our theoretical descriptions of psychological states are linguistically modeled, then perhaps the best analogue of self-knowledge of intentional psychological states is our knowledge of the sense and reference of our linguistic utterances. It is difficult, however, to conceive of this as a form of perceptual knowledge of internal states, or to suppose that we all regularly or universally err with respect to it.

IV

Now, Paul Churchland would certainly object to the argument of the preceding section (and any argument of a similar nature) by protesting that theoretical knowledge is not so "specifically *linguistic* as we have chronically assumed" (Chapter 2, this volume). He would object that it simply begs the question by presuming that theoretical knowledge in natural science and other domains is essentially linguistic in nature; that it consists of meaningful contents that can be expressed in sets of propositions (generalizations, laws, etc.). In place of this traditional view, itself allegedly part of folk psychology, Churchland advances the "prototype activation" model, which treats theoretical understanding as the activation of neural networks operating on connectionist or PDP ('parallel distributed processing') principles (Rumelhart & McClelland 1986) that employ *prototypes* of the types of object they represent.

Via the distribution of excitatory and inhibitory stimuli within the neural system that determines the level of activity of its connected nodes, the system can learn to recognize instances of *F*s (e.g., phonemes, mines, grammatical categories) by forming "complex feature detectors" that enable the system to construct a representation of a prototypical *F*, and to judge whether any particular stimulus object is an *F*, by determining the proximity of the pattern of activation produced by input stimulation to the pattern that constitutes the neural network's representation of a prototypical *F*. This exploitation of connectionist theory is an extension of Churchland's (1979) general attack upon epistemologies that postulate the internal processing of sentences or symbols: He argues that the neural systems that explain the perceptual and theoretical achievements of wolves and prelinguistic children are no different in kind (although no doubt different in degrees of complexity) from those that explain the perceptual and theoretical achievements of linguistically competent adults.

Churchland employs the notion of prototype activation to explain how we can harbor all those false theories of folk psychology even though we have difficulty articulating them in the form of universally quantified empirical laws. He claims that our theoretical understanding of human action involves the subsumption of actions under prototypical generative sequences. However, this returns us to the objection discussed in the first section of this chapter. There simply do not appear to be any prototypical generative sequences for human actions. There are no prototypical generative sequences concerning aggression, dishonesty, and suicide, for example: People are aggressive, are dishonest, and commit suicide for a wide variety of reasons, and aggression, dishonesty, and suicide have a wide variety of causes – for the reason noted earlier. Our classificatory prototypes for human action are attuned to the *representational* dimensions of human action. A wide variety of physical behaviors (raising my hand, moving a switch on a shock generator, tampering with a colleague's brake cable, etc.) are all discriminated by social agents as instances of aggression, insofar as they all involve the agent's representation of his or her behavior as directed toward the injury of another. Since behaviors are constituted as actions and identified by these representational dimensions – at least according to the classificatory descriptions of folk psychology – there is no limit to the kinds of causes they can have and, therefore, not much hope for prototypical characterizations in terms of them.

No doubt there are regular generative relations between types of neurophysiological states and physical behaviors. But there is no reason to suppose that these are discriminable by lay agents, or that they can be identified with the lay generalizations relating intentional psychological states and actions that can be roughly articulated and endorsed by most layfolk and that are advanced by many scientific psychologists.

This is not to deny that we employ prototypes of human actions. It is just to deny that our prototypes for human actions are causal sequences. It is neither to deny that we employ nonlinguistic prototypes in perceptual judgment. As Mary Hesse (1974) has argued, there must be a high degree of agreement with respect to our basic perceptual discriminations in order for the learning and employment of language to be possible, and hence there must also be involved in this process some form of nonlinguistic theory of the kind that Churchland champions. Connectionist theory and the prototype activation model serve as a decent (although by no means the only possible or viable) account of the basis of this agreement that makes our linguistically informed perceptual and theoretical achievements possible.

That is, Churchland provides a neurophysiological account of a basic form of perceptual discrimination that serves as an enabling condition for the development of language and linguistically informed perceptual and theoretical judgments. Without any justificatory argument, he then assumes that this account can be extended to provide a theoretically sufficient account of all forms of perception and theoretical knowledge, including those that are linguistically informed.

I do not think Churchland gives us any good reason for supposing that this is so. One very basic difference is as follows: As Mary Hesse also notes, our linguistically informed and articulated theories often override our original prototypical perceptual discriminations. Our perceptual discriminations are modifiable by linguistic negotiation, unlike the perceptual discriminations of wolves and very young children. Without language and without the articulated, disputed, and defended claims of Copernican theory, we would probably never have come to see the heavens in the Copernican fashion that Churchland so eloquently recommends.

My concern, however, is not to deny the possibility that connectionist theories can be extended to account for the forms of perceptual and theoretical knowledge that can be articulated and communicated by human agents, or to belabor the prima facie differences between the theoretical achievements of wolves and human astronomers. This theoretical possibility, in fact, does not pose any threat to the ontology of folk psychology by casting doubt upon the linguistic informity of human perception and theoretical knowledge. The linguistic modifiability of human perception and cognition supports the folk-psychological assumption that human perception and cognition are linguistically informed. This assumption does not presuppose or preclude any theoretical account of its psychological or neural implementation. Connectionist theories of human perception and cognition are thus not inconsistent with the assumption that human perception and cognition are linguistically informed. They may be inconsistent with psychological accounts of linguistic informity in terms of computations performed upon "mental representations" in a "language of thought" (Fodor 1975). That is, however, quite a different matter.

More to the point, this theoretical possibility does not undermine the general account of self-knowledge advanced in the previous section. On the contrary, it tends to support it. Our linguistically informed theoretical knowledge is intimately tied to our ability to articulate the contents of our theories. If linguistically informed theoretical knowledge involves a direct representational relation between neural systems and the external world, as claimed by connectionist theory, rather than an internal relation to mental representations, then there is no longer any good reason to treat self-knowledge as a form of internal perception or any analogue of it.

V

Throughout this chapter, I have argued that we would not be obliged to reject the ontology of folk psychology even if our folk-psychological explanations turned out to be regularly inaccurate or inadequate. We would still have good evidential grounds for maintaining the existence of such states in the face of such explanatory failure. I have done so not because I lack faith in the ultimate explanatory adequacy of folk psychology. I do not. I have, rather, been engaged in what I consider to be a holding operation, to defend the preservation of our intuitions about the reality of such phenomena in the face of some justifiable doubts about the contemporary adequacy of folk-psychological explanations. This is because I believe that the primary threat to folk psychology is, in fact, not empirical but conceptual: It derives precisely from the common commitment to the principles that ground the thesis of eliminative materialism.

It needs to be stressed that Churchland never seriously addresses the question of the supposed empirical inadequacy of folk psychology. He claims that it has remained largely unchanged since the time of the Greeks. This is patently false. The folk-psychological explanations avowed by the medievals are strikingly different from the folk-psychological explanations avowed by contemporary folk: These days, one does not hear much about 'acedia' (Altschule 1965), for example.[2] In any case, theoretical constancy over time is epistemologically neutral: It may be indicative of "conceptual inertia" or empirical success. Churchland claims that folk psychology is "stagnant": It is not fertile in extending its forms of explanation to novel domains. Yet many hold that Freud's achievement was to do precisely that.

Contemporary social psychology is the closest scientific psychological analogue of our everyday folk-psychological accounts of human actions. It advances intentional explanations of human actions undreamt of by the Greeks or medievals. Churchland provides no general methodological critique of the theoretical achievements of contemporary social psychology. He does not, for example, impugn the evidential basis of the theoretical achievements documented in the 22 volumes of *Advances in Experimental Social Psychology* (edited by L. Berkowitz and published by Academic Press).

Churchland's eliminativist argument ultimately depends upon the generally recognized irreducibility of the categories of intentional folk-psychological descriptions to the categories of neurophysiology. He presumes that this reductive failure is a *consequence* of the explanatory inadequacy of folk psychology: "Folk psychology's explanatory impotence and long stagnation inspires little faith that its categories will find themselves neatly reflected in the framework of neuroscience" (1981, p. 75). Churchland, of course, assumes that we should not accept psychological theories that do not "smoothly" reduce to neurophysiology. This assumption suggests that the normative thesis of eliminative materialism rests upon the following conditional claim: If folk psychological theories do not smoothly reduce to neurophysiological ones, then they are empirically inadequate.

I do not propose to engage the normative thesis of eliminative materialism directly. I want instead to highlight the defeasibility of the conditional claim on which it is based. Just about everyone in the debate about the future of folk psychology agrees about the irreducibility of folk-psychological theories to neurophysiology. If we grant this claim, then if scientific social psychology can independently demonstrate its empirical adequacy (by reference to standard criteria such as successful prediction and fertility etc.), this conditional claim can be falsified.

I believe that it can, with the following qualification: At the end of the day, there is some point to Churchland's negative characterization of contemporary folk psychology, including contemporary social psychology; for, despite its recognized achievements, contemporary social psychology has no comprehensive general theory of human action but represents a set of rather piecemeal generalizations about such phenomena as 'cognitive dissonance', 'risky shift', 'destructive obedience', and 'bystander apathy'. Problems of experimental replication and generalizability have led some theorists to doubt the empirical progressiveness of social psychology (Smith 1972; Gergen 1982), and others to talk about the "crisis" in contemporary social psychology (Elms 1975; Parker 1989).

There are a variety of explanations of the crisis – and a multitude of recommendations about how to resolve it. In conclusion, I want to suggest my own interpretation. Throughout its history, social psychological science has been dominated by the principles of materialism and atomism. Practitioners have invariably conceived of psychological phenomena in terms of atomistic internal states, theoretical descriptions of which are held to make indirect reference to brain states. I have elsewhere (Greenwood 1989) documented the methodological inadequacies of this approach, and I believe these suffice to explain the contemporary malaise in social psychology. I believe an empirically adequate social psychology will be developed only when it embraces a social relational conception of contentful psychological states – one that recognizes the social embeddedness of characteristically human beliefs, emotions, motives, and so forth (Greenwood 1991b).

The point may be made in the following fashion. Contemporary social psychology (like most of academic psychology) was based upon Wilhelm Wundt's atomistic experimental analysis of sensations. Although later generations of behaviorists and cognitive psychologists rejected Wundt's introspective method, they retained the principles of behavioral and psychological atomism and isolative experimental analysis. Yet

Wundt himself did not think that intentional psychological phenomena such as beliefs and emotions could be adequately conceived and studied in this fashion, arguing that such social relational phenomena are best studied through their social products:

There are other sources of objective psychological knowledge, which become accessible at the very point where the experimental method fails us. These are certain products of common mental life, in which we trace the operation of determinate psychical motives: chief among them are language, myth, and custom. (Wundt 1900, p. 31)

Wundt's own *Völkerpsychologie* (1900–1920) – the original 'folk psychology'– represents a form of (causal-explanatory)³ theoretical psychology of action (anticipated by Vico, Herder, and Kant) that has been systematically ignored by scientific psychologists, including social psychologists. The primary reason for the "degeneracy" of this "research program"⁴ is its systematic neglect by practitioners, not its intrinsic or empirically demonstrated inadequacy. It has quite simply never been given a theoretical chance.

Whether it will in the future remains to be seen. What I want to stress here is that it will not so long as practitioners *remain* committed to an atomistic conception of folk-psychological phenomena. Churchland predicts that folk psychology will be an explanatory failure. I suggest that if this proves to be correct, the most likely reason will be that practitioners continue to endorse the atomistic reductive constraints of eliminative materialism. If they reject these constraints, the theoretical prospects for folk psychology are much more open and optimistic.

Notes

1. This empirical claim can be, and has been, disputed (Wellmann 1988), but the very fact that it does appear to be a legitimate empirical claim (rather than a contradiction in terms) itself demonstrates the inadequacy of Churchland's account of the semantics of folk-psychological descriptions.
2. The difference between medieval folk psychology and contemporary folk psychology does not by itself indicate the inadequacy of either. Churchland simply ignores the theoretical possibility that the ontological states referenced in folk-psychological explanations may change over time because the ontology of folk psychology is itself transformed in historical time (and may vary cross-culturally). Thus the emotions and motives of medievals may have been different from ours because the contents of their psychological states may have been different from ours (Greenwood 1991b).
3. I stress that this form of theoretical psychology is causal explanatory in order to dissociate this account from the neo-Wittgensteinian interpretation of folk psychology, which also stresses the social relational nature of folk-psycho-

logical phenomena, but denies causal-explanatory status to folk-psychological explanations (e.g., Peters 1958; Winch 1958). A social-relational account of folk-psychological phenomena does not itself entail a denial of the causal-explanatory status of folk-psychological explanation (Greenwood 1991b), although the neo-Wittgensteinians may have had some legitimate grounds for criticizing the applicability of traditional Humean accounts of causal explanation to the folk-psychological domain (Greenwood 1989).

4. It is worth recalling that the concept of "progressive" and "degenerating" research programs comes from Lakatos (1970), who insisted on the methodological virtues of retaining "degenerating research programs" to ensure a comparative measure of theoretical progress and to leave open the possibility that such programs might stage a comeback and become "progressive" again. (See his account of the varying fortunes of Prout's hypothesis during the nineteenth century.)

References

Altschule, M. D. (1965). "Acedia: Its Evolution from Deadly Sin to Psychiatric Syndrome." *British Journal of Psychiatry*, 111:117–119.

Berkowitz, L., & LePage, A. (1967). "Weapons as Aggression-eliciting Stimuli." *Journal of Personality and Social Psychology*, 7:202–207.

Churchland, P. M. (1979). *Realism and the Plasticity of Mind.* Cambridge: Cambridge University Press.

Churchland, P. M. (1981). "Eliminative Materialism and Propositional Attitudes." *Journal of Philosophy*, 78:67–90.

Churchland, P. M. (1984). *Matter and Consciousness.* Cambridge, Mass.: MIT Press.

Churchland, P. M. (1986). "Cognition and Conceptual Change: A Reply to Double." *Journal for the Theory of Social Behavior*, 16:217–221.

Elms, A. C. (1975). "The Crisis of Confidence in Social Psychology." *American Psychologist*, 30:967–976.

Fodor, J. (1975). *The Language of Thought.* Cambridge, Mass.: Harvard University Press.

Gergen, K. J. (1982). *Towards Transformation in Social Knowledge.* New York: Springer-Verlag.

Goldman, A. I. (1970). *A Theory of Human Action.* Princeton: Princeton University Press.

Greenwood, J. D. (1989). *Explanation and Experiment in Social Psychological Science.* New York: Springer-Verlag.

Greenwood, J. D. (1990a). "The Social Constitution of Action." *Philosophy of the Social Sciences*, 20:195–207.

Greenwood, J. D. (1990b). "Two Dogmas of Neo-Empiricism: The Quine–Duhem Thesis and the Theory-Informity of Observations." *Philosophy of Science*, 57:555–574.

Greenwood, J. D. (1990c). "Self-Knowledge: Inference, Perception, Articulation." *Theoretical and Philosophical Psychology*, 10:39–48.

Greenwood, J. D. (1991a). "Self-Knowledge: Looking in the Wrong Direction." *Behavior and Philosophy*.

Greenwood, J. D. (1991b). *Relations and Representations: An Introduction to the Philosophy of Social Psychological Science*. London: Routledge.

Hallpike, C. (1979). *Foundations of Primitive Thought*. Oxford: Clarendon.

Hanson, N. R. (1958). *Patterns of Discovery*. Cambridge: Cambridge University Press.

Harré, R. (1970). *The Principles of Scientific Thinking*. Chicago: University of Chicago Press.

Harris, P. (1989). *Children and Emotion*. Oxford: Basil Blackwell.

Hesse, M. (1974). *The Structure of Scientific Inference*. London: Macmillan.

Hesse, M. (1976). "Models Versus Paradigms in the Natural Sciences." In L. Collins, ed., *The Use of Models in the Social Sciences*. London: Tavistock Press.

Kuhn, T. (1970). *The Structure of Scientific Revolutions*, 2nd ed. Chicago: University of Chicago Press.

Lakatos, I. (1976). "Falsification and the Methodology of Scientific Research Programmes." In I. Lakatos & A. Musgrave, eds., *Criticism and the Growth of Knowledge*. Cambridge: Cambridge University Press.

Leslie, A. M. (1988). "Some Implications of Pretense for Mechanisms Underlying the Child's Theory of Mind." In J. W. Astington, P. L. Harris, & D. R. Olson, eds., *Developing Theories of Mind*. Cambridge: Cambridge University Press.

Levy, R. (1984). "Emotion, Knowing and Culture." In R. Shweder & R. LeVine, eds., *Culture Theory: Essays on Mind, Self, and Emotion*. Cambridge: Cambridge University Press.

McGinn, C. (1979). "Action and Its Explanation." In N. Bolton, ed., *Philosophical Problems of Psychology*. London: Methuen.

Olston, D., & Astington, J. (1986). "Children's Acquisition of Metalinguistic and Metacognitive Verbs." In W. Demopoulos & A. Marras, eds., *Language Learning and Concept Acquisition*. Norwood, N.J.: Ablex.

Parker, I. (1989). *The Crisis of Modern Social Psychology*. London: Routledge.

Peters, R. S. (1958). *The Concept of Motivation*. London: Routledge & Kegan Paul.

Rumelhart, D. E., & McClelland, J. L. (1986) *Parallel Distributed Processing: Explorations in the Microstructure of Cognition*, Vol 1: *Foundations*. Cambridge, Mass.: MIT Press.

Smith, M. B. (1972). "Is Experimental Social Psychology Advancing?" *Journal of Experimental Social Psychology*, 8:86–96.

Triandis, H. (1980). *Handbook of Cross-cultural Psychology*. Boston: Allyn & Bacon.

Wellmann, H. M. (1988). "First Steps in the Child's Theorizing About the Mind." In J. W. Astington, P. L. Harris, & D. R. Olson, eds., *Developing Theories of Mind*. Cambridge: Cambridge University Press.

Winch, P. (1958). *The Idea of a Social Science*. London: Routledge & Kegan Paul.

Wundt, W. (1900–1920). *Völkerpsychologie*, Vols. 1–10. London: Allen & Unwin.

4 Connectionism, eliminativism, and the future of folk psychology

William Ramsey, Stephen Stich, and Joseph Garon

I. Introduction

In the years since the publication of Thomas Kuhn's *Structure of Scientific Revolutions* (1962), the term "scientific revolution" has been used with increasing frequency in discussions of scientific change, and the magnitude required of an innovation before someone is tempted to call it a revolution has diminished alarmingly. Our thesis in this chapter is that if a certain family of connectionist hypotheses turn out to be right, they will surely count as revolutionary, even on stringent pre-Kuhnian standards.

There is no question that connectionism has already brought about major changes in the way many cognitive scientists conceive of cognition. However, as we see it, what makes certain kinds of connectionist models genuinely revolutionary is the support they lend to a thoroughgoing eliminativism about some of the central posits of commonsense (or "folk") psychology. Our focus in this chapter is on beliefs or propositional memories, though the argument generalizes straightforwardly to all the other propositional attitudes. If we are right, the consequences of this kind of connectionism extend well beyond the confines of cognitive science, since these models, if successful, will require a radical reorientation in the way we think about ourselves.

Here is a quick preview of what is to come. Section II gives a brief account of what eliminativism claims, and sketches a pair of premises that eliminativist arguments typically require. Section III explores how

Copyright © 1991 by William Ramsey, Stephen Stich, and Joseph Garon. Thanks are due to Ned Block, Paul Churchland, Gary Cottrell, Adrian Cussins, Jerry Fodor, John Heil, Frank Jackson, David Kirsh, Patricia Kitcher, and Philip Kitcher for useful feedback on earlier versions of this essay. Talks based on the essay were presented at the University of California, San Diego, Cognitive Science Seminar and at conferences sponsored by the Howard Hughes Medical Foundation and the University of North Carolina at Greensboro. Comments and questions from these audiences have proved helpful in many ways.

we conceive of commonsense psychology and the propositional attitudes that it posits. It also illustrates one sort of psychological model that exploits and builds upon the posits of folk psychology. Section IV is devoted to connectionism. Models that have been called "connectionist" form a fuzzy and heterogeneous set whose members often share little more than a vague family resemblance. But our argument linking connectionism to eliminativism will work only for a restricted domain of connectionist models, interpreted in a particular way; the main task of Section IV is to say what that domain is and how the models in the domain are to be interpreted. In Section V we illustrate what a connectionist model of belief that comports with our strictures might look like, and go on to argue that if models of this sort are correct, then the outlook for commonsense psychology is bleak. Section VI assembles some objections and replies. The final section is a brief conclusion.

Before plunging in, we should emphasize that the thesis we propose to defend is a *conditional* claim: *If* connectionist hypotheses of the sort we shall sketch turn out to be right, so too will eliminativism about propositional attitudes. Since our goal is only to show how connectionism and eliminativism are related, we shall make no effort to argue for the truth or falsity of either doctrine. In particular, we shall offer no argument in favor of the version of connectionism required in the antecedent of our conditional. Indeed, our view is that it is still early – too early to tell with any assurance how well this family of connectionist hypotheses will fare. Those who are more confident of connectionism may, of course, invoke our conditional as part of a larger argument for doing away with the propositional attitudes.[1] But, as John Haugeland once remarked, one man's *ponens* is another man's *tollens*. And those who take eliminativism about propositional attitudes to be preposterous or unthinkable may well view our arguments as part of a larger case against connectionism. Thus, we would not be at all surprised if trenchant critics of connectionism, like Fodor and Pylyshyn (e.g., 1988), found both our conditional and the argument for it to be quite congenial.

II. Eliminativism and folk psychology

'Eliminativism,' as we shall use the term, is a fancy name for a simple thesis. It is the claim that some category of entities, processes, or properties exploited in a commonsense or scientific account of the world do not exist. So construed, we are all eliminativists about many sorts of things. In the domain of folk theory, witches are the standard example. Once upon a time, witches were widely believed to be responsible for various local calamities. But people gradually became convinced that there are better explanations for most of the events in which witches had been implicated. There being no explanatory work for witches to do, sensible people concluded that there were no such things. In the scientific domain, phlogiston, caloric, and the luminiferous ether are the parade cases for eliminativism. Each was invoked by serious scientists pursuing sophisticated research programs. But in each case the program ran aground in a major way, and the theories in which the entities were invoked were replaced by successor theories in which the entities played no role. The scientific community gradually came to recognize that phlogiston and the rest do not exist.

As these examples suggest, a central step in an eliminativist argument is typically the demonstration that the theory in which certain putative entities or processes are invoked should be rejected and replaced by a better theory. That raises the question of how we go about showing that one theory is better than another. This question is notoriously difficult to answer. It would be widely agreed, however, that if a new theory provides more accurate predictions and better explanations than an old one, and does so over a broader range of phenomena, and if the new theory comports as well or better with well-established theories in neighboring domains, then there is good reason to think that the old theory is inferior, and that the new one is to be preferred. This is hardly a complete account of the conditions under which one theory is to be preferred to another, though for our purposes it will suffice.

But merely showing that a theory in which a class of entities plays a role is inferior to a successor theory is plainly not sufficient to show that the entities do not exist. Often a more appropriate conclusion is that the rejected theory was wrong, perhaps seriously wrong, about some of the properties of the entities in its domain, or about the laws governing those entities, and that the new theory gives us a more accurate account *of those very same entities.* Thus, for example, pre-Copernican astronomy was very wrong about the nature of the planets and the laws governing their movement. But it would be something of a joke to suggest that Copernicus and Galileo showed that the planets Ptolemy spoke of do not exist.[2]

In other cases the right thing to conclude is that the posits of the old theory are reducible to those of the new. Standard examples here include the reduction of temperature to mean molecular kinetic energy, the reduction of sound to wave motion in the medium, and the reduction of genes to sequences of polynucleotide bases.[3] Given our current concerns, the lesson to be learned from these cases is that even if the commonsense theory in which propositional attitudes find their home is replaced by a better theory, that would not be enough to show that the posits of the commonsense theory do not exist

What more would be needed? What is it that distinguishes cases like phlogiston and caloric, on the one hand, from cases like genes and the planets on the other? Or, to ask the question in a rather different way, what made phlogiston and caloric candidates for elimination? Why wasn't it concluded that phlogiston is oxygen, that caloric is kinetic energy, and that the earlier theories had just been rather badly mistaken about some of the properties of phlogiston and caloric?

Let us introduce some terminology. We shall call theory changes in which the entities and processes of the old theory are retained or reduced to those of the new one *ontologically conservative* theory changes. Theory changes that are not ontologically conservative we shall call *ontologically radical*. Given this terminology, the question we are asking is how to distinguish ontologically conservative theory changes from ontologically radical ones.

Once again, this is a question that is easier to ask than to answer. There is, in the philosophy of science literature, nothing that even comes close to a plausible and fully general account of when theory change sustains an eliminativist conclusion and when it does not. In the absence of a principled way of deciding when ontological elimination is in order, the best we can do is to look at the posits of the old theory – the ones that are at risk of elimination – and ask whether there is anything in the new theory that they might be identified with or reduced to. If the posits of the new theory strike us as deeply and fundamentally different from those of the old theory, in the way that molecular motion seems deeply and fundamentally different from the "exquisitely elastic" fluid posited by caloric theory, then it will be plausible to conclude that the theory change has been a radical one, and that an eliminativist conclusion is in order. But since there is no easy measure of how "deeply and fundamentally different" a pair of posits are, the conclusion we reach is bound to be a judgment call.[4]

To argue that certain sorts of connectionist models support eliminativism about the propositional attitudes, we must make it plausible that these models are not ontologically conservative. Our strategy will be to contrast these connectionist models, models like those set out in Section V, with ontologically conservative models like the one sketched at the end of Section III, in an effort to underscore just how ontologically radical the connectionist models are. But here we are getting ahead of ourselves. Before trying to persuade the reader that connectionist models are ontologically radical, we need to take a look at the folk-psychological theory that the connectionist models threaten to replace.

III. Propositional attitudes and commonsense psychology

For present purposes we assume that commonsense psychology can plausibly be regarded as a theory, and that beliefs, desires, and the rest of the propositional attitudes are plausibly viewed as posits of that theory. Although this is not an uncontroversial assumption, the case for it has been well argued by others.[5] Once it is granted that commonsense psychology is indeed a theory, we expect it will be conceded by almost everyone that the theory is a likely candidate for replacement. In saying this, we do not intend to disparage folk psychology, or to beg any questions about the status of the entities it posits. Our point is simply that folk wisdom on matters psychological is not likely to tell us all there is to know. Commonsense psychology, like other folk theories, is bound to be incomplete in many ways, and very likely to be inaccurate in more than a few. If this were not the case, there would be no need for a careful, quantitative, experimental science of psychology. With the possible exception of a few die-hard Wittgensteinians, just about everyone is prepared to grant that there are many psychological facts and principles beyond those embedded in common sense. If this is right, then we have the first premise needed in an eliminativist argument aimed at beliefs, propositional memories, and the rest of the propositional attitudes. The theory that posits the attitudes is indeed a prime candidate for replacement.

Though commonsense psychology contains a wealth of lore about beliefs, memories, desires, hopes, fears, and the other propositional attitudes, the crucial folk-psychological tenets in forging the link between connectionism and eliminativism are the claims that propositional attitudes are *functionally discrete, semantically interpretable* states that play a *causal role* in the production of other propositional attitudes, and ultimately in the production of behavior. Following the suggestion in Stich (1983), we shall call this cluster of claims *propositional modularity.*[6] (The reader is cautioned not to confuse this notion of propositional modularity with the very different notion of modularity defended in Fodor [1983].)

The fact that commonsense psychology takes beliefs and other propositional attitudes to have semantic properties deserves special emphasis. According to commonsense:

1. When people see a dog nearby, they typically come to believe *that there is a dog nearby.*
2. When people believe *that the train will be late if there is snow in the mountains,* and come to believe *that there is snow in the mountains,* they will typically come to believe *that the train will be late.*
3. When people who speak English say that "there is a cat in the yard," they typically believe *that there is a cat in the yard.*

And so on, for indefinitely many further examples. Note that these generalizations of commonsense psychology are couched in terms of the *semantic* properties of the attitudes. It is in virtue of being the believe *that p,* that a given belief has a given effect or cause. Thus commonsense psychology treats the predicates expressing these semantic properties, predicates like "believes *that the train is late*", as *projectable* predicates – the sort of predicates that are appropriately used in nomological or lawlike generalizations.

There is a great deal of evidence that might be cited in support of the thesis that folk psychology is committed to the tenets of propositional modularity. Perhaps the most obvious way to bring out folk psychology's commitment to the thesis that propositional attitudes are *functionally discrete* states is to note that it typically makes perfectly good sense to claim that a person has acquired (or lost) a single memory or belief. Thus, for example, on a given occasion it might plausibly be claimed that when Henry awoke from his nap, he had completely forgotten that the car keys were hidden in the refrigerator, though he had forgotten nothing else. In saying that folk psychology views beliefs as the sorts of things that can be acquired or lost one at a time, we do not mean to be denying that having any particular belief may presuppose a substantial network of related beliefs. The belief that the car keys are in the refrigerator is not one that could be acquired by a primitive tribesman who knew nothing about cars, keys, or refrigerators. But once the relevant background is in place, as we may suppose it is for us and for Henry, it seems that folk psychology is entirely comfortable with the possibility that a person may acquire (or lose) the belief that the car keys are in the refrigerator, while the remainder of his beliefs remain unchanged. Propositional modularity does not, of course, deny that acquiring one belief often leads to the acquisition of a cluster of related beliefs. When Henry is told that the keys are in the refrigerator, he may come to believe that they haven't been left in the ignition, or in his jacket pocket. But then again he may not. Indeed, on the folk-psychological conception of belief, it is perfectly possible for a person to have a long-standing belief that the keys are in the refrigerator, and to continue searching for them in the bedroom.[7]

To illustrate the way in which folk psychology takes propositional attitudes to be functionally discrete, *causally active* states let us sketch a pair of more elaborate examples.

1. In commonsense psychology, behavior is often explained by appeal to certain of the agent's beliefs and desires. Thus, to explain why Alice went to her office, we might note that she wanted to send some e-mail messages (and, of course, she believed she could do so from her office). However, in some cases an agent will have several sets of beliefs and desires each of which *might* lead to the same behavior. Thus we may suppose that Alice also wanted to talk to her research assistant, and that she believed he would be at the office. In such cases, commonsense psychology assumes that Alice's going to her office might have been caused by either one of the belief/desire pairs, or by both, and that determining which of these options obtains is an empirical matter. So it is entirely possible that on *this* occasion Alice's desire to send some e-mail played no role in producing her behavior; it was the desire to talk with her research assistant that actually caused her to go to the office. Had she not wanted to talk with her research assistant, however, she might have gone to the office anyhow, because the desire to send some e-mail, which was causally inert in her actual decision making, might then have become actively involved. Note that in this case common-sense psychology is prepared to recognize a pair of quite distinct seman-tically characterized states, one of which may be causally active while the other is not.

2. Our second illustration is parallel to the first, but focuses on beliefs and inference rather than desires and action. On the commonsense view, it may sometimes happen that a person has a number of belief clusters, any one of which might lead him or her to infer some further belief. When that person actually does draw the inference, folk psychol-ogy assumes that what he or she inferred it from is an empirical question and that this question typically has a determinate answer. Suppose, for example, that Inspector Clouseau believes that the butler said he spent the evening at the village hotel, and that he said he arrived back on the morning train. Suppose Clouseau also believes that the village hotel is closed for the season, and that the morning train has been taken out of service. Given these beliefs, along with some widely shared background

beliefs, Clouseau might well infer that the butler is lying. If he does, folk psychology presumes that the inference might be based either on his beliefs about the hotel, or on his beliefs about the train, or both. It is entirely possible, from the perspective of commonsense psychology, that although Clouseau has long known that the hotel is closed for the season, this belief played no role in his inference on this particular occasion. Once again we see commonsense psychology invoking a pair of distinct propositional attitudes, one of which is causally active on a particular occasion while the other is causally inert.

In the psychological literature there is no dearth of models for human belief or memory that follow the lead of commonsense psychology in supposing that propositional modularity is true. Indeed, until the emergence of connectionism, just about all psychological models of propositional memory, except those urged by behaviorists, were comfortably compatible with propositional modularity. Typically, these models view a subject's store of beliefs or memories as an interconnected collection of functionally discrete, semantically interpretable states that interact in systematic ways. Some of these models represent individual beliefs as sentencelike structures – strings of symbols that can be individually activated by their transfer from long-term memory to the more limited memory of a central processing unit. Other models represent beliefs as a network of labeled nodes and labeled links through which patterns of activation may spread. Still other models represent beliefs as sets of production rules.[8] In all three sorts of models, it is generally the case that for any given cognitive episode, like performing a particular inference or answering a question, some of the memory states will be actively involved, and others will be dormant.

Figure 1 shows a fragment of a "semantic network" representation of memory, in the style of Collins and Quillian (1972). In this model, each distinct proposition in memory is represented by an oval node along with its labeled links to various concepts. By adding assumptions about the way in which questions or other sorts of memory probes lead to activation spreading through the network, the model enables us to make predictions about speed and accuracy in various experimental studies of memory. For our purposes there are three facts about this model that are of particular importance. First, since each proposition is encoded in a functionally discrete way, it is a straightforward matter to add or subtract a *single* proposition from memory, while leaving the rest of the network unchanged. Thus, for example, Figure 2 depicts the result of removing one proposition from the network in Figure 1. Second, the model treats predicates expressing the semantic properties of beliefs or

SEMANTIC NETWORK

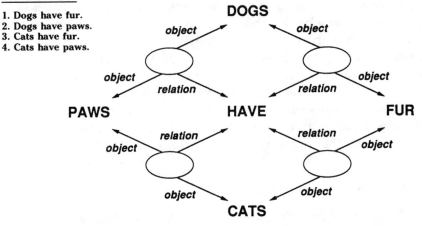

Figure 1

memories as *projectable*.[9] They are treated as the sorts of predicates that pick out scientifically genuine *kinds*, rather than mere accidental conglomerates, and thus are suitable for inclusion in the statement of lawlike regularities. To see this, we need only consider the way in which such models are tested against empirical data about memory acquisition and forgetting. Typically, it will be assumed that if a subject is told (for

SEMANTIC NETWORK

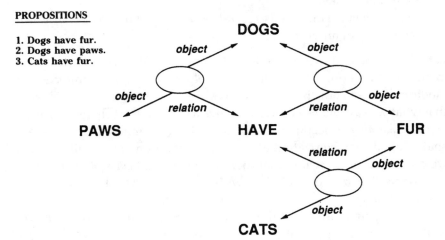

Figure 2

example) that the policeman arrested the hippie, then the subject will (with a certain probability) remember *that the policeman arrested the hippie.*[10] And this assumption is taken to express a nomological generalization; it captures something lawlike about the way in which the cognitive system works. So while the class of people who *remember that the policeman arrested the hippie* may differ psychologically in all sorts of ways, the theory treats them as a psychologically natural kind. Third, in any given memory search or inference task exploiting a semantic network model, it makes sense to ask which propositions were activated and which were not. Thus, a search in the network of Figure 1 might terminate without ever activating the proposition that cats have paws.

IV. A family of connectionist hypotheses

Our theme in the preceding section was that commonsense psychology is committed to propositional modularity, and that many models of memory proposed in the cognitive psychology literature are comfortably compatible with this assumption. In this section, we describe a class of connectionist models that, we argue, are *not* readily compatible with propositional modularity. The connectionist models we have in mind share three properties:

1. Their encoding of information in the connection weights and in the biases on units is *widely distributed*, rather than being *localist*.
2. Individual hidden units in the network have no comfortable symbolic interpretation; they are *subsymbolic*, to use a term suggested by Paul Smolensky.
3. The models are intended *as cognitive models*, not merely as *implementations* of cognitive models.

Later in this section, we elaborate further on each of these three features; in the next section, we describe a simple example of a connectionist model that meets our three criteria. We are, however, under no illusion that what we say will be sufficient to give a sharp-edged characterization of the class of connectionist models we have in mind. Nor is such a sharp-edged characterization essential for our argument. It will suffice if we can convince the reader that there is a significant class of connectionist models that are incompatible with the propositional modularity of folk psychology.

Before saying more about the three features on our list, we would do well to give a more general characterization of the sort of models we are calling 'connectionist', and introduce some of the jargon that comes with the territory. To this end, let us quote at some length from Paul Smolensky's lucid overview:

> Connectionist models are large networks of simple, parallel computing elements, each of which carries a numerical *activation value* which it computes from neighboring elements in the network, using some simple numerical formula. The network elements or *units* influence each other's values through connections that carry a numerical strength or *weight*. . . .
>
> In a typical . . . model, input to the system is provided by imposing activation values on the *input units* of the network; these numerical values represent some encoding or *representation* of the input. The activation on the input units propagates along the connections until some set of activation values emerges on the *output units*; these activation values encode the output the system has computed from the input. In between the input and output units there may be other units that participate in representing neither the input nor the output; these are often called *hidden units*.
>
> The computation performed by the network in transforming the input pattern of activity to the output pattern depends on the set of connection strengths; *these weights are usually regarded as encoding the system's knowledge* [emphasis added]. In this sense, the connection strengths play the role of the program in a conventional computer. Much of the allure of the connectionist approach is that many connectionist networks *program themselves*, that is, they have autonomous procedures for tuning their weights to eventually perform some specific computation. These *learning procedures* often depend on training in which the network is presented with sample input/output pairs from the function it is supposed to compute. In learning networks with hidden units, the network itself "decides" what computations the hidden units will perform; since these units represent neither inputs nor outputs, they are never "told" what their values should be, even during training. (Smolensky 1988, p. 1)

One point must be added to Smolensky's portrait. In many connectionist models the hidden units and the output units are assigned a numerical "bias" which is added into the calculation determining the unit's activation level. The learning procedures for such networks typically set both the connection strengths and the biases. Thus in these networks the system's knowledge is usually regarded as encoded in *both* the connection strengths and the biases.

So much for a general overview. Let us now try to explain the three features that characterize those connectionist models we take to be incompatible with propositional modularity.

1. In many nonconnectionist cognitive models, like the one illustrated at the end of Section III, it is an easy matter to locate a functionally distinct part of the model encoding each proposition or state of affairs represented in the system. Indeed, according to Fodor and Pylyshyn (1988, p. 51), "conventional [computational] architecture requires that

there be distinct symbolic expressions for each state of affairs that it can represent." In some connectionist models an analogous sort of functional localization is possible not only for the input and output units but for the hidden units as well. Thus, for example, in certain connectionist models, various individual units or small clusters of units are themselves intended to represent specific properties or features of the environment. A strongly positive connection strength from one such unit to another might be construed as the system's representation of the proposition that if the first feature is present, so too is the second. In many connectionist networks, however, it is not possible to localize propositional representation beyond the input layer. That is, no particular features or states of the system lend themselves to a straightforward semantic evaluation. This can sometimes be a real inconvenience to the connectionist model builder when the system as a whole fails to achieve its goal because it has not represented the world the way it should. When this happens, as Smolensky (1988, p. 15) notes,

it is not necessarily possible to localize a failure of veridical representation. Any particular state is part of a large causal system of states, and failures of the system to meet goal conditions cannot in general be localized to any particular state or state component.

It is connectionist networks of this sort, in which it is not possible to isolate the representation of particular propositions or states of affairs within the nodes, connection strengths, and biases, that we have in mind when we talk about the encoding of information in the biases, weights, and hidden nodes being *widely distributed* rather than *localist*.

2. As we just noted, there are some connectionist models in which some or all of the units are intended to represent specific properties or features of the system's environment. These units may be viewed as the model's symbols for the properties or features in question. However, in models where the weights and biases have been tuned by learning algorithms, it is often not the case that any single unit or any small collection of units will end up representing a specific feature of the environment in any straightforward way. As we shall see in the next section, it is often plausible to view such networks as collectively or holistically encoding a set of propositions, although none of the hidden units, weights, or biases are comfortably viewed as *symbols*. When this is the case, we call the strategy of representation invoked in the model *subsymbolic*. Typically (perhaps always?) networks exploiting subsymbolic strategies of representation will encode information in a widely distributed way.

3. The third item on our list is not a feature of connectionist models themselves but, rather, a point about how the models are to be interpreted. In making this point, we must presuppose a notion of 'theoretical' or 'explanatory' level which, despite much discussion in the recent literature, is far from being a paradigm of clarity.[11] Perhaps the clearest way to introduce the notion of 'explanatory' level is to place it against the background of the familiar functionalist thesis that psychological theories are analogous to programs that can be implemented on a variety of very different sorts of computers.[12] If one accepts this analogy, then it makes sense to ask whether a particular connectionist model is intended as a model at the psychological level or at the level of underlying neural implementation. Because of their obvious, though in many ways only partial, similarity to real neural architectures, it is tempting to view connectionist models as models of the implementation of psychological processes. And some connectionist model builders endorse this view quite explicitly. So viewed, however, connectionist models are not *psychological* or *cognitive* models at all, any more than a story of how cognitive processes are implemented at the quantum mechanical level is a psychological story. A very different view that connectionist model builders can and often do take is that their models are at the psychological level, not at the level of implementation. So construed, the models are in competition with other psychological models of the same phenomena. Thus a connectionist model of word recognition would be an alternative to – and not simply a possible implementation of – a nonconnectionist model of word recognition; a connectionist theory of memory would be a competitor to a semantic network theory, and so on. Connectionists who hold this view of their theories often illustrate the point by drawing analogies with other sciences. Smolensky, for example, suggests that connectionist models stand in relation to traditional cognitive models (like semantic networks) in much the same way that quantum mechanics stands in relation to classical mechanics. In each case the newer theory is deeper, more general, and more accurate over a broader range of phenomena. But in each case the new theory and the old are competing at the same explanatory level. If one is right, the other must be wrong.

In light of our concerns in this chapter, there is one respect in which the analogy between connectionist models and quantum mechanics may be thought to beg an important question; for although quantum mechanics is conceded to be a *better* theory than classical mechanics, a plausible case could be made that the shift from classical to quantum mechanics was an ontologically *conservative* theory change. In any event, it is not clear that the change was ontologically *radical*. If our central thesis in this chapter is correct, then the relation between connectionist models and more traditional cognitive models is more like the relation between the caloric theory of heat and the kinetic theory. The caloric and kinetic theories are at the same explanatory level, though the shift from one to the other was clearly ontologically radical. In order to make the case that the caloric analogy is the more appropriate one, it will be useful to describe a concrete, though very simple, connectionist model of memory that meets the three criteria we have been trying to explicate.

V. A connectionist model of memory

Our goal in constructing the model was to produce a connectionist network that would do at least some of the tasks done by more traditional cognitive models of memory, and that would perspicuously exhibit the sort of distributed, subsymbolic encoding described in the previous section. We began by constructing a network – we shall call it network A – that would judge the truth or falsehood of the sixteen propositions displayed above the line in Figure 3. The network was a typical three-tiered, feed-forward network consisting of sixteen input units, four hidden units, and one output unit, as shown in Figure 4. The input coding of each proposition is shown in the center column in Figure 3. Outputs close to 1 were interpreted as 'true' and outputs close to zero were interpreted as 'false'. Back propagation, a familiar connectionist learning algorithm, was used to "train up" the network, thereby setting the connection weights and biases. Training was terminated when the network consistently gave an output higher than 0.9 for each true proposition and lower than 0.1 for each false proposition. Figure 5 shows the connection weights between the input units and the leftmost hidden unit in the trained-up network, along with the bias on that unit. Figure 6 indicates the connection weights and biases further upstream. Figure 7 shows how the network computes its response to the proposition *dogs have fur* when that proposition is encoded in the input units.

There is a clear sense in which the trained-up network A may be said to have stored information about the truth or falsity of propositions 1 through 16, since when any one of these propositions is presented to the network, it correctly judges whether the proposition is true or false. In this respect, it is similar to various semantic network models that can be constructed to perform much the same task. There is, however, a striking difference between network A and a semantic network model like the one depicted in Figure 1. For, as we noted earlier, in the semantic

	Proposition	Input	Output
1	Dogs have fur.	11000011 00001111	1 true
2	Dogs have paws.	11000011 00110011	1 true
3	Dogs have fleas.	11000011 00111111	1 true
4	Dogs have legs.	11000011 00111100	1 true
5	Cats have fur.	11001100 00001111	1 true
6	Cats have paws.	11001100 00110011	1 true
7	Cats have fleas.	11001100 00111111	1 true
8	Fish have scales.	11110000 00110000	1 true
9	Fish have fins.	11110000 00001100	1 true
10	Fish have gills.	11110000 00000011	1 true
11	Cats have gills.	11001100 00000011	0 false
12	Fish have legs.	11110000 00111100	0 false
13	Fish have fleas.	11110000 00111111	0 false
14	Dogs have scales.	11000011 00110000	0 false
15	Dogs have fins.	11000011 00001100	0 false
16	Cats have fins.	11001100 00001100	0 false

Added Proposition

17	Fish have eggs.	11110000 11001000	1 true

Figure 3

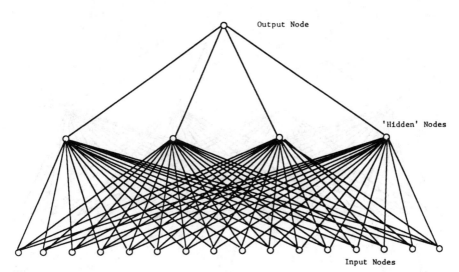

Figure 4

Network A

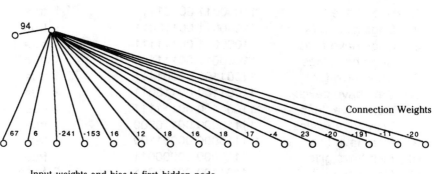

Input weights and bias to first hidden node
in network with 16 propositions.

Figure 5

network there is a functionally distinct subpart associated with each proposition, and thus it makes perfectly good sense to ask, for any probe of the network, whether or not the representation of a specific proposition played a causal role. In the connectionist network, by contrast, there is no distinct state or part of the network that serves to represent any particular proposition. The information encoded in net-

Network A

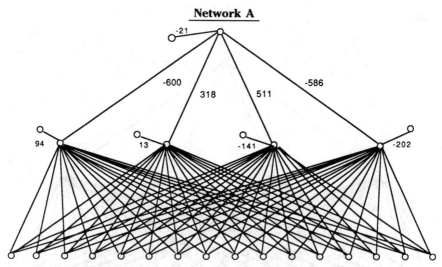

Weights and biases in network
with 16 propositions.

Figure 6

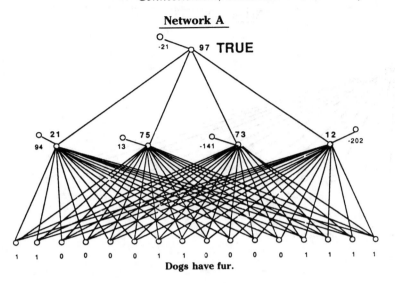

Figure 7

work A is stored holistically and distributed throughout the network. Whenever information is extracted from network A, by giving it an input string and seeing whether it computes a high or a low value for the output unit, *many* connection strengths, *many* biases, and *many* hidden units play a role in the computation. And any particular weight or unit or bias helps to encode information about *many* different propositions. It simply makes no sense to ask whether or not the representation of a particular proposition plays a causal role in the network's computation. It is in just this respect that our connectionist model of memory seems radically incongruent with the propositional modularity of common-sense psychology; for as we saw in Section III, commonsense psychology seems to presuppose that there is generally some answer to the question of whether a particular belief or memory played a causal role in a specific cognitive episode. But if belief and memory are subserved by a connectionist network like ours, such questions seem to have no clear meaning.

The incompatibility between propositional modularity and connectionist models like ours can be made even more vivid by contrasting network A with a second network – we shall call it network B – depicted in Figures 8 and 9. Network B was trained up just as the first one was, except that one additional proposition was added to the training set (coded as indicated below the line in Figure 3). Thus network B encodes

Network B

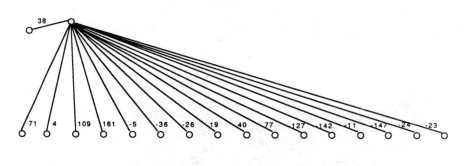

Input weights and bias to first hidden node
    in network with 17 propositions.

Figure 8

all the same propositions as network A plus one more. In semantic
network models, and other traditional cognitive models, it would be an
easy matter to say which states or features of the system encode the
added proposition, and it would a simple task to determine whether or
not the representation of the added proposition played a role in a
particular episode modeled by the system. But clearly, in the connectionist network, those questions are quite senseless. The point is not

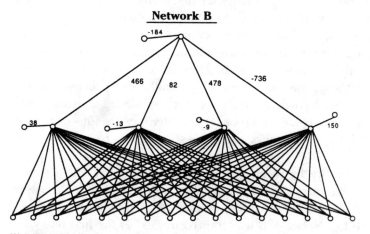

Weights and biases in network
    with 17 propositions.

Figure 9

that there are no differences between the two networks. Quite the opposite is the case; the differences are many and widespread. But these differences do not correlate in any systematic way with the functionally discrete, semantically interpretable states posited by folk psychology and by more traditional cognitive models. Since information is encoded in a highly distributed manner, with each connection weight and bias embodying information salient to many propositions, and information regarding any given proposition scattered throughout the network, the system lacks functionally distinct, identifiable substructures that are semantically interpretable as representations of individual propositions.

The contrast between networks A and B enables us to make our point about the incompatibility between commonsense psychology and these sorts of connectionist models in a rather different way. We noted in Section III that commonsense psychology treats predicates expressing the semantic properties of propositional attitudes as projectable. Thus *"believes that dogs have fur"* or *"remembers that dogs have fur"* will be projectable predicates in commonsense psychology. Now both network A and network B might serve as models for a cognitive agent who believes that dogs have fur; both networks store or represent the information that dogs have fur. Nor are these the only two. If we were to train up a network on the 17 propositions in Figure 3 plus or minus a few, we would get yet another system, which would be as different from networks A and B as these two are from each other. The moral here is that though there are *indefinitely* many connectionist networks that represent the information that dogs have fur just as well as network A does, these networks have no projectable features in common that are describable in the language of connectionist theory. From the point of view of the connectionist model builder, the class of networks that might model a cognitive agent who believes that dogs have fur is not a genuine kind at all, but simply a chaotically disjunctive set. Commonsense psychology treats the class of people who believe that dogs have fur as a psychologically natural kind; connectionist psychology does not.[13]

VI. Objections and replies

The argument we set out in the preceding five sections has encountered no shortage of objections. In this section we try to reconstruct the most interesting of these, and indicate how we would reply.

Objection 1: Models like A and B are not serious models for human belief or propositional memory.

Of course, the models we constructed are tiny toys that were built to

illustrate in a perspicuous way the features set out in Section IV. They
were never intended to model any substantial part of human propositional memory. But various reasons have been offered for doubting that
anything like these models could ever be taken seriously as psychological
models of propositional memory. Some critics have claimed that the
models simply will not scale up – that although teaching a network to
recognize fifteen or twenty propositions may be easy enough, it is just
not going to be possible to train up a network that can recognize a few
thousand propositions, still less a few hundred thousand.[14] Others have
objected that whereas more traditional models of memory, including
those based on sentencelike storage, those using semantic networks,
and those based on production systems, all provide some strategy for
inference or *generalization* that enables the system to answer questions
about propositions it was not explicitly taught, models like those we
have constructed are incapable of inference and generalization. It has
also been urged that these models fail as accounts of human memory
because they provide no obvious way to account for the fact that suitably
prepared humans can easily acquire propositional information one
proposition at a time. Under ordinary circumstances, we can just *tell*
Henry that the car keys are in the refrigerator, and he can readily record
this fact in memory. He does not need anything like the sort of massive
retraining that would be required to teach one of our connectionist
networks a new proposition.

Reply 1: If this essay were aimed at defending connectionist models of
propositional memory, we would have to take on each of these putative
shortcomings in some detail. And in each instance there is at least
something to be said on the connectionist side. Thus, for example, it just
is not true that networks like A and B don't generalize beyond the
propositions on which they have been trained. In network A, for example, the training set included:

Dogs have fur	Cats have fur
Dogs have paws	Cats have paws
Dogs have fleas	Cats have fleas.

It also included

Dogs have legs

but not

Cats have legs.

When the network was given an encoding of this last proposition, however, it generalized correctly and responded affirmatively. Similarly, the network responded negatively to an encoding of

Cats have scales

although it had not previously been exposed to this proposition.

It is important, however, to see that this sort of point-by-point response to the charge that networks like ours are inadequate models for propositional memory is not really required, given the thesis we are defending in this chapter. For what we are trying to establish is a *conditional* thesis: If connectionist models of memory of the sort we describe in Section IV are right, *then* propositional attitude psychology is in serious trouble. Since conditionals with false antecedents are true, we win by default if it turns out that the antecedent of our conditional is false.

Objection 2: Our models do not really violate the principle of propositional modularity, since the propositions the system has learned are coded in functionally discrete ways, though this may not be obvious.

We have heard this objection elaborated along three quite different lines. The first line – let us call it objection 2a – notes that functionally discrete coding may often be *very* hard to notice, and cannot be expected to be visible on causal inspection. Consider, for example, the way in which sentences are stored in the memory of a typical von Neumann architecture computer: For concreteness we might suppose that the sentences are part of an English text and are being stored while the computer is running a word processing program. Parts of sentences may be stored at physically scattered memory addresses linked together in complex ways, and, given an account of the contents of all relevant memory addresses, one would be hard put to say where a particular sentence is stored. But nonetheless each sentence is stored in a *functionally discrete* way. Thus, if one knew enough about the system, it would be possible to erase any particular sentence it is storing by tampering with the contents of the appropriate memory addresses while leaving untouched the rest of the sentences the system is storing. Similarly, it has been urged, connectionist networks may in fact encode propositions in functionally discrete ways, though this may not be evident from a casual inspection of the trained-up network's biases and connection strengths.

Reply 2a: It is somewhat difficult to come to grips with this objection, since what the critic is proposing is that in models like those we have constructed, there *might* be some covert functionally discrete system of propositional encoding that has yet to be discovered. In response to this objection, we must concede that indeed there might. We certainly have no argument that even comes close to demonstrating that the discovery of such a covert, functionally discrete encoding is impossible. Moreover, we concede that if such a covert system were discovered, then our argument would be seriously undermined. We are inclined, however, to think that the burden of argument is on the critic to show that such a system is not merely possible but *likely*; in the absence of any serious reason to think that networks like ours do encode propositions in functionally discrete ways, the mere logical possibility that they might is hardly a serious threat.

The second version of objection 2 – we shall call it objection 2b – makes a specific proposal about the way in which networks like A and B might be discretely, though covertly, encoding propositions. The encoding, it is urged, is to be found in the pattern of activation of the hidden nodes, when a given proposition is presented to the network. Since there are four hidden nodes in our networks, the activation pattern on presentation of any given input may be represented as an ordered 4-tuple. Thus, for example, when network A is presented with the encoded propositions *Dogs have fur*, the relevant 4-tuple would be (21, 75, 73, 12), as shown in Figure 7. Equivalently, we may think of each activation pattern as a point in a four-dimensional hyperspace. Since each proposition corresponds to a unique point in the hyperspace, that point may be viewed as the encoding of the proposition. Moreover, that point represents a functionally discrete state of the system.[15]

Reply 2b: What is being proposed is that the pattern of activation of the system on presentation of an encoding of the proposition *p* be identified with the belief that *p*. But this proposal is singularly implausible. Perhaps the best way to see this is to note that in commonsense psychology, beliefs and propositional memories are typically of substantial duration; and they are the sorts of things that cognitive agents generally have lots of, even when they are not using them. Consider an example: Are kangaroos marsupials? Surely you have believed for years that they are, although in all likelihood this is the first time today that your belief has been activated or used.[16] An activation pattern, however, is not an enduring state of a network; indeed, it is not a state of the network at all except when the network has had the relevant proposition as input. Moreover, there are an enormous number of other beliefs that you have had for years. But it makes no sense to suppose that a network could have many activation patterns continuously over a long period of time. At any given time, a network exhibits at most one pattern of activation. Thus, activation patterns are just not the sorts of things that can plausibly be identified with beliefs or their representations.

Objection 2c: At this juncture, a number of critics have suggested that long-standing beliefs might be identified not with activation patterns, which are transient states of networks, but, rather, with *dispositions to produce activation patterns*. Thus, in network A, the belief that dogs have fur would not be identified with a location in activation hyperspace but with the network's *disposition* to end up at that location when the proposition is presented. This *dispositional state* is an enduring state of the system; it is a state the network can be in no matter what its current state of activation may be, just as a sugar cube may have a disposition to dissolve in water even when there is no water nearby.[17] Some have gone on to suggest that the familiar philosophical distinction between dispositional and occurrent beliefs might be captured, in connectionist models, as the distinction between dispositions to produce activation patterns and activation patterns themselves.

Reply 2c: Our reply to this suggestion is that while dispositions to produce activation patterns are indeed *enduring* states of the system, they are not the right sort of enduring states; they are not the discrete, independently causally active states that folk psychology requires. Recall that on the folk-psychological conception of belief **and inference**, there will often be a variety of quite different underlying **causal patterns** that may lead to the acquisition and avowal of a given belief. When Clouseau says that the butler did it, he may have just inferred this with the help of his long-standing belief that the train is out of service. Or he may have inferred it by using his belief that the hotel is closed. Or both long-standing beliefs may have played a role in the inference. Moreover, it is also possible that Clouseau drew this inference some time ago, and is now reporting a relatively long-standing belief. But it is hard to see how anything like these distinctions can be captured by the dispositional account in question. In reacting to a given input, say *p*, a network takes on a specific activation value. It may also have dispositions to take on other activation values on other inputs, say, *q*, and *r*. But there is no obvious way to interpret the claim that these further dispositions play a causal role in the network's reaction to *p* – or, for that matter, that they do not play a role. Nor can we make any sense of the idea that on one occasion the encoding of *q* (say, the proposition that the train is out of service) played a role whereas the encoding of *r* (say, the proposition that the hotel is closed) did not, and on another occasion, the reverse was true. The propositional modularity presupposed by commonsense psychology requires that belief tokens be functionally discrete states capable of causally interacting with one another in some cognitive episodes and of remaining causally inert in other cognitive episodes. In a distributed connectionist system like network A, however, the disposi-

tional state that produces one activation pattern is functionally inseparable from the dispositional state that produces another. Thus, it is
impossible to isolate some propositions as causally active in certain
cognitive episodes, while others are not. We conclude that reaction
pattern dispositions won't do as belief tokens. Nor, so far as we can see,
are there any other states of networks like A and B that will fill the bill.

VII. Conclusion

The thesis we have been defending in this essay is that connectionist
models of a certain sort are incompatible with the propositional modularity embedded in commonsense psychology. The connectionist models in question are those that are offered as models at the *cognitive* level,
and in which the encoding of information is widely distributed and
subsymbolic. In such models, we have argued, there are no *discrete,
semantically interpretable* states that play a *causal role* in some cognitive
episodes but not others. Thus there is, in these models, nothing with
which the propositional attitudes of commonsense psychology can plausibly be identified. If these models turn out to offer the best accounts of
human belief and memory, we shall be confronting an *ontologically
radical* theory change – the sort of theory change that will sustain the
conclusion that propositional attitudes, like caloric and phlogiston, do
not exist.

Notes

1. See, for example, Churchland (1981 and 1986), where explicitly eliminativist
   conclusions are drawn on the basis of speculations about the success of
   cognitive models similar to those we shall discuss.
2. We are aware that certain philosophers and historians of science have
   actually entertained ideas similar to the suggestion that the planets spoken
   of by pre-Copernican astronomers do not exist. See, for example, Kuhn (1970),
   ch. 10; and Feyerabend (1981), ch. 4. However, we take this suggestion to be
   singularly implausible. Eliminativist arguments cannot be that easy. Just
   what has gone wrong with the accounts of meaning and reference that lead
   to such claims is less clear. For further discussion on these matters, see Kuhn
   (1983) and Kitcher (1978, 1983).
3. For some detailed discussion of scientific reduction, see Nagel (1961), Schaffner (1967), Hooker (1981), and Kitcher (1984). The genetics case is not
   without controversy. See Kitcher (1982, 1984).
4. It is worth noting that judgments on this matter can differ quite substantially. At one end of the spectrum are writers like Feyerabend (1981), and
   perhaps Kuhn (1962), for whom relatively small differences in theory are

enough to justify the suspicion that there has been an ontologically radical change. Toward the other end are authors like Lycan, who writes: "I am at pains to advocate a very liberal view. . . . I am entirely willing to give up fairly large chunks of our commonsensical or platitudinous theory of belief or of desire (or of almost anything else) and decide that we were just wrong about a lot of things, without drawing the inference that we are no longer talking about belief or desire. . . . I think the ordinary word 'belief' (qua theoretical term of folk psychology) points dimly toward a natural kind that we have not fully grasped and that only mature psychology will reveal. I expect that 'belief' will turn out to refer to some kind of information-bearing inner state of a sentient being . . . but the kind of state it refers to may have only a few of the properties usually attributed to beliefs by common sense." (Lycan [1988], pp. 31–2.) In our view, both extreme positions are implausible. As we noted earlier, the Copernican revolution did not show that the planets studied by Ptolemy do not exist. But Lavoisier's chemical revolution *did* show that phlogiston does not exist. Yet on Lycan's "very liberal view," it is hard to see why we should not conclude that phlogiston really does exist after all: It is really oxygen, and before Lavoisier "we were just wrong about a lot of things."

5. For an early and influential statement of the view that commonsense psychology is a theory, see Sellars (1956). More recently the view has been defended by Churchland (1970, 1979), chs. 1 and 4; and by Fodor (1987), ch. 1. For the opposing view, see Wilkes (1978), Madell (1986), and Sharpe (1987).

6. See Stich (1983), p. 237.

7. Cherniak (1986), ch. 3, notes that this sort of absentmindedness is commonplace in literature and in ordinary life, and sometimes leads to disastrous consequences.

8. For sentential models, see John McCarthy (1968, 1980, 1986) and Kintsch (1974). For semantic networks, see Quillian (1966); Collins and Quillian (1972); Rumelhart, Lindsay and Norman (1972); Anderson and Bower (1973); and Anderson (1976, 1980, ch. 4). For production systems, see Newell and Simon (1972), Newell (1973), Anderson (1983), and Holland et al. (1986).

9. For the classic discussion of the distinction between projectable and non–projectable predicates, see Goodman (1965).

10. See, for example, Anderson and Bower (1973).

11. Broadbent (1985); Rumelhart and McClelland (1985, 1986, ch. 4); Smolensky (1988) and Fodor and Pylyshyn (1988).

12. The notion of 'program' being invoked here is itself open to a pair of quite different interpretations. For the right reading, see Ramsey (1989).

13. This way of making the point about the incompatibility between connectionist models and commonsense psychology was suggested to us by Jerry Fodor.

14. This point has been urged by Daniel Dennett, among others.

15. Quite a number of people suggested this move, including Gary Cottrell and Adrian Cussins.

16. As Lycan notes, on the commonsense notion of belief, people have lots of them "even when they are asleep" (Lycan 1988, p. 57).

17. A similar objection was suggested to us by Ned Block and by Frank Jackson.

118   *William Ramsey, Stephen Stich, and Joseph Garon*

References

Anderson, J. (1976). *Language, Memory and Thought*. Hillsdale, N.J.: Lawrence Erlbaum Associates.

Anderson J. (1980). *Cognitive Psychology and Its Implications*. San Francisco: W. H. Freeman.

Anderson, J. (1983). *The Architecture of Cognition*. Cambridge, Mass.: Harvard University Press.

Anderson, J., & Bower, G. (1973). *Human Associative Memory*. Washington, D.C.: Winston.

Broadbent, D. (1985). "A Question of Levels: Comments on McClelland and Rumelhart." *Journal of Experimental Psychology: General*, 114:189–192.

Cherniak, C. (1986). *Minimal Rationality*. Cambridge, Mass.: MIT Press.

Churchland, P. (1970). "The Logical Character of Action Explanations." *Philosophical Review*, 79:214–236.

Churchland, P. (1979). *Scientific Realism and the Plasticity of Mind*. Cambridge: Cambridge University Press.

Churchland, P. (1981). "Eliminative Materialism and Propositional Attitudes." *Journal of Philosophy*, 78:(2): 67–90.

Churchland, P. (1986). "Some Reductive Strategies in Cognitive Neurobiology." *Mind*, 95: 279–309.

Collins, A. & Quillian, M. (1972). "Experiments on Semantic Memory and Language Comprehension." In L. Gregg, ed., *Cognition in Learning and Memory*. New York: Wiley.

Feyerabend, P. (1981). *Realism, Rationalism and Scientific Method: Philosophical Papers*, Vol. 1. Cambridge: Cambridge University Press.

Fodor, J. (1987). *Psychosemantics: The Problem of Meaning in the Philosophy of Mind*. Cambridge, Mass.: MIT Press.

Fodor, J., & Z. Pylyshyn. (1988). "Connectionism and Cognitive Architecture: A Critical Analysis." *Cognition*, 28:3–71.

Goodman, N. (1965). *Fact, Fiction and Forecast*. Indianapolis: Bobbs-Merrill.

Holland, J., Holyoak, K., Nisbett, R., & Thagard, P. (1986). *Induction: Processes of Inference, Learning and Discovery*. Cambridge, Mass.: MIT Press.

Hooker, C. (1981). "Towards a General Theory of Reduction," Parts I, II & III. *Dialogue*, 20:38–59, 201–236, 496–529.

Kintsch, W. (1974). *The Representation of Meaning in Memory*. Hillsdale, N.J.: Lawrence Erlbaum Assoc.

Kitcher, P. (1978). "Theories, Theorists and Theoretical Change." *Philosophical Review*, 87:519–547.

Kitcher, P. (1982). "Genes." *British Journal for the Philosophy of Science*, 33:337–359.

Kitcher, P. (1983). "Implications of Incommensurability." In P. Asquith & T. Nickles, *PSA 1982* (Proceedings of the 1982 Biennial Meeting of the Philosophy of Science Association), Vol 2. East Lansing, Mich.: Philosophy of Science Assoc.

Kitcher, P. (1984). "1953 and All That: A Tale of Two Sciences." *Philosophical Review*, 93:335–373.

Kuhn, T. (1962). *The Structure of Scientific Revolutions*. Chicago: University of Chicago Press; 2nd ed. (1970).

Kuhn, T. (1983). "Commensurability, Comparability, Communicability." In P. Asquith & T. Nickels, eds., *PSA 1982* (Proceedings of the 1982 Biennial Meeting of the Philosophy of Science Association); Vol. 2. East Lansing, Mich.: Philosophy of Science Association.

Lycan, W. (1988). *Judgment and Justification*. Cambridge: Cambridge University Press.

McCarthy, J. (1968). "Programs with Common Sense." In M. Minsky, ed., *Semantic Information Processing*. Cambridge, Mass.: MIT Press.

McCarthy, J. (1980). "Circumscription: A Form of Non-monotonic Reasoning."*Artificial Intelligence*. 13:27–39.

McCarthy J. (1986). "Applications of Circumscription to Formalizing Common-Sense Knowledge." *Artificial Intelligence*, 28:89–116.

Madell, G. (1986). "Neurophilosophy: A Principled Skeptic's Response."*Inquiry*, 29:153–168.

Nagel, E. (1961). *The Structure of Science*. New York: Harcourt, Brace & World.

Newell, A. (1973). "Production Systems: Models of Control Structures." In W. Chase, ed., *Visual Information Processing*. New York: Academic Press.

Newell, A., & Simon, H. (1972). *Human Problem Solving*. Englewood Cliffs, N.J.: Prentice-Hall.

Quillian, M. (1966). *Semantic Memory*. Cambridge, Mass.: Bolt, Branak & Newman.

Ramsey, W. (1989). "Parallelism and Functionalism." *Cognitive Science*, 13:139–144.

Rumelhart, D., Lindsay, P., & Norman, D. (1972). "A Process Model for Long Term Memory." In E. Tulving & W. Donaldson, eds., *Organization of Memory*. New York: Academic Press.

Rumelhart, D., & McClelland, J. (1985). "Level's Indeed!: A Response to Broadbent." *Journal of Experimental Psychology: General*, 114:193–197.

Rumelhart, D., McClelland, J., & the PDP Reserach Group. (1986). *Parallel Distributed Processing*, Vols. I & II. Cambridge, Mass.: MIT Press.

Schaffner, K. (1967). "Approaches to Reduction." *Philosophy of Science*, 34:137–147.

Sellars, W. (1956). "Empiricism and the Philosophy of Mind." In H. Feigl & M. Scriven, eds., *Minnesota Studies in the Philosophy of Science*, Vol. 1, Minneapolis: University of Minnesota Press.

Sharpe, R. (1987). "The Very Idea of Folk Psychology." *Inquiry*, 30:381–393.

Smolensky, P. (1988). "On the Proper Treatment of Connectionism." *The Behavioral & Brain Sciences*. 11:1–23.

Stich, S. (1983). *From Folk Psychology to Cognitive Science*. Cambridge, Mass.: MIT Press.

Wilkes, K. (1978). *Physicalism*. London: Routledge & Kegan Paul.

5 Being indiscrete

John Heil

I. Eliminativism and scientific progress

Ours is an age in which it is impossible not to be impressed by science. Skepticism about scientific progress, like skepticism generally, is an attitude no one is able to take seriously outside the study. From Quine (1960, 1969) we have learned that epistemology and ontology are continuous with psychology and physics. What we can know, indeed what we can reasonably believe, is determined by our psychological endowment, the features of which are, if discoverable at all, empirically discoverable. Our regard for entities is proportioned to the standing accorded them by empirical theories in which they figure.

In such a climate it is scarcely surprising that discussions of propositional attitudes and other content-bearing mental conditions have tended to link the fate of such things to their prospective role in appropriately scientific theories of mind. (See, e.g., Churchland 1979, 1981, 1985; Stich 1983; Ramsey et al., Chapter 4, this volume.) Must we tolerate the existence of beliefs, desires, intentions, and actions? Or is talk about these simply part of an outmoded folk idiom? The answer to these questions, it will be said, hinges on our assessment of the place such items can be expected to occupy in an articulated science of mind. For the moment, perhaps, we are in no position to forgo beliefs and desires. There are, however, indications that psychological explanation stands to benefit from their elimination. Or, if the prospect of a nonin-

This essay was begun during a National Endowment for the Humanities fellowship year at the University of California, Berkeley. It was inspired by "Connectionism, Eliminativism, and the Future of Folk Psychology" (Ramsey et al., Chapter 4, this volume), delivered by Stephen Stich, on which I was invited to comment for a conference on "The Future of Folk Psychology" at the University of North Carolina at Greensboro in the spring of 1988. A version of the introductory pages appears as a portion of "Intentionality Speaks for Itself" in Silvers (1988). I am grateful to the National Endowment for Humanities for support during 1987; to the Department of Psychology, University of California, Berkeley, for providing office space and hospitality; and to my colleague Alfred Mele for much discussion on the topics taken up here.

tentional psychology has a paradoxical ring, we might envision the elimination of *psychology*. The point is often made rhetorically: *Might not complete accounts of intelligent behavior omit entirely reference to content-bearing states and processes?*

A negative response seems merely obstructionist: Only a fool or a philosopher with an axe to grind could imagine it worthwhile to stick up for common sense. Science, we recall, has a way of surpassing our expectations, of accomplishing what we had judged to be unaccomplish-able. What is possible is whatever is scientifically thinkable, and what is thinkable scientifically is anybody's guess. When science and philosophy square off, the smart money is on science.

Against this background, it is idle to insist that any theory having as a consequence that we altogether lack beliefs, desires, and other content-ful mental states is false a priori. To be sure, we may worry that such a theory, if true, could neither be taken seriously nor accepted: Takings and acceptings would be mere fictions. And we swoon at the prospect of a theory that, if apt, must be simultaneously unbelievable and indubita-ble: Belief and doubt must go the way of witches and phlogiston. A doctrine with these remarkable features seems, not to put too fine a point on it, conceptually *volatile*. In setting out to abolish beliefs, it relinquishes its claim to be a theory we ought reasonably to believe. In the same way, we may be hard put to see how it could be thought to be *true*: Truth is precisely the sort of semantic "doodad" the theory bids us scorn.

Considerations of this sort ensure that anyone wishing to promote a theory that countenances a denial of content-bearing states of mind runs a nonnegligible risk of incoherence. Incoherence, however, though trou-bling, may be a small price to pay for impressive theoretical advance. An incoherent doctrine can turn out to be obliquely perspicuous. The point is explicit in Wittgenstein's *Tractatus* (1921/1960, sect. 6.54): "My propo-sitions serve as elucidations in the following sense: anyone who under-stands me eventually recognizes them as nonsensical, when he has used them – as steps – to climb beyond them. (He must, so to speak, throw away the ladder after he has climbed up it.) He must transcend these propositions, and then he will see the world aright." Certain truths may be such that attempts to express them are bound to be frustrated. Theories purporting to express such truths could be called *Kierkegaar-dian*.

The hypothesis that nothing at all possesses intentional content is evidently Kierkegaardian. It obliges us to envision a world indis-tinguishable by its human inhabitants from our world, but one bereft of intentionality. In that world, there are no beliefs, wants, or intentions. There are, to be sure, sentences (or sentencelike entities and episodes) in which the words "belief," "want," and "intention" occur. In such a world nothing is true or false, though, again, the words "true" and "false" turn up from time to time in utterances and inscriptions. A theorist who denies representational content has it that *our* world is *that* world. Were this so, the claim that it is so would not be *true*. It would not be false either: *Nothing* would be true or false. This is simply an intriguing, if kinky, consequence of the theory. It cannot be believed or asserted – it cannot even be true – in a world that satisfies it. The difficulty comes, not in imagining a world satisfying the theory, but in making sense of the claim that our world is or might be such a world. That claim could have a sense only in a world in which it is false. It does not follow, however, that it is false, but (at most) that if it has a truth value – if it is *either* true or false – it is false.

Let us suppose, then, at least for the sake of the present discussion, that the abandonment of content-bearing mental states, whatever its liabilities, ought not to be rejected solely on the grounds that it is, when advanced, apparently self-defeating. It may *show* somehow what it cannot *say*.[1]

II. The demise of 'folk psychology'

Philosophers aiming to abolish content – 'eliminativists' – inevitably begin with the assertion that ordinary talk about beliefs, wants, memories, images, dreams, and the like is embedded in a 'folk theory' of behavior. Words like "believe," "desire," "remember," "imagine," and "dream" belong to the specialized vocabulary of this folk theory, and only in that context does the jargon of intentionality take hold. Folk theory, however, is held to be manifestly deficient. It is precisely because psychology has traditionally cleaved to the aim of extending and refining folk theory that the discipline has failed to keep pace with genetics and nuclear physics. Indeed, folk psychology, like astrology, phlogistic chemistry, and Aristotelian kinematics, provides a clear-cut example of a "stagnant or degenerating research program" (Churchland 1981).

What exactly is folk theory supposed to include? It would never occur to most of us to describe our everyday talk about our own and others' beliefs, desires, and dreams as the expression of a *theory* of behavior. To be sure, we do, from time to time, take up theories in assessing our own and others' actions. The influence of Freud and the explosive growth of the "self-help" industry guarantee as much. Those bent on challenging folk psychology, however, have something more perfidious in mind. Systematic psychology, they contend, is continuous with an implicit 'ur-theory,' the roots of which lie in the intentional vocabulary we learn at our mother's knee. Like any theoretical vocabulary, the intentional idiom is theory-laden: We master it only by way of mastering the theory in which it is embedded. In broad outline, that theory depicts intelligent agents as harboring psychological states with intentional content – beliefs, desires, images, and the like. These conspire in complicated ways to produce behavior. Understanding or explaining an instance of behavior involves identifying its intentional psychological background.

Eliminativists do not deny that folk theory serves us well enough as an everyday heuristic. Attempts to refine and extend it, however, reveal that "it suffers explanatory failures on an epic scale" (Churchland 1981, p. 76). Folk theory, for instance, is unrevealing about "the nature and dynamics of mental illness, the faculty of creative imagination, or the ground of intelligence differences between individuals." Folk theory fails to illuminate "the nature and function of sleep, . . . the common ability to catch an outfield fly ball on the run, or hit a moving car with a snowball, . . . the internal construction of a 3-D visual image from the subtle differences in the 2-D array of stimulations in our respective retinas, . . . the rich variety of perceptual illusions, . . . the miracle of memory . . ." (Churchland 1981, p. 76). This is not to say that we ordinary folk-theorists have set out to explain such things and failed. Rather, empirical psychologists who have persisted in framing explanations in folk-theoretical terms have made little headway in the enterprise. In contrast, workers operating outside the intentional domain seem to be on the road to genuine theoretical advance:

If we approach *homo sapiens* from the perspective of natural history and the physical sciences, we can tell a coherent story of his constitution, development, and behavioral capacities which encompasses particle physics, atomic and molecular theory, biology, physiology, and materialistic neuroscience. That story, though still radically incomplete, is already extremely powerful, outperforming [folk theory] at many points even in its own domain. . . . [T]he greatest theoretical synthesis in the history of the human race is currently in our hands. (Churchland 1981, p. 75)

One may resist the conceit that we employ folk theories in everyday accounts of intelligent action. For the moment, I shall not. Nor shall I dispute the disputable claim that ordinary intentional modes of explanation are seriously deficient.[2] Let us pretend that folk theorizing is widespread, that it is indeed degenerate, and that, in contrast, the burgeoning disciplinary hybrid, *cognitive science*, affords hope for progress and discovery. It is not, of course, that cognitive science has produced vastly superior accounts of human thought and action. Rather, as the passage just quoted indicates, its proponents find much in it that is exciting and promising.[3] Further – and for my present purposes what is most significant – some of the most riveting new approaches offer explanations of intelligent activities that seem pointedly to omit appeal to intentional states and processes. On this matter there is diversity amid agreement. Some eliminitivists favor purely *syntactic* theories of mind, explanations that depend solely on *formal* properties of mental occurrences (see, e.g., Stich 1983). Others wish to promote explanations couched exclusively in *neuralese* (Churchland 1979, 1981, 1985). Still others imagine that 'connectionist' theories – those built around 'parallel distributed process' (PDP) models of cognition – are the wave of the future (see, e.g., Ramsey et al., Chapter 4, this volume; Rumelhart et al. 1986).[4]

Even if none of these approaches to mentality turned out to be correct in detail, one might still wish to draw a general moral. The present direction of cognitive science offers scant comfort to the friends of intentionality. It seems possible, and to some, likely, that our best theories of behavior will have no place for familiar intentional states and processes, that they will leave no room for beliefs, wants, dreams, and images. As theories evolve, ontological allegiances shift. Intentional items, appealed to in folk theories, may decline in explanatory stature. From such speculations, it is but a short step to the conclusion that there are no especially good reasons to suppose that there are, or ever have been, any beliefs, wants, dreams, and images. The argument may be summarized as follows.

1. Beliefs, wants, images, and the like belong to, and so depend on, a folk theory of intelligent behavior.
2. This folk theory seems bound to be replaced by better theories.
3. Recent work in cognitive science suggests that these better theories are likely to omit reference to beliefs, wants, and images.
4. There is, then, no reason to suppose that there are any intentional entities, any beliefs, wants, or images.

The conclusion is, as it stands, importantly ambiguous. It might be taken merely to license the thought that a mature cognitive science will feature an intentional vocabulary not smoothly isomorphic with everyday folk terminology. On such an interpretation we might expect the development of theories incorporating, for instance, appeals to "finer-grained" intentional states and processes. Thus construed, the conclusion is innocuous. Indeed views of this sort have always been common in mainstream cognitive psychology. (See, e.g., Anderson 1985, ch. 5.) When we scrutinize considerations advanced against commonsense mental categories, however, it is clear that, more often than not, something stronger is intended. Problems thought to beset traditional psychology evidently stem from perfectly general features of intentional states and processes. As a result, the eliminativist argument is most naturally regarded as supporting the conclusion that intentional goings-on *generally* will be left behind as science marches forward.

The eliminativist argument, it should be borne in mind, hinges on our accepting the suggestion that our intentional vocabulary is inextricably tied to an empirical theory of behavior. Once this connection is established, the fate of beliefs, wants, dreams, and images is linked to the fate of this empirical theory. If the theory is found wanting, we should be obliged to abandon the intentional vocabulary it legitimates. The case is no different in principle from many in the history of science. The demise of a theory makes for the demise of its ontology. Theoretical posits survive theories only to the extent that they find a home in a successor theory. We ought to accept, then, according to this argument, the potential elimination of intentionality. And when we look at the direction in which research in cognitive science seems to be moving, we shall be obliged to reckon elimination as rather more than a mere abstract possibility.

It is tempting to accept the outlines of this characterization but insist that folk theory is in fact in decent condition. As long as we consider everyday explanations of everyday actions, this seems right. Opponents of folk theory, however, are not inclined to dispute these informal successes. The issue is not whether, at some relatively shallow level, intentional categories suffice, but whether, at a much deeper level, they bear any interesting relation to reality. The failure of elaborations of folk categories – the failure, that is, of traditional intentional psychology – suggests to many that it may not.

Again, it is tempting to resist the conclusion on the grounds that contemporary intentionalistic psychology is not nearly so feeble as eliminativists would have us believe. This is a plausible response, perhaps, though it is not one I shall pursue here. My heart would not be in it. In any case, so long as we accept the notion that intentional categories are tied to an empirical theory of behavior, we must also accept the contention that our grounds for assigning reality to intentional goings-on hinge on the empirical viability of that theory. When it comes to empirical theories, philosophers are scarcely in a position to pass judgments on their respective merits and liabilities from the armchair. The interesting philosophical moves in the debate have been made already, in linking the intentional idiom to theories of behavior.

III. Eliminating content

Suppose we are led to accept the idea that states of mind are nothing more than posits of an ur-theory of behavior. And suppose we come to agree with eliminativists that this theory is "ripe for replacement." This in itself need not oblige us to forsake items to which the abandoned theory appeals. Elimination requires, in addition, that there be nothing singled out by a successor theory that plausibly corresponds to those items. It has been argued that this condition is indeed satisfied, at least for the propositional attitudes, when the envisaged successor is a 'connectionist' theory of a certain kind. The argument presumes at least a rudimentary grasp of connectionist architectures, however, so I shall provide a sketch of these before moving on.[5]

Connectionist models of cognition differ from traditional computational models in several respects. Perhaps the most significant difference lies in their nonlocal, 'distributed encoding of representations':

From conventional programmable computers we are used to thinking of knowledge as being stored in the state of certain units in the system. In [connectionist] systems we assume that only very short term storage can occur in the states of the units; long term storage takes place in the connections among units. . . . This is a profound difference between [the connectionist] approach and more conventional approaches, for it means that almost all knowledge is *implicit* in the structure of the device that carries out the task rather than *explicit* in the units themselves. (Rumelhart et al. 1986, p. 75)

The idea is perhaps best illustrated by means of a diagram depicting, schematically, the structure of a simple connectionist network. (See Figure 1.)

Provided with an interpretation of each input and output unit and an assignment of "weights" to connections between units, a network of this sort could be used to "model" various psychological processes. Incoming sources of stimulation activate particular input units, and a pattern of activation spreads through the network, culminating eventually in an activation level at the output unit. The output of the network will be a function of its input together with connection strengths among units. As the network "learns," these weights are adjusted until output is "appropriate" to input. Consider a simple network rigged to distin-

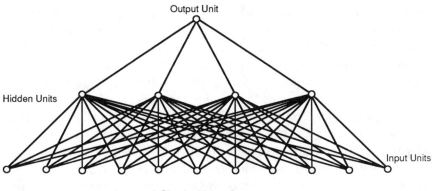

Figure 1.

guish species of birds. Input units might be provided with interpretations by being assigned particular bird *features*. A unit that was assigned
the feature "hooked bill," for instance, would be activated by hawks but
not by robins. Its level of activation is passed through the network via
connections it bears to higher-level units. Weights on these connections
allow the activation level in one unit to raise the activation level in some
units and to inhibit it in others. The addition of intermediate-level
uninterpreted "hidden units" provides the model with impressive computational power it would otherwise lack.

A network of this sort that acquired the knack of identifying species of
birds would, in Rumelhart et al.'s terminology, harbor *implicit* knowledge of those species. Knowledge of blue-crested finches, for instance,
would be represented in the model not by a particular connection, unit,
or list of features but, rather, by a unique global activation state. We
have seen that it is this aspect of network models, the "distributed"
character of their "representations," that their proponents regard as
sharply distinguishing them from earlier, computer-inspired hierarchical models. And it is the distributed nature of connectionist representations that, according to some, threatens the theoretical status of propositional attitudes.

The argument is founded on the idea that propositional attitudes
possess – essentially – a triad of characteristics that prevent their being
instantiated in connectionist systems of the sort illustrated here. Propositional attitudes are, according to Ramsey, Stich, and Garon, for instance, *"functionally discrete, semantically interpretable* states that play a
causal role in the production of other propositional attitudes, and ultimately in the production of behavior" (Ramsey et al., Chapter 4, this

volume). Connectionist networks of the relevant type fail to instantiate propositional attitudes, though – apparently – not because they lack attitudes toward propositions. Connectionists routinely describe their models as, for instance, possessing knowledge, or as capable of learning to judge the truth and falsity of propositions. Indeed, Ramsey et al. tell us that values on input units "represent some encoding or *representation* of the input"; that "connection strengths . . . are *usually regarded as encoding the system's knowledge*"; that "it is often plausible to view such networks as collectively or holistically encoding a set of propositions."[6] Indeed the authors provide a simple model (dubbed "network A") that they indicate is designed to "judge the truth or falsehood of . . . sixteen propositions."

Why not say of a system that *judges it true* that dogs have fur, as theirs does, that it *believes* that dogs have fur? We cannot say this because the judgment in question is "stored holistically and distributed throughout the network." Propositional attitudes, in contrast, are taken to require *functionally discrete* realizations. Although a suitably tuned network might be said to have attitudes toward definite propositions and even *knowledge*, it cannot be said to instantiate propositional attitudes.[7]

Granting the model, one may feel less confident of its proponents' assessment of folk theory. Despite their claims to the contrary, there is, so far as I can tell, nothing to prevent us from interpreting connectionist models as exemplifying belieflike states. Though "widely distributed," a belief might nevertheless be taken to have a restricted causal role. This would be so, for instance, if the system exhibited one set of causal powers in virtue of instantiating one belief, another set in virtue of instantiating a different belief, and so on for every belief ascribable to the system. A system that "judged . . . *dogs have fur* to be true" would respond to inputs differently from one that did not so "judge" or one that "judged" *dogs have fur* to be false. Responses would be affected, in addition, by whatever else the system "judged" to be so (and by much more besides). We shall return to this point presently.

Connectionists may aver that the holistic character of connectionist systems is, as Ramsey at al. put it, "radically inconsistent" with the ascription of propositional attitudes to those systems. But why should we agree? At least one noted folk psychologist has insisted for years that beliefs and desires *necessarily* function holistically: "Every judgment is made in light of all the reasons in this sense, that it is made in the presence of, and is conditioned by, that totality" (Davidson 1970/1980, p. 40). Indeed, this idea plays a central role in Davidson's use of a partitioning model to accommodate certain sorts of irrational thoughts and deeds, namely, those that arise from mental causes that are not reasons for what they cause. Such mental causes fail to be reasons, according to Davidson, precisely because they include *more* than isolated clusters of beliefs and desires. (See Davidson 1982, 1986.) More recently, Davidson has been at pains to distance himself from those who take states of mind to be discrete, sentencelike entities: "Of course people have beliefs, wishes, doubts, and so forth; but to allow this is not to suggest that beliefs, wishes, and doubts are *entities* in or before the mind, or that being in such states requires there to be corresponding mental objects" (Davidson 1987; see Heil 1988). Connectionist networks, if anything, provide rather more satisfactory models of Davidsonian agents than do old-style computational models.

Ramsey et al. regard it as important that, on a commonsense – though not on a connectionist – view, beliefs can be added and subtracted to a system one at a time. The matter is difficult to evaluate. The authors themselves provide an illustration of just what must be done to reconfigure a network so that it "encodes" a single additional proposition, *dogs have fur*. The resulting network, network *B*, they say, "encodes all the same propositions as network *A* plus one more." Again, the point must be not that propositional items cannot be added (or subtracted – by reversing the process?) singly, but that doing so requires system-wide modifications.

Why, in any case, should anyone imagine that folk theory is committed to a conception of belief in which beliefs can be inserted into or extracted from an agent without retuning that agent in myriad ways? This, at any rate, is at odds with a plausible holistic conception of belief. On such a conception, if I lose the belief that the keys are in the refrigerator (Ramsey et al., Chapter 4, this volume), I must lose, as well, countless other beliefs – beliefs about actions leading up to my hiding the keys, the milk carton they are next to, how likely they are to be discovered by my teenage son, and so on.

One may, of course, doubt that Davidson has managed to capture the central features of commonsense theory. Whether or not he is right, however, it is scarcely obvious that ordinary appeals to beliefs and other propositional attitudes *necessarily* require such things to be discrete entities. For some theorists, notably Fodor, they certainly seem to be (see, e.g., Fodor 1975). But, despite proclamations to the contrary, Fodor's is *not* the only game in town.

Perhaps connectionists would insist that these remarks fail to take account of important *causal* disparities between connectionist and folk-theoretical systems. Thus, Ramsey et al. (Chapter 4) remind us that it is characteristic of folk psychology that

1. When people see a dog nearby, they typically come to believe *that there is a dog nearby*.
2. When people believe *that the train will be late if there is snow in the mountains*, and come to believe *that there is snow in the mountains*, they will typically come to believe *that the train will be late*.

It is unlikely (1) that we are meant to imagine that a properly fashioned network, when given appropriate dog-indicating inputs, ought *not* to "encode the proposition" that there is a dog nearby or (2) that networks are to be designed so that on encoding the propositions that *the train will be late if there is snow in the mountains* and that *there is snow in the mountains*, will not "typically" come to encode as well the proposition that *the train will be late*. Networks, then, might mimic systems described folk theoretically. Their doing so, however, would be explicable by reference not to propositions encoded but, rather, to (something like) the obtaining of various connection strengths over the system. Semantic features of the network (if any) seem not to be *causally* relevant to its operation. Hence, although it might operate in accord with familiar folk principles, it would not act *on* those principles.

In this context, it is important to realize that the networks we have been discussing are intended by their creators to characterize goings-on at the *psychological* level. Were this not so, were networks taken, as they sometimes are, as *implementations* of psychological theories – models of their neural realizations, for instance – then folk theorists might be perfectly happy to concede that causal principles operating at the under-lying level could be connectionist in character. Indeed the notion that psychological states are neurally distributed is nowadays a physiological commonplace (see, e.g., Lashley 1950). The eliminativist argument, then, requires that we consider a connectionist model intended to cap-ture *psychological*, as distinct from neural, occurrences.

The point is a difficult one to assess. On the one hand, connectionist models seem to touch on psychological matters only at the edges, only at their input and output stages. "Hidden units" are posited so as to obtain psychologically appropriate outputs given particular inputs. Looked at this way, the models appear to be black boxes, and it is unclear *what* it is that accounts describing their operation describe: maybe the boxes' hardware, maybe higher-level principles in accord with which that hardware is operating.

On the other hand, one may easily doubt that there is but a single *psychological* level. Psychological events (my believing that *p* on the basis of my believing that *q*, for instance) could well turn out to have a finer-grained underlying psychological – perhaps connectionist – basis. Consider a simple example. Suppose I decide to give myself the disposition to form beliefs in accord with *modus ponens*. There are at least two ways I might accomplish this. I might set out to instill the principle itself, perhaps by memorizing it. Or I might undertake to imbue some other, perhaps very different, principle, one that, once acquired, would result in my forming beliefs in accord with *modus ponens*. My doing this might, as it happens, be a more efficient means to my end, given certain facts about me. Similarly, it could easily be imagined that an efficient way for Mother Nature to ensure that we satisfy folk-theoretical principles is by endowing us with a connectionist psychological architecture.

A worry remains. Folk theory, according to Ramsey et al. (Chapter 4), is committed to "propositional modularity." Consider a simple example. Suppose I believe that *if there is snow in the mountains, the train will be late* and that *there is snow in the mountains*. Suppose I believe, as well, that *the train is late*, not, however, on the basis of these other two beliefs. I believe that the train is late, perhaps, because I have been *told* by the ticket agent that it is late, or because I am standing in the station and can *see* that it is late. Cases of this sort have been widely discussed in epistemology. They conjure a picture of doxastic agents in which beliefs may individually influence or fail to influence other beliefs. Schematically: S may hold *p*, *q*, and *r*; *q* and *r* may each provide evidence for *p*; yet S may hold *p* on the basis of *q* but not *r* – or vice versa – or S's holding *p* may be based on something else altogether – wishful thinking, for instance. This picture, or something like it, captures a fragment of folk theory, perhaps, but, Ramsey et al. contend, it is not reflected in connectionist networks in which propositions are "holistically encoded." In such networks, representations are not "functionally discrete."

Even if all this were correct, however, even if folk theory were committed to "propositional modularity," it is unclear how extensively the theory would have to be revised in order to accommodate the connectionist model. On the one hand, we have seen already that connectionists are not averse to talk of adding (and presumably subtracting) "encoded propositions" one at a time. On the other hand, according to one familiar folk-theoretical account of belief formation, it might plausibly be supposed that, even when S fails to hold *p* on the basis of *r*, *r* might play *some* role in S's holding *p*: S may not have held *p* on the basis of *q* had he not held *r*. Even when we take so-called *basing* relations to be causal, we need not suppose that other beliefs are causally inert, that the psychological or epistemic basis of a given belief is functionally isolated in some absolute sense from an agent's doxastic background. The Davidsonian maxim quoted earlier is apt here: "Every judgment is made in light of all the reasons in this sense, that it is made in the presence of, and is conditioned by, that totality."

A second reason to doubt that connectionist architectures are at odds with ordinary conceptions of propositional attitudes is, in some respects, more fundamental. When we say that S holds *p* on the basis of *q* but nor *r*, or that S does *A* because he wants *x* not because he wants *y* (although he wants both *x* and *y*, and each mandates his *A*ing), we are deploying counterfactually loaded locutions. We suppose, for instance, that had S not held *p*, then, despite his holding *r*, he would not, *ceteris paribus*, have held *q*; had S not wanted *x*, then despite his wanting *y*, he would not, *ceteris paribus*, have done *A*.[8] Such counterfactuals are, as we suppose, made true (or false) by S's psychological condition. That condition could, for all anyone knows, be captured by a connectionist model featuring "distributed representations." A model might, for instance, be such that had it not encoded the proposition that *q*, it would not have come to encode the proposition that *p*, although, given that it encoded *q*, it would have come to encode *p* whether or not it encoded *r*. Folk theory certainly seems to embody a broadly causal conception of mind, one that grounds certain counterfactuals. But it need not thereby be committed to a crude "billiard ball" model, any more than it need embrace conceptions of belief and desire that treat these as specialized entities.

We may conclude that a strategy pitting connectionism against folk theory provides scant support for eliminativism. On the contrary, connectionist models of cognition seem most naturally interpretable as hypotheses about the underlying dynamics of beliefs, desires, and the other propositional attitudes. Connectionism may well be at odds with certain conceptions of intentional states – Fodor's, for instance – but this raises doubts, if at all, only for those conceptions. Connectionism, then, poses no special threat to ordinary appeals to beliefs and desires. It remains to be seen whether intentional states can reasonably be regarded as purely theoretical posits.

Notes

1. Of necessity I shall, in common with everyone else, continue to employ an intentional idiom in discussing theories that deny the existence of intentional

content, despite their entailing that this idiom is in some fashion entirely *off base*. Lynne Rudder Baker (1987) is less charitable toward theories of this sort.

2. The latter contention is sometimes buttressed by the observation that folk theories have provided no important advances, no startling discoveries, over the past "two or three thousand years" (Churchland 1981). The explanatory matrix we apply to behavior is not importantly different from that deployed by Plato and Aristotle. It is not obvious, however, why this is so readily taken to be an *objection* to folk theorizing. Change represents progress only when it is for the better. What needs to be, but has not been, shown is that folk theories might be drastically *improved*. Compare a similar complaint someone might lodge against Euclidian geometry: 2,500 years and no new axioms!

3. The refrain is a familiar one (see Dreyfus 1979). The advent of new, largely untried approaches to standing scientific problems inevitably produces euphoria among their adherents. This is due, of course, not to their having *succeeded* but to their not yet having *faltered*. Those in the trenches are, for the most part, more cautious in their pronouncements than those on the outside – journalists and philosophers, for instance. This seems surely to be the case in the recent connectionist rage; see below.

4. It is arguable that connectionism does not, in fact, abandon intentional states and processes, but merely locates these in *patterns* of neural activity rather than in bits of neural hardware or simple state-transitions. Connectionists without philosophical axes to grind certainly seem at home with standard intentional categories.

5. I focus, in what follows, on an argument advanced by Ramsey et al., Chapter 4, this volume – an argument that makes explicit the alleged relation between connectionism and eliminativism.

6. Here and elsewhere, italics are in the original.

7. It is impossible to resist noting in passing that if this is right, we have a knockdown counterexample to the traditional characterization of knowledge as justified true belief.

8. I am offering these not as counterfactual *analyses* of the locutions in question, only as examples of the sorts of counterfactual, they typically imply.

References

Anderson, J. R. (1985). *Cognitive Psychology and Its Implications*, 2nd ed. New York: W. H. Freeman.

Baker, L. R. (1987). *Saving Belief*. Princeton: Princeton University Press.

Churchland, P. M. (1979). *Scientific Realism and the Plasticity of Mind*. Cambridge: Cambridge University Press.

Churchland, P. M. (1981). "Eliminative Materialism and the Propositional Attitudes." *The Journal of Philosophy*, 78:67–90.

Churchland, P. M. (1985). "Reduction, Qualia, and the Direct Introspection of Brain States." *The Journal of Philosophy*, 82:8–28.

Davidson, D. (1970/1980). "Mental Events." In L. Foster & J. W. Swanson, eds., *Experience and Theory*. Amherst: University of Massachusetts Press. Reprinted in Davidson, D. (1980), *Essays on Actions and Events*. Oxford: Oxford University Press.

Davidson, D. (1982). "Paradoxes of Irrationality." In R. Wollheim & J. Hopkins, eds., *Philosophical Essays on Freud*. Cambridge: Cambridge University Press.

Davidson, D. (1986). "Deception and Division." In J. Elster, ed., *The Multiple Self*. Cambridge: Cambridge University Press.

Davidson, D. (1987). "Knowing One's Own Mind." *Proceedings and Address of the American Philosophical Association*, 60:441–458.

Dreyfus, H. (1979). *What Computers Can't Do*, 2nd ed. New York: Harper & Row.

Fodor, J. (1975). *The Language of Thought*. New York: T. Y. Crowell.

Heil, J. (1988). "Privileged Access." *Mind*, 97:238–251.

Lashley, K. S. (1950). "In Search of the Engram." *Society of Experimental Biology Symposium*, No. 4: *Physiological Mechanisms in Animal Behaviour*. Cambridge: Cambridge University Press. Reprinted in F. A. Beach, D. O. Hebb, C. T. Morgan, & H. W. Nissen, eds., *The Neuropsychology of Lashley*. New York: McGraw-Hill, 1960.

Quine, W. V. (1960). *Word and Object*. Cambridge, Mass.: MIT Press.

Quine, W. V. (1969). "Epistemology Naturalized." In *Ontological Relativity and Other Essays*. New York: Columbia University Press, pp. 69–90.

Rumelhart, D. E., Hinton, G. E., & McClelland, J. L. (1986). "A General Framework for Parallel Distributed Processing." In D. E. Rumelhart & J. L. McClelland, eds., *Parallel Distributed Processing* (2 vols.), Vol. 1. Cambridge, Mass.: MIT Press.

Silvers, S., ed. (1988). *Representation*. Dordrecht: Reidel.

Stich, S. P. (1983). *From Folk Psychology to Cognitive Science: The Case Against Belief*. Cambridge, Mass.: MIT Press.

Wittgenstein, L. (1921/1960). *Tractatus Logico-philosophicus*, trans. D. F. Pears & B. F. McGuinness. London: Routledge & Kegan Paul.

6 Two contrasts: folk craft versus folk science, and belief versus opinion

Daniel C. Dennett

Let us begin with what all of us agree on: Folk psychology is not immune to revision. It has a certain vulnerability in principle. Any particular part of it might be overthrown and replaced by some other doctrine. Yet we disagree about how likely it is that that vulnerability in principle will turn into the actual demise of large portions – or all – of folk psychology. I believe folk psychology will endure, and for some very good reasons, but I am not going to concentrate on that here. What I want to stress is that for all its blemishes, warts, and perplexities, folk psychology is an extraordinarily powerful source of prediction. It is not just prodigiously powerful but also remarkably easy for human beings to use. We are virtuoso exploiters of not so much a theory as a craft. That is, we might better call it a folk craft rather than a folk theory. The *theory* of folk psychology is the ideology about the craft, and there is lots of room, as anthropologists will remind us, for false ideology.

What we learn at mother's knee as we are growing up, and what might be to some degree innate, is a multifarious talent for having expectations about the world. Much of that never gets articulated into anything at all like propositions. (Here I am in partial agreement with the new Paul Churchland. He now wants to say that folk psychology is a theory; but theories do not have to be formulated the way they are formulated in books. I think that is a good reason for not calling it a theory, since it does not consist of any explicit theorems or laws.) But now, what is this thing that is folk psychology, if it is not a theory? What kind of a craft is it? I certainly have had my say about that, in *Brainstorms* (Dennett 1978) and in *The Intentional Stance* (Dennett 1987), and I shall not try to telescope all I say there into a summary here. Instead, I shall expand on the similarities between folk psychology and folk physics – two crafts that repay attention, and that *should* be studied with the methods of anthropology, not just the informal methods of philosophers.

I

If we look at folk physics, we discover some interesting anomalies. Folk physics is as effortless, as second-nature as folk psychology, and it keeps us one step ahead of harsh reality most of the time. A pioneering analysis of a portion of folk physics is found in Patrick Hayes's (1978, 1979) work on what he calls the "naive physics of liquids." Consider how robust and swift our anticipations are of the behavior of liquids under normal circumstances.

For instance, if you and I were seated at a table, and I happened to overturn a full glass of water, almost certainly you would push your chair back rather quickly, because you would expect that if you didn't, the water would run off the edge of the table onto your clothes. We do these things *almost* without thinking. But in fact, if the circumstances were slightly different – if there were a lip on the table, or a towel where the liquid was pouring – we would effortlessly have very different expectations, and behave differently. We know about how towels absorb liquids, and about how liquids don't roll up over the edge of lips under normal conditions. These are part of a huge family of expectations we have about liquids, which we would find very difficult to enunciate in a string of propositions – though that is just what Hayes very ingeniously attempted. He tried to do a formal, axiomatic folk physics of liquids. In the folk physics of liquids, he notes, siphons are impossible. So are pipettes – putting your finger over the top of the straw and drawing up the Pepsi. Hayes views this feature as a virtue of his theory because that is what folk physics declares; it is different from academic physics. There is something counterintuitive about both pipettes and siphons. Therefore, if you want to codify à la anthropology what people actually think and do, you want to make folk physics *predict against* such things as siphons and pipettes.

Now when we turn to folk psychology, we should expect the same thing. We should expect that some deeply intuitive ideas of folk psychology will just turn out to be false. Folk physics would say that gyroscopes are impossible, and that sailing upwind is impossible, but we come to learn that they are not, strange as this seems. We were just wrong about these matters, but even after we learn this, the intuitions don't go away; the phenomena still seem counterintuitive. So we might expect that folk psychology, under the pressure of advanced academic psychology and brain science, will similarly come a cropper. Certain deeply intuitive principles of folk psychology, perhaps never before articulated, may have to be given up. (I presume that folk physics never *articulated* the principle that siphons were impossible until siphons were well known to be possible; when siphons were observed, people perhaps said, "Hey wait a minute! Things shouldn't happen that way!") So it would be surprising if we had already articulated the principles of folk psychology that academic psychology is going to undermine – if it undermines any. Rather, we shall find ourselves beset with extremely counterintuitive clashes, and something will have to give. And what very likely will give is parts of folk psychology. That is to say, the craft itself will come to be adjusted to acknowledge the existence of perplexities and peculiarities and contrary predictions that the craft had never before made.

I want to distinguish between craft and ideology, between what we learn to do, and what our mothers and others have actually *told* us the craft was all about when they enunciated the lore, for what the anthropologists tell us is that craft and ideology are often quite distinct. If you ask the native potters how they make their pots, they may tell you one thing and do another. It is not a question of lack of sophistication. Jet airplane pilots tell their students, "This is how you fly a jet plane." They even write books about how they fly jet planes, but often that is not how they fly. They often do not know what they are doing. Now, if you want to study that sort of thing, you should bring the particular talents of the anthropologist to the study, but pending that research I shall hazard some informal observations. I suppose that if we look carefully at the ideology of folk psychology, we find it is pretty much Cartesian – dualist through and through. Perhaps there are also other problems and perplexities within the ideology as it has come down to us through the tradition. But notice that nobody in philosophy working on folk psychology wants to take seriously that part of the ideology. We are all materialists today, so the issue about the future of folk psychology is not whether or not some Cartesian view will triumph. We have apparently just decided that dualism (if it really is, as some have argued, presupposed by "common sense") is an expendable feature of the ideology. The question that concerns us now is whether there are other, less expendable features of the ideology.

Consider what can happen: Fodor, for instance, looks at the craft of folk psychology and tries to come up with a theory about why it works. His theory is that it works because it is good natural history. It is actually an account of what is going on in the head, he thinks. All the things that seem to be salient in the practice of the craft actually have their isomorphs or homomorphs in the head. So he comes up with what he calls 'intentional realism.' He notices that people say things like

Tom believes that p

and

Sam desires that q (actually, nobody ever uses this form, but bend a little!)

From this, we note that there is an attitude slot and a p-or-q slot, a propositional slot. We have two different sources of variation, two different knobs that turn in the folk craft. The reason it works, Fodor thinks, is that in the head there are things that line up with those knobs in a nice way. If the attitude knob has fourteen settings on it, there have to be fourteen different state types in the brain. If the p-or-q knob has an infinity of settings, there has to be an infinity of possible different internal states, each of them distinct and discrete. But that is just one theory about why folk psychology works, and several other chapters in this volume demonstrate that there are some good reasons for thinking it is a bad theory.

It is rather curious to say "I'm going to show you that folk psychology is false by showing you that Jerry Fodor is mistaken." Yet that is pretty much the strategy of Ramsey, Stich, and Garon's chapter, "Connectionism, Eliminativism, and the Future of Folk Psychology." It won't achieve its aim if Fodor is wrong about what is the most perspicuous ideology or explanation of the power of the folk craft. If he is wrong about that, then indeed you would expect that the vision he has of what is going on in the brain would not match what the brain people would discover; but that disparity would not mean that folk psychology as a craft was on the way out, or even that no perspicuous account of the ontology or metaphysics of folk psychology as a craft would survive well on a connectionist day of glory. I think John Heil nicely explains in his commentary how one might imagine that happening. One can also see in Ramsey, Stich, and Garon's own account how they are using folk-psychological terms simply in order to motivate their connectionist models, and explain how they are supposed to work. Why do they feel they must do that, if there is no useful relationship between folk psychology and computational neuroscience? Is it just a temporary ladder that we shall learn to discard? If the ladder works so well, why contemplate discarding it?

We should acknowledge, then, that it does not matter if the folk ideology about the craft is wrong – unless the ideology is taken too seriously! In *The Intentional Stance* (1987; p. 114), I comment at one point that Fodor's theory is a little like a curious folk theory of the common cold: A cold is a large collection of sneezes, some of which escape.

Someone might actually think that that is what a cold was, and might wonder how many more sneezes had to escape before it was over. Fodor's theory is similar: It is that there are all these sentences in the head; some of them come out, and some of them go in, but aside from a bit of translation (between "mentalese" and, say, English), basically they never get changed around all that much.

Some others, such as myself, have tried to give a different analysis of what folk psychology as a craft is, in terms of the intentional stance. I have insisted that far from being most perspicuously treated as (1) discrete, (2) semantically interpretable states (3) playing a causal role, the beliefs and desires of the folk-psychological craft are best viewed as *abstracta* – more like centers of gravity or vectors than individualizable concrete states of a mechanism.

In Chapter 4, Ramsey, Stich, and Garon give some bottom-up reasons for being dubious about this Fodorian triad of views about the nature of psychological states, and I am going to try to give a few slightly different ones – one might call them top-down reasons – by performing a few quasi-experiments drawn from *The Intentional Stance*. (If you have read the book, you are not a naive subject.)

What follows is a joke. See if you get it. ("Newfies" are people from Newfoundland; they are the Poles of Canada – or the Irish of Canada if you are British.)

A man went to visit his friend the Newfie and found him with both ears bandaged. "What happened?" he asked, and the Newfie replied, "I was ironing my shirt, you know, and the telephone rang." "That explains one ear, but what about the other?" "Well, you know, I had to call the doctor!"

The experiment works – with you as a subject – if you get the joke. Most, but not all, people do. If we were to pause, in the fashion of Eugene Charniak, whose story-understanding artificial intelligence (AI) program (Charniak 1974) first explored this phenomenon, and ask what one has to believe in order to get the joke (and here we have a list of propositions or sentences-believed-true, individuated in the standard way), what we get is a long list of different propositions. You must have beliefs about the shape of an iron, the shape of a telephone; the fact that when people are stupid, they often cannot coordinate the left hand with the right hand doing different things; the fact that the hefts of a telephone receiver and an iron are approximately the same; the fact that when telephones ring, people generally answer them; and many more.

What makes my narrative a joke and not just a boring story is that it is radically enthymematic; it leaves out many facts and counts on your filling them in, but you could fill them in only if you had all those beliefs. Now an absolutely daft theory about how you got the joke – and this is probably not fair to Fodor but a caricature of sorts – is this: Enter some sentences (in the ear – exactly the sentences I spoke), and their arrival provokes a mechanism that seeks all the relevant sentences – all those on our list – and soon brings them into a common workspace, where a resolution theorem-prover takes over, filling in all the gaps by logical inference. That is the sort of sententialist theory of cognitive processing that Fodor has gestured in the direction of, but nobody has produced a plausible or even workable version, so far as I know. The sketch I have just given is an absolutely harebrained theory, which nobody could assert with a straight face. Nobody believes that theory, I trust, but note that even if it and all its near kin (the other sentientialist/inference engine theories) are rejected as theories about how you got the joke, our list of beliefs is not for that reason otiose, foolish, or spurious. It actually does describe cognitive conditions (very abstractly considered) that have to be met by anybody who gets the joke. We can imagine running the experiments that would prove this. Strike off one belief on that list and see what happens. That is, find some people who do not have the belief (but have all the others), and tell them the joke. They will not get it. They cannot get it, because each of the beliefs is necessary for comprehension of the story.

II

Ramsey, Stich, and Garon discuss the phenomenon of forgetting one belief out of a list of beliefs. In the connectionist net they display, the way that you forget a belief is different from the way you might forget a belief in a Collins and Quillian network, but the point I would make here is that on either account, we have counterfactual-supporting generalizations of the following form: If you don't believe (have forgotten) that p, then you won't get the joke.

I am prepared, in fact, to make an empirical prediction, which relies on the scientific probity of talking about this list of beliefs, even though they don't represent anything salient in the head, but are mere abstracta. The joke that I just told and you just got is on its way out. It is going to be obsolete in a generation or two. Why? Because in this age of wash-and-wear clothing, the kids that are growing up have never seen anybody ironing. Some of them don't know what an iron looks and feels like, and their numbers are growing. For that matter, telephones are changing all the time, too, so the essential belief in the similarity in shape and heft of the telephone receiver and iron is going to vanish; it is not going to be reliably in the belief pool of normal audiences. So they are not going to get the joke. One would have to explain it to them: "Well, back in the olden days, irons looked and felt like . . . " – and then, of course, it would not be a joke anymore. This example could be multiplied many times over, showing that the power of folk psychology or the intentional stance as a calculus of abstracta is not in the least threatened by the prospect that no version of Fodor's intentional realism is sustained by cognitive neuroscience.

Ramsey, Stich, and Garon also cite some examples to show the presumed discreteness of beliefs on the folk-psychological model. They point out that an explanation can cite a single belief, and beliefs can come and go more or less atomistically – according to folk psychology. Heil comments usefully on what is misleading about this interpretation of such phenomena, so I am going to extend his criticism via a different example. Suppose we explain Mary's suddenly running upstairs by citing her belief that she has left her purse behind on the bed, and her desire to take her purse with her when she goes out. According to the realist interpretation of folk psychology, this would be a case in which we were not speaking metaphorically, and if we happen to speak imprecisely (did she really actually believe just that she had left her purse on some horizontal surface in the bedroom?), this is always correctible in principle because there is a definite fact of the matter, say the realists, as to just which beliefs and desires a person has. Now I take it that in a case like this, what creates the illusion of discrete, separate, individuatable beliefs is the fact that we talk about them: the fact that when we go to explain our anticipations, when we move from generating our own private expectations of what people are going to do, to telling others about these expectations we have, and explaining to them why we have them, we do it with language. What comes out, of course, are propositions. Given the demands for efficiency in communication, we have to highlight the presumably central content features of the explanation or prediction that we have in mind. A distilled essence – in fact, as we have seen, typically an enthymematic portion of the distilled essence – gets expressed in words.

In order to make any sense of what we are doing in the classical way that Fodor suggests, we have to carry a lot of further baggage along. Let me quote Davidson (1975, pp. 15–16): "Without speech we cannot make the fine distinctions between thoughts that are essential to the explanations we can sometimes confidently supply. Our manner of attributing attitudes ensures that all the expressive power of language can be used to make such distinctions." I agree with that. It remains true, however, that in the ordinary run of affairs, large families of beliefs travel together in our mental lives. At one instant, Mary believes that her purse is on the bed *and* believes that her handbag is on some horizontal surface *and* believes that the item containing her comb is supported by the article of furniture one sleeps in, and so forth. Now do all (or many) of these distinct states have to light up and team up to cause Mary to run upstairs? Or is there just one each from the belief family and desire family that are chosen to do the work? If we cling to Fodor's "classical" view of propositional attitudes, these are the only alternatives, and they are exclusive. That is not to say that there could not be overdetermination (e.g., fourteen beliefs and seven desires were ON at that time, but any pair were sufficient to cause the decision), but that there has to be a fact of the matter about exactly which of these discrete beliefs and desires existed at the time, and whether or not it did, or could, contribute to the causation of the decision.

This is related to a point that Heil makes. Folk psychology recognizes, if you like, the holism of belief attribution in everyday life, and in fact boggles at the suggestion that somebody could believe that her handbag was on the bed and not believe any of these other propositions. The idea that you could believe one of these without believing the others – and not just the obvious logical consequences of it, but all of the pragmatic neighbors of it – is something that folk psychology does not anticipate, because it is not as staunchly realist about beliefs and desires as Fodor is.

So it seems to me that the illusion of realism arises from the fact that we do not just use folk psychology privately to anticipate – each one of us – the behavior of one another. In contrast, if chimpanzees, for instance, use folk psychology (Premack 1986), they do not talk about it. They are *individual* folk psychologists, but we are not. We are *communal* folk psychologists, who are constantly explaining to other people why we think that so and so is going to do such and such. We have to talk; and when we talk, because life is short, we have to give an edited version of what we are actually thinking; thus what comes out is a few sentences. Then, of course, it is only too easy to suppose that those sentences are not mere edited abstractions or distillations from, but are rather something like copies of or translations of the very states in the minds of the beings we are talking about.

The fact that we talk has, I claim, an obvious but interesting further effect: Since we talk, and write, we have all these sentences lying around – our own and other people's. We hear them, we remember them, we write them down, we speak them ourselves, and with regard to any such sentence in our language that we encounter or create, we have a problem: what to do with it. We can discard it, forget it, or we can decide to put it in the pile labeled "true" or the pile labeled "false." And this, I claim, creates a rather different sort of specialized state, what in *Brainstorms* I called opinions. These are not just beliefs; these are linguistically infected states – only language users have them. Opinions are essentially bets on the truth of sentences in a language that we understand. My empirical hunch is that a proper cognitive psychology is going to have to make a sharp distinction between beliefs and opinions, that the psychology of opinions is really going to be rather different from the psychology of beliefs, and that the sorts of architecture that will do well by, say, nonlinguistic perceptual beliefs (you might say "animal" beliefs) is going to have to be supplemented rather substantially in order to handle opinions. And I think it is confusion on this score – more specifically, the failure to distinguish between believing that a certain sentence of one's natural language is true, and having the sort of belief that that sentence might be used to express – that has given Fodor's intentional realism the run it has had.

It occurs to me that another feature of this line of thought that Churchland and Stich might like is that if I am right about the distinction between beliefs and opinions, then the following dizzying prospect opens up: Scientists (connectionist heroes of the near future) might "come to the *opinion*" that there are no such things as beliefs, without thereby having to *believe* there was no such thing! If connectionists are right, after all, they are just connectionist systems that on occasion make bets on the truth of various sentences of their natural language. All of their science goes on – at least the public communication and confirmation part of it – at the level of opinions. Although they do not have beliefs, they do have opinions, since they are still using sentences and hence committing themselves to the truth of some of them. But they wouldn't have to say they *believe* that a particular sentence is true; they would just . . . *connect* that it was! Because of the settings of their connectionist networks, they would put that sentence in the "true" pile, but putting that sentence in the "true" pile (even in the "true" pile of sentences you keep stored in your head) is distinct from believing – on the folk-psychological model. (Those of us who are not Fodorians about belief can go on talking about what these connectionists *believe*, but the Fodorians and Stichians among them can consistently be of the *opinion* that they never in fact believe anything!)

I want to say more about connectionism, for I want to throw a few more buckets of cold water on the euphoria expressed if not induced by the connectionist chapters (Churchland, Chapter 2, this volume; Ramsey, Stich, and Garon, Chapter 4, this volume). First, however, I want to make some remarks in favor of connectionism that they do not quite make. Ramsey, Stich, and Garon claim that connectionism is not merely implementation at a lower level of a traditional, hierarchical model, and I want to say something more in favor of that. Here is why I think connectionism is exciting.

Suppose you have what Haugeland (1985) would call a GOFAI (Good, Old-Fashioned Artificial Intelligence) nonconnectionist AI theory: It postulates a certain level at which there are symbolic structures in something like a language of thought, and it has some mechanism for computing over these. Then, indeed, it makes little difference how you implement that. It makes no difference whether you use a Vax or a Cray, a compiled or interpreted language. It makes no difference how you determine the implementation, because all of the transitions are already explicitly stated at the higher level. That is to say, in technical terms, you have a flow graph and not merely a flow chart, which means that *all* the transition regularities are stipulated at that level, leaving nothing further to design, and it is simply a matter of engineering to make sure that the transition regularities are maintained. It makes no sense to look at different implementations, for the same reason that it makes no sense to look at two different copies of the same newspaper. You might get some minor differences of implementation speed or something like that, but that is not apt to be interesting, whereas the relationship between the symbolic or cognitive level and the implementation level in connectionist networks is not that way. It really makes sense to look at different implementations of the cognitive-level sketch because you are counting on features of those implementations to fix details of the transitions that actually are not fixed at the cognitive level. You have not specified an algorithm or flow graph at that level. Another way of looking at this is that in contrast to a classical system, where the last thing you want to have is noise in your implementation (i.e., you want to protect the system from noise), in a connectionist implementation you plan on exploiting noise. You want the noise to be there because it is actually going to be magnified or amplified in ways that are going to effect the actual transitions described at the cognitive level.

This becomes clear if you consider the hidden units in a connectionist network, such as those in the diagrams in Chapter 4. As Ramsey, Stich, and Garon note there, if you subject those hidden units to careful statistical analysis (it is made easier if you view the results in one of Geoffrey Hinton's lovely diagrams showing which nodes are active under which circumstances), you can discover that a certain node is always ON whenever the subject is (let us say) dogs, and never (or very weakly) ON when the subject is cats, whereas another node is ON for cats and not ON for dogs. Other nodes, however, seem to have no interpretation at all. They have no semantics; they are just there. As far as semantics is concerned, they are just noise; sometimes they are strongly active and at other times weak, but these times don't seem to match up with any category of interest. As many skeptics about connectionism have urged, the former sorts of nodes are plausibly labeled the DOG node and the CAT node and so forth, and so it is tempting to say that we have symbols after all. Connectionism turns out to be just a disguised version of good old-fashioned, symbol-manipulating AI! Plausible as this is (and there must be *some* truth to the idea that certain nodes should be viewed as semantic specialists), there is another fact about such networks that undercuts the skeptics' claim in a most interesting way. The best reason for *not* calling the dog-active node the dog symbol is that you can "kill" or disable that node, and the system will go right on discriminating dogs, remembering about dogs, and so forth, with at most a slight degradation in performance. It turns out, in other words, that all those other "noisy" nodes were carrying some of the load. What is more, if you keep the "symbol" nodes alive and kill the other, merely noisy nodes, the system *doesn't* work.

The point about this that seems to me most important is that at the computational level in a connectionist system, no distinction is made between symbols and nonsymbols. All are treated exactly alike at that level. The computational mechanism doesn't have to know which ones are the symbols. They are all the same. Some of them *we* (at a higher level) can see take on a role rather like symbols, but this is not a feature that makes a difference at the computational level. That is a very nice property. It is a property that is entirely contrary to the spirit of GOFAI, where the distinction between symbol and nonsymbol makes all the computational difference in the world.

Having offered my praise, let me turn to what worries me about connectionism. Both connectionist chapters exhibit connectionist networks that have input nodes, output nodes, and hidden units, but all their discussion is about the hidden units. We should pause to worry about the fact that some of the input units (for instance) look much too Fodorian. It looks, indeed, as if there is a language of thought being used to input *Dogs have fur* across the bottom of the system, for instance. It looks as if the inputs are organized into something altogether too much like Fodorian propositions. Could it be that the only reason we are not seeing the language of thought is that we are not looking at the much larger cognitive systems of which these bits of memory are just small subsystems?

This worry is analogous to a concern one can have about traditional AI systems. For instance, Hector Levesque (1984) has described a knowledge representation system (in AI) with some lovely properties, but one of its *un*lovely properties is that there is only one way of putting something into the knowledge base, and there is only one thing the knowledge base can do. Everything goes in by an operation called TELL, followed by a statement in the predicate calculus; the only thing the system can do is permit itself to be subjected to an ASK operation. I submit that any model of knowledge that one can update or enrich only by writing a proposition using the TELL function and that one can use only by extracting from it a proposition via the ASK function is a hopelessly Fodorian sententialist model of a robust knowledge system.

But for all that the connectionist chapters show us, that is what we have in their connectionist models too. We have a memory for which a TELL and an ASK are defined. No other way of tweaking it, or utilizing it, or updating it has yet been defined. This is a serious charge, which I should try to defend with a more specific example. Here, finally, is one more little experiment concerning the structure of human memory. The claim I want to substantiate by it is that what the connectionists have offered us is not an architecture for memory but at best an architecture for perhaps a little subcomponent of memory. When we start making the memory more realistic, we are going to have to add some architectural details that will require some quite different principles.

Here are some questions – personal questions about your own memory – which you should attempt to answer as quickly as you can:

Have you ever danced with a movie star?

Have you ever been introduced to a white-haired lady whose first name begins with the letter *V*?

Have you ever driven for more than seven miles behind a blue Chevrolet?

Most people have a swift yes or no answer to the first question and draw a blank on the others. Imagine how different their responses would be to the following:

Have you ever been introduced to a green-haired lady whose first name begins with the letter *V*?

Have you ever driven for more than seven miles behind a pink Rolls Royce?

First of all, according to anybody's theory of memory it is false that you have stored as Fodorian sentences "I have never danced with a movie star," "I have never driven more than seven miles behind a pink Rolls Royce," and so forth, because that would lead to combinatorial explosion. Think of all the things you have never done, and know you have never done.

Any remotely sane theory of how you answer these questions has to work the following way: When you hear the question, it stimulates your memory, and either it succeeds in tweaking a recollection of an event meeting the condition or it does not. In the case of the first proposition, if no recollection is made, you draw the metaconclusion that *had you ever done it, you would now be recalling it*, and since you are not now recalling it, the chances are that you never have danced with a movie star. The parallel metaconclusion, however, is simply not plausible in the third case, because there is no reason to suppose that had you ever driven seven miles behind a blue Chevy, you would now be recalling it. In order to make sense of this simple, robust feature of human memory, you have to suppose that human memory is organized in such a fashion that you can unconsciously assess the likelihood that the failure of your memory to produce a recollection for you is a sign – it can be treated on this occasion as a premise or datum – from which you unconsciously "infer" the conclusion "I have never done that." That shows a complexity far beyond ASK and TELL that we can establish quite clearly as a feature of human memory. So a good cognitive psychology will have to model that. How can I build a model of human memory that has that rather nifty, easily demonstrated property? Nobody in *non*connectionist cognitive psychology has a good model of that, so far as I know, but then neither do the connectionists.

And until the connectionists can show that their marvelous new fabrics can be fashioned into larger objects exhibiting some of these molar properties of human psychology, we should temper our enthusiasm.

References

Charniak, E. (1974). "Toward a Model of Children's Story Comprehension." Unpublished doctoral dissertation, MIT, and MIT AI Lab Report 266.

Davidson, D. (1975). "Thought and Talk." In *Mind and Language: Wolfson College Lectures, 1974.* Oxford: Clarendon Press, pp. 7–23.

Dennett, D. (1978). *Brainstorms.* Cambridge, Mass.: MIT Press.

Dennett, D. (1987). *The Intentional Stance.* Cambridge, Mass.: MIT Press.

Haugeland, J. (1985). *Artificial Intelligence: The Very Idea.* Cambridge, Mass.: MIT Press.

Hayes, P. (1978). "Naive Physics I: The Ontology of Liquids." Working Paper 35, Institut pour les Etudes Semantiques et Cognitives, Univ. de Genève.

Hayes, P. (1979). "The Naive Physics Manifesto." In D. Michie, ed., *Expert Systems in the Microelectronic Age*. Edinburgh: Edinburgh University Press.

Levesque, H. (1984). "Foundations of a Functional Approach to Knowledge Representation." *Artificial Intelligence*, 23:155–212.

Premack, D. (1986). *Gavagai! Or the Future History of the Animal Language Controversy*. Cambridge, Mass.: MIT Press.

7 Folk psychology is here to stay

Terence Horgan and James Woodward

Folk psychology is a network of principles which constitutes a sort of common-sense theory about how to explain human behavior. These principles provide a central role to certain propositional attitudes, particularly beliefs and desires. The theory asserts, for example, that if someone desires that p, and this desire is not overridden by other desires, and he believes that an action of kind K will bring it about that p, and he believes that such an action is within his power, and he does not believe that some other kind of action is within his power and is a preferable way to bring it about that p, then *ceteris paribus*, the desire and the beliefs will cause him to perform an action of kind K. The theory is largely functional, in that the states it postulates are characterized primarily in terms of their causal relations to each other, to perception and other environmental stimuli, and to behavior.

Folk psychology (henceforth FP) is deeply ingrained in our common-sense conception of ourselves as persons. Whatever else a person is, he is supposed to be a rational (at least largely rational) *agent* – that is, a creature whose behavior is systematically caused by, and explainable in terms of, his beliefs, desires, and related propositional attitudes. The wholesale rejection of FP, therefore, would entail a drastic revision of our conceptual scheme. This fact seems to us to constitute a good *prima facie* reason for not discarding FP too quickly in the face of apparent difficulties.

Recently, however, FP has come under fire from two quarters. Paul Churchland (1981) has argued that since FP has been with us for at least twenty-five centuries, and thus is not the product of any deliberate and self-conscious attempt to develop a psychological theory which coheres with the account of *Homo sapiens* which the natural sciences provide, there is little reason to suppose that FP is true, or that humans undergo

Reprinted from *The Philosophical Review* 94 (1985) by permission of the publisher and the authors.

beliefs, desires, and the like. And Stephen Stich (1983) has argued that current work in cognitive science suggests that no events or states posited by a mature cognitive psychology will be identifiable as the events and states posited by FP; Stich maintains that if this turns out to be the case, then it will show that FP is radically false, and that humans simply do not undergo such mental states as beliefs and desires.

In this paper we shall argue that neither Churchland nor Stich has provided convincing reasons for doubting the integrity of FP. Much of our discussion will be devoted to showing that they each employ an implausibly stringent conception of how FP would have to mesh with lower-level theories in order to be compatible with them. We do not deny the possibility that FP will fail to be compatible with more comprehensive theories; this would happen, for instance, if the correct theoretical psychology turned out to be a version of radical Skinnerian behaviorism. But we maintain that there is no good reason to suppose that it will *actually* happen.

Before proceeding, several preliminaries. First, we shall use the rubric 'event' in a broad sense, to include not only token changes, but also token states and token processes. Thus, non-momentary folk-psychological token states will count as mental events, in our terminology.

Second, we shall take FP to consist of two components: a set of *theoretical principles*, and an *existential thesis*. Many or all of the theoretical principles may be expected to have the general form exemplified by the example in our opening paragraph; that is, they are universal closures of conditional formulas.[1] As such they do not carry any existential import, since they might all be vacuously true. The existential thesis of FP, on the other hand, is the assertion that generally our everyday folk-psychological descriptions of people are true, and that humans generally do undergo the folk-psychological events that we commonly attribute to them. We take it that Churchland and Stich are arguing primarily against the existential thesis of FP; i.e., they are claiming that our everyday folk-psychological ascriptions are radically false, and that there simply do not exist such things as beliefs, desires, and the rest. Thus their argument, as we understand it, leaves open the possibility that the theoretical principles of FP are true but merely vacuously so.

Third, we are not necessarily claiming that FP is fully correct in every respect, or that there is no room to correct or improve FP on the basis of new developments in cognitive science or neuroscience. Rather, we are claiming that FP's theoretical principles are *by and large* correct, and that everyday folk-psychological ascriptions are often true.

Fourth, we want to dissociate ourselves from one currently influential strategy for insulating FP from potential scientific falsification – viz., the instrumentalism of Daniel Dennett (1978, 1981). He says, of beliefs and desires, that these "putative . . . states" can be relegated "to the role of idealized fictions in an action-predicting, action-explaining calculus" (1978, p. 30). They are not what Reichenbach calls "illata – posited theoretical entities"; instead, he maintains, they are "abstracta – calculation-bound entities or logical constructs" (1981, p. 13), whose status is analogous to components in a parallelogram of forces (1981, p. 20). In short, he evidently holds that they are instrumentalistic fictions, and hence that they are compatible with virtually anything we might discover in cognitive science or neuroscience. We reject Dennett's in-strumentalism. We maintain that FP, in addition to providing a useful framework for prediction, also provides genuine *causal explanations*. Al-though an instrumentalistic attitude toward the intentional idioms of FP is compatible with the mere predictive use of these idioms, it simply is not compatible with their explanatory use, or with talk of beliefs and desires as causes. Accordingly, FP requires a defense more vigorous than Dennett's instrumentalism.

I

Churchland's (1981) argument against the compatibility of FP and neu-roscience rests on three considerations. First, "FP suffers explanatory failures on an epic scale" (p. 76). Second, "it has been stagnant for at least twenty-five centuries" (p. 76). And third, "its intentional categories stand magnificently alone, without any visible prospect of reduction" to neuroscience (p. 75). Irreducibility is the main consideration, and it is allegedly reinforced by the other two points: "A successful reduction cannot be ruled out, in my view, but FP's explanatory impotence and long stagnation inspire little faith that its categories will find themselves neatly reflected in the framework of neuroscience" (p. 75).

Let us consider each of Churchland's three points in turn. In elabora-tion of the first point, he writes:

As examples of central and important mental phenomena that remain largely or wholly mysterious within the framework of FP, consider the nature and dynam-ics of mental illness, the faculty of creative imagination. . . . the nature and psychological functions of sleep. . . . the common ability to catch an outfield fly ball on the run. . . . the internal construction of a 3-D visual image. . . . the rich variety of perceptual illusions. . . . the miracle of memory. . . . the nature of the learning process itself . . . (p. 73).

There are at least two important respects in which this passage is misleading. First, while FP itself may have little to say about the matters Churchland mentions, theories based on concepts deriving from FP have a good deal to say about them. For example, cognitive psychologists have developed extensive and detailed theories about visual perception, memory, and learning that employ concepts recognizably like the folk-psychological concepts of belief, desire, judgment, etc.[2] The versions of attribution theory and cognitive dissonance theory considered below in connection with Stich are important cases of theories of this kind. That all such theories are unexplanatory is most implausible, and in any case requires detailed empirical argument of a sort Churchland does not provide.

Secondly, Churchland's argument seems to impose the *a priori* demand that any successful psychological theory account for a certain pre-established range of phenomena, and do so in a unified way. Arguments of this general type deserve to be treated with skepticism and caution. The history of science is full of examples in which our pre-theoretical expectations about which phenomena it is reasonable to expect a theory to account for or group together have turned out to be quite misleading. For example, the demand was frequently imposed on early optical theories that they account for facts which we would now recognize as having to do with the physiology or psychology of vision; this had a deleterious effect on early optical theorizing. Similar examples can readily be found in the history of chemistry.[3]

The general point is that reasonable judgments about which phenomena a theory of some general type should be expected to account for require considerable theoretical knowledge; when our theoretical knowledge is relatively primitive, as it is with regard to many psychological phenomena, such judgments can go seriously astray. There is no good reason, *a priori*, to expect that a theory like FP, designed primarily to explain common human actions in terms of beliefs, desires, and the like, should also account for phenomena having to do with visual perception, sleep, or complicated muscular coordination. The truth about the latter phenomena may simply be very different from the truth about the former.

What about Churchland's second argument, viz., that FP has remained stagnant for centuries? To begin with, it seems to us at least arguable that FP has indeed changed in significant and empirically progressive ways over the centuries, rather than stagnating. For example, it is a plausible conjecture that Europeans in the 18th or 19th centuries were much more likely to explain human behavior in terms of character types with enduring personality traits than 20th century Europeans, who often appeal instead to "situational" factors. (Certainly this difference is dramatically evident in 18th and 20th century literature; contrast, say, Jane Austen and John Barth.)[4] Another example of empirically progressive change, perhaps, is the greater willingness, in contemporary culture, to appeal to unconscious beliefs and motivations.

Another reason to question the "empirical unprogressiveness" argument is that cognitive psychological theories employing belief-like and desire-like events have led to a number of novel and surprising predictions, which have been borne out by experiment. (We discuss some pertinent examples below. For other striking cases the reader is referred to Nisbett and Ross (1980).) Yet Churchland seems to argue as though the (alleged) empirical unprogressiveness of FP is a good reason for taking any theory modelled on FP to be false.[5] This is rather like arguing that any sophisticated physical theory employing central forces must be false on the grounds that the ordinary person's notions of pushing and pulling have been empirically unprogressive.

Furthermore, the standard of "empirical progressiveness" is not very useful in assessing a theory like FP anyway. The typical user of FP is interested in applying a pre-existing theory to make particular causal judgments about particular instances of human behavior, not in formulating new causal generalizations. He is a consumer of causal generalizations, not an inventor of them. In this respect he resembles the historian, the detective, or the person who makes ordinary singular causal judgments about inanimate objects. It is not appropriate, we submit, to assess these activities using a standard explicitly designed to assess theories that aim at formulating novel causal generalizations.

This point emerges clearly when one realizes that much of the implicit theory behind many ordinary (but non-psychological) particular causal judgments has presumably changed very slowly, if at all, over the past thousand years. Both we and our ancestors judge that the impact of the rock caused the shattering of the pot, that the lack of water caused the camel to die, that a very sharp blow on the head caused A's death, that heat causes water to boil, etc. None of these judgments are part of a (swiftly) empirically progressive theory, yet it seems ludicrous to conclude (on those grounds alone) that they are probably false. A similar point can be made about much (although by no means all) of the implicit causal theory employed by historians. These examples serve to remind us that not all folk theorizing is now regarded as radically false.

This brings us to Churchland's third, and most fundamental, argument for the alleged incommensurability of FP with neuroscience: viz., the likely irreducibility of the former to the latter. An ideal intertheoretic reduction, as he describes it, has two main features:

First, it provides us with a set of rules – "correspondence rules" or "bridge laws," as the standard vernacular has it – which effect a mapping of the terms of the old theory (T_o) onto a subset of the expressions of the new or reducing theory (T_n). These rules guide the application of those selected expressions of T_n in the following way: we are free to make singular applications of those expressions in all those cases where we normally make singular applications of their correspondence-rule doppelgangers in T_o. . . .

Second, and equally important, a successful reduction ideally has the outcome that, under the term mapping effected by the correspondence rules, the central principles of T_o (those of semantic and systematic importance) are mapped onto general sentences of T_n that are *theorems* of T_n (1979, p. 81).

We certainly agree that an ideal, or approximately ideal, reduction of FP to natural science would be *one* way of salvaging FP. And we also agree that such a reduction – indeed, even a species-specific reduction – is an unlikely prospect, given that FP is at least twenty-five centuries old and hence obviously was not formulated with an eye toward smooth term-by-term absorption into 20th century science. (A non-species-specific reduction is even less likely, because if FP is true of humans then it can equally well be true of Martians whose physico-chemical composition is vastly different from our own – so different that there are no theoretically interesting physical descriptions that can subsume both the physico-chemical properties which "realize" FP in humans and the corresponding physico-chemical properties in Martians.)

But even if FP cannot be reduced to lower-level theories, and even if lower-level theories can themselves provide a marvelous account of the nature and behavior of *Homo sapiens*, it simply does not follow that FP is radically false, or that humans do not undergo the intentional events it posits. Churchland's eliminative materialism is not the only viable naturalistic alternative to reductive materialism. Another important alternative is the non-reductive, non-eliminative materialism of Donald Davidson (1970, 1973, 1974).

Davidson advocates a thesis which asserts that every concrete mental event is identical to some concrete neurological event, but which does not assert (indeed, denies) that there are systematic bridge laws linking mental event-*types*, or properties, with neurological event-types. He calls this view *anomalous monism*; it is a form of monism because it posits psychophysical identities, and it is "anomalous" because it rejects reductive bridge laws (or reductive type-type identities).[6]

The availability of anomalous monism as an alternative to reductive materialism makes it clear that even if FP is not reducible to neuroscience, nevertheless the token mental events posited by FP might well exist, and might well bear all the causal relations to each other, to sensation, and to behavior which FP says they do.

Churchland never mentions Davidson's version of the identity theory – a very odd fact, given its enormous influence and its obvious relevance to his argument. Instead he argues directly from the premise that FP probably is not reducible to neuroscience to the conclusion that FP probably is false. So his argument is fallacious, in light of token-token identity theory as an alternative possible account of the relation between FP and neuroscience. He is just mistaken to assume that FP must be reducible to neuroscience in order to be compatible with it.

II

Let us now consider Stich's reasons for claiming that FP probably will not prove compatible with a developed cognitive science (henceforth CS). Unlike Churchland, Stich does not assume that FP must be reducible to more comprehensive lower-level theories in order to be compatible with them. We shall say more presently about the way he thinks FP must fit with these theories.

Stich offers two arguments against the compatibility of FP and CS; we shall examine these in this section and the next. The first argument purports to show that the overall causal organization of the cognitive system probably does not conform with the causal organization which FP ascribes to it. The argument runs as follows. Events which satisfy a given sortal predicate of the form ". . . is a belief that p" are supposed to have typical behavioral effects of both verbal and non-verbal kinds. On the verbal side, the events in this class are ones which typically cause the subject, under appropriate elicitation conditions, to utter an assertion that p. On the non-verbal side, these events are ones which, in combination with a subject's other beliefs, desires, and the like, typically cause the subject to perform those actions which FP says are appropriate to the combination of that belief with those other propositional attitudes. But recent experimental evidence suggests, according to Stich, that the psychological events which control non-verbal behavior are essentially independent of those which control verbal behavior – and hence that the cognitive system simply does not contain events which, taken singly, occupy the causal role which FP assigns to beliefs. If these experimental results prove generalizable, and if CS subsequently develops in the direction of positing separate, largely independent, cognitive subsystems for the control of verbal and non-verbal behavior respectively, then we will be forced to conclude, argues Stich, that there are no such things as beliefs.

One of his central empirical examples is a study in attribution theory, performed by Storms and Nisbett (1970). He describes its first phase this way:

Storms and Nisbett . . . asked insomniac subjects to record the time they went to bed and the time they finally fell asleep. After several days of record keeping, one group of subjects (the "arousal" group) was given a placebo pill to take fifteen minutes before going to bed. They were told that the pill would produce rapid heart rate, breathing irregularities, bodily warmth and alertness, which are just the typical symptoms of insomnia. A second group of subjects (the "relax-ation" group) was told that the pills would produce the opposite symptoms: lowered heart rate, breathing rate, body temperature and alertness. Attribution theory predicts that the arousal group subjects would get to sleep *faster* on the nights they took the pills, because they would attribute their symptoms to the pills rather than to the emotionally laden thoughts that were running through their minds. It also predicts that subjects in the relaxation group will take *longer* to get to sleep. Since their symptoms persist despite having taken a pill intended to relieve the symptoms, they will infer that their emotionally laden thoughts must be particularly disturbing to them. And this belief will upset them further, making it all that much harder to get to sleep. Remarkably enough, both of these predictions were borne out. Arousal group subjects got to sleep 28 percent faster on the nights they took the pill, while relaxation subjects took 42 percent longer to get to sleep (Stich, 1983, p. 232).

What Stich finds particularly significant is the second phase of this study. After the completion of the initial insomnia experiments, the members of the arousal group were informed that they had gotten to sleep more quickly after taking the pill, and the members of the relax-ation group were informed that they had taken longer to fall asleep. They were asked *why* this happened, and Nisbett and Wilson report the following pattern of responses:

Arousal subjects typically replied that they usually found it easier to get to sleep later in the week, or that they had taken an exam that had worried them but had done well on it and could now relax, or that problems with a roommate or girlfriend seemed on their way to resolution. Relaxation subjects were able to find similar sorts of reasons to explain their increased sleeplessness. When subjects were asked if they had thought about the pills at all before getting to sleep, they almost uniformly insisted that after taking the pills they had com-pletely forgotten about them. When asked if it had occurred to them that the pill might be producing (or counteracting) the arousal symptoms, they reiterated their insistence that they had not thought about the pills at all after taking them. Finally, the experimental hypothesis and the postulated attribution process were described in detail. Subjects showed no recognition of the hypothesized process and . . . made little pretense of believing that *any* of the subjects could have gone through such processes (Nisbett and Wilson, 1977, p. 238).

It is very likely, given the data from the first phase of the study, that the cognitive mechanisms which controlled the subjects' verbal responses in the second phase were largely distinct from the cognitive mechanisms which influenced their actual sleep patterns. And in numerous other studies in the literature of attribution theory and cognitive dissonance theory, the data support a similar conclusion: the mechanisms which control an initial piece of non-verbal behavior are largely distinct from the mechanisms which control the subject's subsequent verbal accounts of the reasons for that behavior.[7]

Stich, if we understand his argument correctly, draws three further conclusions. (1) In cases of the sort described, there is no cogent and consistent way to ascribe beliefs and desires; for FP typically attributes both verbal and non-verbal behavioral effects to particular beliefs and desires, but in these cases the cognitive causes of the non-verbal behavior are distinct from the cognitive causes of the verbal behavior, and hence neither kind of cause can comfortably be identified with a belief or desire. (2) It is likely that *in general* our verbal behavior is controlled by cognitive mechanisms different from those that control our non-verbal behavior; for the Storms–Nisbett pattern emerges in a broad range of studies in attribution theory and dissonance theory. From (1) and (2) he concludes: (3) It is likely that FP is radically false, that is, that humans do not undergo beliefs and desires.

We do not dispute the contention that in a surprising number of cases, as revealed by studies in attribution theory and dissonance theory, the mental states and processes which cause an initial item of non-verbal behavior are distinct from the states and processes which cause a subject's subsequent remarks about the etiology of that behavior. But we deny that either (1) or (2) is warranted by this contention. And without (1) or (2), of course the argument for (3) collapses.

Consider (1). Is there really a problem in consistently ascribing beliefs, desires, and other folk-psychological states in light of the phenomena described in the Storms–Nisbett study, for instance? No. For we can appeal to *unconscious* beliefs, desires, and inferences. Although FP asserts that beliefs and desires *normally* give rise to their own verbal expression under appropriate elicitation conditions, it does not assert this about unconscious beliefs and desires. On the contrary, part of what it means to say that a mental event is unconscious is that it lacks the usual sorts of direct causal influence over verbal behavior. Thus we have available the following natural and plausible folk-psychological account of the subjects' behavior in the Storms – Nisbett study: their initial non-verbal behavior was caused by unconscious beliefs and inferences, whereas their subsequent verbal behavior was caused by distinct, conscious, beliefs about the likely causes of their initial nonverbal behavior.

In short, FP does not break down in such cases, because one has the option – the natural and plausible option – of positing unconscious folk-psychological causes.

There is a temptation, we realize, to identify FP with "what common sense would say," and to take the fact that the Storms–Nisbett results confute our common-sense expectations as automatically falsifying some component of FP. But this temptation should be resisted. Common sense would not postulate the relevant unconscious beliefs and desires. But once we *do* postulate them, perhaps on the basis of rather subtle non-verbal behavioral evidence, FP seems to yield the *correct* predictions about how the subjects will perform in Storms and Nisbett's study.

Indeed, as we understand the views of psychologists like Storms, Nisbett, and Wilson who cite such studies as evidence that verbal and non-verbal behavior often are under separate cognitive controls, this appeal to unconscious folk-psychological causes is precisely the theoretical move *they* are making concerning such cases. Attribution theory and cognitive dissonance theory give center stage to folk-psychological notions like desire and belief. Accordingly, the dual control thesis is nothing other than the folk-psychological thesis just stated: it is the claim that unconscious beliefs and inferences cause the subjects' initial non-verbal behavior, whereas distinct conscious beliefs (which constitute hypotheses about the causes of their original behavior) cause their subsequent verbal behavior.[8] Notice how Stich himself, in the above-quoted passage, describes the first phase of the Storms–Nisbett study. "Attribution theory," he says, "predicts that subjects in the relaxation group will *infer* that their emotionally laden thoughts must be particularly disturbing to them. And this *belief* will upset them further . . ." (emphasis ours). Now Stich may have in mind a way of reinterpreting these claims so that the notions of beliefs and inference they employ are very different from the FP-notions, but in the absence of such a reinterpretation, his contention that beliefs and belief-generating mechanisms cannot be cogently ascribed to subjects like those of Storms and Nisbett is quite unfounded.

Our construal of the dual-control thesis assumes, of course, that it makes sense to speak of beliefs and other mental events as unconscious. But Storms, Nisbett, and Wilson claim quite explicitly that there can be non-verbal behavioral criteria which warrant the ascription of beliefs and other mental events even when a subject's verbal behavior appears inconsistent with the existence of such events.[9]

It may well be that the appeal to these criteria – and to unconscious beliefs and inferences generally – constitutes an extension and partial modification of traditional FP; but even if it does, this is hardly a wholesale rejection of folk-psychological notions. On the contrary, the very naturalness of the appeal to unconscious folk-psychological causes reflects the fact that the overall causal architecture posited by FP remains largely intact even when we introduce the conscious/unconscious distinction.

So conclusion (1) should be rejected. This means that even if (2) were accepted, FP would not necessarily be undermined. But conclusion (2) should be rejected in any case. From the fact that unconscious mental mechanisms control our non-verbal behavior in a surprising number of cases, one may not reasonably infer that *in general* our verbal and non-verbal behavior are under separate cognitive control. The findings of attribution theory and dissonance theory, although they do caution us against excessive confidence in our ability to know ourselves, fall far short of establishing such a sweeping conclusion. In this connection it is useful to examine the remarks of Timothy Wilson (1985), a leading advocate of the idea of "dual cognitive control" over verbal and nonverbal behavior respectively. Stich makes much of Wilson's position, which he construes as the radical thesis that our own statements concerning the mental events that cause our nonverbal behavior are virtually *never* caused by those mental events themselves. But this is a mistaken interpretation, in our judgment. Wilson articulates his proposal this way:

In essence the argument is that there are two mental systems: One which mediates behavior (especially unregulated behavior), is largely nonconscious, and is perhaps, the older of the two systems in evolutionary terms. The other, perhaps newer system, is largely conscious, and its function is to attempt to verbalize, explain, and communicate mental states. As argued earlier, people often have direct access to their mental states, and in these cases the verbal system can make direct and accurate reports. When there is limited access, however, the verbal system makes inferences about what these processes and states might be (p. 16).

It seems clear from this passage that Wilson is not suggesting that *in general* our utterances about our mental events are generated by cognitive events other than those mental events themselves. Rather, he is acknowledging that people often have direct conscious access to the mental causes of their behavior, and that at such times these states typically cause accurate reports about themselves. Only where access is limited, where the events are not conscious, are our subsequent utterances caused by inferences about likely mental causes rather than by the mental events themselves.[10]

Wilson goes on to suggest that it will typically be events that are results of considerable processing which will be relatively inaccessible to the agent, and that "more immediate states" (such as precognitive states) may be much more accessible (p. 39). Moreover, there are many cases which do seem to involve complex processing in which people exhibit integrated verbal and non-verbal behavior in a way that seems difficult to understand if the systems controlling verbal and non-verbal behavior are entirely independent. Consider engaging in some complicated task while explaining to someone else what you are doing – as in working logic problems on the blackboard as one lectures. It is hard to see how such an integrated performance is possible if the actor has no access to the beliefs which cause the non-verbal portion of his behavior (other than via after-the-fact inferences).

We conclude, then, that neither conclusion (1) nor conclusion (2) is warranted by the kinds of psychological studies Stich cites, and hence that his "dual-control" argument against FP is not successful.

III

The "dual-control" argument does not presuppose any particular conception of how FP must be related to CS in order for the two theories to be compatible. Stich's second argument for the incompatibility of FP and CS, however, does rest upon such a conception. In particular, he requires that beliefs, desires, and the like should be identical with "naturally isolable" parts of the cognitive system; he calls this the *modularity* principle.

Stich does not attempt to make this principle precise, but instead leaves the notion of natural isolability at the intuitive level. Accordingly, we too shall use this notion without explication; we think the points we shall make are applicable under any reasonable construal.

Stich argues that FP probably fails to satisfy the modularity principle *vis-á-vis* CS, and hence that there probably are no such events as beliefs, desires, and the like. He focuses on recent trends within CS concerning the modeling of human memory. Some early models of memory organization, he points out, postulate a distinct sentence or sentence-like structure for each memory. These models are clearly modular, he says, because the distinct sentence-like structures can be identified with separate beliefs. Another sort of model, motivated largely by the desire to explain how people are able to locate information relevant to a given task at hand, treats memory as a complex network of nodes and labeled links, with the nodes representing concepts and the links representing various sorts of relations among concepts. Stich regards network models as "still quite far over to the modular end of the spectrum," however, because in a network model it is generally unproblematic to isolate the part of the network which would play the causal role characteristic of a given belief (1983, p. 239).

But in recent years, he points out, several leading theorists have become quite skeptical about highly modular models, largely because such models do not seem capable of handling the enormous amount of non-deductive inference which is involved in language use and comprehension. Citing Minsky (1981) as an example, Stich writes:

> In a . . . recent paper Minsky elaborates what he calls a "Society of Mind" view in which the mechanisms of thought are divided into many separate "specialists that communicate only sparsely" (p. 95). On the picture Minsky suggests, none of the distinct units or parts of the mental model "have meanings in themselves" (p. 100) and thus none can be identified with individual beliefs, desires, etc. Modularity – I borrow the term from Minsky – is violated in a radical way since meaning or content emerges only from "great webs of structure" (p. 100) and no natural part of the system can be correlated with "explicit" or verbally expressible beliefs (1983, p. 241).

If Minsky's "Society of Mind" view is the direction that CS will take in the future, then presumably modularity will indeed be violated in a radical way.

We are quite prepared to acknowledge that CS may well become dramatically non-modular, and hence that the modularity principle may well end up being refuted empirically.[11] Indeed, if one considers the relation between FP and neuroscience – or even the relation between CS and neuroscience, for that matter – one would expect modularity to be violated in an even more dramatic way. There are tens of billions of neurons in the human central nervous system, and thousands of billions of synaptic junctures; so if the "naturally isolable" events of neuroscience are events like neuron-firings and inter-synaptic transfers of electrical energy, then it is entirely likely that the naturally-isolable events of both FP and CS will involve "great webs of structure" neurally – that is, great conglomerations of naturally-isolable neural events.

So if modularity is really needed in order for FP-events to exist and to enter into causal relations, then the failure of modularity would indeed spell big trouble for the proffered compatibility of FP with lower-level theories. In fact, it also would spell big trouble for the proffered compatibility of *cognitive science* with lower-level theories like neuroscience; thus Stich's style of argument appears to prove more than he, as an advocate of CS, would like it to prove! And indeed, the demand for modularity even spells big trouble for the compatibility of *neuroscience* with physics-chemistry; for, if the natural-kind predicates of physics-chemistry are predicates like ". . . is an electron" and ". . . is a hydrogen atom," then it is most unlikely that entities falling under neuroscientific natural-kind terms like ". . . is a neuron" will also fall under physico-chemical natural kind terms. Rather, neurons and neuron-firings are entities which, from the physico-chemical point of view, involve "great webs of structure."

We point out these generalizations of Stich's argument because we think they make clear the enormous implausibility of the modularity principle as an inter-theoretic compatibility condition. Surely objects like neurons, or events like neuron-firings, don't have to be "naturally isolable" from the perspective of fundamental physics-chemistry in order to be compatible with it; rather, it is enough that they be fully decomposable into naturally-isolable *parts*. Similarly, cognitive-psychological events don't have to be naturally isolable from the perspective of neuroscience in order to be compatible with it; again, it is enough that these events are decomposable into naturally-isolable parts.[12]

The situation is exactly the same, we submit, for folk-psychological events in relation to the events of CS. Perhaps Minsky is right, and the role of a belief (say) is typically played by a vast, highly gerrymandered, conglomeration of CS-events. This doesn't show that the belief doesn't exist. On the contrary, all it shows is that the belief is an enormously *complex* event, consisting of numerous CS-events as parts.[13] After all, we expect those CS-events, in turn, to consist of numerous neurological events as parts; and we expect those neurological events, in their turn, to consist of numerous physico-chemical events as parts.

Stich never attempts to justify the modularity principle as a compatibility condition, just as Churchland never attempts to justify the demand for reducibility. Thus Stich's modularity argument suffers the same defect as Churchland's reducibility argument: viz., it rests upon an unsubstantiated, and implausibly strong, conception of how FP must mesh with more comprehensive lower-level theories in order to be compatible with them. (It is important to note, incidentally, that even though Stich does not demand reducibility, still in a certain way his notion of inter-theoretic fit is actually *stronger* than Churchland's notion. For, even a reductionist need not require that entities falling under higher-level natural-kind sortals should be naturally isolable from the lower-level perspective. A reductionist does require that there should be biconditional bridge laws correlating the higher-level sortals with open sentences of the lower-level theory, but these lower-level open sentences can be quite complex, rather than being (say) simple natural-kind sortal predicates.)

Although Stich offers no explicit rationale for the modularity principle, perhaps he is influenced by the following line of thought:

The propositional attitudes of FP involve a relation between a cognizer and a sentence-like "internal representation" (Fodor 1975, 1978; Field 1978; Lycan 1982). If FP is true, then part of the task of CS is to explain the nature of these internal representations. But CS cannot do this unless internal representations fall under its natural-kind predicates, or at any rate are *somehow* "naturally isolable" within the cognitive system. And if Minsky's "Society of Mind" approach is the direction CS will take in the future, then this requirement will not be met. Hence if the events of FP do not obey the modularity principle vis-à-vis CS, then FP must be radically false.

One reason we have for rejecting this line of reasoning is that we doubt whether propositional attitudes really involve internal representations – or whether they have "objects" at all. (Cf. note 1.) Furthermore, if Minsky's approach did become the general trend in CS, then presumably this fact too would tend to undermine the claim that sentence-like representations are involved in the propositional attitudes – just as his approach already tends to undermine the claim that such representations are involved in the non-deductive inference that underlies the use and comprehension of language.

Moreover, even if the internal-representation view is correct, and even if part of the task of CS is to give an account of these representations, approaches like Minsky's would not necessarily render CS incapable of accomplishing this task. For it might turn out that the "atoms" of CS are the components of Minsky's Society of Minds, and that CS also posits complex, sentence-like "molecules" constructed from these "atoms." The molecules might be *very* complex, and highly gerrymandered. If so, then they won't count as naturally isolable components of the cognitive system when that system is viewed from the atomic perspective; however, they *will* count as naturally isolable from the higher, molecular perspective. (We think it more likely, however, that if the "Society of Minds" approach proves generalizable within CS, then the result will be a widespread rejection of the mental-representation view of propositional attitudes – a view which, as we said, we think is mistaken anyway.)

Another way one might try to defend the modularity principle is by appeal to Davidsonian considerations involving the role of laws in causality. One might argue (i) that FP contains no strict laws, but only so-called "heteronomic" generalizations (Davidson 1970, 1974); (ii) that two events are related as cause and effect only if they have descriptions which instantiate a strict law (Davidson 1967); and (iii) that event-descriptions which instantiate a strict law of a given theory must pick out events that are naturally isolable from the perspective of that theory. From these three claims, plus the assumption that folk-psychological events enter into causal relations, the modularity principle seems to follow.[14]

But suppose an event c causes an event e, where c and e both are naturally isolable from the perspective of FP. Suppose that c is fully decomposable into events which respectively satisfy the sortal predicates $F_1 \ldots F_m$ of an underlying homonomic theory T, and hence that these component-events all are naturally isolable from the perspective of T; suppose also that these events jointly satisfy a (possibly quite complex) description D_1 of T which specifies their structural interconnection. Likewise, suppose that e is fully decomposable into events which respectively satisfy the sortal predicates $G_1 \ldots G_n$ of T, and hence that these component events all are naturally isolable from the perspective of T; suppose also that these component events jointly satisfy a description D_2 of T which specifies their structural interconnection. Now even if c and e do not have natural-kind descriptions under which they themselves instantiate a strict law of T, nevertheless the strict laws of T might jointly entail an assertion of the following form:

For any event x, if x is fully decomposable into events $x_1 \ldots x_m$ such that D_1 $(x_1 \ldots x_m)$ and $F_1(x_1)$, $F_2(x_2)$, and $\ldots$ and $F_m(x_m)$, then x will be followed by an event y that is fully decomposable into events $y_1 \ldots y_n$ such that $D_2(y_1 \ldots y_n)$ and $G_1(y_1)$, $G_2(y_2)$, and $\ldots$ and G_n (y_n).

We see no reason why the causal relation between c and e cannot rest upon a regularity of this form. One either can call such regularities strict laws, in which case claim (iii) above will be false; or else one can reserve the term 'strict law' for the relatively simple nomic postulates of a homonomic theory, rather than the set of logical consequences of those postulates – in which case claim (ii) above will be false. Either way, the Davidson-inspired argument for the modularity principle has a false premise. (Incidentally, we do not mean to attribute the argument to Davidson himself, since we doubt whether he would accept claim (iii).)

IV

We have been arguing that FP-events might well be identical with arbitrarily complex, highly gerrymandered, CS-events which themselves are not naturally-isolable relative to CS, but instead are fully decomposable into *parts* which have this feature. Of course, if FP-events really do exist, then they will have to accord with the causal architecture of FP; that is, they will have to be causally related to each other, to sensation, and to behavior in the ways that FP says they are. Indeed, as functionalists in philosophy of mind have so often stressed, the causal or functional principles of FP are crucial to the very individuation of FP-events; what makes a given event count (say) as a token belief-that-p is, to a considerable extent, the fact that it occupies the causal role which FP assigns to tokens of that belief-type.[15]

So if our non-modular picture of the relation between FP and CS is to be plausible, it is essential that complex, gerrymandered events can properly be considered causes, even if they involve "great webs of structure" relative to lower-level theory. While a detailed discussion must be beyond the scope of this paper, a brief consideration of the causal status of complex events will help to clarify our argument.

Let us say that an event e *minimally* causes an event f just in case e causes f and no proper part of e causes f. We want to advance two claims about minimal causation, each of which will receive some support below. First, even if an event e is a genuine cause of an event f, nevertheless f also might be caused by some event which is a proper part of e; thus e might be a genuine cause of f without being a minimal cause of f. Second, if e causes not only f but also some other event g, then it might be that the part of e which minimally causes f is different from the part of e which minimally causes g.[16]

These two facts are important because they make it relatively easy for events to exist which satisfy the causal principles of FP. If FP attributes both the event f and the event g to a single cause e at time t, and in fact there are distinct (though perhaps partially overlapping) events e_1 and e_2 such that e_1 minimally causes f (at t) and e_2 minimally causes g (at t), this does not necessarily falsify FP. For, e might well have both e_1 and e_2 as *parts*; indeed, it might well have as parts all those events with minimally cause (at t) one or another of various events which FP says are effects (at t) of e. As long as this complex event is itself the effect of whatever prior events FP says are e's causes, the event will be (identical with) e.

The upshot is that FP could very easily turn out to be true, even if modularity is dramatically violated. Not only can FP-events be complex and highly gerrymandered, with numerous naturally-isolable CS-events as parts, but any given FP-event e can cause its effects in a conglomerative manner, with different effects having different parts of e as their respectful minimal causes.[17]

V

Perhaps it will be objected that our analysis is too permissive; that unless we adopt Stich's modularity condition, over and above the requirement that FP-events conform to the causal architecture which FP assigns to them, we impose no non-trivial constraints on the truth conditions of upper-level causal claims; that is, we allow such claims to come out true regardless of the character of the theory that underlies them. We shall conclude by considering this objection.

It is clear that some underlying theories are inconsistent with the truth of some upper-level causal claims. For example, if the world is anything like the way our current chemistry and physics describe it, then possession by the devil cannot be a cause of any psychological disorders, and loss of phlogiston cannot be a cause of the chemical changes undergone by metals when they oxidize. To consider a case which is closer to home, it seems clear that if we are Skinnerian creatures – that is, creatures whose behavior is fully described and explained by the basic principles of Skinnerian psychology – then folk-psychological claims postulating beliefs, desires, and the like as among the causes of our behavior cannot be true.

The worry under consideration is that our non-modular approach to inter-theoretic compatibility is so liberal that it would allow claims of the above sort to come out true even though they seem clearly inconsistent with underlying theory. We shall argue that this worry is ill-founded.

It will be helpful to distinguish two different conceptions or expectations regarding the epistemic role of a radical failure of fit or integration between an upper-level theory and an underlying theory. On the first conception one thinks of this failure of fit as an important epistemic route to the falsity of the upper-level theory, where that falsity may not be obvious otherwise. The idea is that even if direct evidence at the upper level does not clearly point to the falsity of an upper-level theory (and indeed may even seem to support this theory), nonetheless we can detect the falsity of the upper-level theory by noting its failure to fit in some appropriate way with some underlying theory which we have strong reason to believe is true. Clearly, both Stich and Churchland argue in accordance with this conception.

We find more plausible an importantly different conception of the epistemic significance of failure of fit between an upper-level and a lower-level theory. We do not deny, of course, that lower-level theories can be incompatible with upper-level theories. We do doubt, however, whether it is common or typical that one can know that an upper-level theory is false only by noting its failure to fit with a true underlying theory. More typically, when an upper-level theory is false there is direct evidence for this fact, independently of the failure of fit. The incompatibility arises not because of a failure of modularity, but rather because there simply are no events – either simple or complex – which have all the features which the upper-level theory attributes to the events it posits. Crudely put, the idea is that while various theories of juvenile delinquency or learning behavior can be inconsistent with neurophysiological theories or with physical theories, the former are *likely* to be confirmable or disconfirmable by the sorts of evidence available to sociologists and psychologists. It will be rare for a theory to be supported by a very wide range of evidence available to the sociologist or the psychologist and yet turn out to be radically false (because its ontology fails to mesh properly with that of some underlying theory). So our conception suggests a greater epistemological autonomy for upper-level disciplines like psychology than does a conception of inter-theoretic compatibility which incorporates a modularity condition.

We have emphasized this epistemological point because it bears directly on worries about the permissiveness of our non-modular conception. While our approach is by no means trivial in the sense that it allows every upper-level theory to be compatible with every underlying theory, it is permissive and deflationary in that, at least for a wide variety of cases, considerations of fit will not play the sort of independent normative role which they would play under a modularity requirement.

With this in mind, let us return to the examples with which we began this section. Consider first the case of possession by the devil. Like other causally explanatory notions, the notion of possession by the devil is to be understood, in large measure, in terms of the role it plays in a network of causal relations. Possession by the devil causes or may cause various kinds of pathological behavior. Such effects may be diminished or eliminated by the use of appropriate religious ceremonies (e.g., prayers or exorcism). When behavior is due to possession by the devil, there is no reason to suppose that it will be affected by other forms of treatment (drugs, nutritional changes, psychotherapy, etc.). The state of possession is itself the effect of the activities of a being who has many other extraordinary powers.

Now if an event of possession by the devil (call it d) is to be a cause of a certain bit of behavior (e.g., jabbering incoherently), then d must, on our analysis, be identifiable with some event (call it e) describable in terms of the predicates of our underlying theory; and it must be the case that, given this identification, at least most of the other causal generalizations in which d is held to figure, according to the theory of devil-possession, should come out true. (Although our conception of inter-theoretic fit countenances failures of modularity, it does insist that the identifications we make preserve the "causal architecture" of the upper-level theory.) We submit that no matter how large and complex one makes the event e with which one proposes to identify d, and no matter how willing one may be to regard proper parts of e as causally efficacious, there is simply *no* plausible candidate for e which, given our present physical and chemical theory, will make the network of causal claims associated with possession by the devil come out mainly true. That is, there is simply no event e, however complex, which is linked by law to various forms of behavior associated with possession, which is inefficacious in producing such behavior when exorcism is used, which is shown by law to be produced by an agency having the properties of the devil, and so forth.

This example illustrates the general epistemological claim made above. In effect, we have argued that causal claims about possession by the devil are false not because of sophisticated considerations having to do with modularity (or with "smoothness of reduction"), but because the causal architecture associated with possession by the devil is radically mistaken; nothing stands in the network of causal relations with various other events in the way that possession by the devil is supposed to. We can see this immediately by noting that the falsity of claims attributing causal efficacy to devil-possession is, so to speak, directly discoverable without considerations having to do with chemistry, physics, or biology. If one were to run suitably controlled experiments, then presumably one would quickly discover that exorcism does not affect devil-possession type behavior, that certain other therapies do, and so forth.[18]

A similar set of observations seems relevant in connection with the allegation that our approach would permit causal claims about beliefs to be true even if we are Skinnerian creatures. FP asserts that beliefs, desires, and other propositional attitudes are related to one another in many and various ways, over and above their causal relations to sensation and behavior. Skinnerian theory, on the other hand, denies that we need to postulate such richly-interacting internal events in order to explain behavior, and it also denies that such events exist at all. Rather, the Skinnerian claims that the causal chains leading from environmental "stimulus" to behavioral "response" are largely isolated from one another, rather like the various parallel non-interacting communication-channels in a fiber-optics communications line; thus, whatever internal events are involved in any particular stimulus–response pairing will not bear very many significant causal relations to the internal events that are involved in other stimulus–response pairings; that is, the Skinnerian claims that as a matter of empirical fact, the generalizations linking stimuli and behavior are so simple and straightforward that they are incompatible with the existence of internal events which interact in the rich way which folk-psychological events are supposed to interact with one another. So if the Skinnerian is right, then there simply are no internal events, in humans or in other organisms, which bear all the causal relations to sensation, to behavior, and to one another which FP assigns to beliefs, desires, and the like. Thus our non-modular conception of inter-theoretic fit would indeed be violated if humans should turn out to be mere Skinnerian creatures. Accordingly, this conception is not unduly permissive after all.

This example also illustrates the epistemological claims made above. It is satisfaction of the "causal architecture" of FP, by some set of (possibly complex) events in the central nervous system, which is crucial to the truth of FP. Hence if we are Skinnerian creatures, so that the causal architecture assumed by FP is not instantiated in us by any events either simple or complex, then presumably this fact will show up at the level of a relatively coarse-grained analysis of our molar behavior. Stimulus–response laws that are incompatible with the causal architecture of FP will be discoverable, and will be usable to explain and predict the full range of human behavior. Hence it will not be the case that FP seems to be largely true, according to the best available coarse-grained evidence, and yet turns out to be false merely because of failure to fit properly with some underlying theory.

The upshot, then, is that our approach seems exactly as permissive as it should be, and this fact speaks in its favor; by contrast, a modular conception of inter-theoretic fit seems excessively strict, since it is un-motivated and it denies higher-level theories an adequate degree of epistemological autonomy. So, given (i) the notable failure, to date, of behaviorist-inspired psychology's efforts to unearth stimulus–response laws which are applicable to human behavior generally and which undercut the causal architecture of FP, (ii) the fact that folk-psychological notions seem to lie at the very heart of cognitivist theories like attribution theory and cognitive dissonance theory, and (iii) the fact that FP serves us very well in the everyday explanation and prediction of behavior, it seems very hard to deny that in all probability, folk psychology is here to stay.[19,20,21]

Notes

1. Actually, we regard the example in the first paragraph as a schema which yields a whole range of instances when various sentences are substituted for the letter 'p' and various sortal predicates are substituted for the dummy phrase 'of kind K'. (The word 'someone', though, functions as a quantificational term; under appropriate regimentation, it would go over into a universal quantifier whose scope is the whole schema.) We prefer to think of predicates of the form ". . . believes that p" as what Quine (1970) calls *attitudinatives* – i.e., complex one-place predicates constructed by appending a predicate-forming operator ('believes that') to a sentence. On this view, propositional attitudes have no "objects," since they are not relational states. For further discussion see Horgan (1988).
2. For visual perception, see, e.g., Gregory (1970).
3. For example, eighteenth century chemical theories attempted to explain such properties of metals as their shininess and ductility by appeal to the same factors which were also thought to explain the compound-forming behavior of metals. Chemical theories such as Lavoisier's focused just on compounds, and originally were criticized for their failure to provide also a unified explanation of metallic shininess and ductility.
4. For some striking evidence that situational theories are more empirically adequate, and hence that this change has been a progressive one, see Nisbett and Ross (1980).
5. Thus his critical remarks on Fodor (1975), and in general on cognitive psychological theories that take information to be stored in sentential form; cf. Churchland (1981, pp. 78 ff.).
6. In order to elevate anomalous monism into a full-fledged version of materialism, one must add to it an account of the metaphysical status of mental state-types (properties) *vis-à-vis* physico-chemical state-types. The appropriate doctrine, we think, is one also propounded by Davidson (1970, 1974): viz., that mental properties are *supervenient* upon physical ones. Several philosophers recently have developed this idea, arguing that materialism should incorporate some sort of supervenience thesis. Cf. Kim (1978, 1982); Haugeland (1982); Horgan (1981b, 1982b); and Lewis (1983). Also see the papers collected in the Spindel issue of *The Southern Journal of Philosophy*, 22, 1984.
7. For surveys of the relevant literature, see Nisbett and Wilson (1977), and Wilson (1985).
8. At any rate, this is what the dual-control thesis amounts to as regards the Storms–Nisbett study. Other kinds of mental events besides beliefs and inferences might sometimes be involved too.
9. See, for instance, Wilson (1985), pp. 10 ff.
10. Still, one can understand why Stich would be led to attribute the radical dual-control thesis to Wilson, even though Wilson evidently does not actu-

ally hold this view. Stich quotes from what evidently was an earlier version of the above-quoted passage, wherein Wilson said that the function of the verbal system "is to attempt to verbalize, explain and communicate what is occurring in the unconscious system." Admittedly, this earlier wording suggests that in verbalizing our mental states we *never* have conscious access to those states. But the present passage, with its explicit acknowledgment of frequent conscious access, evidently cancels this suggestion, along with any implicit commitment to the radical dual-control thesis.

11. Although we think it quite possible that CS will become non-modular at its most fundamental levels, we also believe that certain higher-level branches of theoretical psychology probably not only will remain modular, but will continue to employ the concepts of FP itself. Attribution theory is a case in point. (By a "higher-level" psychological theory we mean one which posits events that are wholes whose parts are the events posited by "lower-level" psychological theories. More on this below.)

12. It is worth noting another respect in which Stich's (and Churchland's) arguments seem to lead to sweeping and implausibly strong conclusions. Much formal theory in the social sciences involves ascribing to individual actors states which are recognizably like, or recognizably descended from, the FP notions of belief and desire. Within economic and game theory, for example, individual actors are thought of as having indifference curves, utility schedules, or preference orderings over various possible outcomes, and beliefs about the subjective probabilities of these outcomes. Within economic theories of voting or political party behavior, similar assumptions are made. Even among theorists of voting behavior who reject the "economic" approach, typically there are appeals to voters' beliefs and attitudes to explain behavior. (See, for example, Campbell *et al.* (1960).) Clearly, if Stich's modularity requirement and Churchland's smoothness of reduction requirement are not satisfied by the FP notions of belief and desire, then they are unlikely to be satisfied by the notions of utility, degree of belief, and so forth employed by such theories. Thus Stich and Churchland seem to have produced general arguments which, if cogent, would show – quite independently of any detailed empirical investigation of the actual behavior of markets, voters, etc. – that all these theories must be false, at least on their most natural interpretation.

13. A complex event of the relevant kind might be a mereological sum, or *fusion*, of simpler events; alternatively, it might be an entity distinct from this event-fusion. We shall take no stand on this matter here. (The issue is closely related to the question whether an entity like a ship is identical with the fusion of its physical parts, or is instead an entity distinct from this fusion, with different intra-world and trans-world identity conditions.) To our knowledge, the most explicit and well-developed theory of parts and wholes for events is that of Thomson (1977); event-fusions are the only kinds of complex events she explicitly countenances.

14. This Davidsonian argument was suggested to us by Stich himself, in conversation.

15. But as the famous case of Twin Earth (Putnam, 1975) seems to show, an event's causal role is not the only factor relevant to its folk-psychological

individuation. Our *doppelgangers* on Twin Earth don't undergo tokens of the type *believing that water is good to drink*, even though they do undergo events that are functionally indistinguishable from our own token beliefs that water is good to drink. The trouble is that the stuff they call "water" isn't water at all. Cf. Burge (1979).

16. While a full defense of these claims must be beyond the scope of this paper, we think they are required for the truth of many causal statements in contexts where highly developed and precise formal theories are not available. Consider the claims (a) that application of a certain fertilizer causes plants to increase in mean height, and also causes them to increase in leaf width; (b) that following a certain study routine R causes an increase in SAT verbal scores, and also causes an increase in SAT mathematical scores; or (c) that certain child-rearing practices cause an increase in the incidence of juvenile delinquency in certain populations. There is an enormous literature detailing complex and ingenious statistical techniques for testing such claims. (Fischer (1935) is an early classic, inspired largely by problems connected with testing claims like (a); and many books on "causal modeling," like Blalock (1971), discuss procedures that are relevant to (b) and (c).) These techniques might well establish that the three claims are true. Yet the cases described in (a), (b), and (c) can easily fail to be minimal causes: the fertilizer will commonly be a mixture, containing compounds which are inert, or which have other effects on the plant besides those mentioned in (a); and it seems implausible to suppose that every feature or detail of study routine R or child rearing practice C is causally necessary for the above effects. (Typically, we have no practical way of determining what the minimal causes in such cases are.) Thus (a) can be true even though the fertilizer is a mixture of several distinct compounds, one of which causes increase in height (but not increase in leaf width) while the other causes increase in leaf width (but not height). Similarly, (b) can be true even though different aspects of study routine R are responsible for the increases in math and in verbal scores. (See Thomson (1977) for further defense of the claim that genuine causes don't have to be minimal causes.)

17. The point about conglomerative causation is also relevant to Stich's dual-control argument against FP. Even if verbal and non-verbal behavior should turn out to have largely separate minimal causes, FP could be true anyway; for, FP-events might be complexes of the minimal causes, and these complex events might be genuine causes (albeit non-minimal causes) of both the verbal and the non-verbal behavior. (We should stress, however, that we are *not* claiming that if the dual-control thesis is true, then whenever a subject is in some state B of his nonverbal behavioral system and some state V of his verbal system, it will always be possible, consistently with FP, to ascribe to him some single folk-psychological cause of both his verbal and non-verbal behavior. Whether this will be possible depends upon the specific states V and B and upon the behavior they cause. In the Storms–Wilson insomnia experiment, for example, the state B (subjects' attribution of their symptoms to pills) which causes the arousal group to fall asleep is not merely distinct from the state V which causes their verbal behavior (denial that the above attribution had anything to do with their falling asleep); but in addition, these two states cannot, consistently with the causal principles embodied in FP, be treated as components of some single belief.)

18. Of course, it might be that some cases of exorcism appear to be efficacious, but this is only because they involve certain features which are also cited by other, more secular, theories (e.g., reassuring the "possessed" person, giving him attention, etc.). Establishing this can require ingenuity in experimental design, but poses no problem in principle. It is just false that we could never obtain direct experimental evidence (distinct from considerations of modularity or failure of fit) that would make it rational to reject the claim that exorcism is efficacious in itself, by virtue of dislodging the devil.

19. Although we have assumed throughout that folk-psychological events are complex events consisting of lower-level events as their parts, we want to acknowledge that it may be possible to defend the compatibility of FP and CS without this assumption. Jaegwon Kim (1966, 1969, 1973) holds that an event is an entity consisting in the instantiation of a property by an object at a time, and that mental events consist in the instantiation of mental properties by individuals at times. Under this approach, it is unclear whether lower-level events can sensibly be treated as parts of FP-events. Nevertheless, an advocate of Kim's theory of events still might be able to argue that FP-events exist and bear all the causal relations to one another that FP says they do. For he might be able to argue that these events are supervenient upon groups of lower-level events, and that supervenience transmits causal efficacy. Cf. Kim (1979, 1982, 1984).

20. Throughout this paper we have assumed, as is usual, that if everyday folk-psychological statements are indeed true, then there really exist folk-psychological mental events – that is, token desires, token beliefs, and so forth. In fact, however, one of us (Horgan) thinks there are good reasons for denying the existence of events in general; cf. Horgan (1978, 1981a, 1982a). Horgan also thinks that if physico-chemical events exist, then normally there will be numerous classes of physico-chemical events from within someone's head which jointly meet all the causal conditions which would qualify a given class for identification with the class consisting of that person's folk-psychological mental events; and he takes this to indicate that even if physico-chemical events exist, and even if garden-variety folk-psychological statements (including statements about mental causation) are often true, nevertheless there really are no such entities as mental events; cf. Horgan and Tye (1985). We believe that the essential points of the present paper can be reformulated in a way which does not require the existence of mental events (even if physico-chemical events are assumed to exist), and also in a way which does not require the existence of any events at all. But our objective here has been the more limited one of defending FP within the framework of the ontology of events which is widely taken for granted in contemporary philosophy of mind.

21. We thank Stephen Stich, William Tolhurst, and Michael Tye for helpful comments on an earlier version of this paper.

References

Blalock, H., ed. (1971). *Causal Models in the Social Sciences*, New York, Aldine.

Burge, T. (1979). "Individualism and the Mental," in P. French, T. Uehling, and H. Wettstein, eds., *Midwest Studies in Philosophy*, Vol. 4, *Studies in Epistemology*, Minneapolis, University of Minnesota Press.

Campbell, A., Converse, P., Miller, W., Stokes, D. (1960). *The American Voter*, New York, John Wiley and Sons.

Churchland, P. (1979). *Scientific Realism and the Plasticity of Mind*, New York, Cambridge.

Churchland, P. (1981). "Eliminative Materialism and Propositional Attitudes," *Journal of Philosophy*, 78.

Davidson, D. (1967), "Causal Relations," *Journal of Philosophy*, 64.

Davidson, D. (1970). "Mental Events," in L. Foster and J. Swanson, eds., *Experience and Theory*, London, Duckworth.

Davidson, D. (1973). "The Material Mind," in P. Suppes *et al.*, eds., *Logic, Methodology, and the Philosophy of Science*, Vol. 4, Amsterdam, North Holland.

Davidson, D. (1974). "Psychology as Philosophy," in S. Brown, ed., *Philosophy of Psychology*, New York, Harper and Row.

Dennett, D. (1978). *Brainstorms*, Cambridge, MA, Bradford.

Dennett, D. (1981). "Three Kinds of Intentional Psychology," in R. Healey, ed., *Reduction, Time, and Identity*, New York, Cambridge.

Field, H. (1978). "Mental Representation," *Erkenntnis*, 13.

Fisher, R. (1935). *The Design of Experiments*, Edinburgh, Oliver and Boyd.

Fodor, J. (1975). *The Language of Thought*, New York, Thomas Y. Crowell.

Fodor, J. (1978). "Propositional Attitudes," *The Monist*, 61.

Gregory, R. (1970). *The Intelligent Eye*, New York, McGraw-Hill.

Haugeland, J. (1982). "Weak Supervenience," *American Philosophical Quarterly*, 19.

Horgan, T. (1978). "The Case Against Events," *The Philosophical Review*, 87.

Horgan, T. (1981a). "Action Theory Without Actions," *Mind*, 90.

Horgan, T. (1981b). "Token Physicalism, Supervenience, and the Generality of Physics," *Synthese*, 34.

Horgan, T. (1982a). "Substitutivity and the Causal Connective," *Philosophical Studies*, 42.

Horgan, T. (1982b). "Supervenience and Microphysics," *Pacific Philosophical Quarterly*, 63.

Horgan, T. (1988). "Attitudinatives." *Linguistics and Philosophy*, 12.

Horgan, T., and Tye, M. (1985). "Against the Token Identity Theory," in E. LePore and B. McLaughlin eds., *Essays on Actions and Events*.

Kim, J. (1969). "Events and Their Descriptions: Some Considerations," in N. Rescher *et al.*, eds., *Essays in Honor of Carl G. Hempel*, Dordrecht, Reidel.

Kim, J. (1973). "Causation, Nomic Subsumption, and the Concept of Event," *Journal of Philosophy*, 70.

Kim, J. (1978). "Supervenience and Nomological Incommensurables," *American Philosophical Quarterly*, 15.

Kim, J. (1979). "Causality, Identity, and Supervenience in the Mind–Body Problem," *Midwest Studies in Philosophy*, 4.

Kim, J. (1982). "Psychophysical Supervenience," *Philosophical Studies*, 41.

Kim, J. (1984). "Supervenience and Supervenient Causation," *Southern Journal of Philosophy*, 22.

Lewis, D. (1983). "New Work for a Theory of Universals," *Australian Journal of Philosophy*, 61.

Lycan, W. (1982). "Toward a Homuncular Theory of Believing," *Cognition and Brain Theory*, 4.

Minsky, M. (1981). "K-Lines: A Theory of Memory," in D. Norman, ed., *Perspectives on Cognitive Science*, Norwood, N.J., Ablex.

Nisbett, R., and Ross, L. (1980). *Human Inference: Strategies and Shortcomings of Social Judgment*, Englewood Cliffs, N.J., Prentice-Hall.

Nisbett, R., and Wilson, T. (1977). "Telling More Than We Can Know: Verbal Reports on Mental Processes," *Psychological Review*, 84.

Putnam, H. (1975). "The Meaning of 'Meaning'," in K. Gunderson, ed., *Language, Mind, and Knowledge, Minnesota Studies in the Philosophy of Science*, 7, Minneapolis, University of Minnesota Press.

Quine, W. V. O. (1970). *Philosophy of Logic*, Englewood Cliffs, N.J., Prentice-Hall.

Stich, S. (1983). *From Folk Psychology to Cognitive Science: The Case Against Belief*, Cambridge, MA, Bradford.

Storms, M. and Nisbett, R. (1970). "Insomnia and the Attribution Process," *Journal of Personality and Social Psychology*, 2.

Thomson, J. (1977). *Acts and Other Events*, Ithaca, Cornell.

Wilson, T. (1985). "Strangers to Ourselves: The Origins and Accuracy of Beliefs About One's Own Mental States," in J. H. Harvey and G. Weary, eds., *Attribution in Contemporary Psychology*, New York, Academic Press.

8 Folk-psychological explanations
Jonathan Bennett

Before we can reasonably decide anything about the future of folk psychology, we need a better grasp of what it is and how it works. Since folk psychology more or less defines our chief psychological concepts, exploring it is doing conceptual analysis. Many philosophers these days condemn conceptual analysis or condescend to it; I don't join them, but I shall not argue with them here.

In this essay, I hope to contribute to the understanding of folk psychology by setting out the reasons why the generalizations on which folk psychology rests are *explanatory*, reasons that do not require us to get mired in the question of whether those generalizations are *causal*.

I. Intentionality in simple systems?

We must start with the belief–desire–behavior triangle. The founding triangular idea is that a thinking system *does* what it *thinks* will bring about what it *wants*. Two of these three concepts are said to involve 'intentionality'; a better, because more explanatory, label is 'cognitive teleology' – what a system has if it has thoughts that guide it to its goals.

The conceptual structure that this involves is illustrated by the behavior of a thermostat: The thermostat "wants" the room to be warmer, "thinks" that closing the switch will bring this about, and accordingly closes the switch. This structure is not illustrated by the vending machines that have been used for that purpose by Ned Block. He describes a machine that will give you a Coke for a dime when it is in state S_1 and will give you a Coke for a nickel when it is in state S_2 (you get it from S_1 to S_2 by putting a nickel in), and he describes state S_2 as a low-level analog of *desire for a nickel*.[1] This has nothing to be said in its favor. There is no truth of the form "When the machine is in state S_2 it does what it 'thinks' will bring it a nickel"; thus the most elementary, nonnegotiable aspect of intentionality or cognitive teleology is absent. The same applies to the use of a vending machine in the one unsuccessful chapter of Dennett's (1987) book.[2]

Though thermostats are to be favored over vending machines, they should be approached gingerly. I don't side with those who get furious when Dennett writes indulgently of taking the "intentional stance" toward a thermostat; on the contrary, there is something to be learned from doing just that. But there is also something wrong about doing it, as I shall now explain.

All the behavior of the thermostat that might be handled teleologically, or in intentional terms, is explained by a single mechanism, a single kind of causal chain that can be fully described without any use of intentional concepts. We can replace "The thermostat does what it can to keep the temperature of the room close to 68°" with "The thermostat's switch closes whenever its temperature falls to 66° and opens whenever its temperature rises to 70°," and we can explain the latter generalization without any mention of 68° as a goal and without mentioning beliefs and desires or anything like them.

In short, the one intentional account of the thermostat's behavior is matched by a single physicalistic account; and I submit that when that is the case, the latter account should prevail and the former, though perhaps stimulating and interesting for philosophical purposes, is false and should be rejected. For genuine teleology or intentionality, I contend, *the unity condition* must be satisfied. That is, a system x's intentionality is genuine only if

> Some class of x's inputs/outputs falls under a single intentional account – involving a single goal-kind G such that x behaved on those occasions because on each of them it thought that what it was doing was the way to get G – and does not fall under any one mechanistic generalization.

Where that is satisfied, applying intentional concepts to the system brings a conceptual *unity* to some set of facts about it – a set that is not unifiable under a mechanistic description.

The unity condition marks off the systems some of whose behavior falls into intentional patterns that are not coexistive with mechanistic patterns. Only if a system's behavior satisfies that condition, I contend, is it legitimate for us to exploit its intentional patterns in our thought and speech. The marking-off is of course a matter of degree. It rejects intentionality when the intentional pattern coincides with a single mechanistic one; it welcomes it when such a pattern uses thousands of different mechanisms; and it gives an intervening judgment – "intentionality in this case is so-so, permissible but not very good" – for many intermediate cases.

The fuzzy line drawn by the unity condition seems to correspond roughly with much of our intuitive sense of which systems do and which systems do not have thoughts and wants. Consider a chameleon flicking out its tongue and catching a fly with it. One can plausibly think of this activity as goal-pursuing behavior: It wants to eat the fly and thinks that this activity is the way to bring that about. But suppose we find that one uniform physical mechanism controls this pattern of behavior – a relatively simple causal tie between proximity of fly and movement of tongue, and between location of fly and direction of tongue movement, with, in each case, a few parameters in the one governing a few parameters in the other. Thoughtful people will regard this as evidence that the cognitive-teleological account of the behavior was wrong because really only a single mechanism was involved. The plausibility of the response "Oh, so *that's* all it was" is evidence for the truth of the unity thesis.

The thesis also corresponds to the best *defense* there is for using intentional concepts.

The question of the legitimacy of intentional explanations of behavior ought to be faced squarely. Since chemical explanations involve principles that go wider and deeper, and theoretically admit of greater precision, why should they not always be preferred to explanations in terms of thoughts and wants?

Some of the more libertine and "instrumental" ways of talking about intentionality have given the impression that no justification is needed – that it is simply up to us to decide whether we want to talk and think in a certain way about people and thermostats and vending machines and lecterns. I hope that nobody really believes that.

If justification is to be given, there are three prima facie possible ways of doing this: (1) The most completely justifying (were it true), but also the least credible, is the Cartesian thesis that some animal movements cannot be explained chemically but can be explained in terms of thoughts and wants. (2) The next strongest justification is the one yielded by my unity thesis, as I shall explain in a moment. (3) Finally, there is the fact that we often don't know the chemical explanation, which entitles us to use intentional explanations *faute de mieux*.

Evidently (1) is not available in the actual world, and it would be a sad day for belief and desire if (3) was the best we could do. So let us focus on (2), which says that an intentional explanation of the given behavior brings out patterns, provides groupings and comparisons, that a chemical explanation would miss. What the animal did belongs to a class of behaviors in which it wants food and does what it thinks will provide food; there is no unitary chemical explanation that covers just this range of data. This animal seeks food in many different ways, triggered by different sensory inputs, and it is not credible that a mechanistic, physiological view of the facts will reveal any unity in them that they don't share with behaviors that were not food-seeking at all. If this unifying view of the facts satisfies our interests, gives us one kind of understanding of the animal, and facilitates predictions of a kind that are otherwise impossible (e.g., predictions like "It will go after that rabbit somehow"), we have reason for adopting it. These reasons leave us free still to acknowledge that each of the explained facts, taken separately, admits of an explanation that is deeper and more wide-ranging and – other things being equal – preferable.[3]

II. Some objections answered

When I first said this, Davidson thought I had implied that a thing could lose its entitlement to intentional treatment because we discovered a single mechanism underlying all the input–output relations that we had hitherto grouped under some generalization about thoughts and wants.[4] That was a misunderstanding. The line around fully legitimate intentional explanations depends upon whether there is a single mechanism, not on whether we know it.

Peacocke has rejected my unity thesis because it implies "that if we discover a creature that has only one way of catching flies, an intentional explanation of the creature's behavior is spurious."[5] This does not address itself to the question of how the "intentional stance" is to be justified with respect to a given animal, and presumably it is meant as a naked appeal to conceptual intuition. That is all right: If the appeal were a resounding enough success, that would be evidence that I have been talking about something that, however worthy and interesting, is not the conceptual underlay of our ordinary uses of the words "think," "want," "intend," "in order to," and so forth. Peacocke's appeal to intuition, however, has no such success. In fact, there are two different things it might be: One of them is not true, and the other does not conflict with my account: (1) If Peacocke's creature catches flies by a technique that involves one motor kind movement upon receipt of one sensory kind of stimulus, there is no strong intuitive support for the claim that this is cognitively guided, goal-seeking behavior. I would think worse of my theory if it implied that such a creature brought thoughts and wants, or any analogue of them, to bear on its getting of food. (2) If the behavior in question involves one kind of movement upon receipt of a wide variety of different sensory clues, that does look like cognitive teleology, but then it also conforms to the unity condition. I have tended to illustrate the condition by contrasting simple-input/ simple-output with complex-input/complex-output, but I didn't have to. So long as the input side is complex in the right way, the behaviors in question can't be brought under a single nonintentional explanation; and that is all I demand.[6]

I have met the objection that if the legitimacy of the intentional stance depends on the unity condition, then we ought never to have much confidence, of any organism, that it really does have thoughts and wants. "Given how little we know about what in detail goes on in the central nervous systems of animals," the challenge goes, "how could we be entitled to think that a given range of behavior was probably not under the control of a single mechanism?" I think we could easily be entitled to think this. Our generalization implying that the animal does what it thinks will bring it food brings together a certain class of behaviors and a certain class of sensory inputs. Among the behaviors are cases of running, dodging, climbing, digging, swimming, leaping, biting, keeping still, keeping quiet, and so forth – involving lots of different muscles and different uses of some of the same muscles. The sensory inputs include a variety of different kinds of sight, smell, and sound. In the light of all this, we are soberly entitled to suppose that no one mechanism explains all this behavior.

III. Developing the unity thesis

We have a mechanistic generalization if all the relevant inputs are of some one *sensory* kind and all the relevant outputs are of one *motor* kind.[7] The emphasized adjectives are important. If in the relevant class of situations, x is confronted by evidence that something it could do would lead it to food, its inputs all belong to a single kind, namely the kind "constituting evidence that something x can do would lead it to food"; but this is an *evidential* and not a *sensory* kind. What unites the inputs is something that involves the notion of seeming, or of evidence, or the like, and not something that could be stated just in the language of the intrinsic nature of inputs. Similarly, if in the relevant class of situations, x always moves in some way that is likely to get food, those movements belong to the kind "being likely to lead to getting food"; but this is an *instrumental* and not a *motor* kind; that is, it is a kind defined in terms of probable upshot, not in terms of the intrinsic nature of movements.

(Whether a class of situations falls within a single sensory kind depends not on how its members strike us but on how they strike the animal x whose behavior we are trying to explain. Even if it seems to us that the relevant class of inputs have in common only that in each of them there is evidence that some other animal is frightened, it might be that in all of those situations x detects a single characteristic kind of smell, in which case x's inputs in those situations belong to a single sensory kind. On the other hand, it presumably couldn't happen that we find only an instrumental kind of unity among the outputs although there is a motor kind from the standpoint of x.)

A class of situations covered by something of the form "x receives input of sensory kind K_S and makes a movement of motor kind K_M" might *also* be covered by something of the form "x receives evidence that it can do something that will lead to G, and it does that something." But the sensorimotor generalization prevails over the evidential–instrumental one. We are not fully entitled to employ the latter unless that is our only way of brining the phenomena under a single generalization.

So what is needed for a justified intentional explanation, abstractly stated, is a class of behavioral episodes whose inputs all answer to this description and to no "lower" one:

> There is a kind K of movement such that (1) x gets sensory evidence that if it performs a K movement it will get G, and (2) x performs a K movement.

From now on, to keep things simple, I shall focus on the (1) component of the analysis, leaving (2) to tag along unaided.

The unity thesis helps with a problem that is aired at some length in Dennett's first paper on cognitive ethology.[8] There is a tendency to think that any behavioral regularity is probably due to hard wiring ("tropism" or "instinct" are Dennett's terms), or to a low-level acquired stimulus–response pattern. In Dennett's (p. 348a) words:

The oft-repeated, oft-observed, stereotypic behavior of a species . . . is just the sort of behavior that reveals no particular intelligence at all – all this behavior can be explained as the effects of some humdrum combination of "instinct" or tropism and conditioned response. It is the novel bits of behavior, the acts that couldn't plausibly be accounted for in terms of prior conditioning or training or habit, that speak eloquently of intelligence.

But the alternative to oft-repeated kinds of behavior are the behavioral episodes that get reported in anecdotes, and we are assured that real science cannot be based on those. This threatens to close down any gap through which we might conduct a scientific – or at least a respectably disciplined – study of cognition, especially high-level cognition.

Dennett's (p.348 b–c) solution is to say that anecdotes may be all right if we have lots of them, as we do to support our opinions about one another's mental level: "As we pile anecdote upon anecdote, apparent novelty upon apparent novelty, we build up for each acquaintance such a biography of *apparent* cleverness that the claim that it is all just lucky coincidence – or the result of hitherto undetected 'training' – becomes the more extravagant hypothesis." But he does not discuss how piling up anecdotes differs from discovering a behavioral regularity, nor does he spell out what makes an anecdote evidence of "apparent cleverness." I shall make a suggestion about that shortly.

What Dennett calls (apparent) "novelty" is what used to be called "insight." It is a real phenomenon, but in the initial "insight" literature it was often implied to involve intellectual feats that owed nothing to the animal's past experience. If that were really the case, the feats would have to be (if not miraculous) hard-wired, mere tropisms having their first outing, and therefore not evidence of high-level intellect. A better way of viewing such "novelties" is this: The animal solves a "new" problem, or finds a "new" solution for an old problem, by extrapolating or generalizing from its past experience *across an impressively large qualitative gap.* (It probably got across the gap with help from imaginary trial-and-error approaches to the problem, and that is impressive too.)[9] What impresses Dennett about it is the evidence it gives that the animal's successes in achieving its goals are not all products of habit, dumb training, or low-level conditioning. That seems right, but I don't think it is quite central to the issue that Dennett and I are wrestling with. It is an approach to "Is this dumb tropism or something higher?" that seems to offer no help at all with the question "Is this a little higher than dumb tropism or a lot higher?" The account I shall give should help the reader with the second question as well as with the first. The "novelty" or "insight" idea is not something I shall discuss, but I think it can be simply added to what I shall say.

Anecdotes are also made more admissible, Dennett (p. 348d) says, if they report episodes that were controlled by the anecdotalist: "Similar stratagems can be designed to test the various hypotheses about the beliefs and desires of vervet monkeys and other creatures. These stratagems have the virtue of provoking novel but interpretable behavior, of generating anecdotes under controlled (and hence scientifically admissible) conditions." I submit that control has nothing to do with it. When you know what you are looking for, control gives you a better chance of finding it; but that is a practical convenience, and cannot help with the basic problem of how to get scientifically valid results from data that are not about regularities. A solution to that problem has to depend on what the results are, not on how they were arrived at – for example, whether through a controlled experiment or just through passively observing an animal with which one was not interfering at all.

The right solution, I suggest, is as follows: If we cannot bring a given behavioral episode under a generalization about that animal's behavior, we cannot confidently make *anything* of it – that it manifests thoughts and wants or, for that matter, that it comes from instinct or low-level stimulus–response. So we need generalizations about the animal's behavior, which is to say that we need behavioral regularities; and the problem is to say *what marks off the regularities that are evidence of high-level cognition from those that are not*.

Here is what does it: If the generalization that we establish about the animal's inputs and outputs colligates the data under sensory kinds of input and motor kinds of output, it provides no evidence of cognitive mentality; but if it pulls the inputs together in evidential rather than sensory kinds, and if there is no "lower" unity to the inputs, then the behavior in question is evidence that the animal behaves as it does because of beliefs and desires.

What Dennett calls "piling up anecdotes" might be the accumulation of plenty of evidence for a generalization about a class of sensorily diverse inputs and perhaps outputs that are diverse in their motor respects. Reports on such episodes might be called "anecdotes" just because of their sensory and perhaps motor diversity. If they are Dennett's topic, then what he says is right, but his presentation is misleading. Once the content of the relevant generalizations is understood, we can see that there is really no tension or difficulty here at all, and we need not be pushed into giving weight to an unexamined notion of "novelty" or a fundamentally irrelevant notion of "control."

IV. Further use for the unity thesis

It is often held by philosophers of mind that there are senses of "higher" and "lower" that make true something that Dennett has called *Lloyd Morgan's Canon*: "If two hypotheses about an animal equally fit its behavior, and one attributes to it mental capacities that are higher than those attributed by the other, the latter hypothesis should be preferred." If something like this is right, the unity thesis might be seen as the special case of it where the higher attribution involves some cognitive mentality and the lower involves none. In other special cases both competitors would attribute cognitive mentality, but one would attribute more of it, or more complexity or sophistication in it, or the like. This sloppy formulation is meant as a reminder that I have not offered to define the higher–lower distinction, and so a fortiori I have not put myself in a position to defend Morgan's Canon. Those are two nontrivial tasks that I cannot embark on here. In this chapter, I help myself to the assumption that Morgan's Canon is correct when interpreted in conformity with our intuitive sense of what counts as "higher" than what.

If that is right, and if the unity thesis is a legitimate special case, my way of handling the unity thesis could help us to deal with other higher/lower issues. Consider the question: When the monkey gave its warning cry, did it want its companions to *believe there was a leopard nearby* or merely to *climb a tree*? I assume on intuitive grounds that the former is "higher" than the latter: It credits the monkey with a thought about beliefs, whereas the other credits it merely with a thought about movements.

According to my present hypothesis, we should adjudicate between the two by finding the "lowest" evidential property that is possessed by all and only the environments in which the monkey utters that sort of cry. (If that class of environments is marked out by a sensory kind, that undercuts any evidential kind, and the explanation of the cries ought to be something right off the bottom of the intentionality scale.) The rival kinds of evidential property are these:

Low: The environment offers evidence to the calling monkey that that sort of cry will cause the other monkey to climb trees.
High: The environment offers evidence to the calling monkey that that sort of cry will cause the other monkeys to believe there is a leopard nearby.

If we are to be entitled to think High is true of an environment, we must have grounds for attributing to a monkey a belief about the beliefs of other monkeys. What basis could we possibly have for this? Well, the functionalism that explicates our opinions about what monkeys believe must be supposed also to explicate *their* opinions (if they have any) about what other monkeys believe. That is, if they have a concept of belief, it like ours must be supported by the belief–desire–behavior triangle. Fortunately, for my present purposes I can take a somewhat simplified version of this idea. I shall say that an environment satisfies High if:

High*: The environment offers evidence to the calling monkey that

that sort of cry will cause the other monkeys to act in a manner appropriate to the information that there is a leopard nearby.

Of course, any environment that satisfies Low also satisfies High*. But we cannot be entitled to associate the warning cries with a desire to produce the belief that there is a leopard nearby unless they occur in a class of environments that is united under High* but not under Low – nor under anything else that is lower than High*. For example, if the cry is sometimes given when all the monkeys within earshot are visibly in trees already, the entire class of relevant environments may be united by this property:

> The environment presents evidence to the calling monkey that that sort of cry will cause the other monkeys to *be* in a tree,

that is, to go into a tree or, if already in a tree, to stay there. That is different from Low, but it is lower than High* and therefore disqualifies the latter.

So, what is needed for us to be fully entitled to read the calls as intended to produce beliefs rather than to produce behavior is that they occur in a class of environments that represent a vastly complex jumble unless we bring it under the unifying concept of "environment in which it seems to the monkey that a warning call will lead the others to act in a manner appropriate to there being a leopard nearby," or else under some concept that is even higher than that: for example, an "environment in which it seems to the monkey that a warning call will lead the others to act in a manner appropriate to the caller's believing that there is a monkey nearby," or "appropriate to the caller's wanting the hearers to believe that there is a monkey nearby," and so forth.

I offer that as an example of how the structure of my applications of the unity thesis might be used also higher up the ladder, to help bring discipline into questions about which of two competing intentional explanations should be adopted. By these standards it is unlikely that we shall ever be entitled to think that any nonhuman animal has tried to get another to believe something; but I do not say that in criticism of the standards.

V. Descartes on complexity

A consequence of the unity thesis is that an animal can have a goal and the intellectual ability to recognize the means to achieve it only by virtue of having packed into it a large number of mechanisms. Descartes said that a physical replica of a man would not behave in every way like a man, and he gave two reasons for this. Here is one of them:

> Even though [such physical replicas] might do some things as well as we do them, or perhaps even better, they would inevitably fail in others, which would reveal that they were acting not through understanding but only from the disposition of their organs. For whereas reason is a universal instrument which can be used in all kinds of situations, these organs need some particular disposition for each particular action; hence it is morally [*moralement*] impossible for a machine to have enough different organs to make it act in all the contingencies of life in the way that our reason makes us act.[10]

We must agree with Descartes that a purely physically controlled system would need a distinct physical mechanism to ensure obedience to each distinct conditional of the form "In an *E* environment, perform an *A* action," and that our reason puts us in command of countless such conditionals.[11] But if we assume (as I do and Descartes didn't) that the doings of reason are supervenient on physical happenings, we must conclude that reason generates all those conditionals because its activities are supervenient on those of a vast stock of distinct mechanisms taking us causally from initial states to resultant states, including taking us from sensory inputs to behavioral outputs. This is not in any way impossible, and thus is not "morally impossible," whatever Descartes meant by that. He was probably helped to think otherwise by having no idea of how small the working elements of a brain are. He may have been affected also by the assumption that each distinct conditional requires a distinct "organ," that is, a physical arrangement that has no physical overlap with any arrangement governing some other conditional. That assumption is false, of course; there is no reason why two mechanisms should not share most of their matter.

Anyway, we do not have to be materialists to think that a universal instrument must be a compendium of particular instruments. Descartes's thinking otherwise is a sign of his tendency to assume – in Wittgenstein's great phrase – that the mind is a "queer kind of medium" in which things happen that could not possibly happen anywhere else.

So we have to view a thinking, wanting, planning, and goal-pursuing being as a tight cluster of a large number of mechanisms whose overall effect is to make it register evidence about things it can do that will produce some state of affairs and then do those things.

If I have seemed to imply that for an animal to house a mechanism is for some input–output conditional to be durably true of it, I retract that. Most of the relevant conditionals about actual animals are switched on or off according to the animal's state of alertness, sexual satiety, blood-sugar level, and so on. I leave these toggles out of my account for simplicity's sake; in my main line of argument, the omission is harmless.

VI. Some further aspects of intentionality

I have been contending that we are not entitled to apply intentional concepts to a system unless (1) its input/output relations fall into a certain kind of pattern and (2) they satisfy the unity condition. In the next section, I introduce another necessary condition for intentionality or cognitive teleology – one that will occupy the rest of this essay. That, however, will not be an attempt to strengthen my account of what is needed for intentionality so as to turn it into an account of what suffices for it. Other required elements will certainly be missing.

For example, our concepts of belief and desire are probably such as to require that the inner routes from input to output satisfy certain constraints. Searle's "Chinese room" thought experiment seems to indicate that there are such constraints, though it gives us only negative information – that is, it tells us almost nothing – about what they are. One possibility is that a system counts as thinking and wanting only if the following is true:

> If two input/output pairs contribute to a single teleological pattern, that increases the probability that there is some physical overlap between the inner routes that they involve.

Other ideas also suggest themselves. If I were pursuing sufficient conditions (i.e., pursuing all the necessary conditions) for intentionality, I would have to dig into this topic, but I am not, so I shall not.

Again, all actual intellect involves cognitive dynamics: Often enough a given item of sensory input has no immediate effect on behavior but makes a difference to the behavioral upshots of later inputs by affecting the animal's "cognitive maps." Block's vending machine does model that much, because giving a penniless machine a nickel does not make it do anything but changes its cognitive map so as to alter what it does when the next nickel is fed to it. Now, perhaps this is conceptually required. Perhaps if it were clear to us that a given system was not subject to such cognitive dynamics, that would automatically satisfy us that it was not a genuine thinker and wanter. If so, then that is a further necessary condition that I am ignoring.[12]

Well, so be it. I want to tell one part of the story properly, and am content in this essay to leave other parts untold.

As for the phenomena I am setting aside, the ones that are naturally described in terms of cognitive dynamics, *could* they be described in terms of my apparatus of input–output conditionals? That is, if I wanted to enrich my account to take them in, could I do it by moving on from where I am, or would a fresh start be needed? I think a fresh start would be needed. To force the input/output conditionals to cover the phenomena in question, I should have to make them astronomically complicated and astronomically numerous. Indeed, the case for hypothesizing cognitive states that are affected by sensory inputs and that also combine with sensory inputs to produce behavior is just that without that hypothesis we have a horrendous clutter of input–output conditionals.

Still, the story I am telling in terms of such conditionals is a legitimate abstraction from the thicker story. I claim to have made some good use of it, and I now proceed to try to make more. This brings me to where I was at the end of Section V.

VII. Intentionality as a source of explanations

In the account I have been giving, nothing rules out its being a mere *coincidence* that this single system houses a lot of mechanisms whose overall effect is to make the system a *G*-seeker; and if it is a coincidence, the system's intentionality cannot be used to explain its behavior. Here is an analogous case. Suppose that of the cities Joe is acquainted with, he hates all and only those whose city government has a ward system; there are about forty of them, and Joe's emotions about them have forty different reasons, their common political systems being a sheer coincidence. That gives us a generalization on the strength of which we can "unite" Joe's hatred for Detroit with his hatred for Chicago, and so on, but doesn't give us the faintest *explanation* for any of the hatreds or, therefore, any reason to expect that he will hate the next such city that he encounters.

It does give us an explanation for his hatred for Detroit *today*, namely that he has a deep-seated and long-standing hatred for Detroit; what it doesn't do is to give us any carry-over from one city to another. Similarly, the account I have given of intentionality up to here may enable us to explain the animal's going on this occasion from a stimulus of kind *S* to a movement of kind *M*: It has done this often enough to convince us that it has some settled disposition to link this kind of input with that kind of output. But that link between a sensory kind of input and a motor kind of output corresponds to a single mechanism; an explanation that exploits it is, precisely, an explanation that does *not* make use of any intentional concepts.

I have argued elsewhere that the concepts of belief and desire are nothing if not explanatory, and in this essay I shall take that for granted.[13] I shall also work on the assumption that we have something explanatory if we have something that would have licensed a prediction, but not otherwise.

To put intentionality to work, then, we need to be able to explain or predict one link between sensory input and motor output on the basis of links between other pairs – ones in which the sensory kinds (and perhaps the motor kinds as well) are different. If an animal goes after rabbits in a variety of different ways, on the basis of a variety of different sensory kinds of clue, that gives us *some* reason to predict that it will go after rabbits on the basis of kinds of clue that we haven't so far observed it to use; but the account I have given so far doesn't lay any basis for this. That is because it does not rule out its being a coincidence that the relevant cluster of mechanisms exists entirely under a single skin. How, then, can we repair that hole in the account?

(I am not insisting that attributions of beliefs and desires be *causally* explanatory. I don't care whether the kind of explanatoriness that I shall find for folk-psychological statements is causal in nature, and indeed I doubt if the question is determinate enough to be worth addressing. Even further off my path is the question of whether beliefs and desires are causes. *This* question requires us to reify or eventify beliefs and desires, that is, to find not only truth conditions for "*x* thinks that *P*" and "*x* wants it to be the case that *Q*" but also application conditions for the noun phrases "belief that *P*" and "desire that *Q*." It is better to ask whether attributions of beliefs and desires are causally explanatory than to ask whether beliefs and desires are causes;[14] but it is better still to keep causation right out of the picture.)

Suppose there is a single common cause for all the input–output connections that add up to the animal's having a teleological pattern of behavior. Would that provide us with teleological explanations of the behavior? It would do so only if it entitled us, having seen some parts of the pattern, to predict others; and clearly it would not do the latter. If in some astronomically improbable way a single large genetic mutation led to offspring that had a lot of G-getting mechanisms, where the parents had had none, this common cause would not make it legitimate to *explain* anything the offspring did in terms of having G as a goal. The observation of behavioral upshots of some of the mechanisms would not provide valid evidence for the existence of any others of them. Or, to revert to a parallel that I used earlier, we aren't helped to explain or predict Joe's hatred for Detroit through his hatred for Chicago just because both hatreds were caused by a single bad dream.

What we need for explanatoriness is that there should be a unitary causal explanation not merely for

the system's having mechanisms $M_1, \ldots, M_k$,

where in fact its possession of those mechanisms makes it a G-seeker, but for

the system's having a lot of mechanisms that make it a G-seeker.

This is a weaker explanandum in one way, because it does not list the mechanisms. But I am more interested in the respect in which it is stronger, namely its including the fact that the mechanisms make the system a G-seeker.

VIII. One source of explanatoriness: evolution

One way of filling the gap in the account is through an appeal to evolution, and for my purposes a simplified pop evolutionary story is good enough. Of all the potential mechanisms that got a genetic finger-hold on the animal's ancestors through random mutations, relatively few survived; among the survivors were the bunch of mechanisms that make their owner a G-getter, and *that is why they survived*. Why does this animal contain a lot of mechanisms that make it a G-getter? It inherited those mechanisms from a gene pool that contained them *because they are mechanisms that make their owner a G-getter*.

That answers my specifications for something that makes it more than a coincidence that the animal has many mechanisms that are united in their G-getting tendency. And it lays a clear basis for explanations that bring in intentionality. That a species has evolved a G-getting tendency that is manifested in this, that, and the other links between sensory kinds of input and motor kinds of output creates some presumption that it has evolved other links that also have a G-getting tendency. So there is something predictive in this, and thus something explanatory as well.

If there had been no evolution but animals had been produced by a designing designer, the foregoing account would still hold, *mutatis mutandis*, just so long as the designer had included all the G-getting mechanisms in order that the animal should be a G-getter. As has often been pointed out, there is a strong analogy between the workings of evolution and the workings of a person executing a design, and the analogy goes far enough to spread across my present topic.

I have not yet said that without an evolutionary explanation or something sufficiently like it (e.g., a designing designer), we could not use attributions of intentionality to explain or predict. But even if I did, that claim should be sharply distinguished from Dennett's thesis that it is only because we can appeal to what he metaphorically calls "the intentions of Mother Nature" that we are in a position to make fairly determinate statements about the thoughts and wants of animals.[15] My account does not imply that we need help from evolution in order to answer the question, What, if anything, does this animal think and want? The force of "if anything" is that it might be a coincidence that this part of the physical world has packed into it a bunch of mechanisms that give it intentional patterns of behavior; so that even when we have established the whole intentional story, we should hesitate to *tell* it, to *explain* anything in terms of it, unless we are sure that it is no coincidence and that the mechanisms are interconnected in the right way. This is not the same as Dennett's claim that without an appeal to evolution, we cannot establish the story in the first place.

IX. A second source of explanatoriness: educability

Now, consider an animal whose behavior falls under intentional concepts in a very nontrivial way – the generalization about the circumstances under which it seeks G as a goal covers a vast number of different mechanisms – but it does not contain the means for modifying any of this apparatus in the light of its experience. It picks up from its environments all kinds of information about ways to get G, and acts accordingly, but if one of these input–output pairs starts to let it down, leading not to G but to something unpleasant, that does not lead the animal to delete that input–output pair from its repertoire. Nor does it ever add anything to its repertoire in the light of chance discoveries about what works.

I'll bet that there are no such animals. It is vastly improbable that the required kind and degree of complexity should evolve without being helped along by the evolution of a degree of individual adaptability to discovered changes in circumstances. Still, it could happen. The idea is not incoherent or absolutely impossible; we know what it would be like for there to be such behaviorally frozen animals. They would cope successfully and (it would seem) intelligently with their environments, but as soon as these altered a bit in some relevant way, the animals would be incurably in difficulties, and after a modest number of such alterations the animals would be dead.

We can imagine a world in which great behavioral complexity did have great survival value whereas individual adaptability didn't. In such a world, frozen complexity might well evolve, and my demands for intentional explicability would be met. Animals in that world would have richly intentional patterns of behavior – hard-wired instincts generating a multiplicity of fine-grained minutely appropriate ways of behaving whose overall effect would be to make the animal a G-seeker for this or that value of G.

The behavior of such creatures could be explained and predicted intentionally. If an animal has a lot of (for short) G-seeking input–output patterns, that is evidence that they have been selected *because* they let the animal get G; and *that* is evidence that other input–output links that have the same upshot will also have been selected. By the prediction test, therefore, we can use the premise that the animal is a G-seeker to explain a new bit of G-seeking by it; the premise is at least somewhat projectible, and is not a mere summation of observed behavioral episodes. And all this applies *mutatis mutandis* to frozen creatures that resulted not from evolution but from the activities of a designer.

So we can have explanatory intentionality even where there is no educability, just so long as the animal's origin makes it more than a coincidence that it houses a lot of mechanisms whose overall effect is to make it a G-getter. What about the converse? That is, what about educability without evolution or any substitute for it?

Well, consider again the case of educable parents that have an educable offspring with a goal they did not have: The offspring is the locus of a large number of G-getting mechanisms, none of which was present in the parents, their presence in the offspring being the result of a very radical and sheerly coincidental set of genetic mutations. It is to be understood that the offspring's inherited educability extends to its pursuits of the goal G. (I assume the educability to be inherited so as not to make the story more biologically bizarre than is necessary for my purpose.)

This story, though utterly improbable, seems to be coherent and to state a real possibility. If we knew that it was true of a given animal, we could *explain* some of the animal's behavior in terms of its having G as a goal. For (1) its having G as a goal and (2) its being able to learn from experience jointly give us reason to predict that it will pursue G in ways (and on clues) that we have not previously seen it employ. Such a prediction presupposes that the animal *has* previously employed those ways and clues or ones from which it has been able to reach those through some kind of generalization, imagined trial-and-error, "insight," or the like (cf. Section III). That presupposition distinguishes this prediction from the evolutionary case. In the latter, we have some grounds for predicting that the animal will pursue G through a certain input–output pair without knowing anything about its past experience; but of course we have to assume that many of its forebears have experienced that pair, for otherwise the trait linking them could not have been selected. This difference between the two is, on reflection, just what one would expect. What evolutionary adaptability is to a species, educability is to an individual; so explanations in terms of the former are likely to say things about the species that will be said about the individual in explanations in terms of the latter.

X. Appeals to intuition

I have not been inviting you to consider various possible kinds of animal and to judge whether you would be willing to describe such an animal in terms of beliefs and desires. I have not been holding up examples of an educable animal that did not evolve, an evolved animal that is not educable, one that has both features, and one that has neither, and asking you, "Does this strike you, intuitively, as an animal that thinks and wants?" Out at the margins where we are, such appeals to conceptual intuition are not worth much. I have not engaged in them, and do not need them.

My strategy has been different. I argue for the unity thesis, according to which the range of a folk-psychological generalization concerning a particular animal should correspond to a lot of different generalizations relating sensory kinds of input to motor kinds of output. I add to this the premise, argued for elsewhere, that the concepts of belief and desire are legitimate only if they can help to *explain* behavior. That raises the question of how a folk-psychological generalization can be genuinely explanatory, by the acid test according to which what can explain could have supported a prediction. To that I have given the best answers I can find – answers that mercifully spare us from the quicksand question of whether beliefs and desires can be causes.

It happens that those answers, developed in order to satisfy a certain theoretical demand, do also serve to bring the account closer to what intuition demands. In *Linguistic Behaviour* I left educability and evolvedness out of my account of basic teleology. I rightly said that evolution gave the best answer to questions of the form "Why does this animal have that goal?" – that is, "Why is a set of mechanisms with *that* overall tendency packed under one skin?" But I treated this point merely as a question that *might* arise, not as something that is needed if teleological explanations are to be given for the behavior of a not very educable animal.

I brought in educability as helping to mark a certain difference of level:

I thought that some genuinely cognitive teleology ought not to be described in terms of "believes" and "wants" or "intends" but only in terms of more generic notions which I expressed as "registers" and "has as a goal," and I offered educability as part of what makes the difference. I was steering here by conceptual intuitions, and I think I steered a true course. But I did not realize that educability was also playing a stand-by structural role: In the absence of evolution (or divine design), educability would be needed for any concepts of cognitive teleology, even low-level ones, to be applicable.

In my book I offered an example of a lake whose behavior has a preserving-the-local-wildlife pattern, and I said that its apparent teleology is fake because the very same behavior also falls into a simple mechanistic input–output pattern. I implied (because I believed) that that failure to satisfy the unity condition was the sole obstacle to attributing goals to the lake; protests from readers made it clear that this was not intuitively acceptable; and I am now clear that at least part of the shortfall was due to the fact that cognitive teleology, even of an abysmally low-level kind, requires not only the unity condition but also something that makes the teleological generalizations genuinely explanatory. That is the gap I have been trying to fill in the last part of this essay.

Notes

1. Ned Block, "Troubles with Functionalism," in Ned Block, ed., *Readings in Philosophical Psychology, Vol.* 1 (Cambridge, Mass.: Harvard University Press, 1980), pp. 268–305; p. 271.
2. Daniel C. Dennett, In his "Evolution, Error and Intentionality," *The Intentional Stance* (Cambridge, Mass.: MIT Press, 1987), ch. 8.
3. For more along this line, see Jonathan Bennett, *Linguistic Behaviour* (Cambridge: Cambridge University Press, 1976; Indianapolis: Hackett, 1989), sects. 21–22; Daniel C. Dennett, *The Intentional Stance*, ch. 2.
4. Bennett, *Linguistic Behaviour*; Donald Davidson, "Rational Animals," *Dialectica*, 36 (1982):232.
5. Christopher Peacocke, "Demonstrative Thought and Psychological Explanation," *Synthese*, 4–9 (1981):187–217; quoted from p. 212.
6. As for simple-input/complex-output: That would involve an animal whose pursuits of a certain kind of goal were *triggered by* some relatively simple kind of stimulus, with no significant differences among the occasions on the input side, but were *executed by* a variety of different kinds of movements that have in common only their being apt to produce the goal. That would be magic and, therefore, is negligible.
7. Or a class of sensory kinds whose members differ only in different settings of some small number of parameters, and similarly with motor kinds.
8. Daniel C. Dennett, "Intentional Systems in Cognitive Ethology: The 'Pan-

glossian Paradigm' Defended," in his *The Intentional Stance*, pp. 237–268.

9. For an expanded version of these compressed remarks, see Jonathan Bennett, *Rationality* (London: Routledge and Kegan Paul, 1964; Indianapolis: Hackett, 1989), the final section ("Insight").

10. René Descartes, *Discourse on the Method* 5, 6.56f.

11. If two conditionals differ only in having different settings of two or more parameters, they could be kept true by a single mechanism that had reset-table parameters in it. So when I speak of how many distinct conditionals our reason makes true, I mean how many conditionals that differ from one another in more ways than that.

12. The importance of this omission is one of many things that were made clear to me by Sydney Shoemaker's acute, searching, constructive comments on an earlier version of this essay.

13. See Bennett, *Linguistic Behaviour*, pp. 42–44.

14. I here rely on the difference between thing- and event-causation on the one hand and what I call fact-causation on the other. See Jonathan Bennett, *Events and Their Names* (Indianapolis: Hackett, 1988), sect. 8.

15. Dennett, *The Intentional Stance*, ch. 8.

9 Losing your mind: physics, identity, and folk burglar prevention

Simon Blackburn

In this essay I introduce a paradox in much current thinking about physics. The paradox is that physics (and, indeed, any human thought) never identifies causes – real causes. It may give us casual explanations, but these are only ways of pointing toward the real causes, or features in virtue of which effects follow causes. The paradoxical conclusion is that the predicates we use do not express or refer to the causally powerful properties or states. We can head toward the engine room, perhaps, but never get there. I diagnose current eliminativism in the philosophy of mind as largely the upshot of this paradoxical way of thinking. If I am right, its proponents have done a great service, giving us an outward and visible sign of an inner spiritual tangle. I start by saying a little about eliminativism, by way of introducing the way of thinking about physics that, according to me, it depends upon, and thence identifying the paradox.

The prophets of eliminativism may follow one of two models in their attitude to the categories whereby we understand ourselves and other people in terms of what we feel, think, believe, intend, desire. One model is the prophet Isaiah ("From the sole of the foot even unto the head there is no soundness in it"), and the other is John the Baptist ("There cometh one mightier than I after me"). The frequent comparisons of commonsense psychology to caloric theory, phlogiston theory, and demonology suggest the first, whereas the mere belief that in the future something better may turn up, by some standards of accurate prediction, completeness, simplicity, or capacity to deal with borderline cases, gives only the second. It is only in terms of the first model that there is something false in commonsense psychology. The second atti-

This essay owes an unusual amount to discussion and correspondence. I particularly want to thank Ned Block, Philip Pettit, Mark Rowlands, and Marianne Talbot, as well as Jay Rosenberg and the other symposiasts at the Greensboro Colloquium in 1988. A special debt is owed to David Lewis, whose patient incredulity enabled me to avoid many errors.

tude no more suggests that commonsense categories falsify things than it suggests that belief in Newtonian mechanics falsifies the folk view that it is harder to lift a heavy stone than a light one, or that belief in hydrodynamics falsifies the view that there are rivers.

In this chapter I oppose only the stronger doctrine. What is wrong with strong eliminativism is not its saying that a particular mode of description may one day be replaced. I have no quarrel – how could one quarrel? – with the bare possibility of future modes of understanding that somehow improve on those of folk psychology. Equally I have no quarrel with the bare possibility of future modes of understanding that similarly improve on those of folk geography or furniture classification. Again, many of the arguments against commonsense categories detail particular hard cases of belief ascription, and cases where attribution of content is underdetermined.[1] I shall not be concerned with these: There is, after all, no general doctrine that denies a term any application because it is polycriterial, or gives rise to difficult or borderline cases. Finally there is the issue of norms of rationality versus the natural – the issues concerning correctness that burgeon into the rule-following considerations – but I shall not be centrally concerned with these either. Instead I shall argue that what is wrong with current eliminativism is its claim to see how commonsense-psychological description conflicts with science.

I. The theory theory

To engage with eliminativism, I shall make one concession at the outset. This is that commonsense psychology should be identified as being, in some suitable sense, a "theory." For the purposes of this essay, I shall accept that the terms of commonsense psychology get their meaning from an implicit functional definition, or a network of sayings, platitudes even, connecting beliefs, desires, and the rest with typical causes, typical interrelations, and typical effects. Saying that commonsense psychology is a theory, in this weak sense, is inconsistent neither with allowing that it is used to do many things nor with allowing that we often know by observation, or direct access to our own states, what we ourselves and others believe, desire, and so on.[2] If we are to reject the view that it forms a theory, this ought, I believe, to be on the grounds that it suggests an unsustainable asymmetry between my own case (observational, direct knowledge) and the third-person case (theoretical, indirect knowledge), but in this essay I do not pursue that problem.

For eliminativism, the term "theory" in fact functions as a staging post: Because of some considerations commonsense psychology is well regarded as a theory, but theories are corrigible, hence it is corrigible and the question of its replacement may be raised. The view that terms are introduced by implicit functional definition, which I shall call the role or network model of them, does not itself immediately carry implications of corrigibility. Its doing so depends on the corrigibility of the elements of the network – the generalizations that keep commonsense psychological terms in place and enable them to be used in explanation and prediction. It is not obvious how corrigible these are. A sample list includes such statements as:

1. Barring self-control, anger causes impatience and antisocial behavior.
2. Barring a stronger contrary purpose, hunger causes eating.
3. Barring pathological personality or circumstance, the apprehended loss of loved ones causes grief.[3]
4. People generally do what they say they will do.
5. Intending P and Q is normally sufficient for intending P and intending Q.[4]

Suppose we agree that such generalizations underlie commonsense practice, in the sense that if they are denied, commonsense psychology will have no explanatory and predictive use, and no terms with any meaning. Still, the examples do little to show us how commonsense theory is corrigible. For we may have very little idea indeed how scientific progress, or any other, could tempt us to abandon any of them, let alone sufficient of them to count as abandoning the overall commonsense perspective (nobody is concentrating on small adjustments in this debate).

The real danger in using the word "theory" is in supposing that it does this work for us. Stich and Churhland frequently remind us of other "folk theories" that might have once inspired similar certainties but turned out wrong root and branch: folk demonology, folk cosmology, folk dynamics. As Stich roundly puts it: "Nor is there any reason to think that ancient camel drivers would have greater insight or better luck when the subject at hand was the structure of their own minds rather than the structure of matter or of the cosmos."[5] But the question will be whether the certainties – the platitudes exemplified above – of commonsense psychology could be relevantly similar to the mistakes early scientific theory made about force, inertia, demons, motion. It is certainly overplaying anything gained by introducing the word "theory" to suppose that it guarantees such a similarity. Since the role or network view applies to any term, the right point of comparison may be not early cosmology and dynamics, but those other things that camel drivers doubtless got quite right as they skillfully coped with their world: such unpretentious certainties as that generally it takes more effort to lift a heavy stone than a light one, that sunshine warms and wet chills, that people may safely drink water but can drown in it, that a long journey takes more time than a short one, and so on without end. The very generality of holistic considerations and the network model shows that these may be much nearer the right points of comparison than anything more overtly "theoretical." So we have nothing to support the vision of likely error.

The same trap of overplaying what is achieved by introducing the term "theory" is fallen into by Paul Churchland, when he charges that commonsense psychology is likely to be bad theory, since it is both incomplete in its domain and stagnant.[6] Whether or not these are bad signs in science, or at least in research science, they certainly need not be in the loosely knit body of platitudes connecting hunger and attempts to get food, or anger and bad behavior. Nothing in the network model shows that if concepts are suitable for stating truths, the generalizations of the network must be complete by any standard. Nor need they be under pressure to evolve. Perhaps they remain unchanging through the generations because they are certain, like the platitudes about sunshine, rain, and longer journeys taking more time. One man's stagnation is another man's certainty. It is also relevant to point out that the impression of stagnation may be largely an artifact of the philosophical tendency to abstraction – to talking as if the only relevant concepts are belief and desire. If one looks instead at the richer textures of psychological understanding that inform our lives, change is much more readily visible. (It is also noticeable that change typically does not bring falsification: In a future culture, people may not think in terms, for instance, of "falling in love," and they may not do so, but that would not refute the fact that we now do both.)

On the other hand, it will not help to press the other way – to say, for example, that the sample generalizations are incorrigible because close to tautologous, or if we prefer it "criterial" for the states of anger, hunger, intention. For this meets the familiar point that if the criteria for the existence of a state, in terms, say, of what causes it, are a priori, and if there are similar a priori criteria for its consequences, to avoid a pretended a priori status for what is all too visibly a contingent and a posteriori matter, the correlation between the antecedents and the consequences, it must be contingent and a posteriori that any such state exists. Better, then, not to award too grand a status to arbitrary elements of the network. Our success in understanding one another is at least a success in putting behavior into familiar patterns, and it is a contingent fact that those patterns are not disrupted, in one or many instances, sufficiently to baffle the attempt.

II. The sovereignty of physics

We now engage the essential part of the position: the idea that there is sufficient tension between the claims of folk psychology and the increasing body of knowledge of the sciences for it to be in the cards for those sciences to undermine it. The general eliminativist strategy is to try to say something specific about the kind of state that having a belief or desire must be taken to be, and then arguing that there may be no possibility of evolving science countenancing that state.

Within that general strategy there are two ends to work from. One might have a precise and exclusive sense of the states science countenances, and do relatively little to show that psychological states fail. Or, one might think there is something very specific about psychological states such that, without too much precision about science, one can nevertheless see that science cannot countenance them. Of course, one can work from both ends at once. Because it is physical thinking that centrally troubles me, I consider the first the more important.

Let us accept the sovereignty of physics. I take this sovereignty to be an ontological thesis best stated in terms of supervenience: We suppose that fixing all the facts that are discernible to physics fixes everything.[7] This does not deny the existence of things, states, and perhaps properties that supervene on the physical. But it ought to deny that there is a dimension of freedom in the way these things do: It should not be contingent whether, given the physical truth, there is also this or that further truth, of chemistry, or biology, or psychology. David Lewis believes that it will be contingent upon the absence of "alien" properties. But I hope that their absence will be a truth of our physics. If the way the supervening facts overlaid the total physical truth were contingent, God would have to fix something else than the physics: He would have to fix which of the possible relations the overlying truths bear to it. Real sovereignty should mean that there is not this extra thing to do. Only if real sovereignty exists is everything physically fixed. Otherwise the ways in which extra states overlie the physical states would amount to further contingencies, ineradicable 'nomological danglers'. We could well mark the difference by saying that the sovereignty of physics cannot countenance emergent properties, where emergence is thought of as a brute contingent extra, but can countenance supervenient properties. Supervenience is physically fixed emergence.

If there is supervenience, is there to be physical explicability? Clearly the natural or best explanation of a physical thing having a physical property need not belong to physics. In most contexts, the best explanation of this chair being within three miles of Carfax may be that it belongs to me, and this is where I live. The doctrine of the sovereignty of physics implies only that the position of the chair is physically fixed, not that the explanation is the most natural or quickest to give, or that asked for in any particular context. But there should be this connection with explanation: Another God, who knew how the creating God has fixed the physics, could explain why the chair is where it is.

The doctrine of the sovereignty of physics does not entail determinism over time. It does not entail that if God has fixed the physics and the laws at t, he has thereby fixed the states of the world at t'. He may or may not have. Sovereignty is a synchronic doctrine, not a diachronic one. But it should not be read as implying that fixing the physics at a snapshot time t fixes all the facts at t. It might not fix the historical facts at t, such as how big the tree was three years ago, and in principle this might matter to the evolution of physical states after t. To allow for indeterminism, and external facts of this sort, it is best to use two temporal quantifiers: Read the doctrine as saying that anything that fixes all the physical facts at every time, fixes all the other facts that obtain at any time.

We are looking for an argument implying that the sovereignty of physics threatens the existence of psychological states. So which states does a science like physics countenance? The question is ambiguous. It may be asking which states physics allows, and which it disallows. Or it may be asking which states physics describes – which it is bothered with. It is one thing for any science to imply that some state cannot exist, and a quite different thing for it simply to work in other terms. Physics may deny, for instance, that some kind of causation exists ("ghostly mental causation," perhaps) because it would break conservation laws. But it does not deny that chairs exist, just by working in other terms. Chairs are physical things.

Matters apparently stay the same when we think of properties, or states of affairs: chairhood, or being a chair or a chiliagon. Singular reference introduces more freedom in our descriptions of fact: Physics does not work with the predicate "being within three miles of Carfax." Yet surely its sovereignty is consistent with truths of the form "This chair is within three miles of Carfax."

There is a seductive answer to the question of which states physics countenances, which goes like this. Since physics is sovereign, a true theory must be reducible to physics. Folk psychology is a theory; hence if true it must reduce to physics. But reduction implies finding coextensive predicates to give us an "image" of the theory taken over in the larger theory. However, there is no real prospect of there being physical predicates coextensive with those of psychology. Hence, there is no real prospect of psychological theory being true.[8] In this argument the sovereignty of physics is taken to imply that all truths can be given an extension-preserving mapping into truths of that science. The implication is that if "thinking that the ornaments need dusting" cannot be made to correspond to a kind of physical theory, it cannot be true that people think that the ornaments need dusting. But why is this argument more plausible than an equivalent proof that there are no chairs within three miles of Carfax?

I shall come at this problem by considering the dialectic with which Patricia Churchland supports one part of her position. Her concern is to deny that functionalism defends psychology against the requirement of reduction. (Functionalism is here not much more than a label for the role theory, talking of what we do because of our psychological states, and what typically gets us into them.) Functionalism famously deflects the demand for reduction because in talking of functional identities between things we remain indifferent to sameness or difference of underlying physical states and mechanisms. This is true within a science: In physics, radios, resistors, thermometers, and batteries can be made of many different materials. In biology, birds and bees both fly, but the material constitution of their wings and muscles is different. This suggests the possibility of benign cross-classification between psychology and physics. As it is often put, there are "role states" and variable "realizing states." Churchland opposes this rapprochement with two arguments.

Considering the equation of temperature with mean kinetic energy of molecules, she rightly points out that the identity is inapplicable to the temperature of solids, of plasmas, and of empty space. It is unattractive to deny that there is a reduction of temperature to mean kinetic energy of molecules, so the moral she draws is that reduction can be domain specific: Temperature can be one thing in a gas, another in other things. "Though this is called 'multiple instantiability' and is draped in black by the functionalist, it is seen as part of normal business in the rest of science."[9] The moral is that reduction may be relative to a domain: "we may, in the fullness of time and after much coevolution in theories have one reductive account of, say, goals or pain in vertebrates, a different account for invertebrates, and so forth." The implication is that wherever the predicates cross-classify, there is still to be found a physical state that "is" the property (of believing that p or being in pain or whatever) in one thing, and another which "is" the same property in another thing.

The dialectical position is a little confused here. If reduction is allowed to go on in this way, then it will not require extension-preserving translations of predicates of the old theory into those of the reducing theory. It simply will not matter whether there is one physical kind (and term) or many, corresponding to the old term. If there are many, we just say that temperature (or whatever) is one thing in the one case, and another in the others. This gives us a relaxed attitude to the relation between the old predicates and their physical partners, and one would have thought that far from draping such a thing in black, the functionalist is happily celebrating the freedom offered. That no extension-preserving mappings can be found becomes no argument either against functionalism or against the reduction by these standards of any folk theory to physics. So why does Churchland see this claim as difficult for the functionalist and good for the eliminativist? Surely because she sees the underlying classifications as the only real ones, so that the concept of temperature turns out to lack "empirical integrity" once this many–one relation to underlying physics emerges. It is as if God, to know everything, can now avert his eyes from old-style temperature, the original role state, and look only at the differing energies or realizing states. He would need to frame no claims involving temperature, to know everything. Temperature has lost "empirical integrity." In this view physics as it were absorbs the role state into the realizing state, and thus eliminates it.

The same attitude to physics is visible in the second thing that Churchland says. Following Enc she makes the point that mean kinetic energy of molecules in a gas may itself be "variably realized" since identity of mean kinetic energy is compatible with quite different distribution of molecules and directions of motion: A given volume of gas may stay the same temperature as its molecules change position.

To be consistent functionalists should again deny reductive success to statistical mechanics since, as they would put it, temperature of a gas is differently realized in the two cases. If, on the other hand, they want to concede reduction here but withhold its possibility from psychology, they need to do more than merely predict hardware differences between species or between individuals.[10]

Again, the implication is that with the expanded vision that enables us to see the endless variation in molecular position, the overlying role state becomes invisible, that is, reduced, eliminated.

III. Physical thinking

Many readers will be protesting that the last two words of the preceding section should not go together. The identification of role state with realizer state, they say, is certainly a reduction, but certainly not an elimination. Before commenting on that, I shall say a little about whether we should accept Churchland's description of the case in physics.

If a bright learner asks the teacher why we can talk of temperature of a solid, when temperature is mean kinetic energy of molecules, and those in the solid are not moving, it is hardly satisfactory to reply that temperature is one thing in gases and another thing elsewhere. The learner wants to know what justifies our talking of the same property at all, so that a solid and a liquid both can be at 100° Celsius, for instance. And there had better be an answer.

Of course there is. Physics can explain how bodies, liquids, solids, and space can be at the same temperature. In equilibrium thermodynamics the concept of temperature is justified in the first place by the zeroth law, that if two bodies are in thermal equilibrium with each other, and one is in equilibrium with a third, then the other is also in equilibrium with the third.[11] This is what allows for the definition of an equivalence class of systems in thermal equilibrium. The definitions allow for gases, solids, and any other physical system to be in thermal equilibrium with one another. They are when there is no net energy transfer arising from their thermal contact (e.g., from placing the body in the space, gas, or liquid). This will be because of a relation between the mean kinetic energy of molecules in the gas, and whatever makes up the thermal energy of the other system: the vibration energies of molecules in some solids, of molecules and electrons in metals, and so forth.

Should we identify temperature with these "realizations"? Why should we want to? We already defined it as the property two systems have in common when they are each capable of thermal equilibrium with a third. In other words, the fundamental thing to be said about temperature, as about number and most concepts of physics, is that what is needed is a definition of the equivalence relation of having the same temperature as . . . ; this and the further relations necessary to produce a scale are provided, and nothing further need be said about what temperature is, although a great deal can be said about the kind of energy involved, and its source in the kinetic energy of molecules or other properties of the body, gas, space, and so forth. We also see why the consequence Churchland is drawing, that propositions about temperature become invisible to science, is undesirable, to put it mildly:

Why should we reject the salient equivalences as unreal just because we have found a mechanism for them?

One must beware of rewriting the relation between thermodynamics and kinetic theory as if a question of identity and its answer were the main point. In physics, as opposed to philosophical glosses on it, there is simply no use for a statement like "the temperature in this system is . . . " in which it implies, for instance, that over a phase change the temperature has to change. (It was one thing – e.g., kinetic energy of moving molecules – and is now another – e.g., vibration energy of static molecules.) On the contrary, the only use physics has for the form "the temperature is . . . " insists that the temperature of a solid and a gas in equilibrium is the same: 0°C for instance.

It may help to see this if we reflect that the equivalence between two volumes of gas at the same temperature is an equivalence visible to the kinetic theory. Sharing mean kinetic energy of molecules is a concept of the theory and defines an equivalence class of volumes of gases. In fact, given the gas laws, it follows from the equation of pressure with transferred momentum that temperature in a perfect gas must vary with mean kinetic energy: The concept, as it were, forces itself on the subject. Enc is therefore wrong to say that mean kinetic energy is a kind term of kinematics "only by courtesy."[12] One might as well say that energy is a concept of classical dynamics only by courtesy, or (since things of different constitutions each do it) that being in a state of uniform motion in a straight line is a concept of physics only by courtesy. Physics in not at all confined to constitutional kinds (as if it were not a physical truth that differently composed material things might share mass or charge or velocity).

To use a different example, finding what is the same about a closed system of objects at different heights and moving at different velocities in a gravitational field was a great achievement of classical dynamics. It was only by doing this that dynamics identified the equivalence of potential and kinetic energy. The whole point of the concept is that it classifies across difference of "state," where that is conceived in terms of mere spatial array and velocity of constituent particles. For just this reason it would be a misdescription of two such systems to say that energy is "one thing" in one system and another in another, merely because the positions and velocities of the particles are different.

I now present the first part of my paradox. It is essential to physical understanding that its predicates unify. They classify across difference of realization, for the following reason. The basic concept is that of a system in a state. The state is characterized by intensive and extensive magnitudes: Pressure, force, and density are intensive (local) magnitudes; mass, volume, and internal energy are extensive ones. These magnitudes take possible values (the number that are capable of independent fix defines the number of degrees of freedom of the system); the art of the physicist is to find the right variables and the right laws connecting them to give a function for the evolution of one state into another. Now it is absolutely vital to doing this that concepts emerge that cover systems with different forms of thermal energy, or cover changes of "realization" – which allow, for example, for something such as temperature or entropy which applies indifferently across changes of phase from solid or liquid to gas. If there is no unification, there is no scope for conservation across changes, and the central concept of physical thinking disappears.

I sum up this truth about physics in the thesis (T): Physical thinking is essentially a question of finding the one state that covers many realizations. It is forever a question of finding a unifying feature, a pattern in the particular evolutions of systems. If this is finding a role state that permits different realizations, physics deals only in roles; it is role seeking "all the way down." There is no harm in that: Thesis (T) is bland enough, perhaps merely serving to avert a lay misunderstanding of physics as essentially concerned only with microscopic facts or with identity. Thesis (T) opposes the idea that the "states" that physics countenances are to be thought of as literally spatial items, morphologically identified. Nothing could be less true to physics. No controversial functionalism is required to see it as simply false that accelerating at 25 m per second per second "is one thing in this car and another in that cannon ball" or that being able to pass petrol at 25 cc per second is "one thing in this tube of circular cross section and another in that square-shaped one." Remember too that even causal favorites such as solidity indicate only the possession of some property that precludes occupancy of the same space by other things with some properties.

The view of physics that thesis (T) warns against could be called the 'Tractarian' view, although in calling it this I am conscious of pointing to a cluster of thoughts, or images that determine thoughts, rather than to a clear, unique doctrine. In its simplest form, it is the view that physics itself is incapable of describing equivalences between systems that differ in some microscopic configuration – in the spatial array of constituent particles. The idea is that identity of a physical state consists in the spatial configuration of particles, and evolutions of state are changes in this identity over time. Every state is, then, what it is and not another thing; it is a unique combination of a value for each physical parameter at each place. But for it to explain at all, physics must find the one in the many. This means finding properties that answer not merely to configurations of constituent particles (although of course it may also, at some level, find properties that do so answer). The moral drawn from temperature and energy is quite general, and must be if physics is to explain.

I hope that the reader now feels the first stirrings of unease. It is the unique state – the realizing state, or array of magnitudes or tropes or instances of properties at points, that causes. It is here that the "making happen" happens: How, then, can we identify the cause by citing the relational, dispositional, or role-given properties with which physical thinking leaves us? At least in the seventeenth century, the condensation seemed to yield something solid, and (people wrongly thought) something that leads us to intelligible point-by-point causation. But we cannot have that thought any more. We are left only with point-by-point magnitudes for things that are essentially dispositional – electrical charge, for instance – but we are not left with a "quality" that underlies the "power" or a "ground" underlying the disposition, or a state that finally realizes the role. If the property is not identified as a power, or equivalently, if the "state" of it being realized is not identified as a role state, then the categorical, pure presence of an instance at a point will be unknowable to physics.[13]

An especially interesting example of the lure of the microscopic, Tractarian physical state is given by John Haugeland's excellent paper "Weak Supervenience." Haugeland is arguing, as I am, against the need for identity theory. But his example of the problem of identifying the "robust" events of common description with the "mathematical events" of physical theory depends eventually on a Tractarian view of what these events are. His example is the crossing of a pair of waves generated from different ends of a tank. Imagine that as they cross, each crest hits a cork. Haugeland asks which event describable in the language of ultimate physics is identical to the wave hits, and finds none: "When we turn up our microscope, however, and look at the positions and velocities of the water molecules, there isn't a trace of either wave-hit to be found anywhere."[14] But why should one expect to find the events and states of interest to physics by "turning up our microscope"? If fluid dynamics is treated in kinetic theory, the magnitudes characterizing a liquid at a point and time (velocity, viscosity, density, pressure, temperature) are not associated with the specific detail of microscopic states. They are associated with averages of properties of many microscopic entities. The "mathematical events" of physics are therefore sufficiently large-scale to map onto the events of waves traveling and crossing. It is the individual events and magnitudes that do not.

Does a Tractarian vision infect eliminativism? Consider Stephen Stich's discussion of the relation between mind and brain.[15] Trouble arises because, via the notion of a state, commonsense psychology becomes landed with rather specific commitments to the nature of neurophysiological workings. So Stich can urge that the notion of a belief state is undermined if it turns out that one part of the brain is causally responsible for my saying that there is a cat under the bed, and another part for my reaching down to lift it out. The idea is that according to folk psychology one belief state (that the cat is under the bed) is responsible for both the saying and the doing; neuroscience finds two different states separately responsible for the saying and the doing; hence folk psychology is wrong. Notice, however, that typically people tend to say that there is a cat under the bed only when they are disposed to act in whichever way is appropriate to that information, so presumably there typically exists some connection between any different areas of the brain that are involved, ensuring that the one goes into a cat-behaving state only if the other goes into a cat-reporting state. Hence there is room to find a single fact or feature, such as that of having the action and the speech area coordinated. But this will be simply a fact about the organization of the brain (it is not a fact that is "located" anywhere). I suspect that Stich failed to see this counter because of implicit Tractarianism: A count of located neurophysiological states would be blind to that kind of state. In short, unless we are in the grip of the Tractarian vision, the argument is out of court from the beginning. The single-belief state of folk psychology involves no commitment to one or many genuinely internal mechanisms, any more than the single kinematic state of a motor car – being in uniform motion in a straight line, say – requires that anything, let alone any given number of things, is happening inside it.

If predicates are taken in the resolutely functionalist way I am commending, then we are not finding that F-ing is one thing in one object, and another in a second, because they do it by different mechanisms. It might be a different thing, but only if it is a different thing that they are doing. From the functionalist's point of view, the reason is that it is impossible to find a functionally equivalent state across the divide. But that would be a different matter, although English is unfortunately cavalier at the crucial point:[16] For example, the English question "what is flying?" permits either a (quick and easy) role-state answer, or a (long, and variable) realizing – state answer. It may be right too that in many contexts the latter is the more interesting. What is not true is that this undercuts role-state explanation, nor that it threatens the causal efficacy of such states.

Notice, however, that impatience with traditional ("analytical") philosophy of mind might lead a forward-looking eliminativist to resurface here. Perhaps traditionally there were two questions, one scientific and explanatory, and the other more analytic. But why respect the second? Perhaps in a modern climate the question, "What is thought (belief, desire)?" admits of only a scientific construction: Either we are asking for underlying mechanisms, and need to sit at the feet of neurophysiologists, or we revert back to playing with concepts that lack empirical integrity. Alas, there is no escaping metaphysics without doing more of it than the mere hymning of science involves. The eliminativists believe that the sovereignty of physics and the rise of neurophysiology pose a distinct threat to psychological categories. But they cannot make this claim look plausible without giving or presupposing some account of how science threatens role states. They retain responsibility for showing how the undermining works – in round terms, what belief and desire explanation was that it should be shown to have had its day.

IV. Role states and causation

Thesis (T) says that physical thinking is essentially a matter of finding the one feature that covers many realizations. One might call this the "one state," but it is dangerous. We envisage states, very naturally, as things with positions and boundaries, and this spatial imagining is surely responsible for part of the problem. With this caveat in place, I now turn to the idea that finding the causes – the real causes – of events cannot be a matter of identifying a role state, or feature covering variable realizations. I shall illustrate the difficulty – although it is of far greater generality – by thinking of the trouble we have fitting psychology together with causality.

Folk psychology overtly says little about states. If it talks of them at all, it is to talk of us who get into psychological states, not of any states that get into us. If I get into a state of believing that I am Jesus, no doubt things will have gone on in my brain. But there is no first-order project of finding whether the state I have got into is some very state that has got into this part of me. Commonsense psychology gives no reason to think of the states we get into as spatial arrays. None of the platitudes defining folk psychology talk in these terms: As with physics, it is philosophical gloss, not first-order theory that insists. So why impose talk of states and then reify and locate them? The ruling answer goes like this: Folk psychology may confine itself to using predicates – "believes (desires, etc.) that P." But we need a view of the conditions making such ascriptions true. Functionalism is a start. But we want our psychological states to have causal powers, enabling them to affect the real world, and we want them to do so in ways we can see as conforming to the sovereignty of physics. The best way to do this is to identify the states making the ascriptions true, first with neurophysiological and then, hopefully, with physical states. If they will not go into that shape, then so much the worse for them.

This is the heart of the issue, set forth with his usual clarity and force by Lewis, who writes that his argument for identity theory (the identification of role with realizer states) parallels the following, "which we will find uncontroversial":

> Consider cylindrical combination locks for bicycle chains. The definitive characteristic of their state of being unlocked is the causal role of that state, the syndrome of its most typical causes and effects: namely, that setting the combination typically causes the lock to be unlocked and that being unlocked typically causes the lock to open when gently pulled. That is all we need know in order to ascribe to the lock the state of being or not being unlocked. But we may learn that, as a matter of fact, the lock contains a row of slotted discs; setting the combination typically causes the slots to be aligned; and alignment of the slots typically causes the lock to open when gently pulled. So alignment of the slots occupies precisely the causal role that we ascribed to being unlocked by analytic necessity, as the definitive characteristic of being unlocked (for these locks). Therefore alignment of slots is identical with being unlocked (for these locks). They are one and the same state.[17]

Lewis claims three advantages for so thinking. First the states become recognized as "real and efficacious." Second, "unrestricted mutual inter-definition of the state and others of its sort becomes permissible." Third, it becomes intelligible that the state may sometimes occur despite prevention of its definitive manifestations. The alternative he considers preserves the separation of role state and realizer state. But, according to Lewis, this denies efficacy to the former, for a pure disposition is an inefficacious entity.

The previous two advantages are not central to my problem, but I shall briefly register a query about each of them. First, then, mutual definition seems to go on just as well if we stay with the role predicates of commonsense theory: If there is a definition of belief or desire to be had, it will be had whether we think of it as saying what an underlying mechanism is, or instead as defining the truth that someone is believing or desiring. A definition of flying can be had (roughly: staying aloft in a gravitational field without external support) without adverting to any particular mechanism whereby some particular thing does it.

Second, the identification of role and realizer state may seem to solve problems over externally prevented manifestations of state. But this is not clear, for these problems arise as badly with the identification in place as without it. This is easy to overlook, since once we think of the state as an inner spatial presence, it seems evident that it can be there regardless of whether its effects are its typical effects. But what will not be evident is that the internal, realizing state is on this occasion the original role state, for this is now contingent. Consider the lock again. Another lock might share a whole physical part with the original: five disks coming into line, for instance. But it may have a device that prevents this from being enough to open it. (You may also have to whisper the magic word that triggers the minute relay.) The five disks are in line, but it is not unlocked. If we talk the identity way, we have to say that its being unlocked is a composite: its five disks getting into line and its relay tripping. For this lock, it is not true that its being unlocked is its five disks getting into line. Calling the state of being unlocked UL, and that of having five disks in line, S, we learn that the following is not a valid argument:

Lock 1 is unlocked iff it is in state S
So state UL is state S. Lock 2 is in state S
So lock 2 is in state UL
So lock 2 is unlocked

Because lock 2 is not unlocked. Such an argument trades on forgetting that identity "state UL is state S" must be relativized to locks for which it is true that when the five disks are in line, they are unlocked. How to tell which locks these are? That is easy, provided we know when something is unlocked. But difficulties remain in telling when a lock with five disks in line but unopenable is unlocked. For example, if there is a disruption of the typical workings of the first lock, preventing the chain opening, we may say that it is unlocked but jammed. But we may prefer to say that it is still locked. Or, there may be an accidental disruption to the first kind of lock preventing it from getting into the state S, although it now opens when lightly tugged (it is a raped lock: The fifth disk is damaged, and the other four give it its function). Here we are hardly likely to say that it cannot get into the state of being unlocked. The role-state theorist who avoids the identity has exactly this freedom, or (if we want principles for settling the description) this problem. Of the first lock he or she can say that the thing is unlocked but jammed. The role-state theorist can say this because he or she can say that if the occasion were right for manifestation of its disposition (e.g., the rust were out of the way), it would open. Alternatively; he or she can say that it cannot be unlocked, because this is the right occasion for display of the disposition, and the thing will not open. Similarly, if it opens although the state *S* has not come about, the role-state theorist can deny that it is unlocked (forced, rather) if unlocking implies responding by opening to the right kind of input (a key, not a drill).

In other words, indeterminancies of what to think when we would expect a disposition or other functional trait to be manifested but it is not (or not to be manifested but it is) need handling in the same way whether or not the identity is flourished. If there is a disruption between the physical state that normally explains the disposition, and its exercise on an occasion, the identity theorist simply confronts the open question whether to say that the state "is" on this occasion the original state. The theorist's penchant for identity does not tell him or her the answer. And the role-state theorist faces the question of whether this is the "right" occasion for exercise of the role. The same is true of the more urgent case in which paralysis prevents beliefs and desires from becoming manifest. There are some facts about the paralyzed agent that would be expected to lead to the agent's acting in some way, but others that prevent it. Is he or she disposed so to act? The agent would if the occasion were right (i.e., the disability disappeared), but the occasion will not be right; he or she will not talk or act as things are. If this leaves us not knowing what to say, try bringing on the identity theory. Does the agent possess a state that (in him or her) is the belief or desire? It is just as hard to tell. There are difficulties in knowing what to say of such cases: The contingent or kind-relative identification with underlying state makes it no easier.[18]

These were two subsidiary arguments for making the identity – 2arguments parallel, of course, to the famous Davidsonian argument for event-identity between the mental and the physical. In each development the most important issue is the first that Lewis cites: that of causation, and the intuition that *role states do not cause, whereas realizer states do*. Alongside thesis (T) we now have antithesis (A):

> Thesis (T): Physical thinking is essentially a question of finding the one state that covers many realizations.

> Antithesis (A): If one state covers many realizations, it is they, and not it, that are causally relevant (powerful, active).

These are not incompatible, of course, but together they do give us conclusion (C):

(C) Physical thinking is not a question of finding states that are causally relevant.

And this is sufficiently strange to count as paradoxical. If physics is not the discovery of causally relevant states, what is?

So far, I have merely introduced antithesis (A) and done nothing to defend it. First, we need to be clear what it says and does not say. It does not say that role states cannot be cited in causal explanations. They may be, if causal explanation "points toward" causally active states without itself citing them. Thus, to take Jackson and Pettit's example, the fact that someone coughed may be mentioned in explaining why the conductor got angry.[19] But it features in such an explanation, according to them, by pointing us toward the particular state that actually made the conductor angry: Fred's coughing, or perhaps some feature of Fred's coughing on this occasion. We mention role states, on such an account, in order to shrink the domain from which causally relevant particular states must come. In the same way, we might cite a power or disposition, not because, in mentioning these things, we are actually giving the relevant feature, but because it confines the domain within which such a feature exists. Thus we can mention the dormativity of the opium and provide an explanation of someone sleeping, but what we are saying is that there is some other property the opium has, that causes sleep.[20]

For a similar reason antithesis (A) is not denying that role states may be nomologically connected with effects. A causally relevant property will bring about an effect. It will also bring it about that other higher-order properties – relational and dispositional properties – are instanced, and they may then be in a lawlike correlation with the effect. Thus in a gas the increase in kinetic energy of these molecules in this configuration will transfer energy to the thermometer; it also gives it new powers. It brings about that it has some property responsible for extra available thermal energy, and it thereby also brings it about that the gas bears a different energy exchange relationship to many other things. These changes in role state are, however, epiphenomenal: The molecules do the pushing, and the other properties, supervening upon the first, come along for the ride.

Except, of course, remembering the discussion of physics, it will not really be the molecules doing the causing, but (in the first instance) distributions of other parameters of energy and force within them. And if thesis (T) is right, then for all we shall ever know there will be other magnitudes and realizing states beyond those again, all the way down. If our physics stops at some level – say, with electrical charge – then there will still be a quality or qualities realizing that charge. But, as with Cartesian egos, it will be forever hidden how many there are, or what it is, or whether it is the same on odd dates and even dates.

There are other arguments in favor of (A). Writing of the second-order property of being provocative to a bull (i.e., having some property that causes the bull to react), Block says, "Supposing that provocativeness provokes the bull would be supposing a strange sort of overdetermination of the bull's anger. . . . But to suppose that it always happens would be to suppose a bizarre systematic overdetermination."[21] And our dislike of this can be fortified by remembering how easy it is to generate supervening states. To use an example of Lewis's: If the steam in the cylinder is at 190 pounds per square inch (p.s.i.), then it is also in the state of being either at 190 p.s.i., or being full of suspended particles of gold dust. We think the former causes the piston to move, but its being in the latter state does not. Disjunctives states are bad candidates for causal relevance: Quantificational states (someone coughing) and higher-order states (having some property that causes sleep) seem just as doubtful.

If thesis (T) characterizes physical thinking, and antithesis (A) is not short of defense, can we live with conclusion (C)? Perhaps we can. After all, lawlike explanatory relevance is left to us. There is nothing wrong with saying that the mercury column of the thermometer went up because the temperature was rising, even if ("strictly speaking") what made it go up was a succession of microscopic impingings or, rather, the instancing of the properties that ultimately realize all the powers we can ever know about. We might even take a Humean pleasure in reflecting that the ultimate causes of things are forever obscured from us, so that all we can do is mark the patterns they reliably create as events unfold. And it draws some of the sting from the epiphenomenalism of the mental if its causal inefficacy is on all fours with that of changes of temperature or energy levels. Nevertheless, it would be good to put into place some other route to a solution. We ought to reflect that in spite of the shift in our understanding of causation that Newton and Hume brought about, it is not compulsory to describe it by saying that we never identify real causes. It is hard to believe that "being a feature in virtue of which things happen" is itself a transcendental property, forever defying identification. There ought to be a humanly accessible notion of what it is that makes things happen – one we can rely upon in making recipes and controlling events.

V. Higher-order causal relevance

Things at the same temperature form a certain equivalence class, although the thermal energy can be created by many different means. Sameness of temperature is therefore a higher-order property: the possession of some energy source ensuring that no heat is transferred when in thermal contact with any of a class of other things. Now, imagine a chain of events as follows: A thermometer, affected by its thermal contact with something, records a temperature. Suppose it is connected to a further system: A current flow in a wire if the reading is below a certain level. The current in turn triggers a switch, and lights the boiler, raising the temperature. Then there is a good sense in which the system "looks through" which realization of thermal energy caused the reading. It is sensitive equally to the different creations of thermal energy (if the thermometer is flexible enough, by moving molecules, vibration energies, electromagnetic energies, and so on). That is, the current flows regardless of any particular realization of the temperature, and in the same way the boiler lights regardless of any particular configuration of the electrons in the wire carrying the current. The boiler raises the temperature today as it did yesterday. We ought to have a humanly applicable conception of causal relevance, enabling us to say that the system works the same on each occasion: The same features cause the same effect.[22]

Consider now a lock. Think of a burglar as an instrument. The lock's being unlocked can be responsible for the burglars's getting in: It is the feature to cite, and to use if we wish to control the movements of burglars. Its being unlocked is the upshot of its having four disks in line, on this occasion. But that is not the feature the burglar detected, or is perhaps even capable of detecting. Nor is this a problem only about burglars. A much simpler instrument can be sensitive to whether there is no force on the chain, without being sensitive to whether the reason is that there are four disks in line, or five, or anything else. Again, the upshot "looks through" the preceding realization.

A vivid case of this "looking through" is indifference of a physical result to the question of which instance, or instance of a quantification, is realized. The burglar alarm went off because someone was in the room. It was Bill: Bill (or more: some particular result of Bill being in some particular place at some particular time) caused it to go off, but it is still true that it went off because someone was in the room. That is what makes it go off. That is what is supposed to make it go off. It is not as if it malfunctioned. You cannot take it back, saying that it is supposed to go off because someone is in the room, whereas it actually was made to go off by Bill's standing on one foot in a corner of the room. Is this giving in to a "bizarre causal overdetermination" since on a given occasion the instrument will have responded both to some highly particular flux of energy and to someone's being in the room? Surely there is nothing bizarre about it. We simply do not have to choose between these properties as ones whose instancing makes things happen, ones with causal power and relevance.[23]

But does citing anything less than the particular, as we do when we find a common feature in causal transitions, merely leave us with a signpost to something else, which alone has "real" causal relevance? I say no. In finding causal relevance we are finding features, like rising temperature, or carrying current, that are essentially repeatable, but whose presence can be registered, and brought about, by mechanisms that function in the same way on each of many occasions. The one we find in the many can also be one whose being there makes things happen.[24]

So far, I am insisting on having my cake and eating it: separating the role and realizer states but keeping genuine causal efficacy for the role state. It might occur to some to wonder whether this challenges the sovereignty of physics. Again, I say no. The sovereignty of physics requires only that the connection between the role or disposition and the underlying state is explicable. Its sovereignty would be challenged only if there were something it could not explain in (say) the fact of the five disks coming into line, enabling the lock to be opened. But there need not be. In this lock, when the five disks are in line, there is no force opposing the tension of a pull on the chain. So the chain moves. In other locks, there might still be a force opposing the tension of such a pull, when the five disks are in line. In them, the chain will not move. The property or fact of being locked or unlocked is thus explained, and physical explicability does not at all require that we work in terms of states and their identity. We do not have to "identify" the velocity of the car with the application of the energy to the wheels, in order for the velocity to be explicable by the energy.

The intuition I am opposing is probably this. If there is anything other than identity, then there are two things (two states) to be connected: on the one hand, the underlying physical configurations and, on the other hand, the fact that the lock opens when gently pulled. But unless we can squeeze these together, as it were, there is then bound to be a gap for physics to cross, and it will never explain the exact landing point: the very way the categorical state matches up to the disposition. And my rejoinder is that any intuition that there is an explanatory gap here simply transposes into the same intuition that there is an explanatory gap on the identity story: a gap in understanding why or when state *S* is state UL. If we know why the configuration gives rise to the disposition, we know this, but otherwise we do not. Nothing is made more intelligible by the identity.

My claim then is that being unlocked is not an epiphenomenon, rendering literally false folk-burglar prevention – the theory in which we say, "Because it was unlocked, the bicycle rolled downhill" or "Because it was unlocked, the burglar could push it open." The fact that no force opposed the tension on the chain is in perfectly good standing as a fact that matters. It was because of that (which in turn may be because the five disks were in line) that gravity or the burglar met no resistance. Would it be somehow better not to cite the fact of its being unlocked, and only to cite the fact of the disks' being in line? Not at all: Gravity and the burglar "look through" the reason why it was unlocked.

If antithesis (A) was at fault, what of the degenerate cases, such as disjunctive states, or dormativity? Here I can only sketch an approach. Arbitrary disjunctions? The disjunctive state of "having the steam at 190 p.s.i. or being full of suspended particles of gold dust" is not a state that any natural causal system "looks through" to. A cylinder would be in that state by being full of suspended particles of gold dust. But there is (I take it) no normal effect common to that and to being full of steam under pressure. Only if there were would the state begin to stand in the same relation to having the steam as temperature does to a particular molecular distribution, and thence to look like a candidate for causal efficacy. There is no genuine nomological connection between satisfying this predicate and doing anything (perhaps I should say, anything whose unity is visible to a non-Goodmanian, well-behaved categorization of the world). Quantification? A conductor, like a burglar alarm, may be sensitive to someones' coughing. Making someone cough gives us control over that person's temper, a recipe for making him or her seethe, and a causally relevant state of an audience. We have here a system that looks through its realizations, and I see no objection to causal efficacy. Higher-order properties, like the provocativeness of the cape? A bull is certainly a good instrument – the best going – for detecting whether a stimulus is one that provokes bulls. If a change in temperature is causally relevant to the thermometer, why isn't a change in provocativeness causally relevant to changing demeanor in the bull? My own answer to this would be to reverse Block's. What is wrong with citing this feature is not that it is causally irrelevant but that it is explanatorily such a dud: It provides no basis for prediction and no useful recipe for doing things that control bulls. Being told to wave something provocative at the bull is indeed merely being given a signpost: It points me toward the need to discover the properties that cause the reaction. Thus there is virtue in citing temperature: I can control the rise of the thermometer by controlling temperature, without needing to discover anything about the realization of temperature at all.

It may be said that in all these examples the causal efficacy of the role state, like the role state itself, supervenes upon the Tractarian particulars and their evolutions through time. I do not want to deny this, provided we are comfortable with such a property – and provided it is not a subtle invitation to denying that the causal power, the relevance and efficacy of the feature, is real enough.

VI. Physical states

If we have a good idea of how the thermometer can be made to act by the temperature, can we immediately see how we can be made to act by beliefs and desires? Obviously there is a huge gap: Sameness of temperature is at least visible to physics; sameness of belief arguably not.[25] Still working, as it were, from the physical end, the question will be one of defining a more realistic concept of a physical state or property. Presumably physical states include the possession of a physical property by a physical thing; the bearing of physical relations by n-tuples of physical things; the being in complexes of physical states or bearing of amalgams of physical properties by conglomerations of physical things. Nothing in the sovereignty of physics forbids (physically explicable) complexity, amalgamation, or conglomeration.

It is sometimes thought that there should be, because of the following argument. Physics explains by citing laws; there may be a law covering the transition from A to B, and one covering the transition from C to D, but this would not entail that there is one covering the transition from (A and C) to (B and D). This may be true about laws. But physical explicability is agglomerative and transitive, even if law is not. Thus when a system composed of A and B evolves to a subsequent state C and D because of a law L determining C from A, and another L' determining D from B, then even if there is no single law covering this evolution, there is still nothing physically unexplained about it. For an example, consider a body of known weight, position, and temperature $<p,T>$ in a gravitational field of known strength and direction. Suppose a kinematic law K will give a position p' for it after t seconds. Suppose the body consists in a battery passing current through a circuit, and a law of electromagnetics L determines a temperature T' for it after the same interval. At t it will be in a certain position and at a certain temperature, and nothing in this evolution is physically unexplained. The transition from $<p, T>$ to $<p', T'>$ is both determined and explained by physics, even if physics uses two different laws to do it. It is a transition in which nothing is physically inexplicable. God did not have to do anything extra to secure this evolution of state.

Churchland's vision of the relation between special sciences and physics demands coextensions of terms. Will the sovereignty of physics require anything so strong? In the example given, it does not matter if physics has no interest in the particular evolution, and no kind term to pick out the complex states involved. Further examples suggest a two-stage analysis of this phenomenon. The first part allows for "token-token" identity, but the second is less familiar. Consider (to use Fodor's example) the physical process summed up in the geological "law" that meandering rivers erode their outside banks. This is a physical process, and one in principle explicable by fluid hydrodynamics. Yet neither "river" nor "meander" nor "bank" is a term of physics. All that the "reduction" of the law to one of physics, in this relevant sense of the word, requires is that rivers are (each of them) some, but not necessarily the same, kind of flowing liquid; that meanders are (each of them) some, but not necessarily the same, kind of curved configuration; and that banks are (each of them) some, but not necessarily the same, kind of material liable to lose its cohesion under transverse forces. Each token of the type is an event describable in terms of hydrodynamics. If we think these kinds are invisible to physics, then the fact that a kind is thus invisible is no bar to reductive physical explanation. A fortiori it is no motive to "eliminativism" or rejection of the truths expressed in terms of the kind, even given the sovereignty of physics. The coming of hydrodynamics does not prove that there are no folk rivers.

The example takes us only halfway. We are already prepared to believe that bank erosion is a physical process, and we do not mind saying that rivers and meanders are, each of them, something physical. But we might still worry how physical explicability transfers from any given token of the type to the overall explanandum. Would it not require seeing a physical "shape" in what is perhaps invisible to physics: the reason the disjunction of tokens all count as examples of the same type – river, meander, or bank? It is here that the demand for an "image" of the predicate in the explanatory science (physics) reemerges. It is as if it is all very well to explain each token of the type, but unless there is a physical explanation of the tokens constituting and exhausting examples of the type, the original explanandum is not yet touched. Thus it is that more impressive cross-classification is typically introduced via examples like chairs, ornaments, money, and so on. These kinds correspond even less well to physical boundaries. Whether or not they think it undermining, writers generally agree that there is a distinction between classifications that carve nature at the joints and those that do not, and these kinds, reflecting as they do the particular interests of human beings, surely do not.

This thought needs a little attention. Of course, it is true that we distinguish things by other than physical properties; we "look through" things like mass, velocity, shape, conductivity, constitution, and so forth. And a bullheaded attempt to find disjunctive physical kinds underlying most terms of classification, including those that enter into some laws, is fruitless. Again using Fodor's example, it is a law that bad money drives out good, but an attempt to "define" a term like "money" by thinking of the enormous (limitless) potential disjunction of physical kinds of stuff that might serve as money, and then framing "laws" covering that disjunction, is a hopeless way to try to make the law "physically explicable." Even if such a disjunction were somehow created, it is doubtful whether we could think of it as making anything explicable. It would not be the "physical" properties of the members of the disjunction that are responsible for their being there (round bits of metal, printed pieces of paper, cowrie shells, etc.): Nothing visible to physics is tying the bundle together. Since the disjunction threatens to be shapeless, we might insist that it still plays no role in helping us understand why just things of that kind drive out other things of this kind.

But this is the wrong way to go. Instead we must enlarge our gaze to think of the wider system: us-using money, or us-discriminating-chairs. It does not follow from the cross-classification of chairs with respect to properties like mass, material constitution, shape (up to a point), and so on, that there is anything invisible to physics in the wider system. It would be possible, for instance, to construct a physical system, including various receptors, that selects objects in its environment by properties other than weight, mass, and constitution. Think of a robot capable of "sitting" – taking up some position – and sensitive to feedback telling it whether some of its parts are under mechanical stress in that position.

Then think of it discriminating objects on which it can "sit," capable of selecting further among them on the basis of feedback from its own states, and eventually able to mimic our own chair-selecting practices. (If it is complained that we discriminate chairs by features other than whether we can sit on them without strain, imagine the robot endowed with other sensitivities – for example, a sensitivity to the history of production or whatever else matters.) Of course, it will be by physical means that its sensors and feedback mechanisms work. But given the sovereignty of physics, the same is true of us. The whole system of chair discrimination by robot would be physically explicable. Hence, there is no a priori reason why the same is not so of us. In this development the physicalist explanation does not try to complete an inventory of the woods, plastics, metals, and other things that chairs are and might be made of. Nevertheless, the explanation proceeds by finding what is physically common to occasions on which a classification is effected. Notice too that the physical explicability of the classification in turn does not imply that the robots are built identically. As already emphasized, physics is capable of being quite relaxed about what makes two occasions physically similar. A circuit diagram gives a perfectly good physical description of a device, although there are endless different things that can serve as wires, resistors, or capacitors.

Similarly with money: Nobody, of course, has the least idea how it would go in detail, because social facts are one stage farther from physics than psychological ones. But if there is physical explicability of people's desiring things and exchanging things, then there will be physical explicability of Gresham's law, and again without providing the shapeless list of things that can serve as money. The upshot is that it should not be barely asserted that "chair" or "money," let alone "river" or "bank," is a kind invisible to physics, even though it cross-classifies with respect to many physical properties of its members. The supervenience requirement is satisfied in the following sense: By creating the entire physical system, God had done enough to create the use for the kind term. He has also done enough to create a physical relation, with chairs the things in its domain – the things disposed to elicit and sustain the chair verdict from us.

VII. Psychological states

With this much understanding of physical states behind us, the task of this chapter is nearly finished. But I shall close by saying a little about the other end of the relationship.

The subordinate clauses in propositional attitude psychology mention content; the object of the demonstrative is a thought or proposition, not a sentence, nor words nor utterances.[26] Folk psychology is silent about implementation. It makes no claim that there is some "level" of explanation of our thinking that fruitfully relates us to sentences or words. It is therefore not affected by discoveries, such as seem likely to come in the wake of the successes of parallel distributed processing (PDP) architecture for recognitional and other systems, that there is no fruitful level of explanation that sees such things as involved with rules, or words, or syntactically complex instructions and subcognitive processing. Just as a PDP network can "recognize" a sound or a pattern without anything that ought to be called computation, so perhaps, equally without literal computation, we can think that our friend is coming down the street. There is no a priori reason to suppose that because the skill is great, the mechanisms explaining it involve real, but quick and unconscious, cognitive processes. On the other hand, there is no a priori reason against this: The fruitfulness of such a level of analysis is a matter of scientific, not philosophical, speculation.

Will psychology, granted this much independence, ever make a cognitive science? Some see the hostility to treating psychological states as natural objects as implicit in Frege's antipsychologism. It is certainly present in Collingwood, to whom the capacity of a thinker for self-critical change of his or her own beliefs and desires blocked the pretensions of psychology, or anything else, to be a "science" of thought.[27] Similarly, Putnam argues that the business of attributing a mental state, with a certain content to another, always involves issues of judgment seamlessly bringing to bear any of a formless class of cultural, historical, hermeneutic pressures, and the prospect of the outcome of such a process being a scientifically respectable predicate seems very poor.[28] Allied to this are the normativity or rationality constraints governing psychological attribution, and the resulting suspicion that we have an essentially dramatic, rather than descriptive, activity. But the catholicism I have been urging enables physical respectability to gobble up this as well: In principle, a norm-wielding system is not more invisible to physics than a chair-detecting one or a money-using one.

If we make the role-realizer identity, we can say that redescription of states under predicates that reveal their lawlike connections makes good any preceding causal explanation: It is the fund that backs up what is otherwise only a promise. It is essential to this idea of "making good" that the thing described in the initial, lawless way is the thing that can also be described in the later, lawlike way: This is the model common to Davidson and Lewis. Sometimes this model is plausible. The stone balances the scale, not because there is a law that stones do so, but rather, because the stone is the thing of mass x at distance d from the fulcrum. But with unnecessary identities out of the way, there is no analogy to this model in psychological explanation. We can be agnostic about whether psychological explanations can aspire to the condition of laws (even if they do not for us, it is hard to see why they could not for a more simple animal). Whether there is psychological law or not, no redescription of mental states that succeeds in introducing a lawlike connection missing from psychology would make good the psychological explanation. In other words, all we would get would be something citing a different fact about me or my neural states. We might find that "as I believe" or "when I believe" or "upon coming to believe" that p, such-and-such changes happen, and they are lawlikely correlated with others. But we do not thereby get a new lawlike correlation between "a state that is the mental state" of coming to believe that p, and the other changes. Such a filling-out changes the subject. It substitutes mention of something different.

It will be said that I want it both ways: I both want to stress the separateness of role states (role features) and to award them the causal accolade that (it will be said) properly belongs only to realizer states. I reply that it is the opposition that wants it both ways: both to preserve the causal power belonging to the presence of features wide and small, and to succumb to the Tractarian vision, by insisting that the real engine of change is the irredeemably particular configuration of things. And this view, I have argued, renders it invisible to physics, and indeed to all human thought.

Folk psychology is a wonderful thing. It is no wonder that we are baffled by the prodigious knowledge and abstraction, the sheer instrumentation, that enables us to look through the particular features of ourselves and others that might otherwise get in the way, and type us all by our beliefs and desires. The difficulty lies in seizing and sustaining the idea that in so doing we are identifying real features, whose instantiation is causally effective in producing events in the world. In this chapter, I have not addressed all the obstacles to doing this, but I hope I have removed some.

Notes

1. Stephen Stich, *From Folk Psychology to Cognitive Science* (Cambridge, Mass.: Bradford, 1983), esp. chs. 4 and 5.
2. This point is well made in Patricia Churchland, "Replies to Comments," *Inquiry*, 29 (1986):254.

3. Ibid. p. 256. See also Paul Churchland, "Eliminative Materialism and Propositional Attitudes," *Journal of Philosophy* 78 (1981): 71.
4. From J. Fodor, *Psychosemantics* (Cambridge, Mass.: Bradford 1987), ch. 1, sect. 3.
5. Stich, *From Folk Psychology to Cognitive Science*, Stich, p. 229.
6. Paul Churchland, "Eliminative Materialism and Propositional Attitudes." p. 74.
7. This definition is also given e.g., John Haugeland, "Weak Supervenience," *American Philosophical Quarterly*, 19 (1982):93–103.
8. This is my phrasing of the view I take to be implicit in Patricia Churchland's *Neurophilosophy* (Cambridge, Mass.: Bradford, 1986), ch. 7.
9. Ibid., p. 357.
10. Ibid., p. 357.
11. See, for example, C. J. Adkins, *Equilibrium Thermodynamics* (Cambridge: Cambridge University Press, 1983).
12. Berent Enc, "In Defense of the Identity Theory," *Journal of Philosophy*, 80 (1983): 279.
13. I am here grateful to Robert Kraut and George Pappas. The difficulty over solidity is heralded in Locke's ambivalent attitude to the possibility of knowing the qualities, as distinct from just the powers, of things (including microscopical things): Compare, for instance, *Essay*, bk. II, ch. 4, sects. 1 and 6. See also my 'Filling in Space," *Analysis*, 50 (April 1990): 62–65.
14. Haugeland, "Weak Supervenience," p. 100.
15. Stich, *From Folk Psychology to Cognitive Science*, p. 237.
16. I owe David Lewis thanks for pointing out the need for caution here.
17. David Lewis, "An Argument for the Identity Theory," in *Philosophical Papers*, Vol. 1 (New York: Oxford University Press, 1983), p. 100.
18. Lewis reminded me in private correspondence that his target in the paper was not this kind of role state theory but a behaviorism that thought it did know what to say: It had to say that if there was no display of the disposition, the psychological state was absent. I quite accept that this position is unhappy, but my point remains that it is not necessary (nor, as Lewis of course knows, sufficient, since one has to find a principle for selecting locks for which the identity holds) to insist on the identity by way of refuting it.
19. F. Jackson and P. Pettit, "Functionalism and Broad Content," *Mind*, 97 (1988): 381:–400; p. 394.
20. Ned Block, "Can the Mind Change the World?" in G. Boolos, ed., *Essays in Honour of Hilary Putnam* (Cambridge: Cambridge University Press, 1990), pp. 155–156.
21. Ibid., p. 158.
22. The best sustained discussion of the issues that trouble me, in the Davidsonian context of event identity, is the interchange between Ted Honderich and Peter Smith: Ted Honderich, "The Argument for Anomalous Monism," *Analysis*, 42(1982): 59–64; "Anomalous Monism: Reply to Smith," *Analysis*, 43 (1983): 147–149; "Smith and the Lover of Mauve," *Analysis*, 44 (1984):86–89. Peter Smith: "Bad News for Anomalous Monism?" *Analysis*, 42 (1982): 220–224; "Anomalous Monism and Epiphenomenalism: A Reply to Honderich," *Analysis* 44 (1984): 83–86. Honderich's original instinct is also found in F.

Stoutland, "The Causation of Behaviour" in J. Hintikka, ed., *Essays in Honour of G. H. von Wright* (Dordrecht: Reidel, 1976). My position is most similar to that of Peter Menzies, "Against Causal Reductionism," *Mind*, 97 (1988): 551–574.

23. Lewis rightly reminds me that his original example was a bicycle lock, and that cylindrical locks are not commonly used on houses. But "folk burglar prevention" sounded better to me than "folk bicycle theft prevention," so I have let it stand.
24. It is only the particular instance, not the feature, that causes things to happen. Instead of "the instancing" of a feature," we get the event in its full (transcendental) particularity. Pondering this intuition, I find myself reminded of Bradley's hostility to abstraction: the view that only a picture of reality that involves no abstraction (i.e., reality itself) is (really) true, strikes me as very like the view that only the total Tractarian particular causes. But I cannot explore the relationship here. See Stewart Candlish, "The Truth About F. H. Bradley." *Mind*, 98 (1989):331–348, for the "identity" theory of truth.
25. For recent scepticism, see Hilary Putnam, *Representation and Reality* (Cambridge, Mass.: Bradford Books, 1988).
26. Of course, there is a huge literature trying to deny this. Some arguments are canvassed in my "The Identity of Propositions" in S. Blackburn, ed., *Meaning Reference and Necessity* (Cambridge: Cambridge University Press, 1975). Paul Churchland has been active in allowing that intentional predicates can enter causal relations although the relata are abstract, by drawing the parallel with "numerical attitudes" (e.g., *Matter and Consciousness* (Cambridge, Mass.: Bradford, 2nd ed., 1988), ch. 3, sect. 4. Contrast Stich, *From Folk Psychology to Cognitive Science*, p. 243.
27. R. G. Collingwood, *An Introduction to Metaphysics* (Oxford: Oxford University Press, 1940), chs. 11 and 12.
28. Putnam, *Representation and Reality*, passim.

10 "Tractarian states" and folk-psychological explanation

Jay Rosenberg

I

In its day, folk demonology was a theory invoked to explain some peculiar human behavior – and, indeed, occasionally other phenomena as well – and was widely regarded as doing a pretty good job of it. Its day, however, is past. The explanatory jobs once discharged by such folk-demoniac notions as "possession" and "exorcism" are nowadays performed by other, more reputable notions – or they are not undertaken at all, the very phenomena once ostensibly explained having themselves long since disappeared from the science's explanatory agenda.

From the epistemological point of view, many now agree, folk psychology is also a theory, still invoked nowadays to explain some peculiar human behavior – and, indeed, most ordinary human behavior as well – and still widely regarded as doing a pretty good job of it. Its day, in other words, is not yet past. But there are those who claim to have read the handwriting on the wall. They claim that its day is surely passing and that we can already discern why and how the explanatory jobs now performed by such folk-psychological notions as "belief" and "desire" must either be assigned to other, more reputable notions or perhaps not be undertaken at all, the very phenomena ostensibly explained being themselves somehow radically or fundamentally misconceived. Simon Blackburn's quarrel[1] is with such 'eliminativists'. He thinks that they have been reading the handwriting on the wall through bad metaphysical spectacles and that it is time for a change of prescription. My aim in this brief essay is to register a few modest reservations regarding Blackburn's metaphysical qualms.

Editor's note: Some of Jay Rosenberg's quotations refer to an earlier draft of Simon Blackburn's essay, not the revised version printed in this volume. The original quotations have been retained because they remain accurate statements of Blackburn's central thesis.

What it means to call folk psychology a "theory," the parties to this dispute seem to agree, is that thoughts, beliefs, desires, intentions, volitions (or "acts of will"), and other such folk-psychological beasties have the epistemological status of explanatory postulates or posits or hypotheses. Specifically, in the version of the "theory theory," at issue in Blackburn's chapter, beliefs and desires, for example, are postulated or posited *functional states of organisms,* causally mediating between the stimuli to which those organisms are exposed and their subsequent behavior. In Blackburn's story, saying this amounts to embracing a version of the "network theory" according to which the *terms* of folk psychology get their meanings from "implicit functional definitions," characteristically formulable as platitudinous generalizations connecting beliefs, desires, intentions, and so forth, with their typical causes, inter-relations, and behavioral effects.

Blackburn's eliminativists detect a prospectively fatal tension between the claims of folk psychology thus understood and our growing body of scientific knowledge. Their general strategy, he tells us, "is to try to say something specific about the kind of state that having a belief or desire must be taken to be, and then arguing that there may be no possibility of evolving science countenancing that state." It turns out, then, that eliminativists claim to discern the twilight of folk psychology from two perspectives: (1) the Olympian heights of a "scientific realism" that affirms "the sovereignty of physics" and (2) the murky intentional depths of folk psychology's own interior workings.

From the Olympian perspective, the eliminativists interpret the sovereignty of physics as imposing the demand that all true theories be reducible to physics in a sense requiring the construction of extension-preserving mappings of the truths of the reduced theory into truths of the reducing theory, and they proceed to offer counsels of despair regarding the prospective success or failure of the implied project of defining physical predicates coextensive with those of folk psychology.

Blackburn, however, does not propose to counter such counsels of despair with counsels of optimism. His strategy, rather, is to deny that scientific-realist folk psychologists are committed to such desperate projects in the first place. The "reducibilities" genuinely implied by the sovereignty of physics require not that "images" of, for example, the macroscopic geological laws governing riverbank soil erosion be constructible within, say, fluid hydrodynamics, but only that each "token" geological event of the types specified in those laws be an event describable, and thus explicable, in hydrodynamic terms. "The relevant sense of reduction is one that marches in step with physical explanation," –

but physical *explicability* is agglomerative and transitive in ways that belie the demand for coextensive terms in the reduced and the reducing theories.

What could make one think otherwise, according to Blackburn, is a *metaphysical* mistake – "the mistake of supposing that for any physical property there should be a story, in terms of the configuration of some constituent things, saying what it *is*." The basic notion in physical explanation, however, is that of a physical system in a physical state, characterized by quantifiable intensive (local) and extensive magnitudes. "The art of the scientist," he writes, "is to find the right variables and the right laws connecting them to give a function for the evolution of one state into another," and it is vital to the success of this enterprise that concepts emerge that can span systems in different *configurational* states – that is, states narrowly individuated in purely structural terms, for example, "in terms of mere spatial array and velocity of constituent particles." It is the "Tractarian" notion that, in order to be scientifically respectable, states or properties entering into laws at any level of theoretical science's *explanatory* hierarchy must ultimately be identifiable with configurational states or properties of entities postulated at the lowest level of physical science's *compositional* hierarchy that is the mistaken "metaphysical vision" underlying the eliminativists' conviction that the notion of a physical state per se stands in the way of the compatibility of the sovereignty of physics and the truth of folk psychology.

In its essential respects, the story Blackburn tells about the eliminativists' view from their second perspective runs parallel to this one. Within folk psychology's intratheoretic depths, our eliminativists discover an implicit commitment to "Davidson's model": the idea that the intentionally individuated, contentful mental states posited by folk psychology can fulfill their functional-explanatory role vis-à-vis behavior consistently with the sovereignty of physics only if they are ultimately redescribable as physically law-abiding; causally potent "inner" states (first neurophysiologically and, later, microphysically individuated). Here, too, the eliminativists offer their counsels of despair – now regarding the prospective success or failure of the implied project of reconciling the structure of discrete, "syntactic" causal states ostensibly demanded by this Davidsonian model with the connectionistic, nondigital, and "networky" sorts of architectures ostensibly being turned up by actual contemporary neurophysiological research.

Blackburn's aim in the second part of his essay is to "disrupt" this Davidsonian model "of the same state subject to different descriptions, under one of which, if it causes anything, it must have a lawlike connection with its effect." Here, too, his strategy is to resist the idea that the scientific respectability of folk psychology requires us to "make good" its explanations by identifying its posited behavioral and dispositional (functional) mental states with the "underlying" neural or structural (configurational) states variously "subserving" them. Here too, "the sovereignty of physics only requires that the connection between the [functional] disposition and the underlying [physical] state is *explicable*," and, in fact, "physical explicability does not require that we work in terms of states and their identity at all."

Although he has a number of insightful and useful things to say about the illusoriness of various advantages claimed for this version of the identity theory, the crux of Blackburn's critical contention is that the *causal-explanatory* role assigned by folk psychology to its posited mental states no more requires us to identify them with configurational, "Tractarian" states of the fundamental constituents of organisms than did the *physical-explanatory* role of properties entering into the laws of "reducible" special sciences require us to identify them with such structural states. That "we act as we do because of beliefs and desires" will entail that "beliefs and desires are [identical with] causally effective [neurostructural] states, bringing about different movements and behavior," only against the background of a tacit but mistaken metaphysical commitment to the 'Tractarian' idea that no story could reveal the "intrinsic, causally potent features" of any state unless it were an account framed in terms of the configuration of some spatially localizable constituent things and thereby specifying what that state compositionally is. The "initial wrong turning," according to Blackburn, is "that of supposing that the relation to a propositional object or thought, in folk-psychological attributions, is to be construed as the presence of a kind of object with literal spatial position and boundaries, in the head" (or, for that matter, extending beyond the head).

One goes astray, in fact, as soon as one accedes to the idea that, in order to "make good" folk-psychological explanations of conduct in a manner consistent with the sovereignty of physics, there must be some way of individuating the mental states to which those explanations appeal as such (i.e., as mental states) that offers a prospect of subsuming them under narrowly causal lawlike relations, so that it is the occurrence of those states, thus individuated, that makes the difference to behavior. But the *essential* identification of folk-psychological mental states is given by specifications of their contents, and states structurally, configurationally, or compositionally individuated can therefore be related to the mental states identified in the original explanations *not* in the sought terms of identity, but only per accidens.[2] Thus, even if these extensionally individuated states do fall within the scope of some causal covering law, their doing so does not and cannot "make good" the original [functional] explanation in the sense intended.

But now, concludes Blackburn, once such "Davidsonian" arguments for the reification of folk psychology's posited mental states and their (contingent, token) identity with the neurophysiological states or microphysical configurations that variously "subserve" them have been undermined – that is, once we have eliminated the felt need to say in structural terms what a state of belief or desire is – we shall see that claims of the truth of folk-psychological theory are simply unaffected by empirical discoveries, for example, to the effect that there is no explanatorily useful level of neurophysiological or microphysical structural organization of the human brain that instantiates linearities, syntactic articulations, or computational relationships analogous to those characteristic of the content-specifying clauses of the language of "propositional attitude psychology." "The single-belief state of folk psychology involves no commitment to one or many genuinely internal mechanisms, any more than the single kinematic state of a motor car – being in uniform motion in a straight line, say – requires that anything, let alone any given number of things, is happening inside it."

II

So far I have been trying, more or less faithfully, to recapitulate the central contentions of Blackburn's essay as I understand them. I am not confident that I have gotten them all right, but the confusion that surely remains will doubtless emerge as I proceed. The time has come, however, for me to say something *about* the essay, and the first thing I should say that I find a great of deal of what Blackburn has to say both right-headed and congenial. I certainly do not propose to enter the lists on behalf of eliminativism.[3] Folk-psychological eliminativism is only the occasion-conditioned surface theme of the essay in any event. There is also rather a lot of interesting metaphysics *cum* philosophy of science going on in support of that thematic surface, and that is the topic I should like to explore further.

Blackburn appears to be suggesting that there is something basically wrong-headed about appealing *at all* to the metaphysical picture of state- or property-*identity* (a single state or property that is subject to different descriptions or modes of individuation, one of which is somehow fundamental) as part of the proper philosophical interpretation of the ontological relationship of supervenience. What makes it wrong-headed is that it rests on what he calls "the Tractarian mistake" – a misguided metaphysical presupposition roughly to the effect that *structural* or *configurational* properties of systems in some important way are (metaphysically or ontologically) prior to functional or other "supervenient" properties of systems. And if this is indeed what Blackburn intends, there are two questions that should be examined: first, whether appeals to the identity picture are fundamentally motivated by the "Tractarian mistake" and, second, whether in the last analysis the "Tractarian mistake" really is a mistake. I am not certain about the answer to either of these questions.

Before proceeding further, however, a small matter of terminology needs to be clarified. Blackburn's decision to brand as "Tractarian" the metaphysical mistake he discerns, I am convinced, reflects a misreading of the *Tractatus Logico-Philosophicus* and thus unnecessarily maligns the good name of the youthful Wittgenstein. In particular, there is nothing in the *Tractatus* to support the identification of *its* "configurations of objects" with *spatial* (or spatiotemporal) arrays. Although Tractarian ontology is admittedly notorious for its opacities, it is, I think, reasonably clear that references to "space" there predominately invoke the generic mathematical sense of the term, according to which any appropriately structured combinatioral system of elements qualifies as a "space." Thus we find "color space" (whose elements are colors) and "logical space" (whose elements are possible states of affairs). And where the literal (geometrical) sense of "space" *is* in question, we typically find "spatial objects" and "spatial pictures" being contrasted with objects and pictures of other sorts, with space being listed or treated as one among many possible "forms of objects" (2.0121, 2.0241, 2.171).

The story underlying Wittgenstein's talk of "configurations" is complicated, but the significant center of it is Wittgenstein's picture-theoretic resolution of the classical problematic of predication. To put it telegraphically, Wittgenstein argues that one can explain how a bit of language can (be used to) *say* something only if one understands sentences or propositions not as complex linguistic objects, lists, or concatenations of names (referring expressions) but, rather, as "configurations" of names, that is, as linguistic *facts* to the effect that names are related to one another in such and such a way.

3.1432: Instead of, "The complex sign '*aRb*' says that *a* stands to *b* in the relation *R*," we ought to put, "That '*a*' stands to '*b*' in a certain relation says *that aRb*."

And, although Wittgenstein *illustrates* his account by means of a spatial analogy –

3.1431:   The essence of a propositional sign is very clearly seen if we imagine one composed of spatial object (such as tables, chairs, and books) instead of written signs.
         Then the spatial arrangement of these things will express the sense of the proposition.

– there is nothing in this account that demands that *all* (possible) representing elements be spatial or spatially configured – indeed, in *spoken* language, the relevant "configurations" are surely temporal and acoustic – much less that all represented elements in the (atomic) facts be thus depicted. Wittgenstein's Tractarian ontology, in other words, is perfectly compatible with a physics whose fundamental "objects" are not localizable particles with determinate spatiotemporal trajectories but, for example, polydimensional "rolled-up superstrings" or singularities and gradients in some abstruse n-dimensional field.

Differently put, Wittgenstein's focus in the *Tractatus* is not on the questions of "supervenience" and "reduction" but on the question of "analysis." His conclusion is not that structural or (spatiotemporal) configurational properties of physical systems somehow are ontologically or metaphysically prior to functional or other "supervenient" properties of such systems, but that there must be a stratum of *representation* at which "saying that p" is understood and explained in terms of (extensional) picturing relationships between representing systems ("configurations of names") and represented systems ("configurations of objects").

Nevertheless, to return to the mainstream, I am uncertain as to whether there is not something philosophically worthwhile underlying what Blackburn regards as misguided Tractarian intuitions (I shall henceforth call them "structuralist" intuitions), and one thing that makes me so is a subtext that keeps cropping up in Blackburn's own essay: such notions as that of multiple "realizations" of a state or property, of one folk-psychological state's being "subserved" on different occasions by distinct "neuronal setups," or of "a relation between the mean kinetic energy of molecules in the gas, and whatever *makes up* the thermal energy of [an]other system." What does it mean to say that a functional systemic state or supervenient systemic property is "realized by" or "subserved by" or "made up of" this or that other state or property or "set-up"?

As far as I can make out, Blackburn's answer is that the "realizing" or "subserving" states or properties or "set-ups" are the ones referred to in explanations of such functional states or supervenient properties that are formulated in terms of physical concepts applying at the level of the system's components (i.e., the items comprising the system). Consider temperature. Blackburn argues convincingly that there is no reason to identify the systemic property, temperature, with any of its "realization" (kinetic energy of moving molecules, vibration energy of static molecules, etc.), since "we already have it down as the property two systems have in common when they are each capable of thermal equilibrium with a third." Such remarks are inter alia designed to redirect our attention from states and properties of systems to the patterns of changing relations between or among systems. "[The] fundamental thing to be said about temperature . . . is that what is needed is a definition of the equivalence relation of having the same temperature as . . . " The zeroth law of thermodynamics is thus what legitimizes the concept of temperature by allowing the requisite definition of an equivalence class of systems in thermal equilibrium.

Two physical systems, in turn, are in thermal equilibrium when there is no net transfer of thermal energy arising from their contact. Here our attention is drawn to such diachronic processes of systemic *change* or *evolution* as heating and cooling. Is the moral, then, that we should trade in our earlier metaphysical picture of the *property* identity for a correlative picture of *process* identity, by concluding here, for example, that (the process of) heating or cooling is just the flow or transfer of thermal energy from one physical system to another? As I understand Blackburn, the answer is no. Just as there is no reason to identify the thermodynamic systemic property temperature with any of its "realizations," so too there is no reason to identify thermodynamic intersystemic processes of heating and cooling with any of the energy flows and transfers that variously "subserve" them. Heating and cooling are not *identical with* transfers of thermal energy; they are *explained by* transfers of thermal energy. As I read Blackburn, in other words, what he seems to be suggesting is that we replace *identification* by *explicability* in our philosophical accounts of "reduction" and "supervenience" all the way down the hierarchy of physical systems.

But all the way down to *where*? The crucial point is that the explanatory hierarchy at issue here is also a *compositional* hierarchy. To explain the thermodynamic properties of, for example, gases as properties of a "physical system" is already to commit oneself to one sort of "identification" – the identification of samples of gases with collections (or "populations") of certain ontologically more fundamental items, molecules, of which those gases are composed. A sample of gas consists of molecules, and as Sellars has stressed, it "is because a gas is – in some sense of 'is' – a cloud of molecules which are behaving in theoretically defined ways, and, *hence*, in particular cases, places and times behaves in a certain way, that it obeys [such phenomenological-empirical laws as] the Boyle–Charles law."[4]

Where does this compositional hierarchy of physical systems bottom out? The answer, surely, is that it bottoms out in whatever items are not themselves systems of still other items; and the "sovereignty of physics," in turn, implies that it is physical theory that will (ultimately) tell us what these items are. What I want to suggest is that part of what underlies the "structuralist" metaphysical picture that Blackburn wants to reject is the conviction that at this point in the physical hierarchy there is no longer any room for what he calls "non-Tractarian" properties and states. The root intuition, in other words, is that what ultimately legitimizes our explanatory reliance on functional states and properties is that, at the bottom of the compositional hierarchy of physical systems of systems of systems (of, e.g., quarks, or what have you), such properties and states can be "made good" in terms of structural or configurational – or, at least, *non*functional and, in that sense, properly "structuralist" – states and properties. The structuralist intuition, in other words, is that ultimate intelligibility of *how* a physical system does whatever it (functionally) does depends on the in-principle availability of an account of *what* that system (compositionally) is.

The reader will recognize such reasoning as a metaphysical counterpart to Dennett's argument in "Why the Law of Effect Will Not Go Away," according to which explanatory reliance on nested systems of successively more stupid intentional homunculi is justified by the (well-founded) conviction that the resulting "reductive chain" ultimately bottoms out in homunculi *so* stupid that they admit of straightforwardly extensional redescriptions. But if this much, or something like it, is in fact correct – and I would be the first to admit that there much more needs to be said here – it will follow that Blackburn has not quite shown that we should reject the structuralist metaphysical presuppositions he discerns behind functionalist token-token identity theories root and branch. At best, he has shown that we should reject them *branch*, but the *roots* still seem to me to have a lot going for them.

In fact, however, I have some worries about the branches, too. In particular, I am not confident that we can be as sanguine as Blackburn sometimes appears to be about the strategy of *substituting* appeals to the notion of explicability for appeals to the notion of identity, in our accounts of "supervenience" and "reduction," because I am not sure that there is no deep and unavoidable conceptual connection between the picture of "the same thing under different descriptions" and at least one central form of theoretical explanation. More precisely, it may turn out that one defensible aspect of the structuralist metaphysical intuitions that trouble Blackburn is that the way in which explanatory reliance on functional properties is legitimized by its ultimately "bottoming out" in a family of structural properties rests on the possibility thereby established of *reascending* the original (system-compositional) chain of explanations precisely as a chain of token-token identifications of properly "structuralist" states or properties. Something like this, I suspect, may well be the deeper intuition underlying the notion that folk psychology's folksy *"be*causal" explanations qualify as ("allusive") *causal* explanations only if they have somehow succeeded in making reference to "structuralist" states that fall directly under physical causal laws that describe operative causal mechanisms or capture "intrinsic, causally potent features."

If this were arguably correct, however, then, although something would still be wrong with the Davidsonian picture, it would not be its reliance on structuralist metaphysical presuppositions per se. Rather this version of the Davidsonian picture would err by mistaking for a *proximate* constraint on the epistemic legitimacy of individual folk-psychological explanations *in medias res* what is, in fact, a *remote* metaphysical condition of the compatibility of physics' ontological sovereignty with the epistemic legitimacy of folk psychology's functional explanations in general.

Blackburn, as I have noted, insists that such folk-psychological mental states as beliefs and desires are essentially individualized by their contents, and that states structurally, configurationally, or compositionally individuated can therefore be related to the mental states identified in a folk-psychological explanation not in terms of identity but only per accidens. But surely what one needs first to abandon here is not the idea that specific functional states ("tokens") of a person's believing that p or desiring that q are in some sense "identical" with particular physical (e.g., neurological) states of a biological organism but, rather, the peculiar notion that such theoretical explanatory identifications have the same logical form as, for example, "Hesperus = Phosphorus" and so must (granting, for the sake of this argument, a number of Kripke's more contentious theses) be necessary if true.

Such remarks, of course, are an invitation to extended discussion of scientific or physical explanation per se, and it is well known that one can poke about in that rat's nest for quite a long time before one succeeds in scaring up some halfway useful rats. At a bare minimum, we should need to explore in some detail the differences and similarities between the conditions of epistemic legitimacy for *intra*theoretical explanations of individual phenomena and those for *inter*theoretical explanations of (the successes and shortcomings of) "reduced" predecessor theories by their "reducing" successors. I have done some of this elsewhere, but my allotted space is insufficient for me to do any meaningful amount of it here; so I shall not even try.[5]

It is, however, worth remarking that at least part of the "Davidsonian model" appears to be built into the very foundations of folk psychology, in the sense that one can plausibly argue that the *point* of ascribing content to the beliefs and desires posited by folk psychology in the first place is precisely to *facilitate* their playing a mediating role between sensory inputs and behavioral outputs that can be "causal" in a sense acceptable to, for example, physics. To appreciate this, it is worth taking a short trip "back to the rough ground" to remind ourselves of what folk psychology looks like in action. Consider, for example, the following short and wordless drama:

Tom opens a pack of cigarettes, removes one from the pack, and puts it in his mouth. He searches through his pockets. Then he stands up, crosses to his desk, and rummages in a drawer. He closes the drawer, pauses, snaps his fingers, and walks briskly into the kitchen. There he pauses again and peers about, then opens another drawer and rummages inside. He closes the drawer, opens a cupboard, glances inside, and picks up a pack of matches lying on a shelf. Striking a match, he lights the cigarette in his mouth.

Borrowing a term from the theater, let us call this the *blocking* of the scene. This familiar drama readily evokes a parallel commentary:

Tom *wanted* to smoke a cigarette. When he came to light his cigarette, however, he *discovered* that he didn't have any matches, so he went *looking* for some. He *thought* that there might be some in his desk drawer, but *found* that there weren't any there. He *reflected* for a moment about where they might be, then suddenly *remembered* having *noticed* some matches in the kitchen, although he couldn't *recall* exactly where. He *guessed* that they might be in the drawer, but it turned out that they weren't there. Finally, it *occurred* to him to try the cupboard, where he indeed *found* the matches and so was able at last to light his cigarette.

If we were to retain the theatrical metaphor, we might call this the (actor's) *motivation*, but for the time being I shall simply call it the commentary. The *commentary* is folk psychology at work. The question is, What does the commentary do for us that the blocking alone does not do?

On the face of it, the relation between the blocking and the commentary is *explanatory*. One offers such a commentary in the first instance as a way of making sense (a certain *kind* of sense) of the blocking, to answer various "Why?" questions about it. Why did Tom put a cigarette in his mouth? Why did he search his pockets? Why did he rummage through the desk drawer? Why did he pause? Why did he snap his fingers? Why did he go into the kitchen? Why did he open the cupboard?

The answers to such "Why?" questions are typically cast in terms of "becausal" statements:

1. Tom put a cigarette in his mouth because he wanted to smoke.
2. Tom searched his pockets (rummaged in the desk drawer, went into the kitchen, opened the cupboard) because he wanted to find a match [and believed that there were (or might be) matches in his pockets (the desk drawer, the kitchen, the cupboard)].

A *canonical* folk-psychological explanation, in other words, attributes to Tom one or more of a family of *desires* (or *intentions*) – to smoke; to light his cigarette; to find a match – and one or more of a family of *beliefs* (or *convictions*) – that matches are in the desk drawer; that no matches are in the desk drawer; that matches are in the kitchen; that matches might be in the kitchen drawer; that no matches are in the kitchen drawer; that matches might be in the cupboard; that matches are indeed in the cupboard – and it presents a bit of conduct from the blocking as an action directed toward an *end* (the satisfaction of a desire or fulfilling of an intention), guided by matter-of-fact beliefs.

Such folk-psychological "becausal" claims are therefore characteristically *teleological*.

1*. Tom put a cigarette in his mouth *in order to smoke*.
2*. Tom searched his pockets (rummaged in the desk drawer, went into the kitchen, opened the cupboard) *in order to* find a match [believing that there were (or might be) matches in his pockets (the desk drawer, the kitchen, the cupboard)].[6]

As happens with all teleological stories, however, thinking of their "becausal" claims on the model of *causal* explanations consistent with the "sovereignty of physics" immediately gives rise to a variety of problems. First, when the events belonging to a scene's blocking that are adverted to in the explanans of a canonical "becausal" story do happen, they happen *later* than those episodes in the scene's blocking that the "becausal" statements are invoked to explain. Tom put a cigarette in his mouth because he wanted to smoke, but Tom's smoking occurred considerably later; he searched his pockets (rummaged in the desk drawer, went into the kitchen, opened the cupboard) because he wanted to find a match, but, again, Tom's finding a match occurred later than all of these events. The temporal structure of the *blocking* events adverted to in the explanans of such "becausal" claims is incompatible with their being interpreted as causally related, in the ordinary way, to the events specified in the explanandum.

Second, beliefs and desires can be "generic" in ways that objects and states-of-affairs prima facie cannot. Tom can want a match, but no *particular* match, and he can believe that there are matches in the desk drawer without its being the case that there are any particular matches such that he believes of them that *they* are in the desk drawer.

Third, and most troublesome, such "becausal" claims sometimes advert in their explanans to events that *do not happen* (although, were they to happen, they would belong to the story of the blocking). Tom opened the desk drawer because he hoped to find matches there, but no event of *Tom's finding matches in the desk drawer* occurred at all.

What generates such puzzles, of course, is a tacit picture of belief or desire (or, more generally, of thought) as a sui generis "intentional *relation*" between a person and an actual or possible object or state-of-affairs. The ascription of *content* to beliefs and desires, on the other hand – that is, interpreting them not as intentional relations but rather as *representational states* of persons – sorts it all out. It permits such (functional, teleological) "becausal" states to be causal states in the ordinary "structuralist" sense. It is not the later event of Tom's smoking that, qua "final cause," moves him (by its attraction) to put a cigarette into his mouth but the earlier event of Tom's representing himself smoking which, qua (partial) "efficient cause," contributes to the bringing about of that behavior. It is not some (fictional, imaginary, or "subsistent") nonevent of finding matches in the desk drawer that (causally) explains Tom's opening the drawer, but the real event of his (falsely or suppositionally) *representing* there being matches in the drawer that does so.[7]

What I am suggesting, in other words, is that it may be more difficult than Blackburn supposes to pry apart the *representational* role of folk-psychology's posited "inner states" – that is, their having *contents* – from at least a partially Davidsonian conception of their *explanatory* role – that is, their function as mediating *causes*. While the scientific respectability of folk psychology perhaps does not requires us to "make good" its explanations by *directly* identifying its posited functional mental states with those "underlying" neural or structural (configurational) states that "realize" or "subserve" them, the possibility of understanding teleological-*reason* explanations as scientifically respectable, albeit "allusive," *causal* explanations does arguably require that it at least be possible to do so *indirectly* – for example, by (generically) "descending" the compositional-explanatory hierarchy of physical systems to its "structuralist" foundations – that is, to the point at which there is no longer a distinction to be drawn between what a physical system (compositionally) is and what it (functionally) does – and then (specifically) "reascending" that same hierarchy through a series of token-token structural state identifications to reach the believings, desirings, and behavings with which one began. For that, surely, is the least it would take in order that a given functional state could properly be said to be, on this occasion, "realized" or "subserved" by a particular structural or configurational setup at all.

III

Blackburn's rich, difficult, and provocative essay operates on a number of different levels, and it would be folly to attempt in a brief commentary to engage it on very many of them. The eliminativists I have left to fend for themselves, and I am confident that they will do so quite capably. The poor syntactic-engine, causal-role functionalists out there are beset from all sides in this discussion, and even though I am not exactly a paradigm of the kind of functionalist either Blackburn or the eliminativists have in mind, I do have a lot philosophically in common with those folks and would not be surprised on another occasion to find myself arguing rather more directly on their behalf. But the basic charge Blackburn is leveling in his essay is that a certain philosophy of science is shaped by bad metaphysics; and therefore, I have elected to respond to him in the first instance as a metaphysically inclined philosopher of science. The metaphysics of theoretical identifications, states, and causes is indeed ill-understood, and I do not mean to suggest that I have here made even halting steps toward properly sorting it out. But I do hope to have said enough to suggest that it needs more sorting out than Blackburn gives it in his essay before the "Davidsonian" understanding of folk psychology common to causal-role functionalists and eliminativists alike can comfortably be abandoned. My aim in these remarks, then, has been the relatively modest one of suggesting that one of

Blackburn's own passing critical comments, slightly modified, applies to his own work as well: "Alas, there is no escaping metaphysics without doing more of it than [his essay] allows."

Notes

1. Simon Blackburn, "Losing Your Mind: Physics, Identity, and Folk Burglar Prevention," Chapter 9 of this volume.
2. Otherwise put: Content specifications *rigidly* designate mental states (e.g., beliefs and desires). The identity theory under examination requires, however, that "supervening" descriptions *non*rigidly designate states that are (or can be) *rigidly* designated by "subvening" (structural or configurational) descriptions. For that a given mental state supervenes on some structural states is to be a contingent fact, but true statements of identity between objects rigidly designated are necessarily true.
3. As it turns out, I am not an eliminativist myself – although for quite different reasons than Blackburn's.
4. Sellars, "The Language of Theories," in G. Maxwell and H. Feigl, eds., *Current Issues in the Philosophy of Science* (New York: Holt, Rinehart & Winston, 1961), pp. 71–72.
5. To indicate a direction: As I parse it, the claim that, for example, samples of gas "consist of" molecules or "are identical with" populations of molecules abbreviates a rather complicated story regarding the possibility of mapping the fundamental principles of the classical theory of gases into the kinetic theory, enriched by counternomological assumptions, in a manner satisfying the constraints of a double explanatory accountability. See, for example, my "Coupling, Retheoretization, and the Correspondence Principle" *Synthese* 45, (1980):351–385; and "Comparing the Incommensurable: Another Look at Convergent Realism," *Philosophical Studies* 54, (1988):163–193.
6. It is worth noting that there are various other "becausal" claims in the vicinity that are *not* examples of such canonical folk-psychological explanations: (1) Tom wanted to find a match because he wanted to light a cigarette. (2) Tom paused because he was reflecting on (trying to remember) where there might be some matches. (3) Tom snapped his fingers because he suddenly remembered having noticed some matches in the kitchen.

  In (1) the ostensible explanandum itself belongs to the commentary, not to the blocking. In (2), the ostensible explanans is a simultaneous process, not an account of beliefs and desires. In (3), the teleological dimension falls strikingly away: Tom does not snap his fingers in order to suddenly remember having noticed some matches in the kitchen. The general question of *which* folk-psychological "becausal" explanations qualify as (genuine or "allusive") causal explanations, and why, is a fascinating one, but there is no time to pursue it here. (It is clear enough, for example, that there is more to the notion of a *causal* condition than the truth of counterfactuals of the form "If these things had not been true, others would not have been true either," although it is far from clear what more there is to the notion.)

7. I offer a fuller discussion of folk-psychological explanations in a wider, evolutionary, context in my "Attribution and Appraisal: Elements of a Theory of Conduct," ch. 6 of my *One World and Our Knowledge of It* (Dordrecht, Holland: Reidel, 1980).

11 The autonomy of folk psychology

Joseph Margolis

I shall confine the argument that follows to a sketch of a program for supporting a "folk-psychological" orientation to the human world against various strategies for the reduction or retirement of that orientation, and for supporting the thesis that the "folk" orientation cannot be convincingly construed as yielding to a computational model. The full arguments required at every point are not actually supplied, but they could be – and they have been formulated elsewhere, at least in part and promisingly.

I

In an extremely suggestive recent paper, Jaakko Hintikka raises the question that he calls the "main currently unsolved problem" concerning the "function of logic in argumentation and reasoning."[1] He thinks of logic, on the model of game theory, in the following way: "Actual reasoning should not be approached as if it were a chain of deductive inferences. Rather, what the theory of substantial inference is, is the body of principles of belief-changes in the presence of new evidence."[2] He then distinguishes between "definitory rules" – those rules that stipulate or define "which moves are possible, or . . . which moves are admissible" in the game intended – and "strategic rules" – those rules that, for open-endedly extended, even unforeseeable moves that may yet be admitted, reliably yield the "values" sought (the "utilities or payoffs"), say, moving belief in the direction of truth (in the game intended).[3]

Hintikka considers the "metatheorist's" question of the choice of games among alternatives suggested by a situation that invites conceptualization along one line of modeling or another; but he regularly insists that "the notion of strategy in a given game is possible to define only after the definitory rules have been set up": "Definitory rules must be learned first before strategic rules can be as such understood."[4]

Now, with due respect to Hintikka's interesting suggestion, there is reason to say that, in the "game of life," there is no clear disjunction between definitory and strategic rules, there is no prioritizing of definitory rules over strategic rules; approximate definitory rules are themselves altered and reformulated in the light of what appears to be salient or emerging strategies; the game of life is never satisfactorily given finite boundary properties of the "definitory" sort in the manner of a chess game (Hintikka's example); *and* the "definitory" rules of the game of life are never – or never include – invariantly or unalterably the rules of inference of formal logic.[5]

A perspicuous way of putting this point is to say that the "rules of inference" in *life* are themselves posited, abstracted, projected, hypothesized from practices or forms of life in terms of what we take to be the core specimens of reasonable success within the practice – *not* instantiations of the "definitory" rules – *regarding which* there is conjectured to be (effectively possessed) this or that body of information, belief, knowledge and the like, this or that set of formalizable abstract rules of reasoning (more or less), and these or those strategies or heuristics (more or less) leading to what we specify (more or less) as the values of what we take to be the implied game. In short, all such elements are terribly unsettled and *provisional*, stipulated only *within* the "game" of life *as it goes on* and as it permits, possibly even facilitates, survival, individually and collectively, without being entirely clear about how it distributively facilitates *the capture of truth* – itself assessed within the encompassing practice.

On the argument, the "definitory" rules themselves form what we suppose to be the relatively adequate, most inclusive, least alterable – *but not altogether inflexible*, Platonized, finally discovered – rules of reason, conceptually inseparable from the more transient, context-bound, particularized (though generalizable) rules of strategy for our correspondingly incompletely explicit fixed sense of the governing values of our various activities within life itself.

A very nice analogue of this corrective notion has been formulated by John Stachel reflecting on the general practice of insisting on a strong disjunction between the empirical sciences and "formal sciences." Responding to the interesting question, "Can empirical theories influence or even transform logic?" posited by Maria Luisa dalla Chiara in the light of recent puzzles generated in physics, particularly by the development of so-called quantum logic, Stachel opposes the division between the empirical and the formal – the latter paralleled in a way by Hintikka's (seeming) disjunction between definitory and strategic rules – remarking:

A more fruitful approach to the sciences . . . is based upon regarding each of them as a theoretical practice, working upon and transforming given conceptual materials to produce the particular object of knowledge characteristic of that science at a certain stage of its development. The whole hierarchical organization of the sciences into logic, mathematics, the empirical sciences – each earlier term supposedly founded independently of, and serving as part of the foundation for, the later ones – must be rejected as the consequences of an incorrect starting point in the division of formal and empirical sciences.[6]

The deep point of these preliminary observations may be put this way: The convergent import of subscribing to Stachel's recommendation and opposing Hintikka's apparent disjunction (itself intended to move us somewhat in the same direction) captures an essential part of the conceptual intuition of so-called folk psychology vis-à-vis a variety of reductive strategies, both physicalistic and "logical," which suppose that there is no genuinely fundamental theoretical objection to the in-principle abandonment or replacement of all forms of folk psychology.

Hintikka's proposal is a little more sanguine than, and somewhat different from, what we have attributed to him. For one thing, he apparently believes that the *"strategic principles"* involved in nontrivial extensions of question–answer games *"are* roughly *the same in interrogative inquiry and in deductive logic"*; for a second, "the partial parallelism [between the rules of the questioning game and the rules of deduction] extends only as far as we can, or, rather, as far as the inquirer can, assume that nature's answers are unproblematically true ['actually available']."[7] So, for the game Hintikka proposes, there is no ultimate difference between the rules of deductive logic and the rules of question–answer games, where the questions are answerable as true; the question–answer strategies are usually more productive because of the nontrivial nature of the game involved (for instance, "introduc[ing] new individuals into deductive reasoning").[8] So Hintikka does, in principle, allow a certain play where information, answers to questions put, and the like cannot be simply taken as true.[9]

What we want to say, in contrast, more in keeping with Stachel's notion than with Hintikka's, is that deductive ("definitory") rules form a family of idealizations of various sorts extrapolated *from* the more informal strategic "rules" of answering questions and gaining apparent objectives *in* the context of life in which survival, nonmassive failure, and the like are favored, in which values and payoffs are often not very explicitly defined or definable, and in which truth itself may be problematic and questions may be treated as answerable without supposing always that answers may be effectively assessed in terms of bipolar truth-values. Under those circumstances, it is entirely possible that deductive and question–answer strategies may diverge under real-time circumstances; and it may be the case that deductive rules will not be able to be prioritized over the other strategies in any way.

Hintikka, it seems fair to say, would not agree to this kind of informality: It could, for example, subvert his general commitment to a possible-worlds semantics.[10] We, on the other hand, would be inclined to deepen the complexity of the picture of the conditions of life under which deductive and interrogative strategies could be reliably extracted and generalized. The argument of the "folk-psychological" orientation, therefore, is intended in part to question the conceptual grounds on which inherently informal strategies of reasoning – not by any means chaotic or incapable of relatively reliable stabilities in context – can be replaced *in principle* or in *real-world* situations by some antecedently favored would-be simulation of human practice. In effect, the argument concedes at the start that there can be no knockdown proof that the replacement is possible or impossible, and that the dialectical contest has to do rather with reasonable bets about how we should proceed.

II

Having hinted rather broadly at the general strategy for opposing the supposed adequacy of computational models of human reasoning and intelligence, we may continue in a more pointed way by selecting as a metonym of the entire family of related puzzles questions that can be raised about the general problem of linguistic reference that appear to defy computationality in any strong sense – though, of course, our queries are not meant to disallow, retrospectively or even to some extent prospectively (in certain tailor-made circumstances), the piecemeal modeling of finite or very modestly open-ended segments of pertinent human behavior. The idea here is that human *culture* is not reducible to the purely physical or biological order of things,[11] and cannot be adequately analyzed in terms of informational regularities of the sort, say, Hintikka considers, or of any sort thought to be a restriction of some appropriately selected universal causal order,[12] or of any sort that supposes that a completely extensional syntax may be assumed to provide an adequate formal template for the perspicuous replacement of folk-psychological concepts or analyses of belief and desire and the like suited to the cognitive sciences.[13]

The cultural, I claim, is the home of what is most distinctive in human psychology and behavior, and it cannot be convincingly reduced in any of the ways suggested or by similarly motivated strategies. There, puzzles about reference – which, after all, is an aptitude essential to human linguistic behavior – provide good reasons for thinking that that sort of activity (referring) cannot be satisfactorily handled in terms that depart very far from the folk-psychological orientation. As a matter of fact, quite serendipitously, Hintikka plausibly opposes the disjunction between *reference* and *meaning* (a fortiori, the disjunction between the "theory of reference" and the "theory of meaning").[14] Given that important move, we may readily suppose that if the argument holds reasonably well for reference, it will hold just as well for predication. Hence it will hold for linguistic behavior in general; for there can be no question that there are no natural languages that preclude a significant role for enunciative or constative activity, that is, for speech acts in which reference and predication directed to truth (or to truthlike values weaker than the usual bipolar pair) obtain.[15] Also, all or nearly all forms of distinctive human mental life and behavior are deeply dependent on linguistic ability and will not yield to an analysis that is not attentive to the structures of linguistic behavior.

Consider now the following confrontation: No analysis of natural human languages can either eliminate reference altogether or displace its function by any reasonably equivalent alternative linguistic process; and no computer can perform referential functions in the logically distinctive way and within the effective range that humans can, no substitute functions that computers can perform can simulate sufficiently closely the human capacity for reference. On the intended argument, human minds exhibit noncomputerizable processes, and computer simulations of the human mind are, intrinsically, determinately defective in this regard.

We need not, on the finding supposed, deny the occurrence of artificial intelligence; but such intelligence will always be inferior to human intelligence wherever it depends on reference (in the human way). Artificial intelligence (AI) may, of course, be superior in other ways – for instance, where it depends on the brute-force computational powers of particular machines.[16] Also there is no reason (as yet) to suppose that the intelligence of computers is of the same kind as the intelligence of humans, however deficient their current level of approximations may be supposed to be;[17] and there is no reason (as yet) to suppose that human intelligence can be adequately simulated in principle by augmenting the computational capacity of an intelligent machine by adding parallel distributed processing (PDP) competences (in accord with any variant of "the Hebbian learning rule")[18] or by any primary neurophysiological competence that first assumes "that the world is prearranged in an informational fashion or that the brain contains a homunculus" (or that assumes that its mode of learning is Hebbian).[19]

In effect, this means that human intelligence could *include* programmed computational competence as well as an evolutionarily developed learning capacity that was not intrinsically programmed. But it could not be reduced to any organization of such alternative sorts. The theory, in sum, holds that human intelligence is a complex, relatively stable, developmentally open-ended, variably realized, not systematically closed organization that exhibits *culturally formed aptitudes* that cannot be captured conceptually by any combination of informational programming or neurobiological adaptation. Generally speaking, AI theorists or cognitive scientists (neuroscientists) who model neurobiology computationally tend to deny this, whereas neurobiologists skeptical of AI tend to see their own contribution as foundational rather than comprehensive. The latter usually break off their account before analyzing cultural complexities.[20] The thesis, here, is that cultural phenomena are sui generis, emergent with respect to the physical and biological and the informational when confined to the physical and biological, and irreducible to them; *and* that the folk-psychological view of human intelligence obtains only at the level of cultural emergence. Central to the claim at stake is the larger notion that the cultural capacities of persons cannot be described or explained solely in terms of whatever may describe and explain the biological capacities of *Homo sapiens*.

In an obvious sense, these claims are too general and too unguarded. But we have already conceded that there cannot be any unconditionally compelling argument decisive for our thesis in either direction. There is no knockout blow. It may well be that the functioning of large subfunctional modules of the brain – cerebellar processes, for instance, involved in perceptual–motor coordination – may be fairly characterized in computational terms.[21] We may also wonder whether the human mind actually does function in certain distinctive ways that we cannot see how to describe computationally – and, in failing to see that, we may worry about whether we are facing an insuperable barrier (that we cannot show to be insuperable in principle) in our efforts at analysis: since, that is, *we* are analyzing ourselves at what cannot fail to be a folk-psychological level of discourse. Along the same lines, it may also be true that what we take to be logically possible or impossible is itself an artifact to some extent of what, at our present level of reflection, we take it we mean by "discourse," "information," "mind," "thinking," "machines," and the like.[22] Similarly, then, our sense of computer modeling and of neurobiological reduction is contingently dependent on our present level of "folk" analysis.

These sorts of worries, then, are a dead end, although they are not without interest.

III

Let us turn to our narrower project. Here, it will be useful to introduce at least one essential distinction between two sorts of reference or two sorts of uses of expressions like definite descriptions that, on a theory, function referentially or, alternatively, function in a way that could replace a directly referential use. Thus, in an idiom introduced by Keith Donnellan, we may distinguish between the "attributive" and "referential" uses of definite descriptions:

A speaker [Donnellan says] who uses a definite description attributively in an assertion states something about whoever or whatever is the so-and-so. A speaker who uses a definite description referentially in an assertion, on the other hand, uses the description to enable his audience to pick out whom or what he is talking about and state something about that person or thing.[23]

Donnellan regards the attributive use as "nonreferential," though *if* it functioned successfully, it would single out or *denote something* that the description was uniquely true of; and if it did that, then *we* might well concede that *everything we could in principle identify referringly we could also denote attributively*. If we could do that, we could in principle retire reference in favor of uniquely denoting attributive devices – say, in accord with existentially quantified operators ranging over each such attributive device. There you have the Leibnizian vision that W. V. Quine has always been attracted to, the one in virtue of which a number of his followers have supposed that the determination of reference is dependent on the determination of truth but not vice versa.[24]

There are many quarrels that could be raised about the nature of these distinctions – and Quine's thesis. But, for our present purpose, we may say that it would not be unreasonable to hold that the attributive, nonreferential use of descriptions could (*under certain conditions*) obviate the need for a referential use of language in any logical space in which truth was of primary importance. If reference could be thus displaced, then a computational resolution of referential processes could be effected; and if that could be done, then a fully computational account of the linguistic and cultural aptitudes of humans might at least be envisaged – possibly realized. But not otherwise. At any rate, the referring use of expressions appears to be deeply intentional in a way that might well complicate or defeat a fully computational model of linguistic behavior; but the attributive use is not intentional in a similar sense (though it is intentional), and invites a thoroughly extensional treatment of predicates.

So to say that the enunciative function of natural language requires both reference and predication is not meant to disallow in principle the retirement of the referential function by, say, attributive devices. The argument is, rather, that the replacement cannot be achieved under human or real-time conditions. Expressed classically, God (as in Leibniz's account) could have supplied such a predicative language but humans cannot – not merely because they cannot extend the relevant attributive account to *everything* there is, but because in order to apply it to *anything* they would have to know how to apply it to *everything*.[25] Hence, there is no sense to an approximative approach to the displacement problem, bearing in mind the prospect of more and more powerful computers: If it could be done at all, it would have to be done at one stroke. Alternatively expressed, *God's* mind – not man's – may be computationally simulated, but then only God could achieve the simulation intended.

The upshot is that *human* referential success must be context-bound, in the sense that humans could never know whether attributive replacements for referential devices did ever single out – except of course once again in a context-bound sense, which would not help – whatever they succeeded in identifying in a fully referential way. Furthermore, on the argument, the *context* in which reference succeeds could never itself be suitably analyzed or replaced in any way that would favor the attributive replacement of referential expressions: It might well be analyzed in terms of more perspicuous contexts, but it could never get beyond that. The argument, in short, holds that man, not being God, is restricted to referential devices that, in important ways, never escape what P. F. Strawson has dubbed the "story-relative" form of reference;[26] also, it signifies that story-relative reference is not computational in nature.

One could well imagine a computer endowed with sensory capacities, a capacity for self-reference, and a capacity for matching referential and attributive expressions within the limits of its own sensory capacities relative to its capacity for self-reference. In that sense, a computer could function as a sort of brute god precisely in virtue of its limitations. *We* should, however, understand something of those limitations: for instance, its inability to identify, denote, or refer to a large number of things to which we can refer; even *its* inability to identify, denote, refer to, or reidentify ourselves moving through a complex world in which *we* are unable to identify *ourselves in* the attributively displacing sense already mentioned. The idea that the computer could simply add to its brute capacity incrementally, indefinitely on and on, fails to come to terms with the fact that *we* can already function in a restricted way more or less as the computer would, and *we* know that the semblance of a successful attributive strategy would depend on nothing more than the poverty of our immediate world. The point about the impossibility of a gradual increase in the success of the strategy of attributive replacement remains compelling.

If we grant this much, then we should have admitted (1) that (human) reference is always context-bound; (2) that the referential import of context cannot itself be attributively defined or analyzed; (3) that no attributively restricted language could successfully displace natural languages in principle or in real-time terms; (4) that the computer simulation of finite segments of a referentially structured natural language (or thought) always presupposes, but does not itself simulate, the referential competence by which its own competence is assessed as reasonably successful; and (5) that the successful incorporation of every such simulated segment in a more inclusive segment in which the referential use of the former *is* successfully simulated, is subject to the same limitation, and yields no evidence of a progressive or asymptotic gain by which, in principle, *all* such limitations could be retired. Distinctions (1–5) provide a fair sense (metonymically) in which to understand our original challenge regarding the computational nature of human thought. Alternatively put, distinctions (1–5) fix the sense in which no ordering of the apparent formal features of the simulation of successive segments of a natural linguistic or mental space can be counted on to capture the structure of the cognitive competence by which the original phenomena were first generated and humanly managed: The effective computability of the first (the simulation) does not, or does not yet, entail the effective computability of the second (the original phenomena).[27] The first *presupposes* a particular (referential) competence that it does not itself analyze or simulate; the second actually *exercises* that competence, which, on the argument, cannot be analyzed or simulated in whatever way the first can.

Another way of putting our thesis is this: Human reference succeeds in spite of the fact that *we* cannot replace our referential devices by any known strategy of definite and indefinite descriptions; and the computer's ability to do so itself depends on *our* construing *its* impoverished resources in terms of *our* story-relative devices.

IV

The argument just sketched serves a double purpose: First of all, it indicates the likely inadequacy of the computer simulation of human intelligence beyond the power of context-dependent constraints on finite segments of such intelligence: It is probably true that computers cannot capture the "natural" conditions under which humans determine context sufficiently well *for* referential needs. But second, it indicates the likely inadequacy of neurophysiological analyses as well: It is probably true that the cultural, historical, linguistic, and intentional features of human intelligence cannot be satisfactorily analyzed in terms of any idiom economically fitted to biological processes alone. The two lines of argument are clearly different; but they also converge, in the sense that the resources of artificial intelligence are (often) meant to approximate to what the resources of neurobiology are (often) meant to afford a reductive analysis of; but, in any case, the strategies of both are typically taken to be contextless, ahistorical, completely extensional. The requirements of cultural space – only crudely sketched here in terms of the requirements of reference – appear to elude the resources of both.

The telltale symptom of the limitation of the first strategy rests with what has come to be called the "brittle" quality of computer simulation: its insensitivity to context or slightly altered context or open-ended commonsense improvisation "near" the contexts for which it is programmed.[28] John McCarthy, for instance, has explored various ways of providing computer programs with a measure of "common sense" – as by introducing formalized "nonmonotonic" heuristics that bear on the use of computerized logics. This strategy is certainly ingenious and suggestive, but there are no strong grounds for the sanguine expectation that human common sense can be reasonably so captured. McCarthy correctly perceives what is needed to overcome "brittleness," but his own computational proposals betray an ineliminably "brittle" quality at the very point at which they afford heuristic resources for overtaking complete inflexibility. Two constraints suggest why the limitation is probably insuperable: First, it looks as if there could not "possibly exist a program which would, given any problem, divide all facts in the universe into those which are and those which are not relevant for that

problem"; and second, the relevance-heuristic introduced for any particular problem will itself be "brittle" if it is not subject to being overridden
by other contextually pertinent strategies that cannot have been antecedently programmed.[29]

The essential weakness of the second strategy rests with its impoverished vocabulary for description and explanation, on the assumption
of the irreducibility of cultural contents in physicalist and extensionalist
terms.[30]

A third consideration is this. If the problem of reference constitutes a
genuine conceptual difficulty for the computer modeling of the mind,
then there are likely to be additional such difficulties that may be
collected. (And if, of course, the referential difficulty may be satisfactorily overcome, then we should have some reason for thinking that
other supposed difficulties would yield along similar lines.) Probably
they would all be variant forms of the objection that the human "mind"
is not *a closed system* of any sort. By a "system," we mean here at least an
operative domain of (potentially) infinitely many members, the member
phenomena of which are generated from some fixed supply of finitely
many alphabetic or relational elements in accord with finitely many
rules of formation and transformation capable of functioning extensionally and recursively.[31] The referential puzzle we have posed clearly
signifies that the cognitive competence by which the denotative and
predicative resources of natural language and natural thought are
brought to bear on the determinable particulars of the real world is a
competence that cannot be captured in principle or in real-time terms
within the resources of any posited system that, on a theory, could yield
an ideal attributive language by means of which that referential function
could be effectively retired.

The suggestion is that the unsystematizability of reference is due to
the nature and conditions of the functioning of natural language and
languaged thought in actual use; and that those conditions are distinctly
open-ended because they are essentially historically emergent or historicized (profoundly intentional), capable of generating under that condition what appear (*from the vantage of any putative system*) to be new
elements and new rules of formation and transformation not themselves
systematically generable from the bare resources of any given such
system (assumed to be in place).

Such new elements and such new formational and transformational
processes are not in any sense to be construed as magically generated.
They are only *perceived* to be puzzlingly new – and in that sense *are* new
enough – when retrospectively specified in the fixed terms of any

would-be system of computational (or conceptual) powers. If, however, the system supposed, like the emergent novelty adduced, were, in a fair sense, cognitively intransparent (reflexively historicized, horizontally restricted) *artifacts* of our own serial efforts at self-understanding, then the normal admission of such novelty would never produce the notorious Platonic or Socratic paradox that (for instance) Jerry Fodor is so bashfully fond of confessing,[32] that is, the paradox involved in supposing that

there are no theories of concept learning, there *are* theories of fixation of belief [and that] no theory of learning that anyone has ever developed is . . . a theory that tells you how concepts are acquired; rather, such theories tell you how beliefs are fixed by experience – they are essentially inductive logics. That kind of mechanism [Fodor continues], which shows you how beliefs are fixed by experiences, makes sense only against the background of radical nativism. [By a radical nativism, one means] that any engagement of the organism with its environment has to be mediated by the availability of any concept that can eventually turn up in the organism's beliefs. The organism is a closed system proposing hypotheses to the world, and the world then chooses among them in terms explicated by some system of inductive logic.[33]

All conceptual resources reflexively identified are real enough; we cannot actually formulate a concept and a sketch of how it works and then simply deny its reality. (It has no other reality.) But it is only the (supposed) realist standing of the entire *system* of the mind that produces the quandary (Fodor's quandary). Give up the computational model, at least as a comprehensive model of the mind: All the paradoxes associated with invention or conceptual novelty dissolve or need not be further aggravated for Fodor's sort of reason. (That is, the proposal before us is entirely compatible with modular subsystems of the mind, if any can be discovered.) In a word, we isolate, over a changing cultural history, emergent conceptual resources; but we never perceive their generation from any antecedently posited system. The paradoxes are all artifacts of construing in too strong a realist sense this or that particular computational system – *or* of assuming a priori that *some* such molar system must obtain.[34] Arguments to that effect claim that knockout blow we took pains to disallow at the start.

V

The large strategy favored by the opponents of system is bound to be marked by at least two master claims. The first insists that human language and thought, initially characterized in terms of features reflexively reported by competent linguistic and thinking agents, may well be sui generis, essentially unanalyzable in terms of any sublinguistic or subcultural structures assignable anywhere in the physical or biological world. By itself, this would not preclude the possibility that language and thought do form a system. On the contrary, the well-known theories advanced by Noam Chomsky and Jerry Fodor are, precisely, theories that resist the reduction of the relevant phenomena to the terms of any sublinguistic resources while at the same time they insist that language and thinking actually do form nativist (computational) systems of a determinate sort.[35] Such theories are clearly coherent, though they are also eminently contestable.

The first claim may be plausibly strengthened by the argument that there are endogenous conceptual or cognitive barriers involved in the identification and analysis of phenomena essential to the very ability of human inquirers to examine any particular domain. That is, the ability *to speak of language and languaged thinking* may set limits to what may be offered as a reflexive analysis of just those phenomena. For instance, it does no good to insist, in the physicalist manner, that the natural world is composed of nothing but material bodies in motion,[36] *if* one cannot actually provide an analysis *of* language and thought *in* physicalist terms.

Nothing dire need follow regarding the continuous emergence of human language and culture from an originally lifeless physical cosmos: All that that would signify would be that, *under* the endogenous barriers assumed, the analysis and explanation of such phenomena would always be "top-down" (offered in the same vocabulary) and *explanatorily* discontinuous without being materially discontinuous with the rest of nature. In fact, every "bottom-up" analysis *is*, effectively, managed "top-down."[37]

The second claim insists that the human "mind" cannot be identified *with* the brain, or identified merely as an ordered set of determinate attributes *of* the brain.[38] This is not to say that, in speaking of the human mind, we must posit as real a fundamental substance in nature other than matter (apart from any uncertainty we may have regarding the correct analysis of matter). It is only to say that the human "mind" and "mental" phenomena are best construed as events and processes located *in the social space of a historically functioning culture* – grounded, to be sure, in some suitable way in the neurophysiology of the aggregated members of a given community but not directly assignable (as by attribution) *to* mere neurophysiological elements. Short of an effective physicalist reduction or a reduction to an informationally structured biology, we are bound to concede the initial "adequational" discrepancy between the putative nature of physical and biological structures and the features of mental, linguistic, and cultural phenomena; that is, for instance, we are bound to admit that we need to explain how it is that intensionally complex (inten*tion*al) attributes – just those involved in languaged thought and language-dependent behavior – *can* be directly ascribed to structures (the brain, say) that, *ex hypothesi*, lack natures intrinsically defined in just such terms.[39] Where the relevant properties are intrinsically assigned to minds in virtue of a theory of their real natures (a fortiori, a theory of the real nature of whatever they are said to be identical with), it is conceptually unsatisfactory to fail to provide a reasoned account of the congruity between their putative natures and their intrinsic properties. The odd thing is that leading theorists tend either to neglect the matter (Searle, for instance) or to pretend that the requisite resolution is already in hand (Churchland, for instance). Here, folk-psychological theories simply prosper by default.

There is no need to deny that there still are many complexities in the offing. But the main theme of the second master claim simply holds that "mental" processes (at the linguistic and cultural level) are, however "grounded" neurophysiologically, first "located" *in* a culturally shared societal space that cannot itself be reductively analyzed in terms of such interacting neurophysiologies. Here, the following considerations are important: First of all, the detection of the relevant phenomena is achieved "top-down" and under the supposed condition of endogenous barriers; second, their real structure or "nature" is compatible with some form of materialism (as distinct from physicalism) and does not require or favor any dualism of substances (hence, must opt for some emergent, irreducible, complex rather than compound, array of entities and properties); third, there is and must be an (ontic or conceptual) adequation between such natures and such properties compatible with the work of the physical and biological sciences; and fourth, explanation, being itself an activity adequated to the nature of persons and minds, may, by virtue of the failure of reductionisms to break through the endogenous barriers supposed, have to function in terms congruent with folk-psychological concepts, without prejudice to the continuity of nature. In a word, the continuity of nature is not equivalent to the continuity of explanations of nature: Explanations are not logically required to take a homonomic form, except on some version of a reductive physicalism.[40] These are all manageable puzzles, therefore; in fact, merely collecting them confirms the coherence of the folk-psychological orientation.

It would be fair to say that the *emergence* of linguistically and culturally complex phenomena is simply the recto of the conceptual page of which endogenous barriers form the verso – just those that answer to the conceptual impenetrability of language and culture in sublinguistic and subcultural terms. Grant that, and you have pretty well made room for such phenomena's not forming a system in the sense supplied. This is just the reason that reference serves as such a good metonym for the whole of distinctly human life.

Given human history, the retrospective discovery of novel concepts and the like, there will always appear to be some systematic discontinuity between the occurrence of physical and biological regularities and the evolving invention and novelty of the cultural world – in spite of the fact that cultural and psychological phenomena (speaking and thinking, say) invariably manifest themselves in physical and biological processes and do so in characteristically regular (though perhaps not nomologically specifiable) ways. They are in that sense "functional" phenomena (probably not reducible nomologically, distinctions answering to emergent human interests rather than to the homononic possibilities of the physical sciences), but they are not "functional" in the sense of being merely abstract; they are, rather, "incarnate," indissolubly complex at the level at which they obtain and are detected.[41]

That seems to be all that is needed in order to bring the folk-psychological notion into reasonable conceptual accord with the fundamentally *non*intentionalized concepts of the basic physical and biological sciences. That these disciplines diverge at the explanatory level as well is no surprise and produces no theoretical or conceptual anomalies – only empirical difficulties to be overcome.

We may bring all these considerations together in a concrete way by reflecting on the following example. It seems intuitively clear that if, by a relevant situation, one could approximate (after the fact) the conceptual resources of Newtonian physics – that is, if one could formulate a system of concepts rich enough to generate Newtonian physics reasonably drawn from eighteenth-century resources – it is unlikely (possibly even impossible) to supplement that system with any concepts drawn from the same sources or with any additional heuristics for applying those concepts to a wider domain of phenomena, in such a way as to generate quantum physics as well, from the same resources. It looks very much as if *every* simulation of such a pair of achievements would have to be retroactive or question-begging, would never exhibit a regular pattern of conceptual enlargement that could be supposed to form (or approximate) a system suitable for the computational modeling of such scientific theories.[42]

Apart from reference and what reference narrowly implicates, the *cultural* phenomena of the largest sort confronting and challenging the computability thesis must surely include, first, the extension of given conceptual categories to new cases not originally included among the specimen instances by which general terms are first learned or to which they are first applied in learning;[43] second, the creativity or inventiveness of particular human agents whose work cannot be formally derived in any known way from whatever has already been achieved in the culture to which they are contributing;[44] and third, the large-scale divergence and historical novelty of actual, evolving human societies.[45] Without a satisfactory sketch of how to resolve the questions here implied, it is quite premature to disallow the thesis that the human mind is not a system that can be computationally modeled.

VI

A last word. I have now sketched the coherence and plausibility of the original confrontation. This is already a considerable gain, since it is so often assumed that the theory being advanced *cannot* be consistently or convincingly formulated. It is, of course, plainly true that the full pursuit of the argument would involve a sustained analysis of a large number of notoriously difficult issues: for instance, the nature of persons and their "relation" to the members of *Homo sapiens*, the structure of conceptual universals or general terms, the nature of human history, cognition, intentionality, and the like. But these strenuous matters are not eliminable, and they are no easier to analyze for anyone who would oppose the point and purpose of the confrontation with which I began. Hence, there is no compelling objection to the effect that I am merely producing unnecessary complications. If anyone thinks there is, let him or her begin by indicating a more promising way of answering the questions I have posed.

Notes

1. Jaakko Hintikka, "The Role of Logic in Argumentation," *The Monist*, 72 (1989): 3.
2. Ibid., p. 4.
3. Ibid., p. 5.
4. Ibid., pp. 5, 6.
5. Cf. ibid., p. 6.
6. John Stachel, "Comments on 'Some Logical Problems suggested by Empirical Theories' by Professor dalla Chiara," in R. S. Cohen and M. W. Wartofsky, eds., *Language, Logic and Method* (Dordrecht: D. Reidel, 1983), p. 92;

cf. Maria Luisa dalla Chiara, "Some Logical Problems Suggested by Empirical Theories," ibid., p. 75. Stachel's remarks are supportive of this feature of dalla Chiara's account.

7. Hintikka, "Role of Logic in Argumentation," pp. 17, 18, 19, 22.
8. Ibid., p. 18.
9. Ibid., p. 22.
10. See Jaakko Hintikka, "Semantics for Propositional Attitudes," *Models for Modalities: Selected Essays* (Dordrecht: D. Reidel, 1969).
11. See, for instance, Patricia Smith Churchland, *Neurophilosophy: Toward a Unified Science of the Mind/Brain* (Cambridge, Mass.: MIT Press, 1986).
12. See, e.g., Fred I. Dretske, *Knowledge and the Flow of Information* (Cambridge, Mass.: MIT Press, 1981).
13. See, for instance, Stephen P. Stich, *From Folk Psychology to Cognitive Science: The Case Against Belief* (Cambridge, Mass.: MIT Press, 1983). See also Joseph Margolis, *Science Without Unity: Reconciling the Human and Natural Sciences* (Oxford: Basil Blackwell, 1987), esp. chs. 5, 6, and 9.
14. Hintikka, "Semantics for Propositional Attitudes," p. 87. The argument is directed against Quine's well-known disjunction; although it could just as well be argued that, given Quine's holism and his exposé of the dogma of the analytic–synthetic distinction, something like Hintikka's view could easily be developed within Quine's terms of reference. Cf. W. V. Quine, "Notes on the Theory of Reference," *From a Logical Point of View* (Cambridge, Mass.: Harvard University Press, 1953).
15. See Joseph Margolis, *Texts Without Referents: Reconciling Science and Narrative* (Oxford: Basil Blackwell, 1989), ch. 7.
16. I was very kindly supplied by Peter Lupu, a friend, an item from the *New York Times*, Science section by Malcolm W. Browne, published toward the end of 1988, regarding a supercomputer's solution of a mathematical problem that could be checked only by another computer following the same procedure (a Cray 18, borrowed from the Institute for Defense Analysis at Princeton, New Jersey). The problem involved a square lattice and the determination whether a certain combinatorial array could exist (a so-called finite projective plane of Order 10). According to the leader of the group, a Dr. C. W. H. Lam from Concordia University, Montreal, the answer is no. The proof for whether a finite projective plane of Order 12 could exist would apparently involve a computer working 10 billion times faster than today's supercomputers. (I have, I am afraid, lost the date of publication of this intriguing item. But similar cases are bound to arise.)
17. See George N. Recke, Jr., and Gerald M. Edelman, "Real Brains and Artificial Intelligence," in Stephen R. Graubard, ed., *The Artificial Intelligence Debate: False Starts, Real Foundations* (Cambridge, Mass.: MIT Press, 1988); and John McCarthy, "Mathematical Logic in Artificial Intelligence," in the same volume.
18. See D. E. Rumelhart, G. E. Hinton, and J. L. McClelland, "A General Framework for Parallel Distributed Processing," in James L. McClelland, David E. Rumelhart, and the PDP Research Group, eds., *Parallel Distributed Processing: Explorations in the Microstructure of Cognition*, Vol. 1 (Cambridge, Mass.: MIT Press, 1986), esp. pp. 52–55. By "the Hebbian learning rule,"

Rumelhart et al. intend, roughly, the following: "If a [neural] unit, u_i, receives an input from another unit, u_j; then, if both are highly active, the weight, w_j, [the change in the strength of the synaptic connection between the two units], from u_j to u_i should be *strengthened*." Cf. also D. E. Rumelhart and D. Zipser, "Feature Discovery by Competitive Learning," in the same volume. See also D. O. Hebb, *The Organization of Behavior* (New York: Wiley, 1948).

19. See Gerald M. Edelman, *Neural Darwinism: The Theory of Neuronal Group Selection* (New York: Basic Books, 1987), ch. 1, esp. pp. 4, 20–21.
20. On the first, see e.g., Paul M. Churchland, *Matter and Consciousness: A Contemporary Introduction to the Philosophy of Mind*, rev. ed. (Cambridge, Mass.: MIT Press, 1988); and Patricia Churchland, *Neurophilosophy*. On the second, see Edelman, *Neural Darwinism*, pp. 328–330.
21. See J. C. Eccles, *Facing Reality: Philosophical Adventures by a Brain Scientist* (New York: Springer-Verlag, 1970). ch. 1; J. C. Eccles, M. Ito, and J. Szentagothai, *The Cerebellum as a Neuronal Machine* (New York: Springer-Verlag, 1967); Rodolpho R. Llinas, ed., *Neurobiology of Cerebellar Evolution and Development* (Chicago: American Medical Association, 1969); and David Marr, "A Theory of Cerebellar Cortex," *Journal of Physiology* (London), 202 (1969):437–470.
22. See John Stachel, "Comments on 'Some Logical Problems Suggested by Empirical Theories' by Professor dalla Chiara," previously mentioned; and Hilary Putnam, "The Logic of Quantum Mechanics," *Philosophical Papers*, Vol. 1 (Cambridge: Cambridge University Press, 1975).
23. Keith S. Donnellan, "Reference and Definite Descriptions," *Philosophical Review*, 75 (1966): 281–304; reprinted in Jay R. Rosenberg and Charles Travis, eds., *Readings in the Philosophy of Language* (Englewood Cliffs, N.J.: Prentice Hall, 1979), p. 188.
24. See W. V. Quine, *Word and Object* (Cambridge, Mass.: MIT Press, 1960), sects. 37–38; see also Donald Davidson, "Reality Without Reference," *Inquiries into Truth and Interpretation* (Oxford: Clarendon, 1984), and Hilary Putnam, "Reference and Truth," *Philosophical Papers*, Vol. 3 (Cambridge: Cambridge University Press, 1983).
25. See Benson Mates, *The Philosophy of Leibniz: Metaphysics and Language* (New York: Oxford University Press, 1986), ch. 7.
26. See P. F. Strawson, *Individuals* (London: Methuen, 1959), ch. 1.
27. See Alonzo Church, "An Unsolvable Problem of Elementary Number Theory," *American Journal of Mathematics*, 58 (1936): 345–363; and Judson C. Webb, "Gödel's Theorems and Church's Thesis: A Prologue to Mechanism," in Cohen and Wartofsky, *Language, Logic, and Method*.
28. See John McCarthy, "Programs with Common Sense," in *Proceedings of the Teddington Conference on the Mechanization of Thought Processes* (London: HMSO, 1960); "Circumscription – a form of Non-monotonic Reasoning," *Artificial Intelligence*, 13 (1980):27–39; and "Mathematical Logic in Artificial Intelligence."
29. By a monotonic logic, McCarthy means a logic constrained in the following way: "If a sentence p is [deductively] inferred from a collection A of sentences, and if B is a more inclusive set of sentences, then p can be inferred

from *B*." ("Mathematical Logic in Artificial Intelligence," p. 302). Non-monotonic logics are logics in accord with which what is inferred from *B* is not deductive (but reasonable commonsensically, say, in accord with a heuristic governing how to use certain inference patterns), where additional premises would disallow that inference. "For example, [McCarthy offers,] learning that I own a car, you conclude that it is appropriate on a certain occasion to ask me for a ride; but when you learn the further fact that the car is in the garage being fixed, you no longer draw that conclusion" (p. 303). This accords with what he calls "circumscription" – one strategy by which to enlarge the commonsense capacity of artificial intelligence. "*Circumscription* [McCarthy explains] is a formalized *rule of conjecture* that can be used along with the rules of inference of first order logic." That is, it is a form of nondeductive conjecture that is made to function as a rule of inference. A version of the rule is given informally as: "The objects that can be shown to have a certain property *P* by reasoning from certain facts *A* are all the objects that satisfy *P*." ("Circumscription – a Form of Non-monotonic Reasoning," pp. 27, 28). The conjecture, meant to capture an aspect of commonsense reasoning, holds that "*A* includes all the relevant facts and that the objects whose existence follows from *A* are all the relevant objects" (p. 29). McCarthy shows how the rule bears on the solution of the "missionaries and cannibals" problem, for instance. He is entirely clear, of course, about how little is achieved here and how much more is required. The first of the constraints on relevance cited in the text was mentioned, in discussion with McCarthy, by the Israeli logician Y. Bar-Hillel, "Programs with Common Sense" (Discussion, p. 88). The paper is noticeably primitive and is admitted to be little more than a suggestion by McCarthy himself.

30. See Margolis, *Science Without Unity*, chs. 5, 9, and 10; and *Texts Without Referents*, ch. 6.
31. See *Science Without Unity*, ch. 12.
32. See Jerry A. Fodor, *The Language of Thought* (New York: Thomas Y. Crowell, 1975), ch. 1; for instance, pp. 51–52.
33. Jerry A. Fodor, "Fixation of Belief and Concept Acquisition," in Massimo Piattelli-Palmarini, ed., *Language and Learning: The Debate Between Jean Piaget and Noam Chomsky* (Cambridge, Mass.: Harvard University Press, 1980), pp. 144, 152.
34. In the analysis of language and thinking, the most notorious quarrel about the inexorability of a nativist system has, of course, been the extended quarrel between Chomsky and Piaget – which, in a rather comic sense, proved to be quite indecisive on both sides. See *Language and Learning*, esp. Jerry A. Fodor, in "On the Impossibility of Acquiring 'More Powerful' Structures"; also, Herbert A. Simon, *Models of Discovery* (Dordrecht: D. Reidel, 1977); and Louis Hjelmslev, *Prolegomena to a Theory of Language*, rev. ed., trans. Francis J. Whitfield (Madison: University of Wisconsin Press, 1961).
35. See Noam Chomsky, *Rules and Representations* (New York: Columbia University Press, 1980); Jerry A. Fodor, *Representations: Philosophical Essays on the Foundations of Cognitive Science* (Cambridge, Mass.: MIT Press, 1981). See also Jerry A. Fodor, "Discussion," in "On the Impossibility of Acquiring 'More Powerful' Structures," in *Language and Learning* ch. 6, p. 152. Fodor also

claims, in "Fixation of Belief and Concept Acquisition," in the same chapter: "As far as I know, nobody except the nativists has addressed the question of how [a] concept . . . is acquired, and what they have said is that it isn't acquired" (p. 146). But this is preposterous, a mere artifact of Fodor's adherence to the nativist (or "Socratic") conception of thinking. That is, the thesis is an artifact of the thesis in question. Both Piagetian and "neuronal group selection" theories (Edelman) address the questions in other ways; and there are still other ways in which to do so – Wittgensteinian, for instance.

36. See David K. Lewis, "An Argument for the Identity Theory," *Journal of Philosophy*, 63 (1966):17–25; Thomas Nagel, "Physicalism," *Philosophical Review*, 74 (1965):339–356.
37. See Margolis, *Science Without Unity*, chs. 5 and 10. The so-called anthropic principle in recent cosmological speculations in physics pursues an analogous notion, with some interesting results. See, e.g., Brandon Carter, "Large Number Coincidences and the Anthropic Principle in Cosmology," in M. S. Longair, ed., *Confrontation of Cosmological Theories with Observational Data* (International Astronomical Union, Symposium No. 63, 1973) (Dordrecht: D. Reidel, 1974).
38. See, e.g., J. J. C. Smart, "Sensations and Brain Processes," rev., in V. C. Chappell, ed., *The Philosophy of Mind* (Englewood Cliffs, N.J.: Prentice Hall, 1962); Donald Davidson, "Mental Events," *Essays on Actions and Events* (Oxford: Clarendon Press, 1980); John R. Searle, *Minds, Brains and Science* (Cambridge, Mass.: Harvard University Press, 1984).
39. See Joseph Margolis, *Culture and Cultural Entities* (Dordrecht: D. Reidel, 1984), ch. 1; *Texts Without Referents*, ch. 6; Rom Harré, *Personal Being* (Cambridge, Mass.: Harvard University Press, 1984), ch. 4.
40. See, e.g., for the reductive view, Davidson, "Mental Events," p. 41.
41. See Fodor, *The Language of Thought*, Introduction; Hilary Putnam, *Representation and Reality* (Cambridge, Mass.: MIT Press, 1988); and Margolis, *Science Without Unity*, ch. 9.
42. For a sense of the characteristic problems, see Peter Gibbins, *Particles and Paradoxes: The Limits of Quantum Logic* (Cambridge: Cambridge University Press, 1987).
43. This is the fatal weakness of Nelson Goodman's nominalism, which lacks altogether any cognitive resources *for* extending the use of terms. Clearly, the consensual tolerance of societal practice – perhaps best adumbrated by Wittgenstein's notion of "forms of life" and Bourdieu's notion of the *habitus* (itself somewhat Wittgensteinian) – suggests the dynamics for the smooth extension of terms. See Nelson Goodman, "Seven Strictures on Similarity," in Lawrence Foster and J. W. Swanson, eds., *Experience and Theory* (Amherst: University of Massachusetts Press, 1970); Pierre Bourdieu, *Outline of a Theory of Practice*, trans. Richard Nice (Cambridge: Cambridge University Press, 1977). The important point remains that cultural consensus (regarding extension) cannot be captured by biological constraints and weights that may be assigned to neurophysicalogical, specifically perceptual, processes; and Goodman's own notion of "entrenchment" has no structural import suitable for explaining conceptual extension. See Edelman, *Neural Darwinism*, ch. 2;

and Nelson Goodman, *Fact, Fiction, and Forecast* 2nd ed. (Indianapolis: Hackett, 1965), ch. 4.

44. This applies, of course, to Fodor's strenuous efforts to formulate a comprehensive nativism. See, for instance, Jerry A. Fodor, *The Modularity of Mind* (Cambridge, Mass.: MIT Press, 1983; Zenon W. Pylyshyn, *Computation and Cognition* (Cambridge, Mass.: MIT Press, 1985); and Jerry Fodor and Zenon W. Pylyshyn, "Connectionism and Cognitive Architecture: A Critical Analysis," *Cognition* 28 (1988): 3–71. The argument may be adjusted also to count against Piaget, for Piaget supposes that, at every intellectual "level" at which the developing child acquires new cognitive skills, whatever is performed at each level *is* describable in systematic terms at that level. The difference between Fodor and Piaget rests largely with Piaget's constructivist proviso that emergent cognitional powers arise with maturation, that they are not explicable by any recursive or combinatorial process from an original nativist endowment. See Jean Piaget, *Structuralism*, trans. Chininah Maschler (New York: Basic Books, 1970, and "The Psychogenesis of Knowledge and Its Epistemological Significance," in Massimo Piattelli-Palmarini, ed., *Language and Learning*.

45. This counts against Platonism. Fodor, of course, is a self-confessed Platonist. See his *The Language of Thought*; see also Jerrold J. Katz, *Language and Other Abstract Objects* (Totowa, N.J.: Rowman & Littlefield, 1981).

12 A culturalist account of folk psychology

Richard McDonough

It has been claimed that folk psychology (hereafter FP) is an empirical theory, concerned primarily with the explanation of human behavior. Despite our fondness for this theory, we are told that it is falsifiable like any other, and that from what we already know about the brain, it appears likely that it is a radically false theory. So it is at minimum possible and in fact likely that FP, along with its ontology of content states, will have to be replaced by its superior neurobiological competitor. Those who oppose the "advancing tide of neuroscience" are victims of a "conceptual inertia" similar to those who refused to give up cherished beliefs in phlogiston, witches, and crystal spheres in the heavens. (Churchland 1981, p. 90). In order to justify this radical change in our self-conception the eliminativists must (1) show that FP is an empirical theory, and a seriously flawed one, and (2) sketch the outlines of a plausible replacement. I argue that they fail in both projects. In Section I, I show that they mischaracterize FP by reading into it the internalist metaphysics of their own mechanistic worldview, so their argument that FP is fallible misses the mark. In Section II, I sketch an alternative, "personal level" account of FP. In Section III, I argue, based on Wittgenstein's holistic account of meaning, that the personal level is *autonomous*, that it is not "reducible" to an internal mechanism. In Section IV, I show that FP is part of a nontheoretical account of human culture. In Section V, I argue (1) that their "positive" replacements for FP cannot account for human intelligent behavior and (2) that this explains why the eliminativists must, and do, engage in a wholesale redescription of the data. In Section VI, I consider the metaphysical consequences of a post-mechanistic account of persons and sketch three possible scenarios. In

I am most grateful to Norman Malcolm, Christopher Ray, Chong Kim Chong, Jaganathan Muraleenathan, and Cheryl Tang for their extremely helpful comments on an earlier draft of this essay. For discussion of related themes, see McDonough (in press [b and c]).

the first two, a suitable limited place is retained for mechanistic science adjacent to our overall account of intelligence. But in the final, most radical scenario, the framework of neurobiology, with its ontology of neural code states, must be totally eliminated from our explanations of human behavior.

I. What folk psychology is not

Paul Churchland writes that because its "conception of learning as the manipulation and storage of propositional attitudes founders . . . FP provides a positively misleading sketch of our internal kinematics." (1981; pp. 73–74; P. S. Churchland 1980, p. 153; Stich 1983, p. 231). The view that we manipulate propositional attitudes internally is FP's conception. FP is concerned with the "mysteries" (Churchland 1984, p. 1) of "our internal kinematics" and fails in this, "its own domain" (Churchland 1981, p. 75). The eliminativists agree with Searle (1983, p. 230) that "the brain is all we have for . . . representing the world, and everything we can use must be inside the brain." And they think FP agrees with Searle!

This makes clear why Churchland (1981, p. 71) thinks it is so obvious that FP is a theory. Since the nature of hidden mechanisms cannot be settled a priori, and since FP purports to describe hidden mechanisms, it is obviously an empirical theory.

It also makes clear why Churchland (1984, p. 46) thinks that "it would be a miracle" if FP proved to be correct. Since neuroscience avails itself of the most sophisticated techniques of modern science, FP cannot hope to compete with it about our inner mechanisms. So there is almost no chance that FP will not "reduce" to neuroscience. The only question is whether it will reduce smoothly or not. If the former, then FP is a primitive precursor of the superior deliverances of modern science. If the latter, then so much the worse for FP and its ontology of mental attitudes.

But FP is not committed to the metaphysics of internalism which the eliminativists read into it. Only a philosopher in the grip of a picture could interpret the remark "John avoids dogs because he believes they bite" to mean that John has inside him a B-state that causes him to engage in dog-avoidance behavior. In ordinary usage we do not generally say that people have beliefs, and so forth, inside them. We say that persons are *in* states of belief or desire: "She did it in the belief that it was best," and "They did it in the desire to win." (These locutions suggest that beliefs, and so forth, are objective things in which people can share.)

My argument against eliminativism does not depend on ordinary usage. But ordinary usage does not support the view that beliefs, desires, and so forth, are internal states of a person. I call the theory that makes this internalist assumption 'mechanistic folk psychology' (MFP), irrespective of whether MFP is identified as an "old theory" (Churchland 1984, p. 61) or as a "yet to be devised" (P. S. Churchland 1986, p. 295) scientific psychology.

Internalism is an important part of the mechanist paradigm; not only do the eliminativists make this assumption and read it into FP, but their list of "the remaining parties to the debate" (P. M. Churchland 1979, p. 116; Stich 1983; P. S. Churchland 1986) all make it too. Churchland (1986, pp. 461–462) with others (McGinn 1989, p. 353), even regards the only alternative to mechanism as magic. The set of possible positions is narrowed from the beginning to a set that are all mechanistic and all obviously fallible. But as Churchland (1986, p. 239) states, being philosophical requires one to "follow the ball of yarn past [one's] paradigm [to] contemplate [its] coherence within a broader framework." My aim in the present chapter is to examine the mechanistic paradigm from within the broader *cultural* framework on which it is conceptually dependent (McDonough 1989, pp. 18–20; 1990a, sect. V; 1990b, sect. II).

The claim that FP is not committed to the internalist metaphysics does not imply that there are not, in fact, internal mechanisms subserving cognition. The *present* point is the modest one that this metaphysics belongs with Searle or a revised "scientific" psychology and not with the "homey" or "cracker-barrel . . . generalizations" (P. S. Churchland, 1986, pp. 229, 301) of FP proper.

To sum up, *if* FP were a story about stimuli, internal states, and behavior, there would be no doubt that that story is fallible and probably false (or incoherent).[1] But MFP should not be identified with FP proper, so we have as yet neither an adequate characterization of FP nor any reason to believe that it is a fallible theory. Let us now take an unbiased look at FP proper.

II. Sketch of a "personal level" psychology

In this section, I sketch an account of mental content that is modeled on an account of linguistic meaning, and on that basis, a sketch of a "personal-level" psychology. By the linguistic model I do not mean the "sentential" model. My account, derived from Wittgenstein, emphasizes the importance of *use* for the linguistic paradigm. So the first order of business is to clarify Wittgenstein's notion of use.

A. *Wittgenstein's cultural-functionalist notion of use*

It is incorrect to describe Wittgenstein as belonging to "the behaviorist tradition" if this is seen as "clearly consistent with a materialist conception of human beings" (Churchland 1984, pp. 24, 54). By linguistic use Wittgenstein means a certain kind of *context-embedded* behavior, where the context is the cultural context (McDonough 1989, pp. 9–11). I use the word "culture" not in its ordinary sense (e.g., "a man of culture") but, roughly in terms of the totality of human institutions, customs, practices, and so forth. The meaning of an utterance is the relevant *function* (use) of the utterance in the culture. But not all cultural functions are relevant to *linguistic* meaning. The relevant ones are those described in philosophical grammar. This is not textbook grammar but the account of those "conventions" (institutions, etc.) that determine the role of utterances in cultural contexts.

The foundation of my argument is that Wittgenstein's "use theory" is a kind of *functionalist* account of meaning and that it has certain key analogies and disanalogies with its better-known physicalist analogue. One key disanalogy is that Wittgenstein's functional system is a *normative* system. One key analogy is that a linguistic item is *embedded* in the system in the sense that *its identity is determined by its function in that system.* Wittgenstein's "use theory" is the view that the meaning of an utterance is *individuated by its grammatical role in human culture.*

The notion of the content of mental states is modeled on linguistic meaning. The role of the content states emphasized by the eliminativists is that of explaining or predicting behavior. We can also explain and predict behavior by reference to people's utterances. If S sincerely asserts that the *contras* are to be trusted, we have a good idea what sort of behavior to expect from him or her. If we model content states on cases of sincere assertion, then for S to believe that *p* is for S to be in a state that generally issues in behavior similar to that of one who sincerely asserts p. Since the use of an utterance is its "grammatical function," and mental content is modeled on use, the content states are individuated by reference to the same functional role in a culture.

It follows that intentional content is also culture embedded. Opposing the view that intentions "exist in my mind," Wittgenstein (1958, para. 337; 1967, para. 67) writes: "An intention is embedded in human customs and institutions." Mental states are not inner entities *individuated independently of the cultural context*. A mental state is the state of *being in* a certain cultural role. (Recall the ordinary usage that persons are *in* states of belief.)

So Wittgenstein is also a functionalist about content, but he is not, like his materialist analogues, a *causal-role* functionalist. He is a *cultural-role* functionalist, where the relevant functions are not those in a mechanical system but are a subset of the normative functions (the grammatical ones) of a cultural system. I call the standard causal-role functionalism "C-functionalism" and Wittgenstein's grammatical role-functionalism "G-functionalism." FP is committed to G-functionalism. The "functional architecture" (Stich 1983, p. 230) presupposed by FP is the "architecture" of a culture, not that of a machine.

Causal-role functionalism is a well-known position. But the idea that meaning and content are bound up with cultural functions long predates the modern idea of a mechanical system (and of a function in a mechanical system). One reason for the persistent failure to understand Wittgenstein's "use theory" is that the mechanists control the word "functionalism," and therefore, the parallel with Wittgenstein's *prior* culturalist version goes unperceived.

B. A culturalist account of intelligence

The distinctively human intelligent behavior *is* cultural behavior. (What else could it be?) Any acceptable account of human intelligence must, therefore, explain this behavior. The fact that, in Wittgenstein's view, mental states are *identified* by reference to these cultural functions means that FP states are *perfectly* suited to this task. To be in a G-functional state is, bending some mechanistic jargon to opposite purposes, to *instantiate a cultural program*.[2] As such, human behavior is quite predictable. ("That is how a 'cultured' person behaves.")

Wittgenstein's G-functionalism has certain virtues analogous to that of its physicalist counterpart. In standard C-functionalism, a mental state is abstract in the sense that it is a "causal profile" and so is neutral with regard to the "substrate" in which it is "realized." Similarly, in Wittgenstein's G-functionalism the subject's *composition* is irrelevant to the ascription of mental content. What matters is only that their content states are *individuated by reference to the relevant cultural function*. If Martians arrived, what would determine whether we could understand them would be the similarities between our two cultures, not those between our two brains (assuming that Martians have brains).

One can call these G-functionalist principles "causal" if what is meant is that they can be invoked to explain and predict intelligent behavior. What is denied here is that these "causes" *must* be internal. But though this personal-level psychology is not committed to the internalist metaphysics, it has not been ruled out that there are, in fact, internal states that subserve these G-functional states. The internalist is not defined out of the debate. Neither has it been ruled out that the "reduction" to a subserving mechanism goes very roughly or not at all. The eliminativist is not defined out of the debate. Let us now face the question whether G-functionalism places any constraints on the sense in which such states can be subserved by a mechanism.

III. The autonomy of the personal level

A. Holism and autonomy

In his *Tractatus*, Wittgenstein formulated the philosophical foundations of mechanistic theories of meaning and content: (1) Any such theory presupposes the correspondence thesis (i.e., that the structure of the meaning corresponds to a structure in the machine), and (2) that thesis presupposes the picture theory and some form of meaning atomism (McDonough 1986, esp. sect. VIII, 1989, pp. 8–9). In his later philosophy Wittgenstein rejects the mechanistic paradigm on the grounds that meaning (and intentional content) are holistic in a sense that is incompatible with any mechanistic theory of meaning (McDonough 1989, pp. 9–11). So FP is autonomous (i.e., it is "irreducible" to any mechanistic view).

Mechanistic holism: the network theory and connectionism. Some mechanists, however, actually insist on a "holistic" account of meaning. But it is instructive that many of the views that are called holistic are really forms of meaning atomism, or at least are consistent with it. Quine's view, for example, is called holistic on the grounds that propositions can be recanted only in the light of the effects on the whole network. But such a "recant holism" is consistent with propositions having their own semantic content (Fodor 1987, p. 66; Hookway 1988, p. 42). Similarly, the Churchlands call their theory the "holistic" or "network" theory of meaning" (P. M. Churchland 1979, 1981, 1984; P. S. Churchland 1986). Yet they continually refer to "the meanings of the smaller units," "types of brain states [as] role playing elements," "meaning [as a] function of [the] role [playing] elements," and so forth (P. M. Churchland 1979, p. 61; 1984, p. 34; P. S. Churchland 1986, p. 334). Paul Churchland even speculates that scientific discoveries might lead us to construct "a new system of verbal communication . . . distinct from natural language, with a new and more powerful *combinatorial grammar* over *novel elements* forming novel combinations with exotic properties" (1981, p. 87; emphasis added). So deep is the grip of atomism on contemporary thought that most so-called holisms are really just complicated versions of atomism (McDonough 1989, p. 11).

Similar points can be made about connectionist models, but it is less clear what connectionism is. Generally it is promoted as a theory of representation where information is "distributed" over a network of units in a novel way (P. S. Churchland 1986, p. 460; Ramsey et al., Chapter 4, this volume). Patricia Churchland (1986, p. 461) quotes a "clear statement" of the "connectionist manifesto": "The fundamental premise of connectionism is that individual neurons *do not transmit large amounts of symbolic information.* Instead, they compute by being *appropriately connected* to large numbers of similar units" (Feldman & Ballard, 1982, p. 208). Rumelhart et al. (1986) explain connectionism by contrasting short-term storage, where information is encoded in units, with long-term storage, where it is stored in "connections among units." Ramsey, Stich, and Garon, in Chapter 4 of the present volume, have "each connection weight embodying information salient to many propositions."

But all of these variations have some information-bearing units at some stage or other. Even the view that it is the connections between the units that possess information differs only verbally from views that posit information-bearing units. For the connections between units are just a novel kind of information-bearing unit. So all of these still incorporate versions of atomism. And it appears that they are all versions of the picture theory as well, the only difference from normal picture theories being that in these connectionist models the network pictures a *system* of meaning relationships rather than an "individual" meaning.

But there is another version of connectionism which is the exception that proves the rule. Stich (1983, p. 240) cites with approval Winograd's comment that "many phenomena which 'for an observer' can be described in terms of representation may . . . be . . . a structure-determined system with no mechanism corresponding to a representation." In this version, what is eliminated is not merely FP states but *all* representational states! The mechanism subserving "cognition" does not even represent anything. It is merely a mechanism for assigning "true" and "false," or, more accurately, "T" and "F," to suitably encoded bits of input.

So there seem to be two types of connectionism: The first is a mechanistic model of representation, which retains versions of both atomism and the picture theory. The second is the exception that proves the rule, since it eliminates representation as well. Neither "network holism" nor connectionism supports any doubt that mechanistic theories of meaning presuppose atomism and the picture theory.[3] So a genuinely holistic account of meaning is incompatible with these variations on the mechanistic paradigm.

Organic holism. In Wittgenstein's view, linguistic meaning is grammatical function in a culture. The philosophical grammar that describes this function is not a combinatorial grammar. It describes a functional connection between a language and a culture. The cultural "whole" is "composed" of customs, practices, institutions, and so forth, but it is not describable, except metaphorically, as a "network" of "elements." One can call this whole "organic," to distinguish it from wholes that are combinations of separable elements. On this organic holism one cannot even isolate the meaning or content elements for which one wants to find a realization in the brain (McDonough 1989, p. 11). There can be no correspondence between meaning or mental content and brain structure since the former does not have a *structure* in the required sense. Since some such correspondence is the minimum condition required by any "reduction" to a mechanism, FP is irreducible or autonomous.

B. Meaning states and machine states

Patricia Churchland (1986; pp. 381–382) asks, "Why should not . . . a [neural] theory explain the logical and meaningful relations between states at the psychological level. How, a priori, do philosophers know that it cannot? What can be their special source of knowledge?" Later, discussing an "intelligent robot," she writes: "If the elements in its internal [states have] roles that mirror those in [mine] then what else do they need to have meaning? . . . To refuse to assign meaning – as genuine as it gets – to [its] internal states would . . . be . . . a double standard, . . . To bridle here looks like dogmatism" (1986, p. 345, and see p. 346). Her question is important: What more must robot states have to have "meaning – as genuine as it gets"?

The robot's states must be *culture-embedded* in the sense that their identity is fixed by reference to their G-functional role in a culture. But this requirement cannot be satisfied by a mechanistic view. If the identity of these states is determined by their G-function in a culture, then *they are not mechanical states*. And if their identity is determined by the robot's internal causal economy, then their "elements" cannot "mirror" that of the culture because *one cannot even identify the required cultural-role elements*. And this claim is based not on any special knowledge but on our commonplace understanding of the connection of meaning with culture. It is more appropriate to ask what special knowledge leads mechanists to think that one can "reduce" meaning to the state of a mechanism. Their metaphysics of internalism, atomism, and the picture theory would constitute *special* knowledge if those "doctrines" were coherent.

So there is no double standard. Since meaning and content are bound up with a cultural whole, they cannot be encoded in a machine. In fact, only the systematic implementation of a double standard has given the impression that they can.[4] But this fact shows only that FP is irreducible, not that it is ineliminable.

IV. The account of the propositional attitudes as part of a nontheoretical account of human culture

In this section, I argue that FP is not a theory, and then I rebut certain common arguments that it is.

A. *The nontheoretical status of folk psychology*

The account of content is not a theory about internal states, but part of an account of human culture. To ascribe a content state to S is to describe S as functionally embedded in a culture. Could we conceivably do without such ascriptions?

We could not if we want to understand human (cultural) behavior. FP states are perfectly suited for explaining a part of human cultural behavior since the very identity of these states is determined by their G-function in this culture. So we could not give up FP, without loss of explanatory power, unless we could give up our self-conception as cultural beings. Can we do that?

Certainly no ordinary empirical considerations support such a change. We see people speaking English, playing chess, and so forth; so we need to explain their behavior in these institutions. But are even these "observations" theoretical in some sense? Is it a *theory* that I am speaking English, or playing chess? Could neuroscience discover that it is the Chinese that have been speaking English all along, while we have been speaking Chinese? Could neuroscience discover that no one has ever played chess, or, pushing the paradox, that no one has ever done science?

Churchland (1980, p. 153) is surely correct that "there is no Given" if she means that how we are to understand entities, mechanisms, and processes, of whatever kind, is not "given." But our *cultural embeddedness* is not comparable to an entity, mechanism, or process. Wittgenstein (1958, p. 226) writes, "What has to be accepted, the given, is – one could say – *forms of life*." The "given" is not an "entity," and so forth, hidden or otherwise. It consists of the cultural institutions, practices, and so forth, *including those of science itself*, that are presupposed by *any* discriminations or observations. Scientific discoveries themselves rest on judgments, that this is a good observation and that a bad one, that this is confirmed and that not, and so on. The basis for making the discriminations and observations involved in these judgments is the embedding culture – unless, that is, Churchland thinks that such discriminations and observations are themselves "given." The view that there is no"given" counts not for but against the idea that science could undermine anything; for this view, properly understood, *secures* the conceptual dependence of science on its embedding culture. And science cannot challenge that on which its own observational and discriminatory powers depend.

The claim that it is the framework of FP states that is the candidate for elimination is therefore misleading. The so-called problems with FP stem from the notions of meaning and content. But if these are bound up with culture in the manner set forth in Sections II and III, then we cannot give up FP unless we can give up our self-conception as cultural beings. But science is itself conceptually dependent on culture, and therefore, it is inconceivable that we could give up FP. Against this background, let us examine some of the arguments that FP is a theory.

B. *The arguments that folk psychology is an empirical theory*

The arguments that folk psychology is like a theory. The arguments that FP is like a theory include a variety of arguments to the effect that it contains "nomological" generalizations and "causal" principles, that it has "explanatory and predictive" power, and so forth (Churchland, Chapter 2, this volume). I see no reason to oppose these verbal points. The G-functionalist view can support "laws" – "rough and ready ones, at least" (Churchland 1981, p. 68) – that issue directly from the G-function of FP states. One can say what someone does *because* they are in such a state, or *predict* what someone in such a state will do. But it does not follow from this that FP is replaceable. That would follow only if we could do without these specific kinds of "laws," "causes," and so forth; and since these are connected with our self-conception as cultural beings, on which science itself depends, no scientific evidence could be marshaled to give them up.

I consider one argument to show what I mean by calling these arguments "verbal." Churchland argues, in Chapter 2 of the present volume, that by appeal to FP, "one can control . . . the behavior of others . . . by steering [their] cognitive states . . . by relating [relevant] opportunities, dangers, or obligations. . . . How that is possible without an understanding of the . . . empirical regularities that connect . . . internal states and overt behavior [needs to be explained]." The explanation Churchland seeks is easy. He gives it himself. One "steers" S's behavior by informing S of opportunities, dangers, and obligations. There is nothing here that refers to S's *internal* states. Notice how innocently he slides to the statement that steering S's behavior requires understanding their *internal* states. But this internalist metaphysics is something that no serious empiricist should assume. The conditions he mentions – the opportunity to take his rook, the danger of exposing one's queen, the obligation to win fairly – are all naturally handled by a G-functional account of content states. The fact that one can pin the words "nomological," "causal," and so forth, on folk generalizations is verbal. What is not verbal, but what is also unwarranted, is the assumption that these words carry with them the mechanist's metaphysics of internalism.

The argument from the empirical status of FP principles. Referring to an FP explanation, Paul Churchland writes, in Chapter 2 of this volume, "Any principle that allows us to . . . predict one empirical state . . . on the basis of another logically distinct empirical state has to be empirical in character." But if this statement is supposed to show that the framework of FP is replaceable by something *radically unlike FP*, it does not do so. Perhaps any given FP principle is fallible. Suppose it is even possible that the whole framework of FP principles is replaceable. Even so, if one wants to understand intelligent human behavior, then, since that *is* cultural behavior, the new explanations must make reference to *other* G-functional states, the content of which is individuated either by (1) some *other* cultural factors or by (2) a more penetrating insight into our present manner of cultural embeddedness. The assumption that the replacement could be something like neurobiology begs the question about the *limits of the revisability* of our self-conception.

The argument from overlapping domains. In all of its forms this argument involves the idea that FP is continuous with other natural sciences and so is of the same fallible status. In three separate passages, Paul Churchland writes:

We must evaluate FP with regard to its . . . continuity with . . . theories in . . . overlapping domains [with] evolutionary theory . . . and neuroscience, for example. (1981, p. 73)

The continuity . . . of [human] behavior with the . . . animal kingdom is there to behold. (1984, p. 110)

If we define intelligence . . . as the possession of a complex set of appropriate responses to the changing environment, then even the humble potato displays a certain low cunning. No metaphysical discontinuities here. (1984, p. 153)

Patricia Churchland adds:

[Because] man . . . evolved from non-verbal organisms, and [both] behave intelligently . . . it would be viewed with deserved suspicion if it were claimed that we need . . . one sort of theory for verbal organisms, and [a theory with] different structure . . . for non-verbal organisms. (1980, p. 148)

But these all assume that FP does overlap with biology. No doubt, it looks this way, *if* one assumes that both FP and neuroscience describe our "internal dynamics" and thus are constrained by accounts of the accretion of our internal structure over the millennia. But FP is concerned with norms and culture. What do potatoes have to do with customs, institutions, and so forth? It is just not true that the continuity of human cultural behavior with potato "'behavior'" is "there to behold." It must be proved, not assumed, that biology overlaps with the understanding of human culture.

The argument from the context relativity of content. The key view in Stich's argument is that content ascription in FP is "context-relative." Thus, "a sort of Protagorean parochialism is . . . built into [FP] since [for it] people *like us* are the measure of all things, and science should not respect such a parochial view" (Stich 1983, pp. 7, 182). Patricia Churchland describes "Stich's breakthrough" somewhat differently:

[The problem] is that belief ascription is context relative, and depending on interests, [etc.], different criteria are used to specify the content of a given mental state. Even worse, sometimes different criteria . . . give conflicting answers. . . . So [FP] does not have a *single* . . . well defined notion of content, but rather a set of vague notions flying in loose formation. . . . So when anti-reductionists parade these categories [meaning, etc.] in all their [FP] regalia as irreducible, the irony is that it is their lack of empirical integrity that prevents their reduction. . . . Ironically, FP may be irreducible . . . because [it is] dead wrong. (1986, pp. 382–384)

I take this position to be that there is no a priori reason why FP is irreducible, but that if it is, the reason is that it is seriously flawed. The flaws are, first, that content ascription is context-relative, and for that reason there is a possibility of multiple content ascriptions for a given mental state.

Let us consider Stich's version first. I have myself emphasized that FP states are context-embedded, and thus "context-relative" in a sense. But this sense does not entail a Protagorean parochialism. First, imagine an "ideal ascriber" – that is, a person who participates in *all* cultural practices. For such an ideal person, there are no "exotic subjects," no subjects who participate in cultures in which he or she does not, and therefore no limitation of its FP to a parochial viewpoint. The fact that we are not ideal people is *our* limitation, not FP's. Second, there is a sense in which even ordinary ascribers are not limited in their content ascriptions. Although I do not know how to ascribe content to an "exotic" subject, I can learn to participate in that culture. It is not true that FP is limited to persons like us, because *we can become persons like them.* FP is not committed in principle to a pernicious Protagorean parochialism.

Churchland's claim that the context relativity of content gives us only "a set of vague notions flying in loose formation" supports my view. Since human culture is a set of vague institutions "flying in loose formation," and human intelligent behavior is cultural behavior, then to explain that behavior *is* to explain their charted path through their messy cultural context. And since persons are generally participating in *more than one* cultural role, and content ascription is based on such participation, it must reflect this fact. There is nothing mysterious about multiple-content ascription, given these rather mundane and empirically accessible features of human life.

Any account that fails to capture both the context embeddedness of content, and the possibility of multiple content ascriptions, fails to capture the empirically accessible facts of human behavior. In these conditions, the only way it can be made to appear plausible that one can eliminate content states is to engage in the wholesale redescription of human behavior where all reference to human culture-embedded behavior is systematically removed. This is precisely the eliminativist strategy. Ironically, their justification for this redescription, that the concepts of FP lack empirical integrity, shows only that the eliminativists are presupposing an a priori notion of the empirical.

This emerges clearly in their "positive" alternatives to FP.

V. Neural representation and behavior

A. The Churchlands' theory

The "geometrical" model of representation. The Churchlands claim to provide, as he puts it, "a highly general answer to the question how the brain might *represent* the many aspects of the world" (P. M. Churchland 1986, 279). They call this "new" model of representation the "geometrical" model (P. S. Churchland 1986, pp. 452–456) (P. M. Churchland 1986, p. 287;) They claim that it is easily applied to the fundamental problem of sensimotor coordination where "intelligence has its raw beginnings" (P. M. Churchland 1986, p. 279) and that it can be extended to the highest forms of cognitive activity. It is also claimed that this model facilitates an account of the physical realization in the brain of both representation and computation.

They aim to show how a simple creature, a crab, can represent itself and its world so as to behave intelligently in its world: "The basic idea . . . is that the brain represents various aspects of reality by a position in a . . . state space; and the brain performs computations on such representation by means of general coordinate transformations from one state space to another" (P. M. Churchland 1986, p. 280, and also pp. 283–294; P. S. Churchland 1986, pp. 420–450). It seems that the crab's brain contains "topographic maps" of its retinal surface, muscle system, and so forth. It also contains a set of "motor state spaces," "sensory state spaces," and so forth. Each state space can be represented as a "grid." Input, the state of the world, and output, the position of its arms, can be represented as "arrays" of points on the grids. The crab must be able to "project . . . every point on the . . . sensory grid [onto] the corresponding arm position in the motor grid" (P. M. Churchland 1986, pp. 283, 287).

Patricia Churchland (1986, p. 452) applies the same model to the problem of facial recognition: "Suppose, to make it simple, one neuron is sensitive to size of eyes, another to shape of eyes, another to distance between eyes, another to nose length [etc.]." The condition of the possibility of this application is that the phenomena must "involve a feature phase space with as many dimensions as there are recognitionally relevant features."

The geometrical model issues in an account of the physical realization of neural representation and computation. As she puts it, the cognitive phase spaces are realized in a "neuronal phase space," and "the neuronal arrays . . . are doing matrix multiplication" (1986, pp. 455, 417). As

P. M. Churchland puts it, the crab's sensory state space is "represented by [a] physical grid of signal-carrying fibers." Its motor state space is "represented by a second grid of fibers." A third set of "short verticle fibers" connects the two grids. This third set of fibers is the physical realization of the rules that map points from one grid onto the other: "Such a system will compute the desired coordinate transformations to a degree of accuracy limited only by the grain of the two grids, and by the density of their vertical connections" (1986, p. 289).

The strategy is simple. Representations are structures of elements. Brains are structures of elements. Computations are transformations of structures. Brain activity is transformation of structures. So there can be no a priori objection to the view that representation and computation are neurally realized (see McDonough 1989, p. 9). The crab's intelligence is simply a matter of projecting arrays from one grid onto arrays on other grids.

Both Churchlands claim that this model applies to the higher functions. He postulates a "linguistic hyperspace" in the brain where logical and meaningful relations are "reflected as spatial relations of some kind" (1986, p. 305). She says that the higher functions pose no special problem since "the propositional paradigm would be reinterpreted geometrically" (1986, p. 457).

But this model of representation is not new. Wittgenstein formulates the geometrical model of representation (picture theory) in his *Tractatus*. The idea of representations as structures of elements in *spaces* is the central image of that work, and nothing in the *Tractatus* requires a "narrowly syntactic" (P. M. Churchland 1986, p. 305) model of representations. Quite the contrary: The conditions of the possibility of a mechanistic account of a phenomenon require that it be *atomized* into arrays of parts in a space so that it can be *pictured* by arrays of elements in an internal space.

The *Tractatus* also contains, based on its geometrical model of representation, the first modern eliminativist position. Wittgenstein writes, "With certain forms of propositions in psychology, such as 'A believes that p,' and 'A has the thought that p,' etc., it looks as if it were possible for one proposition to occur in another in a [nontruth functional] way." But:

It is clear . . . that 'A believes that p', [etc.] are of the form " 'p' says p": and this does not involve a correlation of a fact with an object, but rather the correlation of facts by means of the correlation of their objects. . . . This shows that there is no such thing as the soul – the subject, etc., as it is conceived in the superficial psychology of the present day. (1917 pars. 541–5.5421)

Propositional attitudes are analyzed away. The "superficial psychology of the present day" (Wittgenstein 1917), which employs those outdated notions, is to be replaced by a radical new self-conception that countenances neither an irreducible unified self nor cognitive states, but instead *constructs the scientifically acceptable* notions of the self and of representations out of the atomistic notions of structure and structural congruences.

It is because, in his *Tractatus*, Wittgenstein laid the philosophical foundations of mechanism generally, and even of its specific eliminativist version, with such clarity that he came to perceive the problems for such theories before they even became an issue in contemporary philosophy (McDonough 1986, pp. 216–244; 294, n. 13). On the use model of his later philosophy, one cannot even isolate meaning or content elements. These are not the sorts of things that can be pictured by a structure, and so they cannot be realized in a structure in a brain, a computer, or anywhere else (McDonough 1989, p. 11). The "geometrical" model is inadequate for explanations of human intelligent behavior.

The "reinterpretation" of the propositional paradigm is really a *redescription* of it in terms of an old metaphysical ideal. On the Churchlands' "highly general" theory of representation, "the many aspects of the world" must, *equally generally*, be mere structures of elements. They must be the sorts of things that can be "mimed" by an internal structure (Churchland 1979, p. 149). "Empirical reality," as the *Tractatus* puts it, "is limited by the totality of objects" (5.5561), so that the possible "configurations" of these objects "produce" all possible states of affairs (2.072, 2.063). Unfortunately, "empirical reality" does not fit this a priori requirement; hence the eliminativists, with the *Tractatus*, must redescribe it to fit their metaphysical ideal.

Redescribing the data to fit a metaphysical ideal. The Churchlands elevate data revision, so to speak, to a science. He tells us that "it would be madness to make it a constraint upon acceptable theory that it explains the 'facts' as they [are] currently conceived" (1979, p. 44). She adds: "It is spectacularly evident that newer theories do not always espouse the explananda of older theories. . . . Neuroscience may fail to explain phenomena characterized in [FP] for the same reason Newtonian physics fails to explain what turns the crystal spheres" (1986, p. 385). One restraint on data revision that is needed in order to keep science honest is, as he admits, that the new scheme can explain "why the old scheme worked as well as it did" (Churchland 1979, p. 45). Although our new theory does not explain how the crystal sphere turns, it can explain why it looks as if one does. Analogously, the eliminativists must be able to explain why it seemed to us that we had beliefs and the like. This requires an accurate description of belief as conceived in FP. This they do not do. The data that they argue are revisable are data described in terms of their concocted theory, MFP. In order to make it appear that the data of FP are revisable, they have *already* revised it in terms of their favorite metaphysical views – internalism and the picture theory. Since I have dealt with internalism, I here focus on the role of the metaphysics of picturing in their strategy.

Given their geometrical model of representation, they must find a geometrical (picturable) *analogue* to meaning and content. The linguistic paradigm is redescribed as the sentential paradigm (P. M. Churchland 1979, pp. 6, 127; 1981, pp. 85, 88; P. S. Churchland 1986, pp. 387–388), a sentence being a structure and hence eminently picturable. Ali's belief that he is the greatest is redescribed as the view that Ali has a sentence structure residing in his cranium. So what they can explain is why it seemed to me (which, by the way, it did not) that Ali has a certain sentence inscribed in his cranium. So when they say that neuroscience may lead us to eliminate beliefs, what they really mean is that it may lead us to eliminate internal states that picture a sentence. *Beliefs* have already been eliminated on metaphysical grounds *before* the empirically motivated revision is even considered. Thus they cannot explain why it even seemed to me that Ali believes he is the greatest.

The eliminativist rewriting of the data of FP is not "for the same reason" as that involving the crystal sphere. The latter was based on genuine empirical considerations, and therefore it resulted in an increase in explanatory power. The revision of the data of FP is based on metaphysical grounds and, therefore, results in a diminishment of explanatory power. The eliminativist faith that with science everything is possible does not result, as advertised, in an enlargement of the domain of the possible. It is built on the strategy of *shrinking that domain*. Given their metaphysics, reality is impoverished a priori of beliefs and, in general, of everything that pertains to human culture-embedded behavior. What is left after the impoverishment are some mechanical proxies for cognition, which are then argued, irrelevantly, to be eliminable on the basis of empirical developments.

Only if one is under the spell of such a metaphysics can it seem so unproblematic to engage in *this kind* of revision of the data. If belief *must* be an internal state, then it cannot be problematic to redescribe the data of FP to fit internalism. If reality *must* be a structure of elements, then it cannot be problematic to redescribe those data to fit the metaphysics of the picture theory. If the data do not fit this requirement, then their lack of empirical integrity must be remedied. But the judgment that the data lack empirical integrity is based on their a priori metaphysics. Eliminativism is metaphysics, not science.

B. Stich's "autonomous behavioral language"

Stich likes to claim that on the narrow causal standard of his syntactic theory of mind (STM) paradigm, cognitive science does not lose any important generalizations. Yet he agrees with Fodor that if we follow his STM strategy, "literally all of . . . the generalizations of commonsense psychology . . . will be unstatable." The explanation for this apparent inconsistency is that he does not view the loss of these generalizations "with much alarm," because he thinks that STM can do the same explanatory and predictive work as FP and "do it better" (Stich, 1983, p. 182). Of course, in order to do this work better, we must, again, redescribe the data: "The formulation of an appropriate terminology for describing the explanada is often an essential step in the growth of a new science" (Stich 1983, p. 169). Stich's strategy of redescription is, however, very different from that of the Churchlands.

Take the act of selling my car. In Stich's view, this behavior is a "hybrid," involving an autonomous component (roughly, a description of the behavior that involves only facts about the entity itself) and a second component that "marshalls historical facts, legal facts, etc." His scientific psychology "'can explain the behavior under an appropriate autonomous description." But we also "need an account of why that behavior, in those circumstances, constituted the act of selling my car," (Stich 1983, pp. 195–196). This second explanation will not, of course, be part of science. Stich (1983, p. 196) admits that he is "not at all sure what an appropriate autonomous behavioral description . . . would be." But let us grant him this autonomous behavioral language. For even so, he has no explanation of intelligent behavior.

My intelligent behavior of selling my car is not explained by providing a narrow causal explanation of my finger movements (in signing the agreement) plus an account of why those finger movements in that context "constitute" the selling of my car. To explain the *intelligent* behavior, one will need an account of why I behave that way *in that context*. And if it is to be a narrow causal (mechanistic) account, this will require that I employ an internal representation of my behavior *in that context*. The Churchlands recognize this. The problem with their view is that they falsify the context so that it can be pictured by a machine structure. Stich (1983, p. 196), by contrast, recognizes full well that a narrow causal account cannot explain the behavior under the normal context-embedded descriptions. His strategy is to split the behavior into two parts, one part that is explainable by narrow science, the other, in a different sense, by appeal to the cultural surroundings. But since intelligent behavior is context-sensitive behavior, severing the link with the context severs the link with intelligence.

To put this another way, even if Stich can provide two sorts of explanations of the two different components of behavior, what explains the fact that the two autonomous components harmonize as they do – pre-established harmony (McDonough 1989, p. 18)? This can be explained, in principle, on a strong or weak RTM model, since these involve representations of the unadulterated context. But since he rejects these theories, he has no explanation of *our intelligent integration with our context.*[5]

C. Conclusion

Stich and the Churchlands have opposite strategies for explaining intelligence. The Churchlands recognize, correctly, that to give a mechanistic explanation of intelligent behavior, one must be able to trace the context-sensitive behavior of the organism into its neural center. Since they conceive the neural center as a structure of elements, they redescribe the context as a similar (picturable) structure of elements. Since the human context is not like that, the distinctive nature of human intelligence is lost. Stich, by contrast, recognizes that human cultural behavior cannot be traced to an inner mechanical state. So he isolates an autonomous physical component, which he believes to be traceable to the brain. But this does not capture the intelligence of the behavior. The only way to explain intelligent behavior on a mechanistic model is to accept either strong or weak RTM, but all of the eliminativists correctly reject these views. It seems to me that the moral of all this is that human intelligent behavior cannot be explained with a mechanistic theory.

VI. The "metaphysical" implications of Wittgenstein's view

My formulation of Wittgenstein's "Copernican revolution in the theory of meaning" is in response to McGinn's view that *Zettel* 608 commits Wittgenstein to a radical antiphysicalist position (McGinn 1986; McDonough 1989). I argue that *Zettel* 608 is *consistent with* the moderate physicalist view that, whereas our utterances under a "semantical" description cannot be traced to the brain, our utterances under some physical description can be. It is, however, possible that Wittgenstein considered a more radical antiphysicalist position. This is suggested in *Zettel* 610, where he remarks, "If this upsets our concept of causality then it is high time it was upset." (See also Wittgenstein 1976, pp. 410–411.) But just how much may it "upset our concept" of causality? It seems that Wittgenstein is not entirely clear how far he must go, but he is in a state of mind analogous to that of the eliminativists when they are speculating about the reconfigurations of our categories that might be necessitated by new developments in science. In the following subsection, I sketch two different views that retain a place for a physical mechanism subserving our behavior; in the subsection after that, I sketch a more radical antiphysicalist possibility.

A. Two moderate physicalistic views

Suppose it is discovered that there is a taxonomy of human behavior under which all human physical behavior can be traced to a neural mechanism. There are various forms this might take.

The brain as a syntactic engine. Suppose a taxonomy is found that issues in a "syntax" for both the brain and behavior. The brain is a "syntactic engine." Since cognitive states are culture-embedded states, such a discovery would not contribute to cognitive psychology per se. The discovery of a neural syntax could be of interest to the cognitive theorist, but only as a discovery in an *adjacent* field. The connection of the brain to behavior is relevant to meaning and content, but only in the minimal sense that the raw material for meaning or content ascriptions is neurally encoded. Its interest would depend on what, specifically, is discovered. (Is the neural syntax the same in all people? Is it like that of natural language, or of one natural language in particular? Is it like that of some artificial language? And so on.) The discovery of a neural syntax would be the discovery only that persons are under a specific physical constraint in their linguistic capacity. It would only help to explain why our *expression* of thought and meaning takes the particular *physical form* that it does.

Two versions of syntax eliminativism. Suppose the taxonomy of brain and behavior (both physically described) under which the correlations are found isolates units so minimal (or so maximal) that they are even syntax-blind. Even so, nothing physical fails to have a physical explanation. Physical behavior is neurally encoded but not in a way that reflects syntax (McDonough 1989, p. 5 n23). This *may* force a radical change, not in our self-conception but in our conception of language. Which kind of change depends on answers to other questions, particularly the question of whether syntax is essential to language. Suppose one answers yes. Then one must give some other account, presumably a *culturalist* account, of the role of syntax. (The question What is the cultural role of syntax ascription? would become an important question.) On the other hand, if one answers no, then one must hold that the notion of syntax is, at best, a convenient fiction, or at worst, a falsification of the phenomenon of language. Although these two views are very different, they both amount to kinds of "syntax eliminativism." In the first, a cultural role for syntax is retained but syntax has no neural physical reality. In the second, there is not even an essential culturalist role for syntax. But with both alternatives, neither semantics nor syntax is neurally based; thus there is no *physical constraint* on linguistic ability other than the general one that people must have a high degree of neural integrity.

Connectionism may be a version of syntax eliminativism. Although there is no reason to believe that FP is committed to discrete cognitive states (Heil, Chapter 5, this volume), let us pretend for the moment that common sense is committed to discrete syntactic states. The discovery that the brain works on connectionist lines would be the discovery that the taxonomy on which the *physical correlations* obtain diverges from these commonsense notions. We should have to give up the view that discrete syntactic states have a neural reality. We would have to change our views about the physical means by which we *implement our intelligence*. But this is irrelevant to the content states of FP, since these are modeled on "use" (G-function), not on syntax.

B. *Neurobiology eliminativism*

Let us call the view that we must give up the FP framework "FP-eliminativism." Wittgenstein's view is the opposite of this. He regards FP as nontheoretical, and mechanistic science as parasitic on FP and limited in its pretensions (McDonough 1989, pp. 18–21). The two views are *reverse mirror images* of each other. One can, therefore, define a position that is the precise opposite of FP-eliminativism. Let us call "neurobiology eliminativism" (NB-eliminativism) the view that no physical neural regularities underlie intelligent human behavior.

Perhaps it turns out that we cannot fashion any taxonomy of the brain and behavior under which all cognitively associated human physical behavior[6] can be traced to the brain. It was already clear that neuroscience cannot explain human intelligent behavior as such. What is new in the present, more radical scenario is that not even all cognitively associated human *physical* behavior can be traced to an internal physical mechanism. Since all finger movements are caused by muscle twitchings, and those by nervous impulses in the arm, and so forth, the physicalistic discontinuity must lie deeper in the organism. Assuming that the neuroscientists are correct in saying that the brain is the deepest *physical center* of human behavior, it is likely that the discontinuity lies there. This would mean that some physical impulses that go out from the brain cannot be traced to any physical mechanism inside it. We must deny the moderate physicalistic view that everything physical must have a physical explanation. If only a small portion of our cognitively associated physical behavior cannot be traced to physical states of the brain, then the framework of physicalistic neuroscience is still of some utility for explanation of our physical behavior. But if much or all of our cognitively associated physical behavior is only culturally explainable (e.g., if the best explanation of why I moved my finger is that I wanted to sign the check), then the framework of physicalistic neurobiology must be eliminated from the explanation of our cognitively associated physical behavior. That framework would have to go the way of caloric, phlogiston, and crystal spheres in the heavens.

It is important to be clear about what is claimed here. First, there is a well-established science of neurobiology that has made important contributions to the study of the brain and the organism. This science refers to such respectable entities as neurons, dendrites, and carbonium ions. The unbiased observer (unburdened by the mechanistic ideology) is justified in looking forward to learn what sort of principles may be discovered by this science in the future. But one hears mention of a more ambitious science of neurobiology (not only in the popular media, but even in philosophical books and journals) that refers not only to the above-mentioned respectable entities but also to "neural codes," "communication between cells," and so forth. It is this latter "framework," plus its ontology of neural code states and the like (not respectable neuroscience), that is a serious candidate for elimination.

Second, what is eliminated in this "radical" scenario is only an extreme *physicalistic* neurobiology. It is still possible that a reconfigured neurobiology can be retained. There are various possibilities. One of these is that brain states are identified by reference to the history of the organisms that have them. The brain is irreducibly organic in the sense that its "structure" is specifiable only by reference to the history of the organism (i.e., biology may turn out to be biology rather than a branch of physics; see Wittgenstein 1967, p. 608; 1976, pp. 410–412).

C. The empirical status of neuroscience

These three views are arranged in order from the least to the most radical. In all three, the semantical and content states are ineliminable because they are neither theoretical nor traceable to the brain. All three are forms of physicalistic neuropsychology eliminativism. There can be no cognitive science in that sense. With both variants of case *A*, however, the physicalist can take comfort in the fact that all human behavior under some physical description or other can be traced to the brain. So in these first two views, an appropriate, if limited, place for mechanistic science is retained *adjacent* to our account of intelligence. Although it is a mistake to ask what makes people "work" (Churchland 1984 p. 46) – unless one is asking about their salary, goals, and so forth – there is something working inside them that places a physical constraint on human physical 'implementations" of intelligence. The generalizations, if there are any, linking English brains to Chinese brains, human brains to dog brains and Martian brains (if Martians have brains), which the eliminativists fear are missed by FP (Stich 1983, p. 136; P. S. Churchland 1986, p. 378), can be picked up with these alternatives.

But in the final, most radical option there is some physical behavior that cannot be traced to the physical brain. In the extreme case, this requires the total elimination of the physicalistic neurobiological framework from the explanation of human behavior. The line of thought leading to this third possibility is the reverse image of that leading to folk-psychology eliminativism. The differences are that what the folk-psychology eliminativist sees as mere fallible theory (folk psychology) the neurobiology eliminativist sees as nontheoretical and that what the folk-psychology eliminativist sees as the advancing tide of neuroscience the neurobiology eliminativist sees as a collection of question-begging arguments and thinly disguised metaphysics.

This third option might seem too radical to consider in the present "scientific" age. But neuroscience is a mere empirical theory, and is insisted to be so by even its most uncritical defenders. Although the eliminativists like to claim that "the greatest theoretical synthesis in the history of the human race [is] currently in our hands" (Churchland 1981, p. 75; see also Stich, 1983, p. 246), in their more sober moments they admit otherwise. Paul Churchland (1981, p. 75) acknowledges that the neuroscientific account of human behavior "is still radically incomplete." Patricia Churchland (1986, p. 346) tells us that although we must assume that "we are paradigmatic representers . . . we don't know . . .

what it is for a system to have representational states." Stich (1983, p. 14) acknowledges that the usual story about neural explanations of behavior "is at the moment no more than hopeful science fiction," and confesses to "a nagging suspicion that our confidence may be misplaced." (In fact, this story is not even science fiction but is more akin to the genre of science fantasy.)[7]

Despite this occasional candor, it will not be easy to initiate a critical examination of the mechanistic paradigm. Since the French Enlightenment, mechanism has come to be seen as commonsensical. The conceptual inertia resulting from the entrenchment of the mechanistic worldview has led to the conviction that mechanism *has to be true*. (We have even seen it suggested that if the ultimate explanation for my going to the party is that I wanted to go, then we are committed to magic!) But there is no real cause for alarm among genuine empirical scientists. The present critical examination is not an attack on science. It is only the extreme *mechanistic* picture of persons that is challenged, and this in only a limited sense. For the present critique is a version of the Copernican view, prefigured in the German Enlightenment, that mechanistic science probably does have *some* important place in our account of persons. But its limits must be set by an intelligence (in this case, a culture) on which it is conceptually dependent and which it cannot, in principle, explain (McDonough 1986, pp. 279–281, n. 74–75); 1989, p. 12; 1990, sect. II; in Press [a], sect. V).

Notes

1. Eliminativists generally regard FP as committed to a host of other sophisticated views: that mental states are "viewed as some sort of relations to representational entities" (Stich 1983, p. 129); that beliefs have "components, often labeled 'concepts' " (Stich, 1983, p. 78); that persons are sentential information processors (Churchland 1980, p. 152); and so forth. For my present purposes, however, it is sufficient to focus on their more "modest" assumption that it presupposes the metaphysics of internalism.
2. One commonly hears it said that mechanical systems instantiate a "program." But this usage is derivative and metaphorical. It is persons who, literally, instantiate a *cultural program* (the priority of culturalism).
3. It is noteworthy that in his first departure from the extreme-meaning atomism of the *Tractatus*, Wittgentstein anticipated the kind of mechanical "holism" exemplified by the network theory. He considered types of meaning "holism" which are compatible with the *Tractatus* view that meaning is "realizable" in a mechanism (Wittgenstein 1975, sect. VII, p. 69). These "mechanistic holisms" include versions of the picture theory, where the minimal pictures are pictures of *systems* of propositions, and in which a modified notion of meaning elements is retained (1975, sect. VIII, pp. 82–86).

4. The argument is not that one cannot build an intelligent robot. If we did build such a contraption, then its cognitive states, like ours, would have to be *culture-embedded states*. But then one could not trace its intelligence "further in the direction of the centre" (Wittgenstein, 1967, p. 608) to its internal mechanical structure. So this creature *would be a person not a machine*. Neither would its intelligence be any more "artificial" than ours. This is one reason why the popular "argument from contraptions" is irrelevant to the *philosophical* issue involved.

5. Stich (1983, pp. 87–91, 207) notes the ambiguity in Fodor between strong and weak RTM. He finds the existence of the ambiguity puzzling, and he calls weak RTM "pointless." I view Fodor's schizophrenia more charitably since it is the inevitable consequence of taking seriously the mechanistic enterprise of wanting to explain *unadulterated* human behavior. The virtue of "strong" RTM is that on it people *really understand* their context. The problem is that it commits one to an occult notion of representational states (McDonough 1986, sect. VI. 3, and pp. 270–271, n.15; 272–273, n. 18; 274, nn. 27 and 29; pp. 276–277, n. 32; 279–281, nn. 73–75). So weak RTM is the only remaining possibility. It satisfies the mechanistic requirement of narrow causal typing of representation states. But to explain unadulterated human behavior, these "narrow" states must *somehow* explain the "semantically based" regularities exhibited in human life. Fodor honestly admits that he does not know how they can do this. The only reason the eliminativists escape his schizophrenia is that they are eager to trade *the humanity* in our behavior for a preconceived form of explanation. Thus, in a sense, Fodor is right that his theory, however problematic, is the only game in town – the only *mechanistic* game that purports to explain *human* behavior. But mechanism is not the only possibility.

6. I say "cognitively associated" physical behavior since what we are interested in is the explanation of *intelligent* behavior, under some physical description, by reference to the framework of NB. I am describing a scenario in which heartbeats, meaningless twitches and so forth, are still "neurally centered," whereas the physical behavior by means of which we implement our intelligence is not.

7. McGinn (1986) argues that there *must* be mechanisms underlying consciousness but that we cannot, in principle, know them. This "defense" of mechanism is instructive because (1) it is premised on how much we really know about such alleged mechanisms (which is next to nothing) and (2) it illustrates that the certainty with which the mechanistic worldview is believed is more akin to that of an ideological or religious fervor than it is to rational belief.

References

Churchland, P. M. (1979). *Scientific Realism and the Plasticity of Mind*. Cambridge: Cambridge University Press.

Churchland, P. M. (1981). "Eliminative Materialism and the Propositional Attitudes." *The Journal of Philosophy*, 78: 67–90.

Churchland, P. M. (1984). *Matter and Consciousness*.Cambridge, Mass.: MIT Press.

Churchland, P. M. (1986). "Some Reductive Strategies in Cognitive Neurobiology." *Mind*, 95:279–309.

Churchland, P. S. (1980). "Language, Thought, and Information Processing." *Nous*, 14:147–170.

Churchland, P. S. (1986). *Neurophilosophy*. Cambridge, Mass.: The MIT Press.

Feldman, J. A., & Ballard, D. H. (1982). "Connectionist Models and Their Properties." *Cognitive Science*, 6:205–254.

Fodor, J. A. (1987). *Psychosemantics*. Cambridge, Mass.: MIT Press.

Hookway, C. (1988). *Quine: Language, Experience and Reality*. Oxford: Basil Blackwell.

McDonough, R. (1986). *The Argument of the "Tractatus": Its Relevance to Contemporary Theories of Logic, Language, Mind and Philosophical Truth*. Albany: State University of New York Press.

McDonough, R. (1989). "Towards a Non-mechanistic Theory of Meaning." *Mind*, 98:1–22.

McDonough, R. (1990). "The Limits of the Enlightenment." *Language and Communication*, 10(4):255–265.

McDonough, R. In press (a). "Wittgenstein's Refutation of Meaning Skepticism." In Klaus Puhl, ed., *Meaning Skepticism*. Berlin: De Gruyter.

McDonough, R. In press (b). "Wittgenstein's Critique of Mechanistic Atomism." *Philosophical Investigations*.

McDonough, R. In press (c). "Plato's Anti-mechanistic Account of Communication." *Language and Communication*.

McGinn, C. (1986). *Wittgenstein on Meaning*. Oxford: Basil Blackwell.

McGinn, C. (1989). "Can We Really Solve the Mind–Body Problem?" *Mind*, 98: 359–366.

Rumelhart, D. E., G. E. Hinton, & J. L. McClelland. (1986). "A General Framework for Parallel Distributed Processing." In Rumelhart, D. E., & McClelland, J. L., eds., *Parallel Distributed Processing* (2 vols.), Vol 1. Cambridge, Mass.: MIT Press.

Searle, J. (1983). *Intentionality*. Cambridge: Cambridge University Press.

Stich, S. P. (1983). *From Folk Psychology to Cognitive Science: The Case Against Belief*. Cambridge, Mass.: MIT Press.

Wittgenstein, L. (1917). *Tractatus-Logico-Philosophicus*, trans. D. F. Pears & B. F. McGuinness. London: Routledge & Kegan Paul.

Wittgenstein, L. (1958). *Philosophical Investigations*, trans. G. E. M. Anscombe. Oxford: Basil Blackwell.

Wittgenstein, L. (1967). *Zettel*. Trans. by G. E. M. Anscombe & G. H. Von Wright. Oxford: Basil Blackwell.

Wittgenstein, L. (1975). *Philosophical Remarks*, trans. Raymond Hargreaves and Roger White. Oxford: Basil Blackwell.

Wittgenstein, L. (1976). "Cause and Effect: Intuitive Awareness," trans. Peter Winch. *Philosophia*, 6:409–461.

Author index

Subject index